City of Sin and Splendour

Writings on Lahore

Edited by Bapsi Sidhwa

PENGUIN BOOKS

PENGUIN BOOKS
Published by the Penguin Group
Penguin Books India Pvt Ltd, 11 Community Centre, Panchsheel Park, New Delhi
110 017, India
Penguin Group (USA) Inc., 375 Hudson Street, New York, New York 10014, USA
Penguin Group (Canada), 90 Eglinton Avenue East, Suite 700, Toronto, Ontario,
M4P 2Y3, Canada (a division of Pearson Penguin Canada Inc.)
Penguin Books Ltd, 80 Strand, London WC2R 0RL, England
Penguin Ireland, 25 St Stephen's Green, Dublin 2, Ireland (a division of Penguin
Books Ltd)
Penguin Group (Australia), 250 Camberwell Road, Camberwell, Victoria 3124,
Australia (a division of Pearson Australia Group Pty Ltd)
Penguin Group (NZ), cnr Airborne and Rosedale Roads, Albany, Auckland 1310,
New Zealand (a division of Pearson New Zealand Ltd)
Penguin Group (South Africa) (Pty) Ltd, 24 Sturdee Avenue, Rosebank,
Johannesburg 2196, South Africa

Penguin Books Ltd, Registered Offices: 80 Strand, London WC2R 0RL, England

First published by Penguin Books India 2005

Anthology copyright © Penguin Books India 2005
Introduction and selection © Bapsi Sidhwa 2005

The copyright for individual pieces vests with the authors or their estates

ISBN-10: 0143 03166X   ISBN-13: 9780143031666

For sale throughout the world except Pakistan

Typeset in Venetian by Mantra Virtual Services, New Delhi
Printed at Baba Barkhanath Printers, New Delhi

To Parizad,
the quintessential Lahori

Contents

Introduction: City Beloved

Bapsi Sidhwa

I have spent most of my life in Lahore, and the city of eight million provides the geographical location of my novels. The city's ambience has moulded my sensibility and also my emotional responses. To belong to Lahore is to be steeped in its romance, to inhale with each breath an intensity of feeling that demands expression. This is amply illustrated by the bouquet of essays, verse, chronicles and memories that celebrate this anthology.

The very spelling of this hoary city causes one to indulge in linguistic antics—as I did in my first novel, *A Pakistani Bride*:

> Lahore—the ancient whore, the handmaiden of dimly remembered Hindu kings, the courtesan of Moghul emperors—bedecked and bejeweled, savaged by marauding hordes—healed by the caressing hands of successive lovers. A little shoddy, as Qasim saw her; like an attractive but aging concubine, ready to bestow surprising delights on those who cared to court her—proudly displaying Royal gifts.

According to popular myth, Lahore or Loh-awar (from the Sanskrit word 'awar' or fort) was founded by Lav or Loh, one of the sons of the legendary Rama. But Lahore as we know it today owes its splendour to the Mughal emperors. Emperor Akbar moved his capital to Lahore in 1584 and built its massive fort; Emperor Jehangir and his son Shah Jehan—the indefatigable builder who commissioned the Taj Mahal—extended it. Shah Jehan also commissioned the terraced Shalimar Gardens.

But it is the Badshahi Mosque, its massively billowing marble domes ignited by the setting sun as one approaches the city from the Ravi bridge, that conjures up the image of Lahore for me. Reputed to be the world's largest mosque, it is laid out like a jewel before the main gate of Lahore Fort. Both structures originally stood on the banks of the Ravi, but the depleted river has meandered into a new course a couple of miles to the north. The Badshahi Mosque, its elegant proportions and the way it is situated in relation to the city, is sheer architectural poetry. For, above all, Lahore is a city of poets. Not just giants like Allama Iqbal or Faiz Ahmad Faiz, but a constellation of poets. Given half a chance, the average Lahori breaks into a couplet from an Urdu ghazal, or from Madho Lal Hussain or Bulleh Shah's mystical Punjabi verse, and readily confesses to writing poetry.

But if I toss up the word 'Lahore' and close my eyes, the city conjures up gardens and fragrances. Not only the formal Mughal Gardens with their obedient rows of fountains and cypresses, or the acreage of the club-strewn Lawrence Gardens, but the gardens in thousands of Lahori homes with their riot of spring flowers. The trees bloom in a carnival of jewel-colours—the defiant brilliance of kachnar, bougainvillea and gulmohur silhouetted against an azure sky. And the winter and spring air are heady—they make the blood hum. On summer evenings the scent from the water sprinkled on parched earth signals respite from the furnace of the day—for the summers are as hellish as the winters are divine.

There is a certain route I follow when I take visitors to my favourite Lahori landmarks. From my house in the cantonment near the old Lahore airport we drive to Mall Road. Believed to be part of the famed Grand Trunk Road that ran across the breadth of India from Peshawar to Calcutta, it has been grandly renamed Shahrah-e-Quaid-i-Azam, after the founding father of Pakistan. But old names, like old habits, die hard, and it is still commonly called Mall Road. Shaded by massive peepal and eucalyptus trees, its wide meridians ablaze with seasonal flowers, the avenue provides an impressive route for the dignitaries being wafted in their darkened limos to the Government House. Past the delicate pink sprawl of the British-built High Court and the coppery Zamzamah, the cannon better known as 'Kim's Gun' after Kipling's young hero, past the deadly little fighter jet displayed on the traffic island a little further along the road, our tiny Suzuki noses through the congestion of trucks, horse-drawn tongas, bullock carts and scooter-rickshaws to Data Sahib's shrine on Ravi Road.

One of the earliest Muslim saints to visit India, Data Gunj Baksh was embraced by all communities including the Hindus and Sikhs. I was regularly hauled to the shrine as a child. My mother had a committed and confidential relationship with the saint and was forever asking him to either grant her some favour, or thanking him for having granted it. On those visits, prompted by her gratitude, she would insert one or two crisp ten-rupee notes in the collection box just inside the grills of the tomb window. Sometimes, when the resolution of a particularly knotty problem merited extra thanks, she would also donate a *deg* or cauldron of sweet or savoury rice. The shrine provides food at all hours, and the path to the shrine is lined with merchants hawking enormous degs of steaming rice and lentils. Once the deg is paid for, two men haul it on bamboo struts to a comparatively vacant distribution lot a few yards away, and immediately a long line of labourers and beggars materializes before it as if beamed down from an airship. The labourers hold out the flaps of their shirts, and the women portions of their ragged dupattas, to receive the saucerfuls of rice ladled out by the hired help. It is alleged that the saint saved Lahore during the '65 and '71 wars with India. Sikh pilots are believed to have seen hands materialize out of the ether to catch the bombs and gentle them to the ground. How else can one explain the quantity of unexploded bombs found in the area? They can't all be blamed on poor manufacture, surely.

From Data Sahib's, I take my visitors to the monumental Lahore Fort. Running along one side of the old walled city, it is your standard Mughal bastion with thick, impenetrable stone walls, tall ramparts and neatly constructed turrets from which small cannons were fired long ago. One enters the fort through dwarfing gates that open on the wide canyon of the 'elephant walk'. The walk's gradual granite incline is marked by a series of small steps placed wide enough apart to accommodate an elephant's stride. As an awed child, I once watched three richly caparisoned elephants conjure the spirit of bygone empires as, trunk to tail, they lumbered up the ancient path for some visiting dignitaries.

The walk leads to a spread of open courtyards and halls bordered by marble pillars and arching canopies, and finally we arrive at the million-mirrored Sheesh Mahal, the queen's and princesses' private chambers. If my preferred guide has not already attached himself to us, he can be counted on to do so now. Respectful and non-insistent, a rare quality in this indigent breed, he appears always to be loitering inside the fort. He leads us with a somewhat diffident air of mystery to the darkest portion of the Sheesh Mahal and, fetching a tiny box of matchsticks from the depths of his baggy shalwar, strikes a match. (The striking of a Lahori match is a chancy thing. It might ignite a sterile spark that produces no fire, or it might produce a weak fire that gutters out if not nursed.) Holding the anaemic fire like a fledgling in the cupped palms of his hands, the guide finally cajoles it into a robust flame and holds it aloft. For a few seconds all the little mirrors imbedded in the arches and vaulting ceilings of the chamber burst into flames and, as the guide slowly moves his arm about, the flames dance like a glittering chorus of Broadway fireflies.

Akbar's son, the emperor Jehangir, is buried in the magnificent Shahdara mausoleum near the fort. Jehangir's wife Nur Jehan's own small, darkly crumbling tomb lies in the mausoleum's shadow, as the empress had expressly wished it. Its gloomy domed decrepitude is visible from the Grand Trunk Road, and although I remind myself to visit it each time I pass it on my way to her husband's tomb, I have yet to do so.

Lahore was captured by the famous Sikh warrior Ranjit Singh in 1799, and after his death, the city was swallowed up by the British to satisfy the Empire's boa-constrictor appetite. Maharaja Ranjit Singh died in Lahore, and his samadhi is set in a complex of religious buildings and gardens next to the Badshahi Mosque. I visited the samadhi once in the 1980s, when the Sikh demand for a separate state was at its most fervent in India. It was around the same time that an Air-India plane was hijacked by a group of Sikh separatists. I remember the plane's insistent drone above our house; it was desperately seeking permission to land at the Lahore airport. The Pakistani authorities, nervous of being implicated in the hijacking, would not allow it to land until it was almost out of fuel and their Indian counterparts' appeals had become frantic. The Sikh hijackers routinely surrendered to the Pakistani commandos and were shunted off to jail to await trial.

Lahore's old city, built by the Mughals and fortified by a wall which has since crumbled, is a city within the city, and is the nucleus around which modern Lahore has shaped itself. The wall was breached by gates, some of which are still standing.

There is another Lahori haunt that cannot go without mention. It is the Hira Mandi or 'diamond market': 'hira' or 'diamonds' are a euphemism for the alluring dancing girls who ply their trade in this bazaar. Comprising a thick jostle of narrow streets and rickety buildings in the old city, Hira Mandi lies on the other side of Lahore Fort and is undoubtedly one of Lahore's liveliest spots. Here the girls dance and flirt, and sing the verse of Lahore's poets, selling romance as much as they do sex.

My evening forays to the district with friends are infrequent, however, and very few guests are treated to the perilous drive through its narrow lanes. On spotting women in the car the men will bend to peer in and make lewd comments. Once when the window was open, a couple of men poked their hands in to muss up our hair, and asked the men: 'Where're you taking these birds to? Take us with you!' Peeping out the car window through my dark glasses, wrapped in a shawl, curious and at the same time nervous that someone might recognize me despite my attempts at disguise, I watch the reactions of my guests. They are infected by the gaiety of shouted banter and by the colour and movement in the brightly lit streets. Unlike the corpse-like lassitude of the girls penned in their separate cages in the notorious red-light district of Bombay, the dancing girls of Lahore display an impressive animation of gesture and speech. This is in unhappy contrast also to the dispirited women penned in their homes in the more respectable neighbourhoods of an increasingly puritanical, segregated and Islamicized Lahore.

This then is the ancient city, described before Partition as the 'Paris of the East', which insinuates itself in each of the pieces in this anthology. After all, it is the city in which our memories are lodged, and where the people who are dear to us live. But at times I have felt that the magnificent tombs of Lahore, the mosques and gardens, and the colonial edifices built by the British, form only an essential background; it is the people who throng Lahore's bazaars and streets and inhabit the city's buildings that occupy centre stage. And therein lies the emotional landscape of my writing, the memories I draw upon in my novels.

For me, growing up in Lahore as a child, this metropolis with its chequered history and historical sites was compressed into tiny pockets of familiarity: they provided me with many of my characters. Godmother, Slavesister, Mother, Father, the Junglewallas, Toddywallas, Bankwallas and the host of other wallas in *Ice-Candy-Man*, *The Crow Eaters* and *An American Brat*.

Next to the Birdwood Barracks was my home on Warris Road, and down the street on Jail Road—opposite the Salvation Army complex with its glass-shard encrusted walls—the one-and-a-half-room home of Tehmina Sahiar. It was my haven, my refuge from the chill air of violence that swept Lahore during Partition and disrupted all our relationships.

Although she was not related to us, 'Tehmina aunty', or 'Mottamumma' as she was called by some, was dearer to the Parsee community of Lahore than a blood-relative might be, and she commanded an esteem afforded only to sages. At least that is how I viewed her as an adoring and grateful child, and that is how I have portrayed her in her reincarnation as 'Godmother' in my novel *Ice-Candy-Man*. Godmother could be—in a typically nutty Parsee way—delectably eccentric.

In my first novel, *The Pakistani Bride*, much of the story is set in Lahore. We observe Lahore through Qasim, a Kohistani tribesman from the Afghan frontier, as he wanders through the city with his adopted daughter Zaitoon perched on his shoulders. With them we stroll down Anarkali, the crowded bazaar named after the beautiful girl who was bricked in alive by Emperor Akbar because his son, Prince Salim, was determined to marry her.

I was always uneasy with the story of Anarkali. It was inconsistent with everything I had heard about the judicious character of the gentle monarch. Mughal princes, after all, were almost obliged to fall in love with dancing girls: it was a rite of passage, a means of acquiring carnal sophistication and courtly manners. How then could Akbar call such a vengeful punishment upon a young girl whose vocation compelled her to seduce princes?

What I recently learnt gives Anarkali's story a more credible twist.

Anarkali was neither a dancing girl nor, as some suggest, a handmaiden to one of the queens. She was in fact one of Akbar's junior wives. This version gives a more serious complexion to the transgression— one that smacks of royal adultery and incest—and thus liable to invite the dire punishment meted out.

In the excerpts from my novels that I've included in this anthology, I have taken a few liberties with the text for the sake of brevity and continuity. Compiling this anthology gave me a chance to make friends and read engaging new material. I thank all the authors who have so readily and generously contributed to this collection. I also thank my lovely editors at Penguin, Diya Kar Hazra and Sakshi Narang, for their able handling of this anthology and Ravi Singh for his ready support; also Anjali Puri for her editorial help. Khushwant Singh and Soli Sorabji I want to thank for being such genial friends, and my daughter Parizad for her literary and aesthetic sensitivity and help. And, as always, my husband Noshir for his support.

Sadly, Ijaz Husain Batalvi and Ashfaq Ahmed have passed away since I began putting this anthology together. Ijaz Husain Batalvi was as keen to see his essay 'Kipling's Lahore' published in this collection as I was eager for him to see it. A leading lawyer, scholar, literary critic and writer, he had the ability to engage with all age groups. His enthusiasm and intellectual curiosity were infectious.

Ashfaq Ahmed and Bano Qudsia were known as the Elizabeth Barrett Browning and Robert Browning of Lahore. A man of striking good looks and presence, Ashfaq was not only a gifted literary writer, he also wrote hugely popular radio and television plays. *City of Sin and Splendour: Writings on Lahore* has the unique honour of publishing Ashfaq Ahmed and Bano Qudsia for the first time in India.

PART I

ERA AFTER ERA

On the Banks of River Ravi

Muhammad Allama Iqbal

Lost in its own silent rhythm, the Ravi sings its song.
In its undulating flow I see the reflections in my heart—
The willows, the world, in worship of God

I stand at the edge of the flowing water
I do not know how and where I stand—
In the wine-coloured dusk
The Old Man shakily sprinkles crimson in the sky

The day is returning to where it came from
This is not dew; these are flowers, gifts from the sun
Far off, a cluster of minarets stand in statuesque splendour
Marking where Moghul chivalry sleeps
This palace tells the story of time's tyranny
A saga of a time long spent

What destination is this?
A quiet song only the heart can hear?
A gathering of trees speaks for me.
In midstream, a boat hurtles by
Riding the relentless currents,
Darting beyond the eye's curved boundary.

Life flows on this river of eternity
Man is not born this way; does not perish this way
Undefeated, life slips beyond the horizon,
But does not end there.

—Translated by Parizad N. Sidhwa

This poem is taken from *Bang-e-dara*, published by Sheikh Ghulam
Ali and Sons Ltd.

The Travels of Fray Sebastian Manrique in the Panjab, 1641

E.D. Maclagan

Chapter LXVI—In which is given an account of a most splendid and famous Memanè, or Banquet, which Prince Assofokan gave to the Great Mogol [Emperor Jehangir].

Before my departure from the City of Laòr, loquacious rumour proclaimed that the Padchà was going to visit his father-in-law, Prince Assofokan, and congratulate him on having regained his health. I seized the opportunity of seeing the magnificent and splendid Banquet which this Prince gave to his Lord and Emperor. And availing myself of the full liberty which I had, to enter where the limits of etiquette allowed, I also obtained leave to enter with a companion,[1] who went with me, a gallery over the principal hall of the baths of which I have already given a sufficient account. A eunuch took us thither, warning us not to make the slightest noise, and that if we found it necessary to make one in expelling the imperative and importunate phlegm, we should go to other separate rooms which he showed us; then, instructing us also not to leave before he came to fetch us, he went away.

In this principal hall of the Bath the banquet was given. Besides the immovable fixtures with which it was already ornamented, there were added on this occasion rich carpets of silk, silver and gold, which, covering the floor, served as terrestrial tables, in conformity with the custom of the country, and as chairs and seats for the guests gracing them with their presence. And although they reject and consider as useless high tables, they approve, however, the use of grand and rich

This extract is taken from Zulfiqar Ahmad's *Notes on Punjab and Mughal India*, published by Sang-e-Meel Publications.

stands; indeed on this occasion there were in the four corners of the
Hall as many such stands each one of five steps, and all beautifully
covered and decorated with Persian cloths of gold and silver. These
served as buffets and sideboards, and all were covered with divers
vessels of gold, on which the eye-sight could tarry, distinguishing in
some a variety of encrusted stones, in others, in place of them, the
finest shining enamel, which varying in material blended in colouring.
This most superb display was accompanied by various large perfume
vessels methodically placed round the hall, and small silver pans of
extraordinary workmanship, in which burnt the most delicate perfumes
composed of different confections of amber, Aguila² and civet, and
other odoriferous mixtures, which blending in one, gratified without
offending, and soothed the sense of smell. At the entrance to this
beautiful hall there was, on one side, a seven-headed Hydra, made of
silver, and of admirable workmanship, moderately large, and enamelled
with greenish scales; from its renascent heads it ejected thin jets of
sweet-smelling water, which falling into a large trough of the same
material kept it always half full; for though on the one hand it
discharged the water which it received, on the other, it always remained
at the same level for the washing of feet, which, according to Mogol
manners, is one of the most essential points of their ceremonious
etiquette. In the middle of this gilt/ and very rich treasure-room was
placed a desterchanà³ (or table-cloth, in our language) of the thinnest
and whitest cotton, which instead of natural and scented flowers, was
ornamented with artificial ones of gold and silver interwoven in the
cloth itself. In the principal place of this table were two large and
beautiful cushions of plain gold cloth, and over these other smaller
cushions of silver cloth, also plain. This was all the apparatus of the
Imperial table; indeed it lacked serviettes, which they do not use. To
this, when it was time, the Emperor entered accompanied by a very
large retinue of lovely and gallant ladies, who came in front of him
most richly dressed in mileques⁴ or cloths of gold, the gold and silver
groundings of which were variegated with designs of coloured silks.
They wore on their neck collars of gold, with costly strings of pearls,
and their heads were adorned with silver-embroidered wreaths. Behind
this bevy of lovely women came the Emperor between his mother-in-
law and his daughter, bringing in the former on his right hand and

the latter on his left. Immediately behind, followed the hereditary Prince, Sultan Darà Sucur, who brought on his right hand his Grandfather, Assofokan.

When the whole of this company arrived at the entrance of the banquet hall, they commenced immediately to play in the neighbouring and corresponding rooms many and various kinds of instruments. As soon as the Padchá was/ seated at the table between the cushions which I have spoken of, having at his shoulders two venerable dames, who were standing with most costly fans to keep away the importunate flies, both his father-in-law and mother-in-law, and also their children suddenly went on their knees in front of His Highness, who stretching out his hand to his mother-in-law, raised her up and calling her Mother made her sit at his right hand; a favour which was so much esteemed by her husband as well as by the grandchildren, that they immediately made great and profound tassalimas[5] to the Padchà, thereby showing him how much they valued his gracious act; and he, to enhance it, ordered them also to sit down to table, which they did not do until the third command, and then they seated themselves at the end of it, the Princes placing their grandfather in their midst. All these ceremonies of submission and prostration finished, when all were now seated in the order which I have said, there were presently heard most gentle and soft voices which from various choirs sang of the battles and victories in which His Majesty had overcome his enemies. At the sound of this well concerted and gentle harmony of voices and instruments, the arrangements for the washing of hands also commenced. It was done in the following order. First entered four most lovely girls, Prince Assofokan's relations, and daughters of great Lords. The whiteness/ and ruddiness of their faces and the reddish colour (*el rubio*) of their hair were able to compete with the greater whiteness which frigid Boreas produces; and though equal to them as far as fairness of complexion goes, yet, these [the women of the North] could not fail being inferior in grace, elegance and beauty; for the cause of these accomplishments being heat, which governs and harmonizes pose, action, movement and grace of conversation; we may well say, where it is wanting, what Catullus said about the beauty of Quincia,—*Nulla in tam pulchro corpore mica salis.*[6] These four extremes of beauty approached in a manner capable of creating envy in the Cyprian Goddess herself,—for gravity, gaiety and spiritedness,—and thus they brought, divided among them, the requisite vessels for washing the hands of His Imperial Majesty. Drawing near, after the Royal ceremonies, one of them spread in front of him a cloth of white satin, which she carried in her hands, another put on it a most costly vessel of gold inlaid with most perfect precious stones of great value. These vessels are much better contrived than ours, as being deep in the middle and the hollow space being covered with a thin grating, the water and saliva passes below, without leaving in sight on the upper cover the loathsome clotted phlegm. This vessel being placed before him, another girl arrived with a ewer of the same material and value,/ and she poured out the water in which he washed his hands, receiving from the last of these Ladies the towel on which to wipe them. This washing ceremony over, the ladies having retired, twelve others entered, who although of inferior rank to the former, nevertheless were not unworthy of being able to appear with confidence in any presence. These, after having presented the hand-washing vessels to the Princes with a little less ceremony than the first had used with the Padchà, retired. Now the food was brought in by another door to the sound of noisy instruments,— Kettle-drums, Borgondas, and Vacas,[7] instruments almost similar to our own trumpets, but making confused and mournful noises. The banquet arrived in costly dishes of gold, which the Eunuchs brought, very gaily attired in Industane style, with trousers of various coloured silks, and white coats of the finest, transparent cloths, with which, displaying the precious odoriferous unguents with which they were perfumed, they also covered their brown and swarthy skins. Four of the principal of these placed themselves near His Majesty, doing nothing but deliver the courses which the other eunuchs brought to two most lovely damsels kneeling on either side of the Padchà. These placed the eatables before him alternately, and in the same order they offered him water as beverage, and took away the dishes which were no longer required.

I marvelled and was astonished to see observed among those—— so much politeness and order; and no less did I admire the abundance and diversity of the dishes and eatables. Among these there were also some which we use, principally many kinds of pastry, cakes, and different

confections of sweets, made by some slaves, who had been with the
Portuguese of Ugulim,[8] with so much perfection and art that the
Emperor, surprised at the novelty, asked his Father-in-law who were
the makers of such elegant confections, and being told that they had
been made by Franguini[9]——he replied aloud, as if astonished, *Truly
the Franguis would be a great people, were it not for three grave faults; in the first place,
they are Cafars* (i.e. a people without religion);[10] *in the second, they eat pork;
and thirdly, they do not wash the parts by which replete nature expels the excess of their
material paunches.'* This——conversation finished, the dinner, which
had lasted more than four hours, also came to an end, the tables
being taken up with a million prolix ceremonies, which I do not
describe, as I have to describe and relate to the curious Reader another
million, more important and substantial, owing to their being the
cause and chief end of the visits which it is His Majesty's custom to
make to the most important of his vassals. And so, as an agreeable
and festive dessert to this visit, twelve young dancing girls entered,
whom we will leave in silence, in their depravity, as a subject unfit for
Christian ears, on account of the lewdness and immodesty of their
dresses,[11] gestures and actions,——And turning to the chief and centre
(*medula*) of this——company, I say that three lovely damsels appeared
in the midst, gaily and richly dressed, bearing in their hands three
large and costly vessels of gold filled with most precious stones, such
as Diamonds, Balazios,[12] Pearls, Rubies, and other valuable gems, the
contents of the three plates being, according to rumour, valued at
more than seven hundred thousand rupees. A most savoury and valuable
mouthful would this be for a poor man; but it should be less valued
by a Monarch among the richest of the world, the Lord of thirty-
seven Kingdoms and provinces (of which, later on, we will give a
special and veridical account),[13] and the possessor of immense treasures
of gold, silver and precious stones, were this Prince not subject to a
devouring avarice,—another Marcus Crassus,—in his desire to
accumulate treasure; and well he showed it. Indeed, taking but little
interest in the dances and shows which they gave him, he leisurely
looked at and handled all those jewels, which, I believe, was due to/
his counting them;——the Lyric, said in his first satire[14]:

Congestis undique saccis,
Indormis inhians, & tanquam parcere sacris,
Cogeris, aut pictis tanquam gaudere tabellis.

The festivities having arrived at this stage, our Eunuch also arrived to look for us, saying that it was time for us to go, because, if we should remain to the end, it would be very difficult for us. At this warning, we left at once, following our guide, who, so as not to take us through the multitude of Imperial guards, led us by some underground passages by which we arrived in the street, where rewarding him for his trouble and care, we proceeded to our lodgings. As these were very far away, before we arrived at them, we had to traverse with much labour numerous squares and streets, but we considered our trouble well repaid in having witnessed so much grandeur, and matters so strange to our Europe.

Notes:

1. Apparently Fr. de Crasto, since at the end of the banquet they returned together to their lodgings, and Manrique was lodging with Fr. de Crasto.
2. Lignum aloes, see Hobson-Jobson, old ed., p. 258; new ed., p. 335, s.v. 'eagle-wood'.
3. Dastar-Khwan, a round piece of cloth or leather etc., spread on the ground, on which the food is laid, and around which the guests squat.
4. I [E.D. Maclagan] am indebted to Babu Manmohan Chakravarti for a reference to Blochm. Ain. i, p. 92, where a gold cloth is mentioned under the name of 'milak'.
5. Taslim: a respectful mode of salutation.
6. 'So fair a body and not a grain of wit.' Cat. Lxxxvi, 4. The ordinary reading is 'magno' not 'pulchro.'
7. I [E.D. Maclagan] have not found out what these words represent: possibly, Vaca=baja. It has been suggested to me that Borgondas may='barg-andaz'; etc., melody thrower, barg being a Persian word for melody; on the other hand they may not be Indian words at all.
8. Hugli.
9. An adjective derived from Frangui, sc. Firinghi.
10. Kafir.
11. See p. 87, note 6 [in the original book].
12. A kind of ruby. Hobson-Jobson, old ed., p. 39; new ed., p. 52, sv. 'balass'.
13. Sc. In chapter lxxvi, pp. 409–415.

14. Hor. Sat. I, i, 70.
   On every side the numerous bags are piled,
   Whose hallowed stores must never be defiled
   To human use; while you transported gaze,
   As if, like pictures, they were formed to please.
                                                Francis

Akbar's Capital: Jewel in the Sikh Crown

Fakir Syed Aijazuddin

Few cities in modern Pakistan can claim a longer uninterrupted lineage than Lahore, the capital of the province of Punjab. Certainly none has taken quite such insouciant advantage of its inheritance. For over a thousand years, Lahore has gradually encroached on its rural surroundings. It now sprawls inelegantly over an area covering thirty square miles of urban congestion. Northwards it has stretched up to and beyond the embankment built by the Mughal Emperor Aurangzeb in 1662 to protect it from the vagaries of the unpredictable river Ravi, while westwards it has overleapt the flow of the river to race towards Sheikhupura and Shahdara. Contained in the east since 1947 by the international border with India, Lahore has begun to surge inexorably southwards in the direction of its ancient companion, the second largest city of Punjab, Multan. In time it will undoubtedly engulf and absorb distant villages like Raiwind just as, over the years, it has assimilated hamlets such as Baghbanpura, Shahu-ki-garhi, Kot Lakhpat and Nawan Kot, which have long lost their separate identity and are now seamless suburbs of Lahore.

The history of Lahore can be traced reliably as far back as the seventh century A.D. Beyond that point in time, its chronology, like any other ancient genealogy, becomes a matter of supposition, inference or belief. The original foundation of Lahore or Loh-awar (from the Sanskrit word *awar* or fort) was attributed, according to a popular myth, to Lav or Loh, one of the sons of the legendary Rama. An early

This extract is taken from Fakir Syed Aijazuddin's *Lahore: Illustrated Views of 19th Century*, published by Mapin Publishing.

historian, the Alexandrian geographer Ptolemy writing in A.D. 150, mentioned a city called *Labokla* which may or may not have been Lahore, and the Chinese traveller Hieuen Tsang, who visited the Punjab almost five hundred years later in 630, spoke of a large city near Jalandhra (identified by scholars with modern Jullundur) populated by many thousands of Brahmin families. Each allusion appeared to yield some evidence of identification with a community of increasing prominence—whether a town or a city or even perhaps a small province—located close to the Ravi.

Its siting on the banks of one of the five rivers which threaded through the fertile Punjab basin to form the skein of the mighty Indus, its strategic location at a point where the abrasive interests of the kingdoms of Afghanistan and Persia often collided and clashed with those of northern India, and its commercial potential as a warehouse clearing southbound goods from Kashmir and northbound grain and produce from Multan gradually made Lahore into a powerful presence, a lodestone of sorts destined to exercise an almost gravitational pull on the course of Punjabi history.

The Muslim Afghans of Kerman and Peshawar were drawn to Lahore which they attacked in 682 when it was under the rule of the Hindu Chauhan dynasty. Three centuries later, Sabaktin, Governor of Khorassan, marched into the region and subdued the local Raja Jaipal. However, it was Sabaktin's son, Mahmud of Ghazni, who in 1022 finally drove out Jaipal's successor and with him the ruling Hindu dynasty out of the Punjab permanently. Mahmud placed Lahore under the control of his favourite Malik Ayaz, and so monumental were the latter's efforts in rehabilitating the city that he too acquired a legendary status, being accredited with the extraordinary feat of rebuilding the city during the course of a single night. Lahore continued to be governed by viceroys representing the Ghaznavid kings and for a period, between 1098 and 1114, it became the temporary capital-in-exile while the house of Ghazni, ousted from its home, tried to recover its Persian and Turan possessions.

In its early days, the Punjab remained essentially a vassal province. Its history mirrored the fortunes of the ruling dynasties. The fall of the Ghaznavids and their replacement by the Ghorians brought about a reciprocal shift in the allegiance of the satrap at Lahore and when any predators, such as the Ghakkar tribe, sensed a weakness they were quick to move into the vacuum, as they did in 1203 when they captured Lahore. The Ghakkars were soon expelled by Muhammad Ghori and his lieutenant, Qutbuddin Aibak. The conversion of the Ghakkars to Islam did little to decrease their hostility towards the Ghori monarch who was murdered by them in 1206. And then Qutbuddin, originally a slave, made himself the ruler of Lahore. He died four years later, as a result of an accident while playing *chougan* (the forerunner of modern horse-polo). He was buried 'like a treasure in the bowels of the earth' at Lahore.

Twelve years later, Sultan Jalaluddin of Khowrazm made an incursion into the Punjab and took Lahore, but he was driven away by the hordes of Changez Khan. The hordes, commanded by Changez Khan's general Turtai, chased the Sultan northwards from Sind, through Multan as far as Lahore, pillaging and scourging the country they moved through. Then satiated they returned to Ghazni.

For the next three hundred years, the spectre of the Mongols remained a relentless threat to whichever administration controlled the Punjab. They could be resisted, they could be repelled, they could on occasions be routed, but they could not be exorcised. While Lahore was to enjoy periods of comparative stability, for example, under the governorship of Sher Khan (a relation of Ghiasuddin Balban) when he 're-peopled the towns and villages of Lahore, which had been devastated by the Mongols, and appointed architects and superintendents to restore them' (Latif, 1892, p. 16, quoting from *Tarikh-i-Feroz Shahi*), the Mongols bore down again and again with a force that seemed to replenish itself after each onslaught. In the saga of bloody wars, combats, skirmishes, duplicity and rebellion that typified the history of the Punjab during this period, two events, both connected with the Mongols, were of great significance for Lahore—one was Timur's crossing the Indus in the autumn of 1398 on his way to capture Delhi and the other, which occurred 125 years later, was the occupation of Lahore by Babur in 1524.

Timur never came to Lahore; he preferred to make his authority felt from a distance by the effective expedient of a well-timed chastisement. He drained Lahore of its wealth. When his appointee as governor, Malik Shekha Khokar, reneged on a promise to forward tribute to his new master, Timur sent a punitive expedition led by his grandson to teach the defaulting viceroy as well as the inhabitants of Lahore, a lesson. They returned with a plunder of 'money, goods and horses'. Babur, on the other hand, found it necessary himself to subdue his recalcitrant viceroy, Dowlat Khan Lodi, and, after allowing his greedy troops to pillage the city, he had its streets burnt in reprisal for their resistance. In both incidents, the Mongols that Lahore had seen appeared no better than a destructive rapacious scourge, stripping every place they entered until there was nothing left to flay when they discarded it, denuded of all vestiges of wealth, property or civic order. Lahore was to see the Mongol descendants of Timur and Babur return before the century was out, though this time not in the guise of fearsome invaders but as the dynasty of civilised Mughals, settled and secure, who had made India their home and were to spend the next three hundred years of their lives in governing their war-won empire.

Within days of Babur's death in the winter of A.D. 1530, one of his sons, Mirza Kamran, then the governor of Kabul and Qandahar, saw an opportunity for himself as a candidate for the throne of Delhi. He hurried to Lahore and appropriated it by stratagem before the new ruler Humayun could secure it for himself. Humayun indulgently overlooked this sibling challenge and confirmed his younger brother's claim to the city. Ten years later, when Humayun was forced from his kingdom by Sher Shah Suri and he fled with his family out to Lahore for sanctuary, he assembled his nobles in the garden built by Mirza Kamran (of which now only a fragment remains stranded on an island in the river Ravi), directing 'that all the principal inhabitants of the city from seven to seventy years of age (young and old) should attend' (Jouher, 1882, p. 26). To no one's surprise, least of all to Humayun's, Mirza Kamran had made a separate peace with Sher Shah, having secretly ceded the Punjab to his brother's enemy. The brothers parted and left Lahore, Kamran for his estates in Kabul where he was met by a blinding ordered by Humayun for his habitual treacheries, and a sightless death in Arabia in 1557; and Humayun to a future of eleven years of exile and ultimately a triumphant restoration to the throne of his father.

During the years when Humayun was in exile, Sher Shah Suri, a gifted administrator, brought about a feeling of confidence and stability within the country by laying roads, improving communications and reorganising the revenue collection system. Lahore, though, had no place in his scheme. He thought it was situated too far inland to be an effective bulwark against marauders and regretted that he had not razed it to the ground. Scarred experience had warned him 'that such a large city should not exist on the very road of an invader, who, immediately after capturing it on his arrival, could rollect his supplies and organise his resources there' (Quoted in Latif, 1892, p. 24). For that contingency he built the monolithic fort at Rohtas (later completed by his son Salim Shah) on the far side of the fifth Punjabi river, the Jhelum, more than 100 miles to the west of Lahore.

The contribution of the Mughal dynasty to Lahore could be summarised as providing it with gardens, palaces and tombs. The first garden had already been laid by Mirza Kamran during Humayun's time. It was left to the young Akbar, illiterate but intuitively gifted, to build its first permanent palace. Becoming emperor at the premature age of thirteen, he was only in the second year of his reign when he was obliged to come to Lahore from where he supervised a spirited campaign against Sikandar Shah Suri; and again it was from Lahore that he repelled the ambitions of his half-brother Mohammed Hakim Khan. Akbar stayed on this latter occasion 'at the house of Mahdi Qasim Khan, in the citadel' which might explain why Akbar felt impelled to build his own palace there. According to the *Ain-e-Akbari*, which was compiled soon after Akbar transferred his capital to Lahore in 1584: 'His Majesty plans splendid edifices, and dresses the work of his mind and heart in the garment of stone and clay. Thus mighty fortresses have been raised, which protect the timid, frighten the rebellious, and please the obedient. Delightful villas, and imposing towers have also been built. They afford excellent protection against cold and rain, provide for the comforts of the princesses of the Harem, and are conducive to that dignity which is necessary for worldly power' (Abu'l Fazl, 1939,I, p. 232).

Akbar could not have found a plinth more appropriately symbolic of 'worldly power' than the elevated foundations of the old citadel of Lahore, on which he built grand apartments for his personal use and accessible halls of audience to make his regal appearances in before his *omrahs* and the general public. To accommodate the growing bureaucracy which actually administered the expanding Mughal empire, he constructed a warren of smaller vaulted chambers. His confidant and chronicler, Abu'l Fazl, wrote admiringly of this period of Lahore's florescence: 'During the present reign the fortifications and citadel have been strengthened with brick masonry and, as it was on several occasions the seat of government, many splendid buildings have been erected and delightful gardens have lent it additional beauty. It is the resort of people of all countries whose manufactures present an astonishing display and it is beyond measure remarkable in populousness and extent' (Abu'l Fazl, 1949, II, p. 317). Although in the ensuing reigns, Lahore would continue to develop and expand, it would never attain the same importance as it did as Akbar's capital during the twelve continuous years of his occupancy until 1598, nor would it ever compete with the other two cities—Agra and Delhi—associated with this golden period of the Mughal empire.

Jehangir's ideas of the kind of empire he wished to rule over were no less grandiose than those of his father, but before he could implement them, he needed to suppress, soon after his accession in 1605, an early challenge to his authority from his son Khusrau. Rebellion seemed to come instinctively to Mughal princes; treason pulsated through their veins. A brother thought nothing of usurping the right of his real brothers, and many an oedipean son conspired covertly, if not openly, against his father. Jehangir recognised this almost hereditary weakness only too well. He had succumbed to it himself on one occasion when he declared his opposition to Akbar. Confronted, in turn, he chased Khusrau who had fled to Lahore and, after catching him, he showed the same leniency to the person of his son as he had himself received at the hands of his forgiving parent. As a fond father Jehangir spared the person of Khusrau. As the remorseless emperor he made him endure the trauma of being paraded, humiliated and helpless, before seven hundred of his failed supporters who had been impaled upon stakes embedded in double rows from the garden of Mirza Kamran to the city gates of Lahore.

By the tenth year of his reign, settled and secure, Jehangir ordered Abdul Karim in March 1615 to build for him a handsome palace at Lahore. Two years later he visited the completed additions Abdul

Karim had made within the walled fort and gave them his unqualified approval. 'Without exaggeration', he dictated, 'these are mansions delightful and charming and habitations lovely and attractive, exquisitely fine and elegant, adorned throughout with paintings and engravings, the work of artists of the age. The sight was charmed with a view of verdant gardens'. Even though much of what he had ordered to be constructed in the Lahore Fort was later to be remodelled by his successor Shah Jahan, Jehangir's personal style and taste, emulated just short of competition by his nobles, established influential standards of urbane and gracious living in the city that began to radiate around the Fort. William Finch, a merchant who visited the city in 1611, lauded it as being 'one of the greatest cities of the East'. Walking in and around it, he observed: 'The castle or towne is enclosed with a stronge brick wall, having twelve faire gates, nine by land, and three openings to the river: the streets faire and well paved, the inhabitants most Baneans and handicrafts men; all white men [Mughals] of note lying in the suburbs. The buildings are faire and high, with bricke and much curositie of carved windows and doores.'[1] Lahore's prosperity continued under the governorship of Asaf Khan, appointed by his brother-in-law Jehangir in the closing years of his reign.

Immediately after Jehangir's death in 1627, Lahore became the symbolic prize in the contest for the Mughal throne between his two sons—the designated successor Shah Jahan and his younger brother Prince Shahryar. At the time of his father's death, Shah Jahan had more or less been exiled to the Deccan; therefore, he had to rely entirely upon the tactical adroitness of his father-in-law Asaf Khan who was present at court to protect his interests. Shahryar, instigated by Jehangir's ambitious widow Nur Jahan (who also happened to be his mother-in-law and Asaf Khan's sister), raised his standard over Lahore and appropriated the imperial coffers to pay for an army of mercenaries to fight on his behalf. A battle between the two proxy forces took place just outside the city and Lahore soon fell to the victor, appropriately to the prince who had been born within its walls thirty-six years earlier as Prince Khurram and was now proclaimed through the *khutba* read in all the city's mosques as the new Emperor Shah Jahan.

For Shah Jahan, holding his court at Lahore in the first year of his reign was like a homecoming. Not only was he born and suckled there (his nurse Dai Anga was later to build a splendid mosque in the city, funded undoubtedly by her royal charge) but many of his happiest memories were associated with the city and its environs. With time on his hands and the imperial coffers restored to his control, he saw to it that the Lahore fort apartments were remodelled. Personally he made some distinctive additions to them, such as the perfect Moti masjid or Pearl mosque designed for the private use by the royal family. Although Shah Jahan shifted his residence to Agra, each visit by him to Lahore injected a fresh infusion of vitality to the architectural improvement of the city and provided inspiration to like-minded nobles and grandees, prominent amongst whom were his mentor Asaf Khan (whose palace at Lahore cost a reputed 20 lakhs to construct), Hakim Alimuddin later honoured as Wazir Khan who built one of Lahore's most beautiful and enduring mosques, and Ali Mardan Khan whose fertile ingenuity in creating Shalimar Gardens in 1642 enabled his royal master to enjoy the delights of Kashmir without having to leave the plains of the Punjab. Many of Lahore's admired monuments—Asaf Khan's tomb, Wazir Khan's *baradari*, the Chaburji garden and its iridescent entrance built by a Mughal princess in 1646, the enamelled Gulabi Bagh gateway constructed by Mirza Sultan Beg in 1655—belong to this period.

Had Shah Jahan been succeeded by his eldest son, the aesthetic Dara Shikoh, the fortunes of Lahore might have taken a different upward course. In the event, when Aurangzeb (Shah Jahan's third son) deposed his father in 1658, Lahore found itself for the third time witness to the conflict between yet another generation of Mughal princes claiming the throne. Dara Shikoh, following his defeat at Agra, hurried to Lahore and after clearing the treasury of its hoard amounting to over a crore of rupees worth of silver, gold and bullion, left in haste for Multan. In time he too fell casualty to the steely ambitions of Aurangzeb and suffered an ignominious end. Symbolically, no trace remains today of the sumptuous palace said to have been built by Dara Shikoh; instead, the grand Badshahi Masjid ordered by Aurangzeb has dominated the skyline of Lahore for the past three hundred years.

After the death of Aurangzeb in 1707, and until the emergence of the Sikhs as a political force in the Punjab with the establishment of the deceptively diminutive Sukerchakia chieftain Ranjit Singh at the end of the 18th century, Lahore was relegated to a subordinate position. It continued to thrive commercially but sank to a provincial level both in the eyes of the introvert Government centred at Delhi and in the smaller minds of its viceroys who governed the Punjab in its name.

At the end of the turbulent eighteenth century, Lahore's history took a significant turn. Although threatened once again by an invading Afghani—this time by the grandson of Ahmad Shah, Shah Zaman— Lahore's unity and in some considerable measure its credentials as the prime city in the Punjab were to be restored by the young Sikh chieftain Ranjit Singh. He obtained a grant of the city from the departing Shah Zaman in 1798 and in the heat of the following July, he marched towards the walled city to enforce his claim. Collaborators met him at Shalimar gardens where he had encamped on 6 July and arranged to open the Lahori and Shahalami gates to admit his forces. The next day he took possession of the royal citadel, ousting its uneasy occupants. In 1799, the last year of the century, Ranjit Singh, an unknown barely nineteen years of age, declared himself master of Lahore, the city with a pedigree of a thousand years.

Having established himself at Lahore and after a raucous coronation on 12 April 1801, Ranjit Singh quickly organised a mint to issue currency and then proceeded upon a series of campaigns to extend his control over other Sikh and Hill states in the surrounding Punjab. Being a Sikh, the city of Amritsar held more than a political significance for him and by 1802 he had included it in his expanding realm. In the ensuing years he controlled Ludhiana, Kangra (the most crucial of the mainly Rajput hill states to the north), Kasur, the eastern areas up to the Attock river, Multan, and by 1820 Peshawar, Kashmir and distant Ladakh. It was an achievement that evoked pride amongst his supporters and envious apprehension amongst the ranks of his enemies, particularly the British on his eastern borders.

In an effort to contain his permeating influence, a treaty was negotiated in 1809 between Charles Metcalfe representing the British and Ranjit Singh by which the British obtained an undertaking from him to accept the river Sutlej as the dividing border between them. In exchange, they agreed to recognise his undisputed authority over territories north of the Sutlej provided he did not interfere with the possessions of the Sikh Cis-Sutlej Chiefs under their protection. Both undertook to maintain 'perpetual friendship' between the British Government and the State of Lahore. For the next fifty years, the British observed Ranjit Singh rule and his successors mismanage his Sikh kingdom; for the remaining fifty years of the nineteenth century the vanquished Sikhs watched the British reign over the Punjab.

II. 19TH CENTURY LAHORE OBSERVED

Throughout his life Ranjit Singh remained essentially suspicious of any power that showed itself weak enough to negotiate with him. The public compromise he made with the British in 1809 did not deflect him from taking measures privately to protect and if necessary to defend his own interests. Three years after the Treaty of Amritsar was put into effect, Colonel David Ochterlony, whom Ranjit Singh had invited to Lahore to attend the nuptial celebrations of his eldest son Kharak Singh in 1812, noticed that he had ordered the reinforcement of the city walls. Reporting upon what he had seen Ochterlony wrote to his superiors at Delhi: 'He has built and is building a very thick wall and ramparts around the city with a deep and broad ditch, and that the Palace is in like manner surrounded by a deep and broad ditch, the whole faced with brick and the earth thrown inwards, so as to form a very broad rampart with bastions at intervals at a considerable distance from the Palace walls.'

In the initial years of Ranjit Singh's rule, few visitors enjoyed the facility extended to Ochterlony to tour Lahore with freedom. Ochterlony himself had encountered considerable hostility from suspicious courtiers who tried to dissuade the Maharaja from allowing the Britisher such free access. They remonstrated about his 'great confidence and seeming attachment' to the visitor. Ranjit Singh's response to them (as reported by Ochterlony) was characteristically disarming: 'He first said that I seemed a good kind of man, and spoke otherwise favourably, but on their observing that such was our way that we conciliate only to deceive, and requested him to be more careful, he replied that he had invited me to Lahore and must now show me every attention, but if they had given their advice before he would not have asked me to come there.'

As Ranjit Singh's political stature increased, Lahore once again became the fulcrum of the Punjab. Its markets thronged with dealers of all sorts of commodities—grain, fruit, shawls, arms, even mercenaries, and, to Ranjit Singh perhaps the most valuable item of them all—horses. His hospitality became legendary and no visitor who had been exposed to it could ever forget the heady profusion of gifts and other marks of attention which greeted him from the moment they entered his realm. The welcome accorded to William Moorcroft, the veterinary surgeon who came to Lahore in May 1820, became a much-repeated pattern. An escort greeted him at the borders, trays of sweetmeats, food, money and provisions were supplied, and accommodation arranged at convenient stages. In Moorcroft's case, he was lodged at Shalimar gardens to rest and prepare himself before he was received in audience by his munificent host.

The personal largesse Ranjit Singh showered upon his guests fell within an immediate circle. Stepping out of it, the visitor was likely to see aspects of the city which tended to vitiate the impression of grandeur created at the court. Moorcroft, for example, when taken around the 'very populous' inner city by its governor Fakir Nuruddin, noted in his journal: 'The streets were crowded to an extent beyond anything I have ever witnessed in an Indian city. The houses were in general of brick, and five storeys high, but many were in a very crazy condition. The Bazar follows the direction of the city wall, and is not far distant from it. The street is narrow, and this inconvenience is aggravated by platforms in front of the shops, on which the goods are displayed under projecting penthouses of straw to protect them from the sun and rain. Through the centre of the remaining contracted space runs a deep and dirty drain, the smell from which was very offensive. The population consists of Mohammedans, Hindus, and Sikhs, the former in the greatest number. I saw no building of any size or magnificence, except the mosque of the Nawab Wazir Khan. The wall of the city was still under repair, and 3000 men are said to be on work on it and upon the moat which the Raja was about to add to the defences. The place, however, could oppose no effectual resistance to European assailants.' (Moorcroft, 1841, I, pp 105–6).

A later account of the city, provided by Alexander Burnes who headed a delegation to the Sikh Court in July 1831, echoed many of Moorcroft's observations of a decade before: 'In our evening rambles at Lahore, we had many opportunities of viewing this city. The ancient capital extended from east to west for a distance of five miles; and had an average breadth of three, as may be yet traced by the ruins. The mosques and tombs, which have been more stably built than the houses, remain in the midst of fields and cultivation as caravanseries for the traveller. The modern city occupies the western angle of the ancient capital, and is encircled by a strong wall. The houses are very lofty; and the streets, which are narrow, offensively filthy, from a gutter that passes through the centre. The bazars of Lahore do not exhibit much appearance of wealth; but the commercial influence of the Punjab is to be found at Umritsur, the modern capital. There are some public buildings within the city that deserve mention. The King's mosque [the Badshahi Masjid] is a capacious building of red sandstone, which had been brought by Aurangzebe from near Delhi. Its four lofty minarets still stand, but the temple itself has been converted into a powder magazine. There are two other mosques, with minarets, to proclaim the falling greatness of the Mohammedan empire; where the 'faithful', as everywhere else in the Punjab, must offer their prayers in silence' (Burnes, 1834, III, pp. 158–59).

Burnes continued his narrative with a brief description of the tomb of Jehangir at Shahdara, which he called 'the finest ornament of Lahore . . . a monument of great beauty'. He regretted its vulnerability to the river Ravi, which 'capricious in its course . . . has lately overwhelmed a portion of the garden wall that environs the tomb'. Another object of his admiration was the Shalimar garden '—a magnificent remnant of Moghul grandeur'. He described it as being 'about half a mile in length, with three successive terraces, each above the level of the other. A canal, which is brought from a great distance, intersects this beautiful garden, and throws up its water in 450 fountains to cool the atmosphere. The marble couch of the Emperor yet remains; but the garden suffered much injury before Runjeet Sing obtained his present ascendancy. The Maharaja himself has removed some of the marble houses; but he has had the good taste to replace them, though it be by more ignoble stone' (Burnes, 1834, III, pp. 160–61).

In Burnes's observations one reads clues to Ranjit Singh's attitude towards Lahore. He had no pretensions to being another Shah Jahan and therefore never felt the urge to build on an imperial scale. Unlike Aurangzeb, he had no need to construct another house of prayer to rival the Badshahi Mosque—he already had the Golden Temple at Amritsar. Lahore as a city represented to Ranjit Singh yet another possession, a temporal prize to be coveted like one of his fabled jewels or his caparisoned thoroughbred horses. His feelings for them were raw, selfish and possessive, nourished by the admiration he saw in the eyes of his audience. In Lahore, just as he had grasped its historic citadel and put it to his own hardy use or desecrated the Badshahi Mosque and converted it into a functional ammunition store, he stripped many of the more striking monuments in the city of their ornamental decoration and distributed their parts elsewhere to be re-assembled in a pastiche of their original style. Under Ranjit Singh's rule, the citizenry of Lahore recovered a sense of pride in their heritage; because of him, they often sacrificed the very cause of that pride.

A map of Lahore—prepared in 1837 by a British Captain, W. Gordon, a member of the British delegation led by Sir Henry Fane that came to attend the marriage ceremonies of Kunwar Nau Nehal Singh (Ranjit Singh's grandson)—shows Lahore as still contained within the bounds of the walled city. The large *havelis* that sprang up during Ranjit Singh's time—notable amongst them, the splendid ones of Nau Nehal Singh (now a Government School) and of Wazir Dhian Singh (today occupied by squatters)—were built within the protective walls of the city. The areas outside the city, particularly towards Shalimar, were overspread with gardens and country estates.

The death of Maharaja Ranjit Singh in June 1839 brought to an abrupt end the period of comparative stability and tranquillity enjoyed by the residents of Lahore. In imitation of the Mughal wars of succession, conflicts broke out between Ranjit Singh's heirs, egged on by their Dogra advisers, until almost everyone lost—with the singular exception of the foxy Raja Gulab Singh who in the melee secured Kashmir for himself. A contemporary account of the state of panic and disorder that disrupted life in the city has been provided in a translation of the court chronicle for 1841, the year of Sher Singh's assumption of his father's teetering throne:

'During these days when the sacred book of kingship had become scattered and upset in its pages, all the *silahbands* and the attendants upon the platoons gathered together in large crowds of thousands outside the gates of the fort of Lahore and inside it and began to cause various kinds of trouble and molestation to the various men who went or came and teased especially the attendants of the state and the glorious chieftains. Whenever people rode from their mansions and came towards the fort, they began to strike with sticks the face of the horses and the backs of the servants accompanying them and turned them out in great disgrace, uttering many improper and rude words. Apart from the general chaos and confusion, there was indiscipline among the regular troops, for vapours of mischief, revolt and rebellion had gathered together in their brains, whether they were high or low, noble or gentle, and had upset altogether their wisdom and their sense, and the words of being true to salt, to be full of the spirit of sacrifice, to be obedient and loyal seemed to have been removed or erased from the tablets of their hearts by the revolutions of the times. The various figures of dispute, enmity and mischief seemed to have impressed great and small pictures upon the mirrors of their hard hearts.'

'What account,' the chronicler asks sadly, 'should be given of this mischief-making group which had ... gone towards the garden of Jamadar Sahib Khushal Singh [the site of the present Government House] and had uprooted the pleasant trees of that paradise-like garden and had secured for themselves everlasting misfortune and the store of permanent bad-luck with the result that in the twinkling of an eye the garden which used to have spring always began to look like one smitten with everlasting autumn' (Suri, 1972, pp. 146–47).

The apprehensions felt by right-minded citizens were shared by the British who watched the deterioration at the court of their former ally with deepening concern. The provocation of the first Sikh War in December 1845 and the capitulation of the Sikhs under the terms of the Treaty of Lahore, signed on 9 March 1846, provided the British with the excuse to establish their presence in Lahore, ostensibly to protect the young Maharaja Dalip Singh who had been placed on the throne after the assassination of his half-brother Sher Singh in September 1843. A contingent of troops was quartered in the Fort on a temporary basis, the understanding being that they would remain only until the end of the year. Political dialogue between the British Government and the Sikh Darbar was the responsibility of Henry Lawrence, designated the Resident at Lahore. Before the year was out, the stay of the British troops had been extended until Dalip Singh attained his majority in another eight years. By 1847, barracks and bungalows had been constructed in Anarkali to house the garrison and a large Residency built (now the Civil Secretariat) adjacent to Anarkali's tomb to accommodate Lawrence.

The period between 1846 and 1849 enabled Henry Lawrence to put into place, through the mouthpiece of the otherwise ineffective Sikh Darbar, reforms which gradually stabilised life in the Punjab, but even Lawrence could not reverse the policy of the British Government as it moved inexorably towards annexation. Mulraj's rebellion provided the excuse for Lord Dalhousie's precipitation. According to an apocryphal story, Ranjit Singh was once shown a map of India and upon his enquiring what the area shaded in red indicated, he was told that it represented British possessions. 'Soon all of it will be red,' was his prescient response. It took less than ten years after his death for that prophecy to be fulfilled. On 29 March 1849, at a ceremony convened in the Sheesh Mahal apartments, the Punjab was formally annexed and the British flag unfurled above the ramparts of the Lahore Fort. The red in the Union Jack was visible to the entire city.

Note:
1. Latif (1982), p. 16, quoting from the *Tarikh-i-Feroz Shahi*.

The Beginning of Five Queen's Road

Sorayya Y. Khan

In the beginning, Five Queen's Road belonged to the British. The grandeur of the house, the colonial architecture, and the stream of servants walking in and out of the driveway, made this clear. There was another suggestion, something even a blind person could appreciate. In Lahore, city of infinite smells, it was the absence of any smell at all from the premises of Five Queen's Road that made the house unmistakably British. Part of the reason for this was the indoor kitchen, from which only weakened smells escaped. The other was that nothing of strong fragrance was cooked in it: no garlic, no onions, no chillies. And, any time cinnamon or ginger was used, it wasn't thrown into smoking oil to accentuate every bit of spice, but instead ground to a powder, mixed into a cake batter, and baked in an oven, a procedure which allowed the spices to release the gentlest of their aromas.

The house was John Smithson's idea. Smithson was the Chief of the North West Railways, and the house was built with railway funds. Had he waited a year or two, his request for the house would have been received in the midst of the Second World War and would not have elicited a response. In his proposal, he listed the reasons why the railways should build this house for its chief executive, and only some of them were true. It was possible that guests from home would be more comfortable staying in his own house rather than in hotels, but the new house did not offer more space for entertainment needs; and although he swore it to be true, the events of Partition proved him wrong—the property on Five Queen's Road did not turn out to be a wise investment for the railways. The assessment he submitted to his superiors at home did not include the most pressing and honest reason for his expensive request to build himself a separate house. After ten years of being confined to the railways' own housing colony, the Mayo

Garden, Smithson's patience had simply run out. He believed that he had endured as much of the colony as he possibly could.

The Mayo Garden was a haven of sorts, neat rows of freshly painted bungalows on either side of clean streets that were swept like clockwork twice a day, and in the summer, hosed down every evening. The map inside the locked glass case that met visitors as they turned into the colony was fading, and no one bothered to replace it. New construction, a bungalow here and there, and the expanded children's playground were written in with a marker that did not match the faded shade of the other writing. Smithson knew he could order the map changed, but for once, he wanted someone else to take the initiative. The Mayo Garden was what its name suggested: a garden town. Neat lines of trees had been planted forty years earlier when the colony was built, and they had matured to provide vast tents of green and shade that covered the colony. The rectangular lawns were enclosed with rows of bushes that were precisely as high as they were supposed to be when the malis measured them every few months, and if they were not, they were quickly chopped back. The flowers were beautifully tended, and were sometimes so exemplary in their brilliant beds of purple or red or yellow that the only way it seemed possible for them to have been spared the Lahore dust was if they had been dusted, petal by petal, every morning after the cars sputtered by.

Even so, Smithson did not like what was happening in his colony. He was tired of the neat rows of bungalows, tired of living with the same people with whom he worked. People dropped by his bungalow at all hours of the evening for a glass of whisky or a shot of after-dinner brandy and to ask for favours, among them the opportunity to move in to the colony. They brought gifts with them: Cadbury chocolates from home that were covered in a film of white or melted together in clumps of chocolate in which the peanuts and almonds poked through. Once he had a huge crate of wine gifted to him, and no matter how insistent he was about not accepting it, his guest's insistence outdid his own. Two of his strongest servants were required to unload the crate and carry it into the house. He was a beer drinker with a penchant for the local Murree beer sold in oversize bottles at the market. He had stayed away from wine all his life on principle, having long ago connected wine drinking with idiosyncrasies reserved for women. He never touched a drop of that wine, and he did not serve it at any of the numerous functions that were held in his house.

Smithson had spent many years in India, and besides the success of his railway operation, the size and intricacies of his plaster of Paris model of India were testament to this. He used a topographical map of India as a guide when he created the model, moulding uneven lumps and placing them around the top of the crooked triangle to represent the mountain ranges. The model sat in the middle of his office, covering the span of a dark, sheesham dining-room table built to fit twenty for a sit-down dinner. The fan hung low from the high ceiling, inadvertently fanning more air on the railway chief's model of India than on the staff or visitors or anyone else who was in his office. The placement of his model made it difficult for people to enter his office, and for those who were new to the office or unaccustomed, it was a source of embarrassment, because they often walked directly into the table.

In addition to overseeing his railway system, Smithson spent his years tending to his plaster of Paris model. The white surface was covered with thousands of broken lines that represented the expanse of the railway system in India. There were blue lines for existing rail routes, and purple lines for tracks that were in the planning stages, years away from being laid down. There were green squares to identify railway stations, and orange circles in cities where the railways had their own representatives. The model was also a personal document of Smithson's travels in India. He had drawn in yellow lines to mark all the routes he had travelled, all the places he had visited during his tenure in India. The yellow lines did not cover all of the model, but much of it, enough to leave the impression that he had seen a large part of His Majesty's Empire. Although his work looked perfect, as if he never made a mistake, this was not so. It was only that Smithson had a fail-safe method of making corrections. First, he rubbed off the chalk as best as he could with his handkerchief. Then he pulled out the small bucket of white gypsum powder that he kept underneath the table, and mixed a bit of it with a few drops of water. Finally, he spread the paste with his finger over the part to be modified, and in a matter of seconds, the spot was white again, and before the end of the day, he could draw over it.

His colleagues believed his obsession with the model in his office had to do with his being vaguely related to the first Surveyor General of India, whose idea it had been to undertake the first geographical survey of the country. But Smithson thought of it quite differently, and he staunchly defended his model to his colleagues. It was important to know exactly how the Empire stretched out underneath them, he said. Otherwise, it was bound to slip between their fingers.

Smithson selected the plot for his house, and it exceeded his list of conditions. The site was larger and more open than any he had hoped to find, and in the middle sat a small mound upon which he immediately imagined the house. The location was highly desirable. It was at the crossing of Queen's and Lawrence Roads, minutes away from the Charing Cross police station, and two hundred yards away from Mall Road, which led to the Governor's house. Smithson enlisted the help of a local architect to design the house and sent the blueprints to his brother-in-law's architectural firm in England for advice, even though the era of colonial architecture at home had long passed. It took sixteen months for the house to be completed, and Smithson never missed his daily visit to the site.

The time spent building the house was filled with decisions: the woodwork on the veranda, which fireplaces should duplicate the one in Smithson's office, whether the billiard table should have its own room, and whether any of the doorways would be framed with arches. When the house was complete, there were two simple verandas extending across the length of the front and back of the house, and both were wide enough to comfortably hold a table of four bridge players. Each room had a fireplace, including the library, where Smithson decided to house the billiard table. The library sat in the warmest corner of the house and had tall windows that let in so much winter sun that the fireplace would never once be used. There was only one arch in the house. It dropped from the high ceiling to separate the spacious living and dining rooms, and framed a set of delicate French doors that could be pulled closed on occasion. The locks on the doors were ordered from England, and the decorative fixtures arrived before the house was completed.

But the decisions dearest to Smithson were reserved for the garden. He spent hours considering the landscape of the property, the colours that he wanted to highlight, the placement of the shrubs and trees. Before the roof was laid down, Smithson filled a sketchbook with an artist's renditions of where the bedded terraces of perennials would be, and where he would plant the bougainvilleas that would learn to curl around leads of rope and climb the walls of the yellow house. His desire to garden was recent, but his appreciation for the careful work of planting, weeding and watering was old. When he was a child, and his mother took in laundry to make ends meet after his father died, she grew a garden in the patch of land behind their house and planted neat rows of vegetables. In those years, Smithson had sat on the steps of the kitchen to watch his mother tend her tomatoes, cucumbers, celery and carrots. She was new to gardening, and despite her efforts, it was not uncommon for her plants to barely grow before the leaves ran holes and died. He had fond memories of the one year this did not happen, when in the late summer he had helped his mother pull vegetables of different shapes and colours from the ground.

Smithson delayed the final construction work on the house by insisting that his garden be started before he moved in. He was determined that some flowers should already be blooming and visible from the windows of his library when he did his unpacking. The disgruntled workers were forced to remove their equipment from the sites of his terraced perennial beds. After some arguing, he promised not to lay down his grass until the workers finished their work, and the house stood finished. It was just as well, because it gave him enough time to receive his order of grass-seed from Bengal. He had selected a special variety that promised to withstand the heat of the tropics most resiliently. It was true to its word, and he was able to grow a carpet of green grass that was unparalleled among the other brown, blotchy lawns in Lahore. One or two years later, when almost everything in his garden began to bloom according to plan, he passed his afternoons underneath the gazebo in his garden. The colours he lived with were fabulous. The purple bougainvilleas against the freshly painted yellow house with the backdrop of the blue sky were so striking—the combination of colours seemed wet, as though they had been painted on to a canvas and would never dry. In a strange way, the texture, the depth, the precision of the colours were uniquely Indian. One of Smithson's first impressions of India had been that it was a land committed to the celebration of colours, from the clothes and shoes people wore, down to their jewellery. When he considered the colour contrasts in his garden, he felt pleased, as if he had managed to capture an Indian ethic, only to make it better, present it more clearly.

Smithson dug an intricate series of miniature waterways in his garden to provide an irrigation system for the thousands of flowers he planted. The waterways were tiny ditches only a few inches in diameter that wove through the entire garden, beginning at the well. They were re-dug after the annual monsoon rains washed them away. During the rest of the year, the malis would take turns every evening drawing water from the well and pouring it into the mouth of the system that carried water thousands of square feet. The grass could not be watered this way, and the malis carried water in *mashaks*, buffalo hides looped around their backs, controlling the squirting water from the neck of the hide hanging near their hips. In spring, the blooming flowers and bushes, and their bouquet of jasmine, lavender and queen of the night filled the garden. The breezeless seasons kept the aromas inside the walls of the grounds. The fresh scents piled upon each other from the bottom up, each fresh fragrance pushing from the ground upward in an empire of perfumes that stretched into the baking sky.

Smithson had been in the house six, maybe seven, years when the British decided to quit India. The Empire planned to retreat and in its stead leave behind two separate countries, India and Pakistan. During that summer of 1947, more quickly than he would have liked, his colleagues began boarding the huge ships docked in Karachi's harbour preparing to sail home. Smithson received his orders and, reluctantly, began to prepare for his departure. Although he had known since he arrived in India that the Empire would not persevere forever, he was less prepared to leave than he had imagined. He was not enthusiastic about returning to England, to the quiet life he had led before he acted on his instincts several years after the First World War and joined the service of the Empire. Besides his mother, who lived her life in one room of her house because she was too old and tired to keep up with the housework of a larger space, nothing waited for him at home. Nevertheless, when Smithson received the scheduled date of his departure, he circled the date on his calendar and accepted it as fact. Then he sat down at his desk with a notepad and pen in his hands. He drew up an inventory of his office that included his books and files and the innumerable boxes of maps and papers in the closet behind his desk. He began to consider the items he wanted to take back to England, but before he could detail them, his attention shifted. Instead, he made a list of people to whom he would give his alcohol. He recalled the crate of inexpensive wine his servants had inadvertently moved from the Mayo Garden to Five Queen's Road, and he singled it out not to be passed along to anyone.

Servants filled his trunks with his belongings. Most of what Five Queen's Road housed was railway property: furniture, dishes, wall hangings, bookcases. The books and carpets were his, and so were the rolls of silk he had bought for his mother on his travels to the North West Frontier Province. He knew she would be pleased with the silk, even if she no longer had the energy to sew. The material was softer than any dress she owned, and meticulously hand-embroidered with simple flowers. He wrapped his precious stone collection, after polishing each piece between his long and slender fingers, and he wondered if there would ever be anyone to whom he could present the blue lapis lazuli stones coloured with flecks of gold. He packed his new, framed photographs himself, folding them in sheets and blankets. A few months before his departure, during his last Lahore spring, he hired two photographers to freeze the image of Five Queen's Road for him. One photographer did this on a glass plate to capture colours, and the other one used black-and-white film. Smithson posed in the photographs, standing outside his library next to the bougainvillea in a hand-tailored suit, with the hat on his head slightly tipped forward. He had not wanted to wear a hat, but the photographers insisted that if he did not, the sun would bounce off his high forehead, moist with a permanent film of perspiration, and cause a glare that might ruin the picture. He pointed a cane he never used a few feet ahead of him, pulled his lips taut around his teeth, and stared into the camera with the seriousness of a man unaccustomed to being photographed.

But what he most wanted to take with him, he could not. He wanted the plaster model to accompany him to England, to sit in his house or his office. The reality was, however, that he wouldn't have enough space in either location, and eventually he yielded this point. Before he resigned himself to this, he thought of ways to pack the model. He knew it was too large to fit in a crate. He thought of sawing it up into smaller, more manageable pieces. This was no use, though, since he was sure it would splinter, if not crack, into thousands of pieces. And then, there was still the long journey home to take into account, in the dank bowels of the ship, where the model would surely begin to crumble, succumbing to the moist air. After considering every possibility, he accepted the necessity of leaving the model behind, but not in his office, where he did not expect order to prevail once he relinquished his authority. Instead, he decided to have the model transported to Five Queen's Road. His colleagues thought him silly, and as he supervised the move of the model, one of them chided him for thinking of his house, a railway property, as his own. The remark prompted him into action, and that evening, when Smithson arrived home, he wrote a series of letters to his superiors asking that he be awarded the right to determine the fate of the house. After some persistence, and a curt letter that remarked on the extraordinariness of his request, he received permission to dispose of Five Queen's Road any way he pleased. The only stipulation was that the transaction be registered in the books and the money be returned to the railway coffers from which it had originally come.

*

Smithson spent more time worrying about the fate of Five Queen's Road after Partition than the state of the railways. He declined to participate in the planning and preparing of manuals. He refused to take time to explain procedures to the local staff who would inherit his railway operation. He did not see the point in all the talk of training which some of his colleagues had taken to heart, spending their last days in India behind closed doors trying to squeeze a career of experience into a few weeks of instruction. He was uneasy with this posture. As soon as it had become clear that His Majesty was truly going to give up the Empire, he suffered from spells of paralysis in which he believed that nothing he could possibly do, no amount of training or instruction, could affect the way things were going to turn out once the locals were at the reins. Of course, he wished that the railway operation would continue the way it had, well maintained, running smoothly, and on time. But he had seen the fate of things the British had given up, a restaurant gone cheap and filthy, a shop changing its decor and selling common knick-knacks. It was happening too quickly. After maintaining an Empire as vast as this one, and for so long, this slipshod method of getting out overnight was not dignified, not the way it ought to have been done. It was true, though, there were things even His Majesty and his Lords and Viceroys could not control. It was in the blood of the Indians, this way of behaving, and it wasn't going to change, no matter how much training he offered his staff. A colleague scolded him for his fatalism. 'Do you realize,' he had said, 'how much like an Indian you're beginning to sound?'

His colleague had chuckled, but the comment had surprised Smithson, who always hesitated in drawing such comparisons. He disagreed with his colleague, even said as much; that it was just that they already had done all the work that they could with the railways, the roads, the hospitals, the schools. There were only a few months left, and that was not enough time to do anything more than a ragged job of teaching the locals how to run things.

Five Queen's Road was the exception. Smithson was finding it difficult to walk away. It was hard enough giving it up, but virtually unbearable wondering who would look after it for him when he was gone. Who would tend the flowers, who would make sure the bushes were pruned on time, who would supervise his complicated watering schedule to assure that his flowers bloomed in synchrony? These questions preoccupied him. He had thoughts of turning Five Queen's Road into a museum. In fact, this was the plan most of his colleagues endorsed. That the house should become a railway museum and a storehouse of memorabilia, some of their plans and maps gracing its walls. He also thought of turning it into a library filled with railway material, all the documents that would be left behind, at first of use to the local authorities who would take over, but later, to students, who would pore over the material and decide for themselves how all the work had been accomplished. Smithson was not opposed to these ideas on principle. He considered a museum and library important contributions. It was the idea of turning his house into public property that upset him. The house would fall under the supervision of a vague authority, a committee or an association, and it would be impossible to extract commitments from these people on how the house would be cared for after he was gone.

Smithson made his decision during his last trip to Murree, the hill station he frequented every year. Sitting on a patio in the mountains two hundred miles from Lahore, he resolved to sell the house. He was not dissuaded by the fact that Five Queen's Road had lost value during the summer of Partition, when all over the city, houses left vacant by fleeing refugees were being occupied by whoever got to them first. Smithson had other ideas, and once he was able to accept that the market would give him less than the house he was so proud of was worth, he put all his energy into redeeming Five Queen's Road. He believed that if he attached a significant price to his house at a time when houses could be had for little, people would take notice. He did not consult a commission agent in the business of buying and selling houses for advice on how to arrive at a price for Five Queen's Road. He deflated by thirty-five per cent the only appraisal the railways had made of his house years earlier, and used that value as the base price. Then, he pulled out the thick stack of receipts from a folder marked 'Garden' from his library, and began the task of adding all the figures together. After making the appropriate conversions from pounds to rupees for his overseas orders, he calculated the amount he had spent on his garden over the years. He added this sum to the base price of the house and used the total as the non-negotiable price of Five Queen's Road.

As he had predicted, people took notice. They mentioned how odd it was that he was trying to sell the house. They wanted to know how he had settled on the figure and said it was pittance in comparison to what the house could have brought him a year or two earlier. He might as well have saved himself the trouble, they said, and disposed of the property by giving it away for even less. Whenever he was confronted with these comments, Smithson would patiently explain that he was well aware that most houses could be had cheaply, but was also certain that Five Queen's Road and his garden would not be one of these. And then he would add, as though it had been an afterthought, that much of his garden was imported, the bulbs, for example, the plant food, and the variety of lavender bush that had sailed with him in his quarters, all the way from England.

Smithson interviewed many people, all of them from well-established backgrounds and highly recommended by colleagues at the railway colony or other English friends. He finally settled on the only Hindu who expressed interest in buying his house, Dina Lal, a lawyer and wealthy landlord. He was partly influenced by his own dealings with the man during his tenure in India. At one point, Dina Lal had owned some land that the British had needed for a new railway line, and he had sold it without having to be pressed very hard. But what really impelled him to sell the house to the lawyer was an evening at Dina Lal's residence. The reception was a farewell for an English businessman with whom Dina Lal had been friends. The party was held on a patio that overlooked a small but perfectly manicured garden. Big long candles lit the path in the garden, heating the scent from the jasmine flowers and making their sweet perfume more potent. Later in the evening, Smithson prepared to leave, taking his cue from the commotion in the living room, where furniture was being cleared out of the way and a big rug had been unrolled. Instead, his host asked him to join them inside, and, if he could manage it, stay a little longer.

The performance that followed persuaded Smithson that Dina Lal should become the owner of Five Queen's Road. His house seemed worthy, almost deserving, of the grandeur and majesty of the evening. Smithson knew these evenings with dancing women were common in certain circles of Lahore, but it was rare for an Englishman to witness one of them. It was Smithson's first encounter with such an evening, and everything about it thrilled him. He had heard, along with almost everyone else, that the dancing woman, a Muslim, was Dina Lal's mistress. A beautiful woman dressed in a red peshwa with gold brocade, she moved across the rug. The balls of her feet and her ghungroos, the bracelets of tiny silver bells wrapped around her ankles, answered the beat of the tabla, while the rest of her body moved so fluidly it might have been one long, perfectly honed, extraordinary muscle.

Smithson was enraptured, his face flushed pink as he watched with intense concentration. There was a beauty in the night's performance that saddened him and, for a fleeting moment, made him consider staying on in India, retiring at Five Queen's Road and hosting parties like this one. The evening ended with a string of applause, several encores, and, for Smithson, with the reality that he would be returning to England in a matter of weeks, leaving his house in Dina Lal's safekeeping.

Toba Tek Singh

Saadat Hasan Manto

A couple of years or so after the partition of the subcontinent, the governments of Pakistan and India felt that just as they had exchanged their hardened criminals, they should exchange their lunatics. In other words, Muslims in the lunatic asylums of India be sent across to Pakistan; and mad Hindus and Sikhs in Pakistani asylums be handed over to India.

Whether or not this was a sane decision, we will never know. But people in knowledgeable circles say that there were many conferences at the highest level between bureaucrats of the two countries before the final agreement was signed and a date fixed for the exchange.

The news of the impending exchange created a novel situation in the Lahore lunatic asylum. A Muslim patient who was a regular reader of the *Zamindar* was asked by a friend, '*Maulvi Sahib*, what is this thing they call Pakistan?' After much thought he replied, 'It's a place in India where they manufacture razor blades.' A Sikh lunatic asked another, '*Sardarji*, why are we being sent to India? We cannot speak their language.' The *Sardarji* smiled and replied, 'I know the lingo of the Hindustanis.' He illustrated his linguistic prowess by reciting a doggerel:

Hindustanis are full of *Shaitani*
They strut about like bantam cocks.

One morning, an insane Mussalman yelled the slogan '*Pakistan Zindabad*' with such vigour that he slipped on the floor and knocked himself senseless.

This extract is taken from *Orphans of the Storm: Stories on the Partition of India*, edited by Saros Cowasjee and K.S. Duggal, published by UBS Publishers' Distributors Ltd.

Some inmates of the asylum were not really insane. They were murderers whose relatives had been able to have them certified and thus save them from the hangman's noose. The people had vague notions of why India had been divided and what was Pakistan. But even they knew very little of the complete truth. The papers were not very informative and the guards were so stupid that it was difficult to make any sense out of what they said. All one could gather from their talk was that there was a man with the name of Mohammed Ali Jinnah who was also known as the *Qaid-i-Azam*. And that this Mohammed Ali Jinnah alias *Qaid-i-Azam* had made a separate country for the Mussalmans which he called Pakistan.

No one knew where this Pakistan was or how far it extended. This was the chief reason why inmates who were not totally insane were in a worse dilemma than those utterly mad—they did not know whether they were in India or Pakistan. If they were in India, where exactly was Pakistan? And if they were in Pakistan, how was it that the very same place had till recently been known as India?

A poor Muslim inmate got so baffled with the talk about India and Pakistan, Pakistan and India, that he got madder than before. One day while he was sweeping the floor, he was suddenly overcome by an insane impulse. He threw away his brush and clambered up a tree. And for two hours he orated from the branch of this tree on Indo-Pakistan problems. When the guards tried to get him down, he climbed still higher. When they threatened him he replied, 'I do not wish to live either in India or Pakistan; I want to stay where I am, on top of this tree.'

After a while the fit of lunacy subsided and the man was persuaded to come down. As soon as he was on the ground he began to embrace his Hindu and Sikh friends and shed bitter tears. He was overcome by the thought that they would leave him and go away to India.

Another Muslim inmate had a Master of Science degree in radio-engineering and considered himself a cut above the others. He used to spend his days strolling in a secluded corner of the garden. Suddenly, a change came over him. He took off all his clothes and handed them over to the head-constable. He resumed his perambulation without a stitch of clothing on his person.

And there was yet another lunatic, a fat Mussalman who had been a leader of the Muslim League in Chiniot. He was given to bathing fifteen to sixteen times during the day. He suddenly gave up bathing altogether.

The name of this fat Mussalman was Mohammed Ali. But one day he proclaimed from his cell that he was Mohammed Ali Jinnah. Not to be outdone, his cell-mate who was a Sikh, proclaimed himself to be Master Tara Singh. The two began to abuse each other. They were declared 'dangerous' and put in separate cages.

There was a young Hindu lawyer from Lahore. He was said to have become mentally unhinged when his lady-love jilted him. When he heard that Amritsar had gone to India, he was very depressed: his sweetheart lived in Amritsar. Although the girl had spurned his affection, he did not forget her even in his lunacy. He spent his time cursing all leaders, Hindu as well as Muslim, because they had split India into two, and made his beloved an Indian and him a Pakistani.

When the talk of exchanging lunatics was in the air, other inmates consoled the Hindu lawyer with the hope that he would soon be sent to India—the country where his sweetheart lived. But the lawyer refused to be reassured. He did not want to leave Lahore because he was convinced that he would not be able to set up legal practice in Amritsar.

There were a couple of Anglo-Indians in the European ward. They were very saddened to learn that the English had liberated India and returned home. They met secretly to deliberate on problems of their future status in the asylum: would the asylum continue to have a separate ward for Europeans? Would they be served breakfast as before? Would they be deprived of toast and be forced to eat *chapatis?*

Then there was a Sikh who had been in the asylum for fifteen years. And in the fifteen years he said little besides the following sentence: 'O, *pardi, good good di, anekas di, bedhyana di, moong di dal of di lantern.*'

The Sikh never slept, either at night or in the day. The warders said that they had not known him to blink his eyes in fifteen years. He did not so much as lie down. Only on rare occasions he leant against the wall to rest. His legs were swollen down to the ankles.

Whenever there was talk of India and Pakistan, or the exchange of lunatics, this Sikh would become very attentive. If anyone invited him to express his views, he would answer with great solemnity: 'O, *pardi, good good di, anekas di, bedhyana di, moong di dal of the Pakistan Government*.'

Some time later he changed the end of his litany from 'of the Pakistan Government' to 'of the Toba Tek Singh government.'

He began to question his fellow inmates whether the village of Toba Tek Singh was in India or Pakistan. No one knew the answer. Those who tried, got tied up in knots explaining how Sialkot was at first in India and was now in Pakistan. How could one guarantee that a similar fate would not befall Lahore and from being Pakistani today it would not become Indian tomorrow? For that matter, how could one be sure that the whole of India would not become a part of Pakistan? All said and done, who could put his hand on his heart and say with conviction that there was no danger of both India and Pakistan vanishing from the face of the globe one day!

The Sikh had lost most of his long hair. Since he seldom took a bath, the hair on the head had matted and joined with his beard. This gave the Sikh a very fierce look. But he was a harmless fellow. In the fifteen years he had been in the asylum, he had never been known to argue or quarrel with anyone. All that the older inmates knew about him was that he owned land in village Toba Tek Singh and was once a prosperous farmer. When he lost his mind, his relatives had brought him to the asylum in iron fetters. Once a month, some relatives came to Lahore to find out how he was faring. With the eruption of Indo-Pakistan troubles these visits had ceased.

The Sikh's name was Bishen Singh, but everyone called him Toba Tek Singh. Bishen Singh had no concept of time—neither of days, nor weeks, or of months. He had no idea how long he had been in the lunatic asylum. But when his relatives and friends came to see him, he knew that a month must have gone by. He would inform the head warder that 'Miss Interview' was due to visit him. He would wash himself with great care; he would soap his body and oil his long hair and beard before combing them. He would dress up before he went to meet his visitors. If they asked him any questions, he either remained silent or answered, 'O, *pardi, anekas di, bedhyana di, moong di dal of di lantern*.'

Bishen Singh had a daughter who had grown into a full-bosomed lass of fifteen. But he showed no comprehension of his child. The girl wept bitterly whenever she met her father.

When talk of India and Pakistan came up, Bishen Singh began to question other lunatics about the location of Toba Tek Singh. No one could give him a satisfactory answer. His irritation mounted day by day. And now even 'Miss Interview' did not come to see him. There was a time when something within had told him that his relatives were due. Now that inner voice had been silenced. And he was more anxious than ever to meet his relatives and find out whether Toba Tek Singh was in India or Pakistan. But no relatives came. Bishen Singh turned to other sources of information.

There was a lunatic in the asylum who believed he was God. Bishen Singh asked him whether Toba Tek Singh was in India or Pakistan. As was his wont, 'God' adopted a grave mien and replied, 'We have not yet issued our orders on the subject.'

Bishen Singh got the same answer many times. He pleaded with 'God' to issue instructions so that the matter could be settled once and for all. His pleadings were in vain; 'God' had many pressing matters awaiting 'His' orders. Bishen Singh's patience ran out and one day he let 'God' have a bit of his mind, '*O, pardi, good good di, anekas di, bedhyana di, moong di dal of Wahi-i-Guru ji ka Khalsa and Wahi-i-Guru di Fateh! Jo boley so nihal, Sat Sri Akal.*'

This was meant to put 'God' in his place—as God only of the Mussalmans. Surely if He had been God of the Sikhs, He would have heard the pleadings of a Sikh!

A few days before the day fixed for the exchange of lunatics, a Muslim from Toba Tek Singh came to visit Bishen Singh. This man had never been to the asylum before. When Bishen Singh saw him he turned away. The warders stopped him: 'He's come to see you; he's your friend, Fazal Din,' they said.

Bishen Singh gazed at Fazal Din and began to mumble. Fazal Din put his hand on Bishen Singh's shoulder. 'I have been intending to see you for the last many days but could never find the time. All your family have safely crossed over to India. I did the best I could for them. Your daughter, Roop Kaur. . . .'

Fazal Din continued somewhat haltingly, 'Yes . . . too is well. She went along with the rest.'

Bishen Singh stood where he was without saying a word. Fazal Din started again, 'They asked me to keep in touch with you. I am told that you are to leave for India. Convey my *salaams* to brother Balbir Singh and to brother Wadhwa Singh . . . and also to sister Amrit Kaur . . . tell brother Balbir Singh that Fazal Din is well and happy. Both the grey buffaloes that they left behind have calved—one is a male, the other a female . . . the female died six days later. And if there is anything I can do for them, I am always willing. I have brought you a little sweet corn.'

Bishen Singh took the bag of sweet corn and handed it over to a warder. He asked Fazal Din, 'Where is Toba Tek Singh?'

Fazal Din looked somewhat puzzled and replied, 'Where could it be? It's in the same place where it always was.'

Bishen Singh asked again: 'In Pakistan or India?'

'No, not in India; it's in Pakistan,' replied Fazal Din.

Bishen Singh turned away mumbling, '*O, pardi, good good di, anekas di, bedhyana di, moong di dal of the Pakistan and Hindustan of dur phittey moonh.*'

Arrangements for the exchange of lunatics were completed. Lists with names of lunatics of either side had been exchanged and information sent to the people concerned. The date was fixed.

It was a bitterly cold morning. Bus-loads of Sikh and Hindu lunatics left the Lahore asylum under heavy police escort. At the border at Wagah, the Superintendents of the two countries met and settled the details of the operation.

Getting the lunatics out of the buses and handing over custody to officers of the other side proved to be a very difficult task. Some refused to come off the bus; those that came out were difficult to control: a few broke loose and had to be recaptured. Those that were naked had to be clothed. No sooner were the clothes put on them than they tore them off their bodies. Some came out with vile abuse, others began to sing at the top of their voices. Some squabbled; others cried or roared with laughter. They created such a racket that one could not hear a word. The female lunatics added to the noise. And all this in the bitterest of cold when people's teeth chattered like the scales of rattlesnakes.

Most of the lunatics resisted the exchange because they could not understand why they were being uprooted from one place and flung into another. Those of a gloomier disposition were yelling slogans, 'Long Live Pakistan' or 'Death to Pakistan.' Some lost their tempers and were prevented from coming to blows in the very nick of time.

At last came the turn of Bishen Singh. As the Indian officer began to enter his name in the register, Bishen Singh asked him, 'Where is Toba Tek Singh? In India or Pakistan?'

'In Pakistan.'

That was all that Bishen Singh wanted to know. He turned and ran back to Pakistan. Pakistani soldiers apprehended him and tried to push him back towards India. Bishen Singh refused to budge. Toba Tek Singh is on this side he cried, and began to yell at the top of his voice, 'O, *pardi, good good di, anekas di, bedhyana di, moong di dal of Toba Tek Singh and Pakistan.*' They did their best to soothe him, to explain to him that Toba Tek Singh must have left for India; and that if any of that name was found in Pakistan he would be dispatched to India at once. Bishen Singh refused to be persuaded. They tried to use force. Bishen Singh planted himself on the dividing line and dug his swollen feet into the ground with such firmness that no one could move him.

They let him be. He was soft in the head. There was no point using force; he would come round of his own—yes. They left him standing where he was and resumed the exchange of the other lunatics.

Shortly before sunrise, a weird cry rose from Bishen Singh's throat. The man who had spent all the nights and days of the last fifteen years standing on his feet, now sprawled on the ground, face down. The barbed wire fence on one side marked the territory of India; another fence marked the territory of Pakistan. In the no man's land between the two barbed-wire fences lay the body of Bishen Singh of village Toba Tek Singh.

—*Translated by Khushwant Singh*

The 1988 Show

Emma Duncan

In the West elections are as bland and distant as a television chat show. In Pakistan they are street theatre with audience participation. The scarcity value heightens the excitement: everybody turned out to watch the 1988 show because, they said, they weren't sure when there would be another performance.

Some friends of mine borrowed a first-floor office on a crossroads in British-built Lahore. It had high windows and a carved-wood balcony under which Benazir's last and biggest procession was due to pass. Below were knots of policemen leaning on their sticks and chatting. Groups of men sat on plastic chairs outside the street restaurants slopping up stew with torn-off bits of flat bread while the chefs squatted on platforms above them stirring greasy, spicy meat in huge pots or turning orange chickens on spits. The PPP's green, red and black banners spanned the street. The crossroads was decorated with bright film posters of fat-thighed women and fleshy-faced bandits and candidates' posters in the same school of portraiture: plumping out the faces, doubling the chins, and lending a twist of lascivious brutality to the lips. Some perfectly harmless-looking candidates I knew were painted as overweight thugs.

We, of course, did not go down to the street for our food. It was brought up the ancient dusty staircase from one of the restaurants by a thin boy. The balcony on which we stood and chewed our chicken-legs was in the same style as those that Mogul emperors lean out of in miniatures. But while they were handing out judgements to the crowds below, we were watching what kind of judgement the crowds would make on the tamasha the PPP was laying on.

This extract is taken from Emma Duncan's *Breaking the Curfew: A Political Journey through Pakistan*, published by Penguin Books Limited.

People began to form a thin lining to the procession's route. Some carried banners and flags, most wore a folded cardboard party-hat in green, red and black. Suzuki trucks began to crawl down the road, each sardine-packed with people and flanked by marchers throwing thick handfuls of leaflets into the crowd. The men from the restaurants began to leave their plates and drift over to the roadside. The police, grossly outnumbered, forced themselves on to the road edge and tapped a few shins with their sticks. As the spaces between the vans filled with people, the procession slowed to snail-speed and the shouting rose.

Then round the corner came a lorry fronted by a fifteen-foot picture of Zulfikar Ali Bhutto in a Mao cap, followed by another lorry carrying his daughter. She stood in its open top, turning, waving and smiling, surrounded by hangers-on who also waved and smiled in recognition of the crescendo of adulation roaring through the street. The lorry crept purposefully. The driver must have been steel-nerved, for there was a permanent wedge of young men squashed between the front of the moving lorry and the unmoving crowd. They always just pushed and squeezed their way out before being crushed.

A couple of women on our balcony leant over like pop groupies and yelled 'Bhutto! Bhutto!' making victory-signs at the crowds; but they were drowned by the ambient noise. I asked the girl standing beside me in an embroidered kashmiri shawl whom she was going to vote for. 'The other side,' she said with an apologetic smile. 'My family are rather big business people, and we do not trust the Bhuttos.'

Our air-conditioned Pajero slipped in between a couple of the painted and steel-frilled buses. Each was topped with fifty or so people waving, singing and dancing, like too many cabaret girls sprung out of a birthday cake. The procession edged its way down on the road towards the railway station and the old city where Benazir's great rally was to take place. The buildings got shabbier and older, with carved balconies and classical balustrades, little arched windows and thick, studded wooden doors in arched doorways.

'I've never been here,' said one of the Lahore housewives in the Pajero in a tone of touristic interest. We were in one of the most historic as well as one of the main commercial areas of the city, and just next to the railway station. Perhaps it wasn't that surprising, though: Pakistanis do not seem much stirred by history. The commerce there was grubby, small-scale stuff that her family would long ago have graduated out of. And if she wanted to travel long-distance, she undoubtedly went by plane.

The buses and Suzukis, lorries and Pajeros crept to a stop; only the motor bikes and cycles, edging their way between the vehicles, were moving. The symphony of horns (with voice accompaniment) soon stopped: everybody realised that something important had stalled the procession. Benazir was having a rest.

Small entertainments sprang up quickly in the interval. In a space between two lorries, a crowd cheered on two acrobatic dancers who rolled their stomachs, their hips and their eyes at each other. On the edge of the crowd, three small boys practised the same dance, giggling and wiggling. The usual salesmen with sugar-cane and spiced peanuts and lentils in newspaper cones moved in to take advantage of the captive market. On top of Benazir's lorry, three of her young candidates—an accountant, a lawyer and a man of property—were keeping the entertainment going while she was away. They chanted and threw rose petals on the crowds and the crowds chanted back. The floodlights meant for Benazir lit their smiles, inflated by a brief taste of back-street fame.

PART II

CITY WITHIN A CITY

The Postal Clerk

Saad Ashraf

I

Ghulam was a faithful clerk in the Indian Posts and Telegraphs Department in the Punjab. To him, a government job offered stability and prospects of advancement and, more than that, the respect and awe of his countrymen, including the people of his community. Soon after joining service, Ghulam observed a change in the attitude of people around him; his elders started getting up to greet him and his visitors stood in front of him with the folded hands typical of India. His family, too, started addressing him as Ghulam Sahib instead of calling him by his pet name, Gama. Almost imperceptibly, Ghulam adopted the demeanour of an officer, though he was a mere clerk. His attitude towards others underwent a change, and he wanted his uneducated, rustic and devout wife to address him as 'Ghulam Sahib' too. Even when they made love—in the dark of the night, under the open skies, in the summer, with millions of stars as silent witnesses—the inadvertent use of his pet name would turn off his libido. At such times he felt like being rough with her, but the words of his Anglo-Indian postmaster kept ringing in his ears and held him back. The postmaster had said that the main difference between white people and the Indians was that the latter did not treat their womenfolk properly; which was why the English had come to rule over them.

In 1880, after a tenure of work in his home town, Ghulam was transferred to the provincial capital, Lahore, where he came and stayed with an old family friend, Hakeem Mahir. The Hakeem lived in a four-room house outside the walled city, not far from the Royal Mosque and the red-light area known as Hira Mandi. From the courtyard of his friend's house, Ghulam could see two of the minarets of the Royal Mosque towering high above him into the blue skies, in their full majesty.

Hakeem Mahir came from an old family of hakeems which had specialized for generations in dispensing potions famous for their aphrodisiac qualities. The potions were made by grinding precious stones and then dissolving them in a special secret concoction handed down the generations, which did not affect the intestines or produce flatulence in the stomach. A four-week course was guaranteed to give the greatest pleasure to the male and ensure the total submission of the female. With the British Government firmly installed, and stability having returned to the Punjab, the market for aphrodisiacs had taken a turn for the better. Hakeem Mahir's clientele consisted not only of Lahore's old Mughal and Sikh elite but also the nouveau riche who had emerged by cashing in on their services to the British during the Indian Mutiny of 1857. Among Hakeem Mahir's satisfied clients was the lieutenant governor of Punjab, who had the reputation of being an oversexed individual. It was a popular rumour in Lahore that the lieutenant governor had a homosexual relationship with one of his British assistants. There had been anonymous letters to the Governor General in Calcutta, lodging complaints, but nothing came of them and both the lieutenant governor and the assistant continued working in the same office.

Hakeem Mahir's pharmacy was in a small shop in the bazaar about a mile from his house, on the road which ran through Hira Mandi. Nobody knew how Hira Mandi had come to be located there, though old residents recalled childhood tales told by their elders, who had said this was the main camping ground of the Sikh army of Maharaja Ranjit Singh, then ruler of the Punjab. It was said that a few women of easy virtue had first set themselves up on its outskirts to offer their services to the soldiers, and their number and influence had grown with time. When the Maharaja died and his empire started crumbling some years later, these women, who had by then turned into a sizeable community, started occupying more of the camping ground, until, finally, the army was completely ousted to make way for the red-light area.

On one side of Hakeem Mahir's pharmacy was a large store from which spices and dried herbs were sold wholesale to the shopkeepers of the city. Mohammed, the owner, was an amateur wrestler who would close his shop every afternoon for two hours to head for the nearby arena run by a mute wrestler, Goonga. Goonga had gained fame all over India after having floored the Russian wrestler, Romanovoski, in St Petersburg some years back, even though his opponent had weighed twice as much and was a good nine inches taller. Master-wrestler Goonga had a large photograph, duly framed, hanging in one corner of the shack which served as his office, as evidence of his victory over the Russian. It showed his foot on his adversary's neck, as he lay helpless on the mat, his eyes pleading for mercy. Goonga spent half-an-hour every day teaching Mohammed and his other pupils holds and locks, knowledge that he claimed to have received in inheritance. Goonga imparted all his instructions in sign language. Whenever Goonga felt his instructions were not being properly followed, he would give a practical demonstration and the pupil would find himself on the floor, much like the Russian wrestler, Romanovoski.

The road on which Hakeem Mahir's house and pharmacy stood had been named after Rattan Bai, the teenaged dancing girl from Hira Mandi whom Maharaj Singh, a direct descendant of Maharaja Ranjit Singh, had installed as his mistress in his large haveli a couple of furlongs away. The haveli had been the scene of a gruesome tragedy some decades back when, on a cold December night in 1859, both Rattan Bai and her young paramour were found murdered. Everyone suspected Maharaj Singh, who had been in Mooltan for a week prior to the day of the murder, but had arrived back that day and was seen hovering around his haveli a few hours before the murder. The British had acted swiftly by arresting him as the prime suspect in the double murder of Rattan Bai and her lover and, having found him guilty after a protracted trial, had executed him by hanging him from hastily erected gallows outside the Lahore Fort, in full view of the sepulchre where his great ancestor, Maharaja Ranjit Singh, had been cremated with his queens and concubines.

Thereafter, Maharaj Singh's haveli had remained unoccupied for many years, but during the last decade, it had come to be intermittently occupied by Sikh, Muslim, Hindu and English tenants. A number of those who had lived in the haveli had left the premises in a hurry, with fear writ large on their faces, complaining that they had been disturbed in the dead of the night by the sobs, groans and cries of a young girl pleading for mercy from her killer. They said that this could be none other than Rattan Bai's roaming and restless spirit, which had come to settle matters with her murderer at the place of her demise. A brave young English corporal named William Brandish, who had seen service with the Company's army in Bengal, had declared these incidents to be figments of someone's imagination and had taken the haveli on rent to establish the truth. Brandish slept in the very room where Rattan Bai was said to have met her end, but he too had vacated the premises after a few months when he found the colour of the room turning crimson as night fell.

II

One day when Hakeem Mahir was sitting in his clinic behind the low desk on which he wrote his prescriptions, Ghulam walked in and sat in front of him—a place usually reserved for patients.

'What can I do for you, sahib? Is yours a malady of the heart or the body?' asked Hakeem Mahir jokingly.

'Of both, but primarily that of the heart,' remarked Ghulam.

'Then why don't you do something about it?'

'What can I do? I neither have a house nor servants, nor has my travelling allowance been paid by the government so that I can bring my family here. It will take a couple of hundred rupees to bring them over here and get them settled and there is nobody to hear the plaint of this poor government servant,' said Ghulam.

'Then what can one do for you?' the Hakeem asked.

'Nothing, except that someone should help me get my family here.'

Hakeem Mahir knew that he didn't have the money to loan to his friend. He paused and thought for a moment and then spoke up: 'Why not take another wife and have another family here. Lahore abounds with young and beautiful ladies from noble houses who have nobody to look after them. They are renowned for their art of captivating the hearts of men and for producing sons. Your religion, too, permits you to take another wife in case of a genuine need.'

After Ghulam had sufficiently recovered from this suggestion, he started giving his friend's proposal some serious thought. The wife he had left behind in his home town was backward, spoke rudely, had large hips and big breasts that were soft and supple, and reminded him of flour that had been kneaded with too much water. She wore a lungi and slurped when she ate and, in the past few years, their marriage seemed to have all but broken down, with her spending more and more time on the prayer mat than with him.

Furthermore, Ghulam's boss, Mr Carter, the English postmaster in Lahore, had been happy with his work, particularly with his report on a clerk who, through an error in addition, had been accused of misappropriation. This had helped Mr Carter to present himself as a model of meticulous efficiency before Mr Collins, the deputy postmaster general, who had praised his watchful eye. Mr Collins had promised to recommend a promotion for Mr Carter, and Mr Carter, in turn, had promised a promotion for Ghulam, to the post of deputy superintendent. Ghulam thought that his wife would hardly fit in with his elevated position, if he was promoted.

'I will think about your suggestion, but why should a lady from the nobility want to marry me, a petty clerk, anyway?' questioned Ghulam of his friend, who waited for a more opportune time to reply.

Hakeem Mahir did not forget to follow up on his suggestion. He mentioned the availability of an eligible bridegroom to one of his patients, Mirza Mahmud, a Mughal gentleman originally from Delhi, but now settled in Lahore, who had once mentioned in passing to the Hakeem that he wanted to fulfil his worldly commitments by marrying off his only daughter, Noorani Begum, and then retire to Mecca to spend the rest of his life atoning for his sins. When Mirza heard about the availability of a groom for his daughter, his joy knew no bounds and he spontaneously accepted Ghulam as a future son-in-law. It was true that there was a substantial age difference between the prospective bridegroom and his daughter, but he figured that this could be offset by the many advantages that he might derive from his son-in-law's position as a government functionary, in addition to having his daughter well provided for as long as her husband lived.

Ghulam's marriage with Noorani Begum proceeded along the lines that Mirza Mahmud had hoped for. The couple took up residence in an old neighbourhood of Lahore popularly known as High Haveli, located inside the Taxali Gate, one of the many gates that led into the walled city where Emperor Akbar's old Mughal mint had once stood. High Haveli was a three-storied marbled mansion with thirty rooms that had lost much of its past magnificence with time and with rapidly changing ownership. The mansion was at one time the property of Mughlani Begum, the viceroy of Punjab in the middle of the eighteenth century, who was said to have lived here herself for some time, after marrying a eunuch. It had lately been converted into six five-room units to cater to the requirements of the times.

Noorani Begum was a cultured woman of medium height, with a wheatish complexion. She had good manners, and could recite the poetry of Mir, Ghalib and Sauda. She knew Persian and could quote Hafiz and Saadi. She was a good cook and could make delicious rice puddings with saffron; unlike the wife Ghulam had left behind, who was only adept at cooking vegetables and lentils. Noorani Begum knew how to keep Ghulam happy at home and in bed so he could devote all his time and energy at work in pleasing Mr Carter the postmaster. She once went in a doli through the weaving lanes of Old Lahore to the General Post Office located in Anarkali to call on Mem Carter, who lived there in a bungalow. She had tucked away ten silver rupees bearing Queen Victoria's profile, wrapped in a red satin kerchief, which she pressed in Mem Carter's hands as soon as they were alone. Mem Carter had appreciated this gesture as she had been born in India and was used to its ways. She had smilingly accepted the gift and, in her English-accented Hindustani, thanked Noorani Begum. Soon thereafter, Ghulam had been promoted to deputy superintendent.

But a year later, Mr Carter was transferred to Bombay on a promotion. Ghulam's future would now depend upon the person appointed as the new postmaster in his place. The popular rumour was that Mr Appleby, the postmaster at Allahabad, would fill this post. The reputation of Postmaster Appleby preceded his arrival. He was said to be a person of strict countenance who could take umbrage easily, primarily because his grandfather, a pure white sahib, had married an Indian woman, which made other Englishmen look down upon him. Mr Appleby, in turn, took out all his frustration on his native subordinates. He would scold them in front of others and use invectives in his speech. Even worse, he would cultivate a few favourites and use them as spies to keep a check on the people in his office. While these rumours were still circulating, a newcomer made his appearance at the Lahore Post Office. He was Ramdas, the head clerk from Jallandhar, who had been transferred to Lahore. Ramdas had worked with Mr Appleby, and was, in fact, one of his spies. Appleby had had him transferred to Lahore to size up the people he would be working with, as a prelude to his arrival. Ramdas was a quiet, bespectacled person, about forty years of age, who had already put in half of his life with the Indian post office. Ramdas kept much to himself, observing the babus at work. Whenever somebody asked him about his English postmaster, Appleby, he would say, 'How can I, a lowly clerk, know anything about an English burra sahib?' He did pick up the information, though, that Deputy Superintendent Ghulam had been spreading imagined tales of Mr Appleby's good nature, though he had never seen or met him before. After a week at the Lahore Post Office, Ramdas left for Jallandhar as quietly as he had come, ostensibly to fetch his family.

The great day finally came when Mr Appleby arrived at the Lahore Railway Station by train from Jallandhar. As he emerged from his first-class compartment, he was welcomed by the acting postmaster of Lahore, Mr Griffiths. Mr Appleby, a thin man, over six feet tall, wore a white toupee and spectacles made of wire, and had a tense expression on his face. The only time he smiled faintly was when he met Mr Griffiths. When he shook hands with Ghulam, he muttered a few words, of which Ghulam could make out nothing, but presumed that he was being asked his name.

'I am Ghulam, Deputy Superintendent, Head Post Office Lahore, sir,' muttered Ghulam inaudibly, breathless and nervous on being at such close quarters with his English boss.

'So you are Ghulam,' remarked Appleby, with lips tensed and eyes fluttering.

Could Ramdas, the clerk from Jallandhar, have filled the ears of the sahib with some unkind words about him? There was little sleep for Ghulam that night, as all kinds of thoughts raced through his mind. Noorani Begum tried pacifying him by telling him that this could just be a casual remark made by the sahib, but without much success.

III

Ghulam's first meeting with Postmaster Appleby came a fortnight later, when he was summoned to see him. Ghulam knocked softly at the postmaster's door and only after an authoritative voice from inside gave him permission to enter did he turn the shining brass handle to walk inside. Mr Appleby was busy with some papers in a file and, without raising his eyes, addressed Ghulam, who stood with folded hands in front of him.

'Deputy Ghulam, there have been complaints about the late delivery of *dawk* in the Mian Mir cantonment in the last two weeks. I would like you to make a complete report to me on the subject as soon as possible. Keep an eye on your postmen. I don't want anyone fooling around here. Is this clear?' he said sternly.

'Yes. Yes, sir,' was all Ghulam could mumble on his way out of his boss's office.

When Ghulam had recovered from his first encounter with his postmaster, he decided to take on the task that the postmaster had entrusted to him. He made a list of all the postmen who had made deliveries in the last two weeks in the Mian Mir cantonment, and found that there were four: Chopra, Ali Bux, Ragbir Singh, and the Indian Christian, Stephen, who delivered post in the morning and afternoon shifts on each alternate day. Next, he took out the register in which all the post to be delivered in the Mian Mir cantonment was entered, with the addresses and the date of receipt of the post. The system was foolproof as far as the receipts were concerned, but there was no record of delivery, and too much trust had been placed in the postmen delivering it the same day. Ghulam spent the next few days keeping a tab on all the post for delivery to the cantonment by placing a small identification mark in pencil, from which the date of its collection for delivery by the postmen could be deciphered. Ghulam was amazed to find that Chopra was delivering the post two or three days after its receipt. He found this out by going to the addressee's house and questioning the servants about the date of delivery. With these findings, Ghulam sought an audience with Mr Appleby.

'Yes, Deputy Ghulam, you wanted to see me?' said Postmaster Appleby.

'This postman Chopra very big rascal, sir, keeping dak at his house for two or three days and not delivering the same day. What does this mean, sahibjee?' Ghulam explained in his Punjabi-accented English.

Appleby's jaw dropped by two inches on hearing what Ghulam had just said. It was possible that Chopra was totally honest but delivered the dak late only because he was a lazy scrounger, a category to which Appleby thought most Indians belonged—or there could be something bigger and more sinister than met the eye. In any case, the matter needed investigation.

'Deputy Ghulam, thank you for this information. I will look into this matter personally. A word of caution: don't let anyone know what you have discovered,' said the postmaster.

As soon as Ghulam left the room, Appleby was on the telegraph key in the corner of his office to Captain Rupert, the Superintendent of Police, Lahore, about the urgent need for them to meet in the afternoon for tiffin in the Officers Club in the Mian Mir cantonment.

Captain Rupert, formerly of Hodson's Horse, had been absorbed in the Punjab Police after his retirement from the Company's army on account of his reputation as a ruthless disciplinarian, and his avowed aim in life of 'civilizing these bloody niggers before I die'. He had been given charge of Lahore to get rid of the 'badmashes' who may have taken refuge in the city from other parts of India after the events of 1857.

When Appleby explained the mystery of the late delivery of the post in Mian Mir cantonment, and what Ghulam, his deputy superintendent, had discovered, Captain Rupert was overly excited as the task ahead would provide a break from the routine police work for which he had adequately trained his subordinates. Captain Rupert was considered the top specialist in the use of third-degree methods to break criminals. This had earned him the fear of the most hardened criminals in the province. He was the inventor of the famous 'mirchi danda', a small cane about eight inches long and half an inch in diameter, which was kept immersed in a mixture of oil and green chillies and used only under his personal supervision. In the initial tests of this torture device, Captain Rupert had at first asked the victim to confess his crime, but when the victim had refused and had shouted, 'You white monkey! You mother-fucker Angrez!' Captain

Rupert had coolly asked him to be tied to a charpai with his rear end exposed and, with the care of a surgeon performing a delicate operation, had inserted the device. The effect was instantaneous and the culprit not only admitted to the crime for which he had been hauled up on this occasion, but a few others about which the police had been totally ignorant. Soon the fame of Captain Rupert's invention had spread throughout the province's underworld, and it was said that families that had lived off this vocation for several generations had either left the province or had decided to call it a day and chosen another source of livelihood.

Captain Rupert decided to head the investigation himself and deputed his spies around the hovel where Postman Chopra lived. After a few days of surveillance, a raid on the hovel was carried out in the evening hours, just as the sun was setting behind the river and the dark smoke from the numerous hutments on its banks hung like a long serpent's tail in the crimson sky. A police party, its members dressed as women, arrived at the hovel in dolis and, while a few stood guard outside, two or three quickly seized Chopra and another person who turned out to be Ramdas, the head clerk of the Lahore Post Office and principal henchman of Postmaster Appleby.

It was on a cold and bleak December night that the culprits were produced handcuffed before Captain Rupert in a small ante-room in the red brick building housing the office of the Superintendent of Police. This building was located on the lower Mall not more than a hundred yards from the Government College, recognizable from afar by its gothic spire. Captain Rupert sat in his chair, smoking his pipe. He wore a blue blazer and grey flannel trousers, into which he had changed after eating his dinner of mulligatawny soup and roasted beef, for which he used to dress every night in his dinner jacket.

'So you are the badmashes who have been fiddling with the post in my city. I want to know why,' he said, addressing the two.

'I am innocent. The Head Clerk Ramdas told me to give him the dak and returned the envelopes to me for delivery a day or two later. I am a poor man who has eaten the salt of Queen Victoria. I beg your forgiveness. I am loyal to the sarkar! He is the culprit,' said the postman, pointing his finger at the head clerk. Captain Rupert kept listening to Postman Chopra lying at his feet, while Ramdas, the head clerk, stood silently in the corner with his head bowed.

'And what has the honorable head clerk to say for himself, eh?' said Captain Rupert.

Ramdas stood unmoved.

'I am speaking to you, head clerk! Give me the courtesy of a reply or be ready for the consequences,' said Captain Rupert sharply.

Ramdas remained silent.

By now, Captain Rupert had sized up the situation. It was possible that Ramdas had roped in Chopra for some sinister unknown purpose, and, if so, the matter needed to be investigated.

'Mr Head Clerk, I will leave you and give you some time to think about making a confession. In case you decide not to do so, I am afraid that we'll have to adopt some other measures.' Captain Rupert took out his pocket watch from his blazer and noted the time. The past few hours had been wasted, and nothing had been achieved by the interrogation. He left the room and headed for his office, where he opened the upper drawer of his writing table and took out the corn-cob pipe which his American aunt had presented to him. He started filling the pipe with the local dried tobacco, which the Indians smoked in their hubble-bubbles. He lighted and inhaled the pipe, puffing up his cheeks to get it going. Captain Rupert was in deep thought and his blue eyes had become cold and stony. He opened the second drawer of the table and took out an eighteen-inch-long metal cylinder and a pair of surgical gloves. Stamping out his pipe on a plate, he left the room carrying these items with him to the ante-room where the two suspects were in the same position as he had left them.

Captain Rupert motioned to one of his men and whispered something into his ear. Chopra was led out of the room and a little while later, two men brought in a charpai, a bundle of rope and some cloth. The charpai was placed in one corner of the room and the doors were locked from inside.

'Well, Mr Head Clerk, are you ready to tell us all?' asked Captain Rupert sternly. There was no reply from Ramdas, but the atmosphere in the room had suddenly become tense. Captain Rupert made certain gestures upon which his men seized Ramdas, took off his dhoti, shoved him onto the bed with his bare bottom upended, and tied him firmly to the charpai. A piece of cloth had also been put around his mouth so that only his muffled voice would be heard. Captain Rupert went to work quickly. He took hold of the metal cylinder and gave it a few vigorous jerks in the air, and unscrewed the cap. He then took out a short cane rod, held one end, and with the utmost precision, using the fingers of his other hand as a guide, conducted the operation. Ten seconds later, Ramdas's shrieks were heard through the wad of cloth around his mouth. In another minute, he was coughing violently.

'Are you prepared to tell us everything?' Captain Rupert shouted into Ramdas's ear.

A muffled sound was all that could be heard.

'I think the blighter is still not willing to talk and we will have to deliver another dose,' said Captain Rupert to one of his men, within hearing distance of Ramdas.

Captain Rupert's white-gloved hands went to work again. The muffled shrieks from Ramdas became a bit louder but Captain Rupert pretended not to hear anything. From his own experience, he knew that an additional dose of the mirchi danda was the best insurance against the offender changing his mind. This time Ramdas's body shook with convulsions and his muffled shrieks could be heard.

'Have mercy on me! My body is aflame and I am prepared to tell you all,' shrieked Ramdas. The process had barely taken half an hour. Captain Rupert beckoned to his men to untie Ramdas and bring him to his office as soon as he had recovered.

Ramdas was brought to Captain Rupert's office with tears flowing down his cheeks and was made to sit in front of him.

'Here's pen and paper to write your confession. The British in India are people of principles. We could never rule India if we were not just in our dealings. Take your time, because whatever you write will be taken into account at your trial. I will return after an hour to collect your confession,' said Captain Rupert before leaving the room.

To while away the hour, and to recover from the after-effects that such interrogations had on him, Captain Rupert decided to take a walk in the area around his office. He walked out of the building on to the road that went in the direction of the Royal Fort, bypassing the walled city. The cold, fresh December air hit his face. The dust of the day and the haze in the sky had settled and an uncountable number of glimmering stars lit the clear dark night. The road was deserted except for a few stragglers covered in their blankets, with only their eyes showing, who slunk into the dark on seeing a white sahib coming their way. In the distance, one could hear the sound of solitary hooves as the odd horse-driven carriage made its way to its destination. As he walked alone, Captain Rupert was happy, and proud, that he had made this city so safe that anyone, regardless of skin colour or sex, could venture out alone at any time of the night, without the fear of being accosted or robbed. He kept walking on the dimly lit road till he reached the shrine of a divine who had made Lahore his abode several centuries earlier. The shrine shone in all its splendour and glowed with light, in contrast to the surroundings. A number of bazaars had grown around it and buzzed with activity, despite the late hour. They were full of noisy natives and merchants selling their wares—flowers, food, perfume and incense. The Indians loved a tamasha, whether it was that of a festival or a late-night visit to the shrine of a saint long since dead.

He took out his pocket watch and observed that it had taken exactly half an hour to reach this spot, so he turned on his heel to return to keep the appointment with Ramdas. When Captain Rupert returned to his office, he found Ramdas sitting on a wooden bench in the room. He was in a stupor, but a couple of written sheets were lying on the table in front of him. Captain Rupert picked up the sheets and started reading what Ramdas had written.

Excellency!
By your treatment of a poor servant of Queen Victoria you may have been able to break my body but nothing can break my spirit. I am an Indian and for us our motherland comes first and everything else is of secondary importance. Above all, we are truthful and simple people. So I will tell you the truth. I did take the post from Chopra's home with the purpose of opening and reading what was written in the letters. As you will observe, only the dak of military officers was taken. It is because of them that you rule over Mother India. I planned to kill those who bore ill will against us Indians. I am aware that there are Englishmen who are kind

to us, such as Appleby sahib who treats me like a son, but such individuals are few and far between. How could I know what the sahibs thought of us natives if I didn't read their letters? This was the little I could do for my country. Postman Chopra is totally innocent. He objected to my asking him to keep the dak for a few days before delivery, but I am the head clerk in the Lahore Post Office and superior to him in rank so he could not refuse my orders. Nobody else has anything to do with this. I am writing this down because I know that the English people do not believe what they are told till they have investigated matters on their own. So if you like you can continue probing this matter and waste as much of your time as you want, though to save you the time and effort, I have written the truth.

I remain, sir,
Your most obedient servant,
Ramdas
Head Clerk, Lahore Post Office.

Because of this written confession and subsequent trials by the courts at Lahore, Ramdas was sentenced to transportation for life in the Andaman Islands, and Mr Appleby was asked to proceed on early retirement on the grounds of being too familiar with the natives. Ghulam, the deputy superintendent, was promoted to the rank of a fully-fledged superintendent—the first Indian to hold that post at the General Post Office at Lahore.

The City Within

Samina Quraeshi

THE THIRTEEN GATES

Many older cities once had walls. It was the only way to protect themselves from the hostile outer world, from strange, violent foreigners and sudden, devastating attacks. Certainly, there was great psychological comfort to be derived from the presence of that vast barricade surrounding one's home; even though the barricade might some day fail. Lahore, like most other old walled cities, has long since outgrown her original fortified boundaries, and the overflow of people, businesses, factories, and industries has spilled through the fabled Gates of the wall and spread for miles onto the plains beyond.

The wall no longer stands, much of it removed by the British to maintain control of the city dwellers within, its thirteen ancient gates still signal one's entrance to the fabled City of a Hundred Gardens. Although the wall no longer repels the advances of Chingiz Khan's warriors, in many ways it still signifies what it always has—security, community, the primal sense of 'inside' and 'outside'.

To those who live within its walls, Lahore's Old City is a community in the best sense of the word. A place in which all who dwell there know their environment. A place where one asks, and is asked, fewer questions than when outside. A place where, having entered, one looks for what is familiar rather than what is unfamiliar. A place where, whether resident or visitor, one is fully cognizant of having entered and being 'within' until one has left again. This is the feeling that an imposing portal provides. But when a portal allows one entry to an entire community rather than a room or a house, the sensation of

This extract is taken from Samina Quraeshi's *Lahore: The City Within*, published by Concept Media Pte Ltd.

arrival is intensified. This is the enduring magic of Lahore, the wall, and the city sprawling outward beyond the gates.

As a civic structure, the Old City of Lahore is a remarkable study in planning efficiency; 260,000 people live in an area of one square mile, or approximately 400 inhabitants per acre. There are some 38,000 households in some 20,000 premises or approximately 58 dwelling units per acre. Within its walls there are 3,422,000 square metres of floor space, 135,000 metres of gulleys, streets, roads and drainage lines. The commercial enterprises number over 4300, the primary schools number 65 and the mosques number over 300.

Though the city is constantly rebuilding itself it has maintained over twenty nationally recognised monuments and buildings of cultural value representing its 1500 years of recorded history.

The hierarchy of the bazaars in the Old City appears to radiate outward from the centre, with perfumes, incense and books still clustered close to the centre, at the great Wazir Khan Mosque. These markets are surrounded by jewellery, precious goods and textiles. Next are shoes, fibres, ropes and utensils, evolving into streets of carpenters, locksmiths, blacksmiths, butchers, produce merchants and basketmakers. The *Bazaar-e-Hakimah* or Bazaar of Healers still offers the diagnostic and curative skills of men learned in the arts of healing. The streets are also lined with shops offering medicinal plants, herbs, oils and unguents. Close to and outside the walls come the more industrial trades of the tanners, potters and foundries. Even today, the more industrial modern trades such as lumber, tyres, auto parts and truck building are found outside the wall.

The thirteen legendary gates into the city stand for much more than simple access to a market. They were named for emperors and saints, for ancient landmarks near them, or for where they led. Some of their history has been lost in the mists of time; in this city there is much that is old beyond all memory. They are arranged almost evenly along the circumference of the city wall, facing out in all directions, the imperial city's eyes on the world.

The Kashmiri Gate and the Delhi Gate opened onto the high roads that ran between Lahore and those great places, and it was probably no coincidence that the largest caravanserai near the walls lay outside of the Delhi Gate. The magnitude of the Delhi Gate

Bazaar and its connecting Akbari Mandi and Kashmiri Bazaar convey centuries of bustling activity and trade, in these great markets scaled for trading in enormous loads of grain, nuts, and spices. The Akbari Gate and the Shah 'Almi Gate are named for rulers Akbar the Great and Shah 'Alam Bahadur Shah, and they lead to marketplaces and bazaars which also bear their names. The Mochi Gate leads to the shoemakers' bazaar; its name is a mispronounciation of Moti, the name of an officer of Akbar who lived near this gate.

The Raushnai Gate lies between the Royal Mosque and the entrance to the citadel. This was the principal entrance into the city from the Fort, and it was through this gate that the courtiers, servants, entourages, and even the emperor himself would pass. Before the gate was opened, the Hazuri Bagh, the courtyard in front of the gate, was watered down because of the heat and dust. Then, through a passage formed by several hundred loyal soldiers. His Majesty would pass, with all the glitter and ceremony due such an occasion. The buildings around this gate were all splendidly illuminated at night; hence its name, meaning the 'Gate of Light'.

The Taxali Gate and the Masti Gate are so called for the landmarks nearest to them, although the exact origins of the name Taxali may reach even further back in time. The Masti Gate refers to the Masjid-i Mariam Makani, the mosque of the mother of Akbar, which is nearby. 'Masti' is, in fact, a mispronounciation of the adjective *masjidi*, or 'of the mosque'. The Taxali Gate was named for the Royal Mint which stood near the gate hundreds of years ago. However, the name may have originated even earlier from the Takkas, an ancient tribe once considered the absolute masters of the Punjab plain, whose descendants continue to live in their ancestral domain today.

The original name of the Yakki Gate was 'Zaki', for the truly amazing martyr saint who fell in battle while fiercely defending Lahore from the Mughal invaders. He was beheaded in front of the Yakki Gate; but, being a true champion, the headless body continued to fight for the rest of the day, collapsing—at last—in a quarter of the city nearby. The grateful citizens reverently built two tombs for this hero—one where his head had fallen, and the other where his valiant body finally gave up what was left of his ghost. Both tombs are still sacred sites to this day.

During the reign of Ranjit Singh, visitors of Lahore who entered the city from the gate on the River Ravi were greeted inside by the Emperor's lions, caged on either side of the entrance. In their memory, two bas-relief lion's heads now gaze outward from the beautiful Sheranwala Gate—the Lion's Gate. Some also refer to this gate as the Khizri Gate, for Khizr Elias, the patron saint of running water, who protected the ferries on the river below.

The Bhatti Gate and the Lohari Gate both refer to the trades practised in their vicinity, but these names have been clouded by the passage of time. The Bhatti Gate is named for a clan which eventually became known primarily as brickmakers (*bhatti* means 'brick'). The Lohari Gate refers to the trade of ironsmiths, but it may also refer to the ancient city of Lahore; the city may have been built up from the quarter around this gate.

The smallest gate is the Mori Gate, so called because originally it was used only for the garbage of the city. Over time, what had been only a hole in the wall was enlarged into a proper gate; without, unfortunately, losing its less than savoury name.

Much grew up outside the gates as well. As the gates were closed at night, certain teahouses, inns and shrines outside the gates became known as gathering places for various delights and entertainment: arts, poetry, food specialties, music. Just inside the Delhi Gate, close to the largest caravanserai, was the *hammam* or bath. A grand building erected for the purpose of reviving the weary traveller; it still stands to this day, housing a school in its vaulted and domed caverns.

The caravanserai and resting places outside the walls were places where travellers could find refuge after the gates to the city were closed at night, as well as finding sufficient room for the animals in the caravan. After some time, each developed a particular identity and following, and they were generally referred to as *takias* (pillows) for their warm and comforting role. Certain *takias* became known for their prediliction for poetry, others for philosophical discussion or beautiful music. Whether your taste ran to wrestling matches, exotic food specialties, dancing girls, or courtesans, you could find a *takia* in the shadow of the Lahore wall to indulge you. In time, these centres of culture became identified with certain patron saints or seasonal or religious festivals, some of which continue into the present time.

The new city outside the wall has swept over and erased much of the traces of the old life of Lahore. Still, the wall, and its venerable Gates, stand. Like all of Lahore, the gates are saturated with the heat and dust of the centuries of life that have erupted and simmered around them. It is unthinkable that so much emotion and vitality could have been expended in this red dust for countless centuries without leaving behind some trace, some lingering electric charge or vapour. Perhaps because of that, it requires almost no effort, on a warm night when the jasmine perfume floats in wisps and the stars are like Ranjit Singh's diamonds, to call back the city as it was, in the height of its celestial splendour . . .

On such a night it is possible to walk again through imperial Lahore, queen of cities, crown capital of all the Punjabi kingdoms there have ever been. The citadel rising above the city blazes in royal glory; inside, lost in compelling music, a reclining emperor, surrounded by a festive, laughing and slightly drunken entourage of courtiers, wives, and servants, gazes on the fluid shapes of the women dancing before him. Masters of their art, their small, neat, bejewelled feet and belled ankles whisper and ring on the tiles at the edge of a marble pool; their neat, lithe bodies, wrapped in transparent silk designed to reveal rather than conceal, flicker like the light on the water behind them. The streets lie in velvety darkness, pierced with points of light from the houses. Animals stir in stables; voices are raised, briefly, and in front of a lavish *haveli* music and laughter pour into the warm night. Outside the wall, beyond the closed, massive wooden gates, the caravanserai glimmer in the dark like embers. The street is lined with the dark shapes of the inns and *takias*, lit with smoky lamps, meant to the welcoming. The *takias* string their enticements like beads in the night air on this narrow street. From one drifts exquisitely beautiful music; then, from the next, the emotional rhythms of poetry, read aloud with fervour; a sudden smell of something cooking, warm with spices and oil; strains of the hypnotic music of the dancing girls, lost after a few steps in the sound of men's voices, raised in cheers and abuse of unseen contestants; the soft laughter of women, barely audible in the night air. Above, Lahore sparkles. All around, beyond the city, lies the rich blackness of the Punjab.

A DAY IN THE LIFE OF AZIZ AHMAD

Aziz Ahmad is saving money to buy his own lathe. He has been running his small metal tooling business in the front room of his mother's house, and neither the capacity of the room nor his mother's approval are large. His tools and machines are in the room just inside the door which faces the street and could be rented to a shopkeeper if the house were on a wider street, or one with other shops. But this is a relatively narrow street—only about eight feet wide, and in a residential district. Behind this room are the remains of a courtyard now dimmed by the encroaching floors above. Now only a grate in the middle allows borrowed light and air to filter down to the street level. On each level above, however, more and more light is available to the courtyard areas, drawing rooms, bedrooms and the rooftop apartment.

He climbs up the circular path to the roof often. Past the faded drawing room, now rarely used, he ascends to his mother's room, where she moved after his father died. He passes his grandfather's room with its door always ajar; inside, he knows he would find his grandfather in prayer. He passes his brother and sister-in-law's apartment, which used to belong to his parents. Once on the roof terrace he looks out and scans the innumerable surrounding rooftops. He once figured he could see half of the Old City from his roof. And as his house is at the city's edge near the Lohari Gate, and the current city is built on the mound of previous fallen cities, he can see to the highest part in the centre, and all the rooftops and minarets in between.

His father had told him of secret pathways which wound from roof to roof and which used to aid in the conveyance of goods and information during the riots before and after Partition. He and some friends had often tried to re-discover these routes for less political reasons, but had always run into barricades or chasms which cut short their mission. And how many nights had he counted the stars in the hot, moist months of May and June when his whole family would move their beds to the roof to sleep in hopes of catching the few breezes which would never find the bedrooms below. The roof was a much more desirable place to be now that the family had installed a water closet in the house. Prior to that, the roof had been the place where the 'night soil' was collected before being taken down to the street in the morning.

Aziz Ahmad stretches in the fresh air which he never feels in his tool shop, far below. The roof, he reflects, is the ideal place to be. And especially when the roof performs its supreme service, during *Basant*.

Basant, the Festival of Kites, surfaces quite spontaneously at the end of the winter rains in February. It is spring, the trees are in flower, and everyone in the Old City is carried away by the light-hearted beauty of the kites. Capricious breezes blow and the kite makers get busy bending splints of bamboo and gluing on brightly coloured tissue paper to fashion kites that people will buy to fly over the city. Everyone takes up residence on the roofs to watch and participate as the spring winds whip brilliantly coloured diamond-shaped paper kites into the air in such quantities that you can barely see the sky above. Against that deep, cool blue there will be thousands of kites, criss-crossing like a swarm of crazed butterflies. Boys of all ages, including Aziz Ahmad and his friends, prepare for the event by buying and making kites of tissue and sticks, as well as by craftily applying bits of ground glass to their own kite strings in order to cut the opponent's string and reign victorious over any and all kites in reach of their own.

Because, of course, there is more to this Festival of Kites than a simple celebration of spring. The kites of *Basant* are warriors, glorious opponents who battle for control of all they survey. Once the kite is in the air, it is an open invitation to a severing contest—the *painch*. No permission is necessary and no regrets proffered. A kite's weapon is its *maanjha*—its wickedly armoured string, which the kite flyers of *Basant* spend many days preparing, and the treatment of which is an art in itself. The string is coated in a mixture of rice paste and ground glass to strengthen it and render it capable of slashing through a hapless opponent's *maanjha*. All sorts of other recipes are whispered about: the adding of tamarind and egg yolk to ensure sharpness, repeated polishing to make it smooth. The surface of the string can never be completely smooth. Some small irregularities do remain in the armour coating; it is these fatal flaws that the opposing fighter hopes to find.

Aziz Ahmad and his friends build their own kites for *Basant*; and then, with almost everyone else, they climb to the rooftops of Lahore, to enjoy the spring weather, witness the heroic combat, and gamble, cheerfully and exuberantly, on the outcome. For Aziz, there is a wonderful exhilaration in standing under the clear blue of the sky, holding the tugging string of the soaring kite he controls high above him, and watching the colourful sky as he waits for the first attacker to appear. The kites of *Basant* are beautiful even in combat. They must fly at a considerable height so that the string can harmonise with the flow and direction of the wind. To attack, they must move in a hawklike swoop across the sky, cross their opponent's string and move swiftly up and down to sever the rival string at its weakest point. During *Basant* the sky is alive with kites swooping and swerving, or hovering poised to strike; there is much manoeuvering and dodging, sneaking up on the tail, creeping in at the belly, slashing from the top, zigzagging to mislead the opponent, soaring high to avoid a dangerous entanglement or diving suddenly to escape the killing strike.

These rooftops that Aziz loves so well are versatile spaces, and it occurs to Aziz, as he reflects on this, that perhaps *Basant* is not the only purpose of the rooftops. In this crowded city, where every house and space is filled with people, families, children, business, the rooftops become the one place to find privacy and solitude; especially for young, romantic couples, who dearly desire a few precious minutes away from the ever-vigilant eyes of family and neighbours. On cool, starry nights, the darkened rooftops above Lahore are amurmur with soft voices, musical laughter, and whispered, passionate declarations. Aziz is well aware of this state of affairs; he is, after all, engaged to be married.

Aziz Ahmed knows the Old City well. He is so familiar with the sounds and smells of each lane that he once bet his cousin that if he were to be placed anywhere within the city walls blindfolded, he would still be able to tell the spot. He knows where the best place is to view a wedding procession. He knows where the *tazia* towers are crafted for the *Muharram* procession. He knows where to buy the finest sweetmeats, the tangiest pickles and the tastiest seekh kabobs. He can get from the Lohari Gate to the Delhi Gate in less than 10 minutes, a journey which is normally traversed in no less than twenty minutes. Yet he prefers to stroll slowly through the various *muhallahs,* surveying each widely divergent market area and marvelling at how the merchants have stayed together in their traditional locations over the centuries, despite rivalries and disputes. He sees, but knows by heart, the flower vendors near the Lohari Gate, the pickle vendors, the kite makers in the Masti Gate Bazaar, and the brass utensil sellers of the Kassera Bazzar near the great Wazir Khan's Mosque. And on he walks to the great covered Azam cloth market, the bangle market, the grain market and the rope market in the Akbari Bazaar near the Delhi Gate. He knows everything that his grandfather taught him of the city history; stories about the *muhallahs*, their vendors, their resident heroes or saints; about the city's legendary rulers, past glories, and semi-mythical wealth and power; all the folk tales, myths, songs, traditions, and stories about Lahore. They mix in his head as he walks, swirling and blending with what surrounds him, with all that he perceives, with all of his senses.

The Splendours of Hira Mandi or Tibbi

Pran Nevile

Tibbi mein chal ke Jalwa-i-Parwar Digar dekh
Are ye dekhne ki cheez hai ise bar bar dekh
(Come to Tibbi to watch the splendours of the Almighty.
It's the worthiest of sights, view it over and over again.)

Named after a nobleman fond of wine, women and song, Hira Mandi, or Tibbi in common parlance, situated in the walled city of Lahore, was in its heyday the pleasure-seeker's paradise. It was patronised by the young and the old, the married and the unmarried, the rich and the famous, out for an evening's entertainment in the company of singing and dancing girls. For the young and the unmarried it was an adventure into the forbidden land. Old people frequented it more for mental relaxation than for any sensual stimulation. Married men, bored with their wives and domestic life, sought to experience new delights, intellectual as well as sexual. For the rich and the famous, patronage of Hira Mandi was a status symbol which enabled them to boast of being masters of the most beautiful of courtesans. On their part, the singing and dancing girls, professional to the core, gave all their clients their money's worth. They were at their best when trying to please the affluent among their clients, while the ordinary customers had to be content with a routine performance. It was not always all song and dance, though. Greater delights were reserved for the few who could pay for them.

It would be a mistake to take Hira Mandi for a prostitutes' street,

This extract is taken from Pran Nevile's *Lahore: A Sentimental Journey*, published by Allied Publishers Limited.

which certainly it was not, even though some of its inmates carried on the world's oldest profession for a living. The courtesan's home was essentially a place of culture, particularly in Moghul times, when some of the singing and dancing girls found their way to the Royal court. There they enchanted the nobility, which sometimes included British guests, with their accomplishments in the fine arts: music, poetry and dance. Witty conversationalists, they were engaged to teach etiquette and gentle manners to young men of aristocratic families. The elders visited them to enjoy their amorous company.

With the advent of British rule and disappearance of the old nobility, much of the grandeur of Hira Mandi was lost. But, thanks to the patronage of the new princely states and the emerging landed gentry of Punjab, the pleasure-houses of Hira Mandi continued to thrive. Troupes of singing and dancing girls were engaged to perform before rajas, nawabs and rich landlords. Their presence on the occasion of a wedding was considered to be a status symbol and an auspicious sign. The art of music had been confined to these families of Hira Mandi for generations. They had produced some of the most famous singers of India.

Theatrical companies during the twenties provided some openings for the courtesans of Hira Mandi but it was the advent of cinema in the thirties that came as a real breakthrough for them to display their talents. Later, many of them grew up to be leading stars. Broadcasting saw some others take to singing as radio artists. One of them was Umra-Zia who, with her *nagma* (song) '*Mera sallam leja— Taqdeer ke jahan tak*' overnight became a singing star around 1935.

Meanwhile, Hira Mandi continued to cast its spell on the Lahorias. In the evenings, the place was transformed into one of gaiety and laughter. Soon after sunset, a row of tongas would line up outside Lohari Gate at the portals of Anarkali, where most of the restaurants and bars were located, to convey the revellers to their destinations. These four-seater shining Peshawari tongas, drawn by sturdy horses, would race towards Bhati Gate, proceeding to Hira Mandi via Ravi Road and Taksali Gate. Some of the merry-makers preferred to walk through the walled city. Passing through Lohari Gate they would go straight to Hira Mandi after crossing Chowk Chakia, Lohari Mandi, and Said Mitha Bazar.

Walking through Hira Mandi, one could see the curtained windows behind which the singing and dancing girls entertained their clients. The strains of the sarangi and the beating of the tabla could be heard from outside. One visiting a *kotha* is received downstairs at the entrance by the agent of the establishment and a flower-seller. He is expected to wear these stringed flowers around his wrists before proceeding upstairs. Amidst glittering lights, he takes his seat on the carpeted floor covered with cool while sheets with bolsters to support himself. The singing girls sit in the centre with a team of musicians behind them ready with their instruments to accompany the singer. An elderly woman, acting as impressario, positions herself in a corner holding a silver plate containing betel leaves. After a brief introduction by her, the visitor settles down for an enjoyable evening. On a signal from the matron, one of the singing girls goes around offering betel leaves to the patrons who are expected to make a token present of a silver rupee coin. The singing girls are dressed in shining silk salwars and shirts embroidered with gold or silver threads with the upper parts of their bodies covered with a fine gauze veil. They wear gold pendants, necklaces, bracelets and anklets.

Soon the stage is set for the evening's entertainment by the musicians playing their instruments. The singer gets into her stride as she sings *thumris, dadras* and *ghazals.* She addresses each song to one or the other of the patrons who, enchanted by her sweet smiles and languishing glances, invites her to come closer to him. He rewards her with cash which she accepts gracefully and flings it towards the matron. She responds to the requests of the patrons in turn. The cries of *'Wa Wa' 'Bahut khub', 'Marhaba', 'Mukarar'* from the patrons encourage her to repeat the couplets with gestures to emphasise the meaning of the words. The musicians in turn get into the spirit of the song animating the whole atmosphere. This establishes a rapport between the singer and the listener. At times, the patrons, in a hilarious mood, ask the singer to dance to the tune of the song. The sound of anklebells in unison with music and the graceful movements of her supple body, hands and feet enthral the spectators. The repeated applause encourages her to display her seductive charms. Visiting a *kotha* was indeed an enjoyable experience.

An event celebrated with pomp and show in Hira Mandi was the deflowering of a singing or dancing girl known as the nose-ring opening ceremony. The nose-ring, made of gold or silver, was traditionally recognised as a symbol of her virginity. Its removal signified her initiation into her new profession. The performance of the ceremony was considered an honour conferred on the wealthiest of the aspirants. The payment varied according to the charms of the girl. The ceremony was marked by festivities comparable to those of a wedding in which leading professional households of Hira Mandi and their numerous friends and patrons took part. There were lavish feasts lasting two or three days where the choicest of dishes of meat, kababs and aromatic pulaos were served. Beggars and the poor were fed generously to seek their blessings for the initiation ceremony. For the girl, it was a momentous occasion heralding her entry into the profession. This was followed by a series of briefing sessions where the elder professionals gave her advice and instructions on the secrets of success in her new career.

With the coming of cinema and the film industry taking roots in Lahore, Hira Mandi emerged as a centre for recruiting budding stars: actresses, singers and dancers. Many of them rose to become leading figures in later years. Some others distinguished themselves in singing and acting and attained countrywide fame.

The war days in the forties saw the birth of a new class of patrons of Hira Mandi from among contractors, businessmen and merchants who were making big money. These affluent pleasure-seekers set a new trend and the Hira Mandi inmates spread out to other parts of the city to cater to their needs. This expanding clientele marked the beginning of the call-girl institution. These girls would visit hotels as well as private homes to entertain their customers. However, Hira Mandi continued to prosper. It was made even more lively by the affluent Lalas of the nearby town of Amritsar, whose spending power could not be matched by the Lahorias or even by the landed aristocracy of Punjab who had until then dominated the social scene. Some landlords hailing from West Punjab were Members of the Legislative Assembly. When in Lahore to attend its sessions, they had brought a wave of gaiety to Hira Mandi. But now the Amritsarias surpassed them. Driving to Lahore in their Fords, Chevrolets, Pontiacs, Packards, they would wine and dine at the posh restaurants, Stiffles, Elphinstone or Standard on the Mall and then proceed straight to Hira Mandi for an evening of amusement. They would patronise its blossoming beauties most bountifully, dazzling the Lahorias with their extravagance.

With the passage of time, the practice of inviting singing and dancing girls to add glamour at weddings lost its popularity. There was, however, a revival of a sort during the forties when the rich began organising private *mujra* parties chiefly for their male friends. I vividly remember one such gathering where the top gentry and ruling elite of Lahore were present to witness the performance of the famous singing girl, Tamancha Jan. Sporting shimmering silks, shining jewels and gold pendants, she enthralled the audience with her lilting ghazals and provocative gestures.

Encouraged by admirers and patrons, some of the Hira Mandi beauties even began visiting the racecourse and leading restaurants on the Mall, Metro in particular. The mushrooming film studios of Lahore were always on the look-out for young female artistes. The budding directors, producers and financiers scouting for new talent found these places a happy meeting ground. Some of the girls were lucky enough to be picked up as actresses while some others ended up as mistresses of affluent pleasure-seekers.

I should like to recall some episodes, romantic as well as tragic, associated with Hira Mandi. One of them is about the murder of Shamshad Bai, a fifteen-year-old courtesan of Lahore. The accused, who was her lover, was one of the wealthiest and most influential landlords of Punjab, Nawab Mohammad Nawaz Khan of Dab Kalan. He was a perfect gentleman liked by his numerous friends among whom were Hindus, Muslims and Sikhs. His hospitality was proverbial. When in Lahore, he would stay at the most expensive Flattis Hotel where he held lavish parties at which the choicest of liquors flowed freely. He spent enormous sums of money on singing girls who entertained his friends. When he entered any restaurant on the Mall, the waiters and barmen rushed to serve him. Generous to a fault, he would invite everyone who happened to be there to join him. He had studied at the Chiefs' College where he was popular with the staff and fellow students alike. His marriage to the daughter of Mian Fazal-i-Hussain, the then Education Minister of the Punjab, a memorable event in those days, however, did not curb his high spirits.

He continued to seek pleasure in women and wine. To meet his mounting expenses he sold or mortgaged his landed estates. He travelled like a Moghul prince with his retinue of servants, singers and musicians. When he met Shamshad Bai, he was so smitten by her that he took her with him to his family palace in Jhang. It was there that the murder of Shamshad took place. It is said that Shamshad had teased Mohammad Nawaz when, in a drunken state, he wanted to make love to her. Shamshad gave him a push and he fell off the bed. She continued to laugh. In a rage he pulled out his revolver from under his pillow and shot her dead. What followed was indeed unbelievable. According to the evidence produced during trial, the Nawab continued lying with the dead body of Shamshad for nearly ten hours.

Mohammad Nawaz was convicted for murder by the Session Court. His appeal to the High Court was pending when he died at the young age of 31, the night before Sir Douglas Young, Chief Justice, returned to Lahore from a holiday in Kashmir to hear the case. This was the tragic end of a young lovable patron who doted on Shamshad, the provocative beauty of Hira Mandi.

This was a crime of passion. Our sympathies go to the singing girl unlike in the story I am now going to narrate. Here the lover, 'K.' for the sake of his beloved Zohra Jan willingly reversed his role from patron to pimp. I was told this episode by a noted businessman, who ran a motor financing business those days at Lahore. 'K.' was a landowner of District Sargodha who had enough income from his crops to lead a comfortable life. He used to visit Lahore now and then to spend his evenings in Hira Mandi. It was in the mid-thirties that he fell under the spell of the beautiful Zohra Jan. He had known Zohra Jan for years; in fact, she grew up 'in his hands', as a Punjabi proverb goes. He had been a constant patron of her family for a long time and when Zohra Jan came of age 'K.' was invited to perform the nose-ring opening ceremony. He was anxious to own a motor car to make a good impression on Zohra by taking her out for joy-rides. Having never saved enough money, he had to raise a loan from a motor finance company to buy the car. He agreed to repay the loan in half-yearly instalments to coincide with his yield from the crops. The loan was to be repaid in three years but after receiving only two instalments the finance company had no news of 'K.' or whereabouts. Letters and telegrams brought no response. The finance company sent their representative to Sargodha and reclaimed the car. It was learnt that 'K.' had gone away to Calcutta with a dancing girl from Lahore after selling his lands. He was honest enough to have left the car behind with instructions that it be handed over to the finance company when they come for it. The said businessman forgot all about 'K.' until one day in the early forties when he took some of his friends to Hira Mandi to entertain them. He was accosted there by 'K.' who greeted him warmly and proposed that he should go up to Zohra Jan's *kotha* to hear her singing. He narrated his adventures in Calcutta where he had taken Zohra to help her enter the film line. He told him how he had lost everything in this attempt. Devoted as ever to his fairy queen, he was now helping her settle down in her old profession. Poor 'K.' the patron, had become the pimp.

This reminds me of a couplet I heard from an old jovial pimp about how he had landed in this profession:

> *Jat ke the neem julae*
> *Us pe ban gae darzi*
> *Lote pote ke ban gae kanjar*
> *Ze khuda ki marzi*

(From a semi-skilled weaver, I became a tailor. Then after many ups and downs, by the grace and will of God I rose to the position of a pimp.)

I have not visited Hira Mandi for nearly five decades now though I long to go once again to that memorable haunt of the young and the old where they went in search of joy, fun and amusement.

Kanjari

Adam Zamizad

At age twelve she was pregnant. At seventeen she was singing and
dancing her way into films. At eighteen she was accused of, and
prosecuted for, breaking into her benefactor, producer/director/actor
Jamal's house, and stealing his wife's jewellery and an unspecified
amount of cash. Rumours put it from well over a million to under
seven rupees, and seven paisas, for luck. At twenty-two she married
one of the richest young men in Pakistan.

Up until the age of eleven—once she got over crying for her parents
and her home—she quite enjoyed her new life with her new family.
No thanks to Sarla Bai, her adoptive mother. Sarla was the niece of
the great Amir Bai, the once hugely famous courtesan. Unlike Amir
Bai, she was neither a kind woman nor a loving parent. But Benazeer
had come to love Amir Bai. And she loved to watch the spectacle of
dance and music and poetry that was enacted night after night in
their living room. Far more exciting than any television programme,
or even a film, that she had ever seen. Sarla Bai was a great dancer
and sang sweeter than a nightingale. Some of Benazeer's earliest
memories were of Sarla, dressed in Mughal splendour, dancing her
bells away to the tempo of the tablas, ecstatically singing some of the
best poems of Urdu literature to the magical notes of the sitars and
the sarangis. Cradled in her 'great aunt' Amir Bai's arms, Benazeer
would watch the proceedings with hypnotic fascination. Along with
the throng of admiring guests and clients who sat cross-legged on
the plush Persian carpet in a wide oval of smoke and drink, handing
out ten, fifty, even hundred-rupee notes as if they owned their own

---

This extract is taken from a novel in progress, about a child kidnapped
from her home and brought up in a kotha in Hira Mandi.

mints. It seemed so beautiful, so fantastical—something out of the pages of a book written by angels and fairies.

Neelo and Nimmi, her 'step-sisters', dressed in equal magnificence, danced side by side with Sarla. It was Benazeer's greatest ambition to join them on the floor and give a performance better than the three of them put together. In her innocence, the poor girl did not realize half of what it entailed. For a start, losing the ring worn in the centre of her nose—the *nuth*. It was meant to be the declaration of a would-be prostitute's virginity. To lose it was the start of a working girl's career—that is, selling her maidenhead to her first client and taking on the full responsibilities and life of a *kanjari*.

The unfortunate event to start off that life happened earlier than she or anyone had expected, just before her eleventh birthday. One cool October morning Amir Bai did not come down for her with the usual glass of home-made lassi, to be followed by fried eggs and parathas. After a discreet amount of waiting, Benazeer went up to call her down. She could not wake her up. Amir Bai had died during the night. Benazeer was heartbroken. Not so Sarla Bai. She took on the mantle of a *naiqa*: a sort of Mother Superior of the order of family prostitutes, an office previously held by Amir Bai. The naiqa's word is law, and great and small are supposed to tremble in her presence. The authority goes with the position and not the person, though a tough personality does make things tougher for all concerned. And Benazeer's adoptive mother was tough—no one could deny her that! No one dared complain either. Especially as her iron and flesh persona combined with her efficient management style brought in better business, a higher class of clients, and lots more money . . .

It was Sarla's decision to present Benazeer to the gathered audience three months later, one Thursday evening—considered lucky, being the eve of Holy Friday. The bidding was formally declared open to auction her virginity. The successful bidder in any such auction was not always the highest, in terms of money. Rank and status were also taken into consideration. The policy paid off in the long run, even financially. A kanjari favoured by a man of high status and social standing fetched a much higher price from her other clients, even if, in the earlier stages of the game, the man's name was kept a secret. Two reasons. One, to avoid gossip and rivalry which could erupt in violence and was bad for business. Two, it could then be suggested that no one had come forward with a bid high enough, and that the girl was still a virgin. Then she could be put to bid again. With enough tact and style, this could be repeated several times, making much more money than if it was admitted that the girl had been 'deflowered'.

The lucky ones were offered perks for their silence. Or, if they belonged to 'families of repute', tacitly blackmailed into shutting up. But even if they did blabber, who cared! Such gossip was always going on in Hira Mandi—the jewel market—as it was called; pretty girls being the jewels. This sex-bazaar was also known as the Shahi Mohalla: the Royal Neighbourhood. Set in the heart of the old Mughal Lahore, with its narrow brick roads twisting at odd, unexpected angles, it used to be the nightly haunt of Rajah, Nawab, King, courtier, and son—during the very good very old days!

People saw what they saw, and if they liked what they saw, they paid the price that was asked, and more. What anybody else said was so much rainwater in a flood. Girls of Benazeer's age were said to be 'tight' anyway, and with a little alum to dry up the parts, or a cut here and there, or some animal blood, the splitting of hymen could be faked as and when. After a cruel night for which nothing in the world had prepared Benazeer, her nuth was back on again the next evening. Only, after a time, Sarla made arrangements for private offers rather than public bidding. Too many of the last would have caused too many moustaches to curl up in amused astonishment, custom and tradition notwithstanding.

The Legend of Anarkali

Shahnaz Kureshy

There are far grander monuments in Lahore, but few as evocative of
romance and tragedy as the tomb of the ill-fated Anarkali, the
courtesan who won the heart of a prince only to face the wrath of a
Mughal emperor... or so the legend goes. Who can visit it without
wanting to discover the myths that still cling to it, like moss to an
old stone? You gaze at the exquisite sarcophagus, with its famous
inscription, and are reminded of the much-chronicled beauty of the
young woman whose remains are said to lie in this relic, surrounded
by outhouses, a police station and a mosque. It's the sort of place that
leads you to reflect on the instability of worldly glories and the way
all vanity has of sinking into oblivion with barely a trace.

The chroniclers have had a field day with this seventeenth-century
tale. In his book, *Anarkali: Archives and Tomb of Sahib Jamal,* Nazir Ahmed
Chaudhry writes that according to popular details of the story recorded
by them, the beautiful young woman was the daughter of a Persian
merchant named Ejaz, who fell on bad days. The merchant set out
for Hindustan with his daughter, with the hope of recovering his
fortune. Misfortune struck again when a band of robbers fell upon
his caravan. He was slain and his daughter taken captive by the leader
of the bandits, one Deler Koh. The matter was reported to the Mughal
'nazim' of Kabul, in whose jurisdiction the incident had taken place.
The bandits were caught and the girl was recovered. Raja Man Singh,
then Governor of Kabul, sent her to Emperor Akbar's harem in Lahore.

As the story goes, the monarch gave her the title of Anarkali or
Pomegranate Blossom. She caught the eye of Prince Salim, the
handsome young heir apparent to the Mughal empire, and so taken
was he with her that the affair could not remain hidden for long. His
tutor, Abu'l Fazl, reprimanded him, but to no avail. Matters became
serious when the prince's parents learnt about the love affair. The
king, it is said, was all the more offended because he saw an affair

with a member of his retinue as an intrusion into his private life.

One day, narrates Chaudhry, the emperor was enjoying a soirée in his mirror-encrusted 'Shish Mahal' at the Lahore Fort, also attended by Prince Salim. While Anarkali danced and sang, another slave girl drew the monarch's attention to the mirrors embedded in the ceiling and pillars of the room, which showed her returning the prince's smile. This infuriated the emperor, who left the party in anger, and ordered the arrest of Anarkali. The alarmed prince fled the court with the girl, with the emperor's servants in hot pursuit. They were soon caught, and the emperor passed a death sentence on the unfortunate girl. She was buried alive in an upright position, within brick walls on a platform.

Prince Salim, who escaped punishment, is said to have later paid homage to the dancing girl by building a magnificent tomb over the grave popularly believed to have been hers, on which he inscribed an eloquent and expressive tribute in the form of a Persian couplet carved on the marble cenotaph.

It says,

> 'Ah! Could I see again the face of my lost friend, I would thank my God until the day of Judgement.'

The first report of this incident was recorded in a journal by William Finch, an English businessman who visited Lahore in February 1611 in connection with the indigo trade. He noticed seeing a monument for one of Akbar's wives and he writes:

> Passing the Sugar Gonge is a faire miskite built by Sheeke Fereed beyond it (without the towns, in the way to the gardens) is a faire monument for Don Sha his mother, one of Akabar's wives, with whom it is said Sha Selim had to do (her name was Immacque Kelle, or Pomegranate Kernell); upon notice of which the King (Akbar) caused her to be inclosed quicke within a wall in his moholl, where she died, and the King (Jahangir), in token of his love, commands a sumptuous tomb to be built of stone in the midst of a foure square garden richly walled, with a gate and divers roomes

over it. The convexity of the tombe he hath willed to be
wrought in workes of gold, with a large faire Jounter with
roomes overhead. Note that most of these monuments which
I mention are of such largeness that, if they were otherwise
contrived, would have rooms to entertaine a very good man
with his whole household.

The sarcophagus is made of a block of pure marble of extraordinary
beauty and exquisite workmanship. According to Orientalist E.B.
Eastwick, it is 'one of the finest pieces of carving in the world'.
Inscribed on top of it are the ninety-nine attributes of God and on
the sides is engraved the couplet composed by Jehangir. A chronogram
in the inscription reveals that Anarkali's death occurred in 1599, six
years before Salim became emperor, and that the tomb was constructed
sixteen years later, in 1615, by which time he had already been married
for over five years to Meherunnissa, later Empress Nur Jehan.

Historians do not agree on the authenticity of this tragic tale.
The doubters ask why Jehangir, who faithfully recorded every event
in his life, failed to pen any record of this love affair. Nor has he ever
referred to a monument raised in Anarkali's memory. Another argument
offered is that had such an incident really taken place, Jehangir would
not have been considered trustworthy enough to be appointed successor
to the throne by his father. In Jehangir's own *Waqiat-e-Jahangiri*, which
is considered a reliable record, the prince wrote of his father's
deathbed:

At this crisis my father desiring me to draw near, threw his
arms about my neck, and addressed me in the following terms:

'My dear boy (baba), take this my last farewell, for here we
never meet again. Beware that thou dost not withdraw thy
protecting regard from those that are secluded in my harem;
that thou continue the same allowance for subsistence as
was allotted by myself. Although my departure must cast a
heavy burden upon thy mind, let not the words that are past
be at once forgotten. There are many a vow between us;
break not the pledge which thou hast given me, forget it not.

Beware; many are the claims which I have upon thy soul. Be they great or be they small, do not thou forget them. Call to thy remembrance my deeds of martial glory. Forget not the exertions of that bounty which distributed so many a jewel. My servants and dependants, when I am gone, do not thou forget, nor the afflicted in the hour of need. Ponder word for word on all that I have said, do thou bear all in mind; and again, forget me not.'

This account, the naysayers contend, is a testimony to the sanctity of the father–son relationship and cannot coexist with what they believe is a slave girl's concocted story.

True or not, the story has an extraordinary power, and has fired the imagination of dramatists, writers and film-makers. Aside from Anarkali's own tale, the fate of this monument is a story in itself. Colonel H.R. Goulding, who was associated with the Lahore Municipal works, wrote about the tomb in the *Civil and Military Gazette* in the early 1920s. He recorded that the tomb was converted into a church in 1850, and became known as the First Parish Church of the Protestant community of Lahore. A thousand rupees were sanctioned by the British government to make the necessary alterations for the tomb to serve as a place of worship for the growing congregation of Sunday worshippers. The building was formally consecrated as a church on 14 January 1857. A full-sized organ was substituted for the harmonium that had been in use here for many years. Mr Goulding was a member of the choir when the new organ was installed. As a church, it was a meeting point for British officers in Lahore and remained a place of Christian worship for another twenty-five years.

In the 1880s, Eastwick walked around its premises, collecting material for his *Handbook of the Panjab* and noticed the marble sarcophagus 'removed from its place, and thrust into a dirty closet' where he found it covered with dust and bat-droppings. According to historian S.M. Latif, the remains of Anarkali had been exhumed and reburied under one of the turrets of the building before the tomb was converted into a church.

In 1891, the building acquired a new use when the Punjab Secretariat turned it into a repository of its records and files. The

Secretariat's library was also located here for a period of time.

The structure rests on a raised plinth and one has to climb four steep steps to enter the building. It is clearly a solidly constructed building to have resisted structural damage for so many centuries. However, the fresco work in the interior and the outlines on the exterior have faded with age, and the entire structure, including the dome, have been relentlessly whitewashed since British days. There have been many alterations to the tomb over the years. An outer staircase was constructed and the outlets and openings from the alcoves were sealed. Large windows were also installed. Over time, the underground chamber that housed the body was also filled with dirt.

In 1960, the Pakistan government made efforts to restore the historical building, located in the Civil Secretariat on the Lower Mall, and opened it to the public. However, it still remains home to the Punjab Archives—a rather nice example of historical wealth being kept in a historical monument. The central hall of the tomb has been turned into an archival museum with many valuable paintings, pictures, sketches, stamps and coins kept in this chamber. But, no matter what future uses lie in the destiny of this monument, for the people of Lahore it will always be the tomb of Anarkali; and a city that named a bustling bazaar after the courtesan will continue to be entranced by the story of her short life.

Thought-Nymph

Munir Niazi

Who knows
She may come at last
On the crest of a wave
Hidden in a leaf
In the song of a bird
In this unquiet house
Or in the dawn's cosmic splendour
And when I meet her
I may be able to say
That which I once said
On a morning like this
In a strange town
To another stranger in Lahore.

—*Translated by Daud Kamal*

This extract is taken from *The Poetical Works of Munir Niazi*, edited by Suhail Safdar, published by Pakistan Writings.

From *The Crow Eaters*

Bapsi Sidhwa

FAREDOON JUNGLEWALLA

Jerbanoo had been against the long journey from the very start. Unnerved by the uprooting, by the buffalo attack and the aloof stance adopted by her unfeeling son-in-law, she had ranted, whined and finally resigned herself to martyrdom. Arms akimbo, vindictive eyes snapping, she never failed an opportunity to castigate him. And the journey, fraught with mishap and mild disaster, had given her plenty.

As on that pitch-black night when the wooden wheel of the bullock-cart collapsed on the outskirts of the Rajastan Desert and a jackal suddenly howled into the stillness.

Jumping from the cart, palms on hips, Jerbanoo planted herself solidly before Freddy. Her winged eyebrows almost disappeared in her hairline. 'So, now we are to be devoured by wolves! Why? Because your majesty wishes it! We are to spend the night at the mercy of wild beasts! Why? Because our village ways were not good enough for you! But don't imagine I'm going to dance to your tune all the time. I've come for my daughter's sake and I'm not going to stand this nonsense any longer! You turn right back! You hear me?' she bawled, her eyes shining triumphantly in the glow of the lantern swinging from Freddy's hand.

Freddy turned away silently.

'You obstinate fiend, have you no care for your wife and child? Oh, how can they live at the mercy of your whims . . . you heartless demon!' she cried.

Putli slept through unconcerned. Her mother's tirades had grown so commonplace that the uproar hardly stirred her dreams.

Ignoring Jerbanoo, Freddy set about repairing the wheel. The slighted woman bounced back into the cart and sat quivering on her mattress.

The jackal bayed, his mournful notes amplified by the nocturnal stillness.

Jerbanoo's spine grew rigid and out of sheer disgust and frustration, she howled back.

The jackal caterwauled eerily.

'Owoooo!' went Jerbanoo.

Excited by the discovery of a mate, the jackal launched an abysmal moan.

'Yieeee!' yowled Jerbanoo, and between the two rose the most ghoulish duet imaginable.

His flesh creeping, his beautiful white teeth on edge, Faredoon leaped onto the cart and scrambled into the hut. Hurling himself within an inch of his mother-in-law's face he hissed, 'Stop it . . . Stop that horrible noise or I'll leave you right here . . . I swear!'

Jerbanoo subsided at once. Not so much at the ominous pledge as at the demented gleam in his eyes.

Within two hours they had resumed their journey, soothed and lulled by the hollow toll of the bell hanging from each bullock's neck.

At other times the child had dysentery, Jerbanoo got cramps bathing in a canal, and Putli, stung by a scorpion, almost fell into a well. On these occasions, attracted by Jerbanoo's strident, scolding outcries, the entire populace of several villages was entertained mercilessly to the shortcomings of her son-in-law.

Tiring of this, Freddy addressed himself exclusively to his wide-eyed, diligent wife, and Jerbanoo slumped into a restive, martyred silence.

Two dust-grimed, mosquito-bitten months later, Freddy led his worn beasts into the fertile land of the Five Rivers.

They passed through several villages, green with wheat and gold with mustard. They spent a few days in the golden city of Amritsar and finally came to Lahore.

Faredoon Junglewalla fell in love with Lahore straightaway. His mother-in-law, the corners of whose set mouth had drooped progressively as the journey had gone on, surveyed the bustling, steaming city with bleak eyes. She withheld her comment for the moment, glad of a chance to rest her rattled joints.

Freddy toured Lahore all day, and each hour strengthened his initial love of the ancient city. That evening they parked the cart beneath a shady tree near the Badshahi Mosque. The horizon cradled the sun in a pink fleece, touching the poetic assembly of white domes with a blush, filling Freddy's senses with serenity. The muezzin's cry, suppliant, plaintive and sensual, rose in the hushed air among the domes. Bells tinkled in a diminutive Hindu temple, snuggled in the shadows of the mosque. A Sikh temple, gold-plated, gleamed like a small jewel in the shadows, and Freddy, responsive to all religious stimuli, surrendered his heart to the moment.

In the morning, having decided to adopt the city and try his luck, Freddy approached his wife for the gold. Putli, who had been laying out feed for the bullocks, glanced around with wary eyes.

'Even trees,' she advised sternly, 'have ears.'

Placing a cautionary hand on Freddy's arm, she led him into their room on the bullock-cart.

The baby slept in one corner and Jerbanoo sat cross-legged on her mattress, battling the enervating heat with a palm-leaf fan. At Freddy's entrance she wrinkled her nose at the bazaar smells assailing her nostrils and, fanning herself into a froth, mutely advertised her displeasure of the city.

Freddy's heart trilled in his chest. Jerbanoo's disfavour set the seal on his inspired decision. Like hens settling on eggs, Freddy's mind settled on a smug clutch of smiling thoughts. Right there he took a silent oath that he would never leave Lahore so long as he lived.

Turning his back upon his mother-in-law's pointed histrionics, Freddy watched his wife unbutton the tight bodice beneath her sari blouse. Putli barely came up to his chest. Secure from prying, thieving eyes, she removed the cache that had pressed the flesh of her breasts from the onset of their travels. Carefully handing the cache to Freddy, she began buttoning herself back into her flattening, cotton bodice. Freddy eyed with chagrin the buoyant little breasts as they disappeared. He reached stealthily for a last-minute touch, but her censorious stare, warning him of his mother-in-law, stayed his hand.

There was a certain fixed quality to Putli's humourless eyes, set well apart in the stern, little triangle of her face, that often disconcerted and irritated Freddy. The only time he saw her unwavering gaze dissolve was in bed. Then her long-lashed lids grew heavy with sensuality and there was such dogged and hedonistic devotion in her eyes for him, such a readiness to please and be pleased, that he became her slave.

As soon as Freddy left, Putli flung herself into an energetic orgy of work. In no time at all she had watered the bullocks, started a fire in the coal brazier and set a colander of vegetables and lentils to simmer. All this she did with such economy of motion and efficiency that her mother roused herself guiltily to give a hand. Taking the plate of rice from Putli she began to feed the child.

Freddy systematically found his way to the homes of the four Parsee families settled in Lahore: the Toddywallas, the Bankwallas, the Bottliwallas and the Chaiwallas. None of them practised the trades suggested by their names. The Toddywallas, a large extended family, were the proprietors of a prosperous tea stall, and the Chaiwallas ran a bar. Mr Bottliwalla was a teller in a bank, and Mr Bankwalla conducted classes in ballroom dancing.

An endearing feature of this microscopic merchant community was its compelling sense of duty and obligation towards other Parsees. Like one large close-knit family, they assisted each other, sharing success and rallying to support failure. There were no Parsee beggars in a country abounding in beggars. The moment a Parsee strikes it rich, he devotes a big portion of his energies to charity. He builds schools, hospitals and orphanages; provides housing, scholarships and finance. Notorious misers, they are paradoxically generous to a cause.

The four families were delighted by Freddy's visit and enchanted at the prospect of another family come to swell their ranks.

In two days Freddy had ensconced his family in a flat atop his brand-new provision store in one of the most busy and commercially prosperous areas in town.

The very next evening, rigged out in a starched white coat-wrap that fastened with bows at the neck and waist, crisp white pyjamas and a turban, he drove his cart to Government House.

Parking his splendid bullocks next to restive tonga horses, Freddy strode confidently up to the resplendent guards at the huge iron gates. The guards allowed him in almost at once and Freddy signed his name in the Visitor's Register.

Having thus paid homage to the British Empire, established his credentials and demonstrated his loyalty to 'Queen and Crown', Freddy was free to face the future.

*

When Faredoon Junglewalla, pioneer and adventurer, trotted into Lahore in his bullock-cart at the turn of the century, there were only thirty Parsees in the city of over a million Hindus, Muslims, Sikhs and Christians. Twenty years later, the number of Parsees in Lahore had swelled to almost three hundred. Poor families had drifted in from Bombay and the area thereabouts to settle in the rich North Indian province, gratefully partaking of the bounty that was Lahore. And, of course, original sons of the soil, of whom Freddy justifiably considered himself a member, had enormously proliferated.

Freddy was the undisputed head of this community. He was also spokesman and leader of the Parsees scattered over the rest of the Punjab and the North-West Frontier Province right up to the Khyber Pass. Freddy's willingness and ability to help, to give of his time, to intervene and intercede, were proverbial; his influence with men who wielded power was legendary. They said of him, 'Oh, he has the police in his pocket.' They boasted, 'He has the English sahibs tamed so that they eat out of his hand.' And this was no mean accomplishment, for the aloof, disparaging and arrogant British rarely became pally with the 'natives'.

Faredoon Junglewalla, toady, philanthropist and shrewd businessman, was renowned for his loyalty to his community and friends. People came from afar seeking his help in bagging prime jobs, securing licenses, contracts, permits and favours. They travelled two thousand miles from Bombay, expecting Faredoon to extricate them from 'tight spots', as did Mr Adi Sodawalla, whose brother, Mr Polly Sodawalla, was languishing in a London jail.

Mr Adi Sodawalla, pale, timorous and pleading, sat across the desk from Faredoon presenting his case.

'Tell me everything . . . every detail,' insisted Faredoon.

Mr Adi Sodawalla related the facts honestly and humbly. He glanced every now and then at the heavy-lidded eyes that missed nothing, and he drew courage from the benign and understanding expression on Freddy's handsome face,

Mr Polly Sodawalla, the subject of his brother's narrative, had voyaged to England with a suitcase full of illegal opium, which he had airily sent away to be deposited in the ship's hold with the rest of his luggage. On disembarking, he was too worn out by landing formalities to clear and take along his possessions. Carrying only the suitcase he had had in his cabin, he went to refresh himself at a hotel in Earl's Court. When he sauntered up to claim his luggage the next day, he discovered that one bag, dumped unceremoniously from place to place with the rest of his luggage, had split open, spilling its secret.

The reception committee of customs officers and policemen, patiently awaiting his return, welcomed him with flattering interest and marched him off to jail.

Interpol moved in. Mr Polly Sodawalla could look forward to a long sojourn in His Imperial Majesty's dank prisons.

At the end of his tale, he anxiously watched Freddy sit back in his swivel chair, fold his hands on his chest and tilt back his head to gaze at the ceiling. He could see that Faredoon was angry.

'Cunt! The lazy, stupid cunt!' exploded Freddy slowly. His voice was bitter. 'Do you know how much money your brother would have made if he had succeeded? At least fifty thousand rupees! Even a baby would have known to clear the luggage first. But no. His Imperial Majesty was too tired, he had to go to a hotel to wash behind his ears, he had to curl up on a sofa like a lamb and fall asleep. He deserves to be in jail!'

'You're right, sir. I will break his teeth,' quavered Mr Sodawalla, holding aloft a puny fist for Freddy's edification.

'Now, had he been caught by a vigilant customs officer,' Freddy continued, 'had he been informed upon, he would have my sympathy. I can find it in my heart to help a misguided soul—but I cannot forgive a fool!'

'But he is my brother! I beg you, I implore you for our mother's sake to help him. She has not stopped crying since she heard the news. "Oh, my son will freeze. Oh, he will die of pneumonia," she wails, non-stop. My heart breaks to hear her. You shall have the entire family's undying gratitude—only you can save him.'

Freddy pursed his lips. 'Something will have to be done,' he agreed.
'Not for that lazy bastard's sake, but for the good name of our
community. We can't let it get around that a Parsee is in jail for
smuggling opium!'

Mr Sodawalla sniffed, wiped his eyes with a huge white handkerchief
and raised grateful, supplicating eyes to his brother's anticipated saviour.

The Sodawallas were not well-off. Faredoon financed the entire
rescue of the unfortunate smuggler from his personal funds. An
emissary was dispatched to London with special documents. Influential
connections were entreated and coerced. Faredoon worked incessantly,
and at the end of two months Mr Polly Sodawalla sailed from London,
a free man.

But if Faredoon did not take a penny from the Sodawallas, he had
no scruples about relieving Mr Katrak, a diamond merchant from
Karachi, of fifty thousand rupees.

Mr Katrak, a man with a venerable beard, sat before Freddy, his
trembling hands on a gold-handled walking stick. His son, Bobby, sat
beside him with lowered head. He was a thickset youth of about
twenty-four, his arrogant air momentarily deflated. Freddy approved
of his open-faced, neatly groomed handsomeness, thinking he would
make a good match for Yasmin.

Bobby Katrak owned a gleaming Silver Ghost Rolls-Royce. It had
stately dashboards, two horns that were elaborately curled, rising on
either side of the tinted windscreen like silver cobras, and sundry
silver fittings. He was given to dashing about at reckless speeds and
had rammed the Rolls into an old blind beggar on a busy thoroughfare.
Bobby had panicked and roared away at thirty-five miles an hour. Five
men had noted his number. Even without it, his was, in 1920, the
only Silver Ghost in Karachi.

The old beggar died the next day in hospital.

'I have told him not to drive so fast,' mourned Mr Katrak. 'How
many times have I told you not to go over fifteen? But no! He wants
to "dhoorr-dhoorr" around at thirty-five and even forty miles an hour!
Now look what you've got yourself into. I feel so ashamed having to
give you all this trouble, Faredoon.'

Freddy wagged his head and clicked his tongue kindly at Mr Katrak's
son.

'Bobby, you must do as your father says. It is his privilege to guide you. Now, I don't think it is only your speed that is to blame. The first rule one must observe is to respect the law. You can never run from it . . . though you may get around it! You should have stopped and seized one or two witnesses. There must have been people who saw you were not to blame—with the aid of a little money perhaps? Then you could have reported the matter to the police. But you did not do this and you have complicated things for yourself.'

Faredoon turned to Mr Katrak. 'I talked to my friend—you know whom I mean. I pleaded that the boy is like my own son. He says he will try to get him off the hook. I convinced him it was not Bobby's fault, but since he did not report the accident, the charges are grave. Anyway, my friend promises to help. He will go to Karachi himself to arrange for a couple of witnesses—make a pre-dated report at some police thana or other. . . but,' and here Freddy's inflection rose to a thinly pitched, incredulous whisper, 'the bastard wants fifty thousand rupees!'

Mr Katrak turned pale. He looked at his son, whose head was hanging as low as it ought. He looked at Freddy again and wrote out the cheque.

Freddy gave Mr Gibbons, who was now inspector-general of police, the ten thousand rupees they had agreed upon, and stowed away the remaining forty in his special kitty. This was the kitty he dipped into to help others—and occasionally himself.

BILLY AND TANYA

At this moment in our story, Freddy, Jerbanoo and Putli are in England and Tanya is expecting.

Tanya has eaten. She finds it difficult to keep Billy's late lunch hours. December is bitterly cold in the high-ceilinged, whitewashed, brick-walled rooms, and Tanya has slept curled up beneath a heavy quilt. She has awakened to the slice and crunch of Billy beginning to feed. Slipping out of bed guiltily, she has wrapped herself in a shawl, duty-bound to keep her mute husband company during meals. She sits across the table.

Suddenly she says, 'Don't do that!'

'What?'

'I feel sick. I can't stand that noise! Why do you make such a performance of eating radish? It's only radish!'

'It's good for the liver. Here, have some,' offers Billy. 'Much better for you than pomegranate. You won't feel sick.'

Tanya strikes out, and the proffered plate flies clattering to the floor.

'I want pomegranate!' she pants. 'I want pomegranate!'

Billy is hurt, his faced closed and sullen. Tanya has grown to dread this expression. It could bode the onset of a non-speaking spell that once lasted a full week. She had not been able to penetrate his ice. Confused and terrified, she saw him turn into a monstrous stranger. She could not relate the grim set of his mouth and his accusing, suspicious eyes to the gentle lover she had married.

The cook now replaced Billy's plate, and he began slicing through another radish.

Tanya watched his scowl as he worked his gnashing jaws, and suddenly she threw up.

Billy didn't even glance her way.

Tanya wobbled to her room, stretched out on the bed and told the baby's maid in a faint voice, 'Call sahib, I am going to faint.'

The maid delivered the message and Billy, scared out of his wits, rushed to his wife's bedside. This was a new stratagem reserved by Tanya for dire emergencies.

Billy patted Tanya's hands, rubbed her feet, laid wet towels on her face and sent servants on futile errands to fetch this and that. His frenzied efforts delighted Tanya. She almost wept beneath her swoon-closed lids.

The moment she emerged from her faint, Billy flew to her side, penitent and pale-faced and all lover!

'You don't love me any more,' she whispered.

'I love you. I love you, darling,' he all but sobbed, and it did Tanya good to hear the words she had despaired of.

Dr Bharucha arrived. 'What's the matter?' he asked, sympathetically.

'I want pomegranate,' whispered Tanya.

It was the season for pomegranates. Bazaars rang with the cry of vendors promoting the fruit. Fruit stalls were red with its colourful abundance.

'I'll get you all the pomegranates you want,' cried Billy.

Billy jumped on to his bicycle and pedalled furiously to the fruit shop at the end of Warris Road. The price was too steep and he went on to the Tollington Market. The price was still too high!

Billy rode through crowded bazaar lanes, bargaining and offering outrageously low bids. He abandoned the bazaars and pedalled all the way to the fruit-mandi. Picking his way through swarms of flies, slush and rotting fruit, he at last found what he sought.

Three hours later, Billy returned with the cherished fruit and proudly presented Tanya three yellow-brown pomegranates the size and shape of crab apples.

'Get away from me!' screamed Tanya, flailing her arms and scattering the pomegranates like ping-pong balls.

'But darling, I searched all over.'

'Don't darling me!' screamed Tanya. 'Lahore is full of red pomegranates and you can find only this?'

'But red ones don't have any strength. These have vitamins. Ask any doctor.'

'I don't care!' cried Tanya. 'I didn't ask for vitamins. You're gone for three hours and you get this? I should have guessed!' Tanya jumped from the bed like a fury. She pounced on a pomegranate that had bounced off the wall and rolled beneath a chair and hurled it, smashing through a window. She was red-faced and perspiring. Billy could not restrain her. She pounced on another hapless pomegranate roosting by the dressing table and flung it out of the window. Billy was terrified. He feared for the unborn child. 'I'll get you what you want!' he screamed and scooted from the room.

He returned in three minutes and he found Tanya propped up in bed. Her hair was wet with perspiration and she was gasping with wrath.

'There, is this what you want?' he said, placing a large red pomegranate on her lap. He retrieved it promptly, in case she decided to smash it, too, through the window.

Tanya continued her curious gaping.

Billy peeled the fruit, gathering the juicy, blood-red kernels into a bowl. 'Here,' he said holding the bowl under her chin.

Tanya averted her chin.

Billy sat on the bed stroking her hair. He scooped the kernels into a spoon and fed her.

Billy's renewed ardour lasted a full month. But it was, as before, an infatuation. The infatuation having run its course, he reverted to his true love, money. Tanya was helpless against her fascinating rival. Reacting like an abandoned mistress, she attacked his passion for her adversary, and he hated her for it.

They were both raw with wounds. But Billy's will and tenacity were greater than Tanya's, his effort more single-minded. And Tanya finally gave in to his tyrannies. The only way to please Billy was to be absolutely submissive, and he was getting harder to please.

*

Billy's tyrannies began with sunrise. His eyes opened and urgent signals were transmitted throughout the house by Tanya. The newspaper was rushed to him. With it, Billy hurried to the thunderbox, which he commandeered for the rest of the morning. Since the bathroom was in the front of the house he had a clear view of the drive, part of the portico, and the garden. Billy never closed the bathroom doors. He sat screened from the outside by a thin, reed curtain. The children briefly popped in and out, the children's maid fetched toothpaste or towels, and the bearer sailed in with a cup of tea on a tray.

Now Billy's thunderbox, being part of the dower received from Sir Noshirwan Jeevanjee Easymoney, had to be special. It was! It was large, it was carved, and it was inlaid with brass. When the lid, which was also the backrest, was shut, it looked like a chest.

Enthroned, Billy sipped his tea and read the newspaper. As soon as the cup of tea was emptied, it was replaced by another. Often Billy sent for his ledgers and scrutinized them on his princely perch.

This was the hour of his business audience. Those who wished to see him at his house and at his leisure visited in the morning. One by one the contractors, land agents, purchasers and dealers would cough outside the reed curtain, say, 'Salaam, Sethji,' and state their case. Billy could see them clearly; they could only see the shadow of Sethji, newspaper outspread, seated on some kind of box. If he switched on the light they could see more. And, of an occasional evening when it was dark outside, they saw Sethji in all his glory, lean shanks gleaming between pyjama top and pyjama bottom, brass inlay and carved thunderbox!

Sometimes there were small conferences, with Billy negotiating with a group of men from behind his reed curtain. In fact, Billy's thinking was sharpest at this hour. Here he initiated some of his best deals, including the deal in iron that, at the onset of the war, zoomed him to riches. Billy was as thrifty with his time as with his money.

Billy bathed, transmitting a battery of unspoken signals. His clothes were laid out, his breakfast prepared, and the moment he walked into the dining room, the cook put his buttered egg on the stove. The egg had to be just so, otherwise Billy would walk away, egg untouched, and the household was disgraced.

The house relaxed with Billy's departure to the office. The children suddenly became boisterous, servants shouted to each other and Tanya went for her bath.

To train a household to the extent that they seek only the master's well-being and approbation is no mean achievement. Whereas Freddy governed his house with the aid of maxims, putting his foot down only if someone's conduct was absurd or destructive, Billy kept his foot down all the time. He tyrannized his house, governing chiefly through Tanya. His commandments were directed at her. They were, in order of preference:

Thou shalt not spend money!
Thou shalt not waste.
Thou shalt give me a minutely detailed account of expenses.
Thou shalt obey thy husband and jump to his bidding.
Thou shalt bring up thy children to obey and to love me more
   than they do you.
Thou shalt never require anything.
Thou and thy children shall not disturb me.
Thou shalt switch off all lights and fans.

The commandments continued endlessly. Few, like Billy, have the overriding tenacity to enslave.

PART III

EXITS, ARRIVALS

I Went Back

Krishen Khanna

Habib was a one-eyed peon in my father's office. A silent, docile man who kept to himself, he did what he was told and spoke sparingly. He had a reputation for being innocuous so nobody took much notice of him. He, on the other hand, quietly noticed everyone in great detail, without letting anyone know that he was taking it all in. One early morning in August 1947, he came into my father's office on the pretext of dusting his desk. He edged closer to my father and, while wiping the telephone, murmured in a low voice that my father should not look at him but should listen carefully to what he was going to say. He whispered that he had overheard conversations between a few clerks in the office that he had found most disturbing. He continued to dust and polish with his back to my father, speaking at the same time in hushed whispers. There was a plot, he said, to have a gang of butchers arrive in a couple of days to clean up the office. 'What do you mean by "clean up"?' asked my father. 'They are planning to kill the Hindus in this office,' he replied. Habib had not gone home the previous night. Instead, he had hidden himself in the office and had surreptitiously overheard this conversation. He urged my father to leave Lahore immediately.

As I recall, my father, an official in the Punjab Government's Education Department, had already opted to serve Indian Punjab after Partition. At the time, most people thought such transfers would take effect gradually, and in good time. Quite obviously, this enormous change could not be pushed through overnight, they reasoned. But for my father, Habib's revelations put the matter in a new light. That very morning, he spoke to the head of the Education Department, who, too, had opted for India, and told him the gist of what the peon had said. The two men decided to leave for the Indian side with their families without any fanfare. In the office, no one but Habib knew that they were leaving. At home, we were told to pack and carry only

essentials in the car. We were exhausted when we went to sleep late
that night and were woken up early the next morning without quite
knowing why and where we were going. We sailed through the
countryside as if we were going for a picnic. We were so certain that
we would return soon to deal with the transfer of our properties and
other matters.

The full force of Partition was to be felt a short while later, when
we finally realized that there was no going back. An incident drove
that message home to us. The Registrar of Punjab University, Mr
Madan Gopal Singh, was in Simla along with other officials, trying
to reconstruct records and get things moving. He decided to go back
to Lahore to fetch some records from the University office. Before
leaving, he wrote a brief note to my father, which he ended with the
words, 'See you when I get back, that is, if I get back.' His
apprehension was well-founded. He was murdered on the University
campus.

No one could have imagined that entire populations would be
bludgeoned out and rendered homeless, and that such cruelty and
barbarity would prevail amongst Punjabis. I cannot conceive of any
of my many Muslim friends indulging in the kind of violence that
spread from one part of Lahore to another like a plague. Perhaps the
conversation that Habib overheard had more than a germ of truth in
it. There must have been trained gangs of thugs moving from one
place to another, carrying out the orders of their political mentors
with heartless efficiency.

It was hard to reconcile these bloody events with the nature of our
life in pre-Partition Lahore. It was a city with a fairly evenly balanced
population of Hindus and Muslims, and had developed an amalgamated
culture. I recall the time when we lived on a small road named after
a British worthy called Maclagan. On this small stretch lived members
of almost every religious group. It was not a neighbourhood confined
to a single economic or professional class. There were professors who
taught at Government College; a few lawyers; a small printing press;
the old Parsi Laundry; Captain Dentist Persikaka who spent about as
much time on his stamp collection as on the decaying teeth of the
elders of Maclagan Road; Dr Gurbux Rai, the veteran freedom fighter,
who spent long spells in jail, and was also an excellent homeopath,

taking care of all those who lived on that road; Bawa Sarup Singh, who was some sort of an apothecary and whose children had fair skin and green eyes (the other children believed that Bawaji's children were descendants of Alexander); and there was Ferozdin, a tailor of great repute whose tiny shop had a number of fancy cars parked in front of it. During the days when my father was studying for his doctorate in London, the tailor would come to my mother every day and ask her if she needed anything. There was Bhagatram the halwai, with his son Kaka, who was to run a famous eating house in Delhi after Partition; and finally there was the local paanwalla, affectionately known as Buddhu.

As children, we had open access to any house in the neighbourhood. So many deep and abiding relationships were formed during that period of my life. These friendships ran right across economic boundaries and formed the basis for my future attitude towards people. I continue to feel as much at ease in the company of dhabawallas, the bandwallas who play at weddings, and wayside cobblers, as I do in the presence of sophisticated intellectuals whose mental equipment is probably more efficient than my own. I remember my father's knack for building one-to-one relationships with a whole gamut of individuals. There was Gangaram, who shod the whole family. Once, he and his sons were invited to lunch. A large cloth was spread on the floor and everyone sat around it. We heard approving sounds of mastication as meat was chewed, loud gurgling as water was drunk, and uninhibited and satisfied burps at the conclusion of the meal. Although we had been taught to eat silently with our mouths closed, we had equally been taught not to make fun of those who ate noisily. So while all these sounds were being produced, my brother, sisters and I kept straight faces, suppressing our laughter! When the meal ended, the eldest of Gangaram's sons turned to my father and requested his help in resolving a family problem. The young man complained that his father drank too much and had become the butt of rude and offensive remarks by the urchins who followed him around. When there was pure milk and ghee in the house, what need was there to become a sharabi, the man asked. My father handled this delicate family affair with great aplomb. He made Gangaram promise that he would confine himself to a *pouua* (a quarter) instead of consuming a bottle a day. The sons, too, were persuaded to accept this concession. My father achieved all this without a trace of superiority in his manner.

There were other examples of his gift for handling relationships that ran across social boundaries. He helped Nazar Hussain, his driver in Multan, in a similar way, and held Fateh Din, his peon, in very high regard, for his unerring sense of duty. But most interesting of all is the case of Abdus Salam, who became a Nobel Laureate in physics. Salam's father was the head clerk in my father's office in Multan. As soon as Salam had passed his eighth-class examination with distinction, his father tried to prevail on mine to give him a job in the office. My father refused, and tried to tell Salam's father that his son was made for better things and should continue with his education. A small scholarship was found, and Salam was able to continue with his studies. He went on to top the Matriculation examination in the Punjab, upon which his father became even more insistent that his son be given a post in the office. Once again, my father resisted, and under pressure from him, Salam was sent to study at Government College, Lahore. My father had written to his friend and colleague, Dr Sarvi Chawla, asking him to supervise Salam's studies. We all know what happened thereafter. I sometimes wonder what Salam's fate would have been had my father not insisted on his continuing with his education. Salam's brilliance would surely not have been content to suffer comfortable mediocrity. In the cosmic order of events, my father's role was that of a catalyst. In purely human terms, his actions were pivotal and acknowledged as being so by Salam's father.

In the Lahore we lived in, relationships between members of different communities were also free-flowing and not rigidly determined. There was a code of behaviour that was commonly understood and which provided the basis for day-to-day transactions. Religious differences were recognized and respected but were not allowed to interfere with the normal course of events. Thus, the social fabric of Lahore up till 1947 was a complex unity. It had a richness all of its own. That this was finally shattered is evidence, not of its fragility, but of the powerful political forces that had been hard at work. This happened with the dawning of an age in which relatively small but cohesive and vocal groups of people were able to sway the masses towards violent action. But the fact that a rupture took place is not proof that the complex unity I have described did not exist or that it was brittle and unsustainable. Why can't it be understood that something beautiful was in the making and, given time, it may well have achieved a more lasting character?

The cataclysmic events of 1947 altered the tenor of relationships. Friends and relatives would not be seeing each other for long periods, and for many people, Partition was inexorable and final. Partition meant that future generations would grow up without intimate knowledge of the complex unity that had once existed in Lahore, and would regard each other quite differently from the way we had done.

Against this backdrop, it was heartening to visit Lahore many decades after Partition and to be greeted with a familiar graciousness and hospitality. On an invitation from Pakistan in 1988, a delegation of four artists went to Lahore to participate in the First International Biennale of Art. I was one of the four. We were received with great warmth by a group of artists much younger than us. They were acquainted with our work, which was flattering.

It pleased me no end to find that something of the spirit of Lahore I had known was still alive. In India, we had heard much talk about extremism and fundamentalism, creating an impression of a fierce religiosity that would lead to our being regarded as outsiders. I was bracing myself for polite but formal hosts, who would keep me at arm's length. What I encountered was quite the opposite. As soon as I began to speak in Punjabi, I sensed an easy rapport building up. No one said it openly, but there was a distinct feeling of cultural commonality. I was surprised at the number of woman artists among those I met, most of them very attractive and none of them clad in burkas. They were extremely intelligent and sophisticated and quite different from what I had been led to expect.

At the seminar that was a part of the Biennale, I noticed the same contrast between the official and non-official attitudes that one finds on the other side of the border. There were Pakistani speakers who expressed concern, bordering on anxiety, on the subject of national identity. They were anxious to preserve an Islamic identity in art. As it happened, there was nothing perceptibly Islamic about the Pakistani contributions to the Biennale, apart from restrictions that appeared to have been observed in representing the human figure.

My visit took place during the rule of Zia-ul-Haq, when Islamic norms were being enforced in Pakistan. Shortly before the Biennale opened, there had been an unsavoury incident. The studio of a Christian artist had been raided by angry men who destroyed paintings of 'nude women'. I saw one of these supposedly offensive canvases— it was an abstraction of sorts. I was reminded of what happened to Akbar Padamsee in Bombay in the early fifties. A sanctimonious government tried to indict him for a perfectly harmless painting of a man and a woman, which would not have been attacked had it not been for a title that announced the two were lovers. After much harassment and a lengthy court case, he was acquitted. The lesson we learnt from this incident was that art can be a very potent instrument for causing a furore, and further, that fanaticism is not the monopoly of any single group of people.

At the Lahore Biennale, meanwhile, a surprise was lying in wait for me. The organizers had decided to award gold medals to outstanding works. These were to be handed out by the Governor of Punjab. The hall was full when His Excellency arrived with his retinue and took his place on the stage. I was astonished when my name was called out, but I proceeded towards the stage. The Governor stood there, holding a medal. We looked at each other for a moment, trying to penetrate the changes that time had wrought in our physiognomies, and then he said very softly, 'Krishen?' I nodded in affirmation and said, 'Sajju?' He put the medal down on a table and embraced me. The entire hall burst into clapping. After a moment he turned to the audience to apologize: 'We are very old and dear friends and have not met in forty years.' I was told much later that he was criticized in some newspapers for his behaviour. I suspect that Governor Makhdoom Sajjad Hussain Quereshi, to give him his full name, had outraged those who expected him to be a model of formal rectitude by embracing, in public, an artist called 'Krishen'. He never gave his critics a thought and extended much hospitality during my visit.

No trip to Lahore could be complete for me without a long and leisurely visit to what we knew as Lawrence Gardens, but which were renamed Fatima Jinnah Gardens. My memory of this part of the world is old and very vivid. No matter what political vicissitudes the city may have suffered, it was clear to me that these gardens had maintained their calm and healing presence. Those tending these gardens seemed to have gone about their business untouched by the gory events the city had witnessed. I walked past the zoo and saw the waterbirds that had always nested there. Strolling towards the small hill on which an open-air theatre had been built many years ago under the watchful eye of Principal Guru Dutt Sondhi of Government College, I encountered many trees I had known, first as a child, and then as an adult, when I had gone with a block of paper and a pencil to make a different sort of acquaintance with them. They had not changed and as I stood silently before them, Auden's lines wafted through my mind:

> All statements about what I feel,
> like I-am-lost, are quite unreal:
> My knowledge ends where it began;
> A hedge is taller than a man.

I continued with my wanderings, secure in the knowledge that no matter what I had lost during Partition, no one could ever rob me of these precious communions. I visited all my old haunts and found places that I could recognize, if not the people inhabiting them. I went to Government College and saw a much younger version of myself in photographs of the swimming team, and as an actor in the plays performed in the imposing Central Hall. I visited the streets on which I had lived and those in which I had played, and the house from which we had made our final exit. There it stood, windows and doors bolted, bereft of the garden that my green-fingered father had carefully nurtured. It was about to be pulled down, giving way to economic necessities in the shape of cold, cemented high-rise buildings. The engines of progress would make a clean sweep of it all. The driver who had been conducting me around asked me if I would like to go in. I decided not to.

As we drove away, a thought came into my mind: that much as I loved Lahore and continue to do so, my ejection from this wonderful city was, in a sense, a blessing. Had I stayed here, comfortable with the easy rhythm of Lahore, I might never have become an artist. I might very well have ended up teaching literature in a school or college, taking pride in producing some indifferent verse myself. Instead, I took a circuitous route, which included thirteen years spent working for a British bank, towards a career as a professional artist. And yet, let me end this account with the admission that Lahore has much to do with what I am today. The very thought of Lahore and all my memories of time spent in this city are like a never-ending spring that continues to irrigate my imagination.

A House Divided

Ved Mehta

Ved Mehta returns to his family home in Lahore, lost during the violent partitioning of India and Pakistan, and discovers that the past is history.

On a personal level, I think of partition—when the blood spilling between Hindus and Muslims caused as many as a million people to die and perhaps 11 million to flee newly created Pakistan for independent India or vice versa—mostly in terms of losing our family home in Lahore. Once, in the early years after partition, my father went back to Lahore to get one last good look at our house and perhaps rescue some of his pictures and papers. The house had been appropriated by Muslim squatters and was then occupied by a Muslim family. They feared that he had come to reclaim the building, and they barely let him in. An old Muslim friend advised him to leave the city as quickly as possible if he didn't want someone to put a knife in his back. He did what he was told.

In 1978, I happened to be in New Delhi and met at a publisher's party a scion of an old, distinguished Muslim family, Fakir Sayed Aijazuddin, or 'Aijaz,' a Pakistani journalist. He and his wife, Shahnaz, also a journalist, were there to promote his book *Pahari Paintings and Sikh Portraits in the Lahore Museum*. They were as warm and outgoing as my Punjabi relatives, and we became fast friends. Aijaz invited me to visit Lahore, saying in perfect Punjabi, 'Whatever the experience of your father back then, it is as safe for you to travel to Pakistan nowadays as for us to travel here.'

'Do you have any mementos of your Lahore house?' Shahnaz asked.

'Only one, a member of a pair of finely carved Chinese ebony

This extract is taken from Ved Mehta's 'A House Divided', published by *Time* magazine.

standing lamps which had flanked our sofa in the drawing room,' I said. 'My father insisted on giving it as a wedding present to my eldest cousin, Dharam Bir. He said, "I wouldn't dream of taking it. It looks so well in your drawing room." My father quoted to him a Punjabi couplet: "To one who shares food, it is sugar/ To one who eats alone, it is a toad." Cousin Dharam Bir had no choice but to accept the lamp. He took it back with him to Bombay, where he lived, and because it was already in India, it survived partition.'

They wanted to know if he still had the lamp, and I told them that when I got my own apartment in New York, cousin Dharam Bir insisted that I should become the custodian of the lamp. It has stood in my apartment ever since, an emblem of our lost house.

In 1979, I started to write about my childhood and took the Aijazuddins up on their invitation to go to Pakistan, in the hope of checking my memories and perhaps reviving them.

Both Aijaz and Shahnaz were waiting for me at the airport. Aijaz embraced me affectionately and said, '*Lahore Lahore hai.*'

'Lahore is Lahore' is a common greeting among Lahoris, as if they need constantly to reaffirm that Lahore is superior to all other cities in the world.

Even though it was getting dark, we took a taxi from the airport straight to Mehta Gulli, at 14 Temple Road, a lane on which all my Mehta uncles had built their houses with common walls and contiguous rooflines. We got out of the car at the old address, but the cozy lane had been incorporated into a much larger area, which seemed under development. There was an empty lot where a couple of my uncles' houses had once stood. Some of the other family houses had been replaced by newer, more lavish homes with little yards and alleyways between them. The wall from Mehta Gulli that we used to climb over to get to the little compound of my maternal grandparents was gone, along with their house. In fact, everything was so changed around that I wasn't able to find any of my childhood landmarks. Whenever we knocked at the door of a house, the whole family would appear in force, as if they were worried that we had come to claim the property and wanted to scare us off.

We backtracked to the spot where the taxi had dropped us and to the cul-de-sac in which my father had built his house, at 11 Temple

Road, in 1928. There, surprisingly, not so much as a brick had been disturbed. Even the small white marble slab on which my father's name, DR. AMOLAK RAM MEHTA, had been etched in black letters was still there, set in the cement at the gate. The letters were dirty and somewhat eroded, but there was no mistaking the name.

'I wonder why the tenants didn't put up a sign with their own names on it,' I said.

'They probably like the look of your father's old marble,' Shahnaz said.

'Or maybe they are just lazy,' Aijaz said. 'But some things have clearly changed. The big house of Sheikh Sahib, which stood opposite your gate, is now just a forlorn plot. Where exactly did you put down Sheikh Sahib's water pipe?'

Aijaz had read in a couple of my books that at the suggestion of Sheikh Sahib, our longtime family friend and Muslim neighbor, my father had arranged a few months before partition to install a pipe under the street to carry water from the Muslim's private tube well to our house. We had thought that extra water might help to save our house in case the rampaging Muslim mobs set it on fire, as they were doing to other houses in the area. The masons had done the installation on the pretext of repairing the plumbing so that the other Muslim neighbors would not know what we were doing. Even so, the work had to be done in the dark. In fact, the new political atmosphere was so poisonous that soon after introducing Sheikh Sahib's water, we had begun to worry that we might have compromised our drinking supply.

'The pipe was put down just where we're standing,' I said. I smoothed the dirt, but the bricks under my shoe seemed undisturbed, evenly laid. 'The pipe must still be down there.'

The gate was unlatched. We pushed it open and walked in. Ahead was the little lane that led all the way back to the servants' quarters and the side entrance to the kitchen. To the left were a rose garden my mother had lovingly planted and tended, and a grape creeper she had trained to cover the servants' outhouse. The creeper was laden with thick bunches of grapes, as in our time. It was a hot, still August night, and the grapes' cloyingly sweet scent in the summer air, mixed with the acrid smell of ordure (ubiquitous here as in India), turned my stomach. I coughed and said, 'I can hardly believe that my mother's grapes and roses are still thriving 32 years after we were driven out of our house.'

We turned left into the little rose garden, where the child-high watering tank my father had put in still stood, and walked up the 10 or so steps to the front veranda. 'We've arrived at such a late hour, without giving notice or asking for an appointment. What will the tenants think?' I said in a whisper.

'We thought it would be better to surprise them,' Aijaz whispered back. 'That way, they won't have a chance to deny your request to see the house and think up excuses.'

On the right was the door to my father's corner room. (As in some Victorian houses, he had his own bedroom.) Straight ahead was the front door that led into the drawing room. I rang the bell—my pulse quickened.

The door was opened by two stout, elderly ladies. I told them I had lived in the house as a child and would be grateful for an opportunity to look through it.

The women hesitated, but then it turned out that they were sisters of Dr. Mubashir Hasan, a former finance minister in Zulfikar Ali Bhutto's government and then the secretary-general of the Pakistan People's Party, and that they and Aijaz were distantly related. In any case, they let us into the drawing room, which was sparsely furnished and had a sad look of neglect and disuse.

The two women seemed pleased to have company but were not altogether comfortable. To put them at ease, I said I was glad to see that the grapevine was flourishing.

'I've never eaten better grapes,' the more docile of the sisters said. 'Every season we have more grapes than either one of us can eat.'

'But these ants!' said the older and more domineering sister, who introduced herself as Amartul Aimma Hasan. Neither of them volunteered the name of the quieter sister. Both of them seemed to make a point of speaking in Urdu, the language of the Muslim country. 'You wouldn't believe them if you saw them. Whole hills of them— all ants. You walk in the garden; they bite your ankles off. I have seen mosquitoes plenty, but they are nothing compared to these ants.'

It struck me as odd that the sisters, who had got the house without giving my family a penny, should be complaining about the ants while my father, who had built and added to the house over many years under the pressure of loans and mortgages, hardly ever spoke about losing it.

Aijaz, Shahnaz and I started walking through the house, with the sisters following close behind.

The house was the first *pukka*, or permanent, structure that anyone in the Mehta family had ever owned. It was, by Lahore standards, small and elegant, 2½ stories tall, of brick and mortar, with running water, electric lights and electric ceiling fans. We thought of it as a monument to my father's progress from the windowless mud hut lighted by mustard-oil lamps in which he had grown up to the modern city of Lahore, which even our British rulers called the 'Paris of the Punjab.' As a boy of 10, my father had migrated from the *kucha*, or impermanent, village and come to Lahore for his education, becoming the second person in the family to graduate from a college (his paternal uncle, Ganga Ram, with whom he had lodged in the city in the early years, being the first). Afterward he became a medical doctor and later obtained a coveted government job in the Punjab's public-health department.

Unlike my father's contemporaries, who were also dusting off the traces of village life but were building indifferent houses in small towns or outposts of Lahore, my father wanted to put down his roots in the pre-eminent city of the Punjab. So, when he was 33, married and with two children, he bought a plot of land for his house on Temple Road, the most central and desirable part of British Lahore. As it happened, when my brothers, sisters and I were growing up— there are seven of us—we scarcely ever lived in our own house, because my father's job required periodic transfers to different cities. Consequently, we children were either packed off to boarding school so that our education would not be interrupted or, if we did move with our parents, lived in minute rented cottages in an expensive hill station or in a ramshackle government bungalow.

When I was 11, we finally started living at 11 Temple Road for the first time in my conscious memory. My father had provided for everything. There was a separate room with an attached bathroom for each of us. The walls were painted in distemper, and the floors were finished with marble chips, which shined just as well as the marble slabs in the palaces of rajas. An internal staircase rose from the back veranda past my sisters' rooms to the terraced roof, which had a traditional *barsati*, or rain shelter, at one end and high brick parapets. Like many Lahoris, we used to sleep on cots out in the open during the hot nights, and if it happened to rain, we pulled them in under the shelter, which was used during the day for stacking and storing the cots. We also played on the roof, just sitting around there or flying kites. When coming down, I hardly ever used the stairs; instead, I slid down the beautifully polished teakwood banister, running my feet along the metal balustrades, making them ring and clang as I came down and jumping onto the landings just long enough to take the turn and jump back on the banister.

Although the house was built on a plot of barely 650 square meters and shared common walls with two flanking houses, it seemed ample. On the other side of the lane, across from the rose garden and the main house, was a stall in which to keep a buffalo for fresh milk; a garage, something we had never had before; and an external staircase, which provided a second access to my sisters' rooms so that they could come and go independently. For us, the house was like a castle, our foothold in a city where no less a person than Alexander the Great had left his mark. (One of my older brother's friends was called Secunder, the Hindustani version of the Greek name.)

In the evening, my sisters, our cousins and I would walk up Temple Road to the Mall. We might look into one of the British shops for some sweets or run around in Lawrence Gardens, a British-type park that was a favorite among English and Indian children alike. More often than not, we would stop by the famous cannon Zam-Zammah, the 'fire-breathing dragon,' which stood in front of the Lahore Museum, where Rudyard Kipling's father had been curator from 1875 to 1893. The cannon was constructed in Lahore in 1757, but most everyone I knew believed that the British had hauled it in from London to impose law and order on the anarchistic Indians. It was said that whoever owned the cannon ruled the Punjab and, for all we knew, the world. Like Kim, the eponymous hero of Kipling's 1901 novel, we grew up in its shadow. Because Kim was English, he felt entitled to defy municipal orders and so climbed up on Zam-Zammah. Sitting astride the cannon, he fought off a Muslim child and a Hindu child who, each in turn, tried to take his place. In contrast, we children were not only law abiding but were cowed by the gun. I remember my father once walked me up to it, and I touched its trunnions. I was so mortified by my transgression of municipal orders that I shrank back, even though I thought that by touching the gun I was paying homage to the British crown.

A Lahori friend of mine, the Indian painter Krishen Khanna, also grew up in the shadow of Zam-Zammah. In 1988, some nine years after I went to Pakistan, he went there to sketch the cannon. He brought back scores of drawings, which he used for a series of abstract paintings. I own one of the paintings—nearly two meters tall and more than a meter wide—in which three barely discernible children climb monkey-like on the cannon, as in *Kim*. The painting now hangs in our dining room in New York, commemorating the Lahore of my childhood.

With the Hasan sisters trailing behind, we proceeded through the narrow, wood-paneled corridor beyond the drawing room—called the gallery, because my father had furnished it with rails on which pictures could be easily hung, removed and rotated. In the middle of the little gallery, on the left, was the door to the dining room, which was quite bare. Its fireplace—all the main rooms had fireplaces—seemed not to have been used in years. We stepped into my mother's bedroom, which still had her big *almirah*, or cupboard, built into the wall and resting on two pedestals. Then we walked through the connected bathroom to my father's corner room. It seemed both bedrooms were being used.

Throughout the tour, the Hasan sisters kept up a stream of nervous chatter. 'You say Sheikh Sahib was your father's friend,' the older Miss Hasan said, referring to our old Muslim neighbor. 'But that crafty Sheikh Sahib has never been a friend to anyone ... Your crafty Sheikh Sahib emptied this house. He took all the furniture, pictures and valuables, and furnished a whole other house with them.'

'A lorry pulled up here in the middle of the night and took everything out,' the younger Miss Hasan said.

'He tried to take this house and install his sister-in-law here,' the older Miss Hasan said.

We were now on the back veranda, where an old, bulbous electric fan with banana-leaf blades was slowly turning, barely stirring the miasmic air. We walked up the internal staircase, our footsteps echoing in the mostly empty house. The banister was dusty to the touch, and my sisters' rooms were locked up. On the roof, the chimneys, rain shelter and high brick parapets were all there, but like everything else in the house, they seemed in disrepair. There wasn't so much as one cot, either on the roof or in the rain shelter. We immediately turned back.

The rooms to one side of the courtyard, in which my older brother and I had lived, were also disorienting. My older brother's room was shut up, and mine, which was being used as a prayer room, was bare except for bamboo matting and some bolsters. The single window looking out onto the lane, which had served as my private access to the outside world, seemed permanently sealed with layers of dirty paint.

Everywhere the plaster on the walls and ceilings was cracked, and the whole house had an unkempt, lonely air. The Hasan sisters seemed to have no one else living with them. I asked about all the vacant rooms.

'Oh,' the older Miss Hasan said, 'before we moved in, the house was partitioned between two families.' Her use of the word *partitioned* in reference to our house, and in English, was so unexpected that I caught my breath. 'Now only two of us are living here.'

'Have you ever thought of taking tenants?' Shahnaz asked the women.

'No,' said the older Miss Hasan. 'I'll never give any rooms to tenants. They'd never leave.'

As we went back toward the front of the house, I suddenly noticed that underfoot were not the marble chips that had been used to finish the floors but rough cement. Without realizing what I was doing, I stamped my foot petulantly like a child. 'What did you do with our marble floors?' I cried.

'This house had no *farash* when we moved in,' the older Miss Hasan said distantly.

'*Farash*?' Shahnaz repeated, somewhat puzzled. 'She can't mean, Ved, that your house had no floors for you all to walk on.'

'I distinctly remember my father had all the floors treated with marble chips,' I said. 'I remember the floors were so smooth that I used to slide across them almost like a skater.'

'No! No!' the older Miss Hasan exclaimed, somewhat annoyed. 'I'm telling you, there was no *farash* in the bathrooms.'

It dawned on the Aijazuddins and me at the same time that she was talking not about *farash*—the floor—at all but about the flush system. It was brought home to me with the force of lost memory that when I was growing up practically no houses in Punjabi cities had flush systems. We all had commodes with removable pots, which had to be manually emptied by the untouchables who skulked in morning and night through the back doors of the bathrooms of British, Hindu and Muslim houses. We never knew where they deposited the waste. That was beyond the reach of our curiosity, as were the lives of the untouchables themselves, who, in religion, were considered as polluted as the miserable office of their karma.

I snapped out of my reverie and asked the Hasan sisters what, in fact, had happened to the marble chips on the floors.

'We got them cemented over,' said the older Miss Hasan.

'But why?' I asked.

'They're easier to maintain this way,' she said.

I noticed the sisters were getting edgy. I complimented them on modernizing the bathrooms and thanked them for letting me see the house, and we left.

Outside, as we were walking back to the car, Shahnaz asked, 'What did you think of the two harpies?'

'They seem O.K., I suppose,' I said.

'Do you remember what a point the ladies made about cementing over the floors and putting in the flush system?' Aijaz said. 'They were putting you on notice that they have made substantial improvements, so you couldn't reclaim the house even if you wanted to. They were telling you the house now legally belongs to them.'

'They can have it with our best wishes,' I said. 'My family would never dream of returning to Lahore. They have their lives in India.'

'Your father is probably still listed as the owner of 11 Temple Road in some municipal archives,' Aijaz said.

'Since Hindus can live here only at the peril of their lives, a lot of good that does him,' I said. My Muslim friends and I laughed together nervously.

'Was the house as you had pictured it?' Shahnaz asked.

'Yes,' I said. 'But of course all the rooms seem much smaller than what I'd remembered. That is not surprising, since I last saw the house when I was small.'

'What were your feelings about visiting your old house?' Shahnaz asked.

'I didn't feel much,' I said. 'After all, it was more than 30 years ago that we lived in the house. And anyway, its loss, like partition, is a part of history, which we all accepted long ago.'

'But you must have felt something while standing on the threshold of your own room,' Aijaz said. 'We certainly felt we were standing on the threshold of your past and, in some subtle way, of our own, too. We felt deeply with you for what you had lost—what we all had lost. I found myself remembering the room from your books and picturing you in it, and listening to your conversations about partition with your friend Sohan. Every time I read about his death in your books I feel a pang.'

'Sohan was the first person close to me who died,' I said, remembering my boyhood friend and mentor, who had been killed by a Muslim in the partition riots. 'But I was 13 then, and I have long since come to terms with his death—insofar as one can come to terms with the innocent death of anyone one has been close to.'

Aijaz and Shahnaz became silent, and we stood there for a moment without knowing what to say. On an impulse, I hugged them both. They were Muslims living in Pakistan, but they seemed in every way like members of my extended family.

Ranamama

Urvashi Butalia

It was around 10 o'clock on a warm summer night in 1987 that I found myself standing in the veranda of a rather decrepit old house in a suburb of Lahore. A dusty bulb, hanging from a single plaited wire, cast a pale light on the cracked pistachio green walls. I was nervous, somewhat frightened, and also curious. The enormity of what I was about to do had only just begun to dawn on me. And predictably, I was tempted to turn around and run. But there was nowhere to run to. This was Lahore; it was night; women did not walk out into deserted streets—or indeed crowded ones—alone in search of non-existent transport.

So I did what I had come to do. I rang the bell. A short while later, three women came to the barred window. I asked if this was the house of the person I was in search of. Yes, they said, but he wasn't there. He was away on 'tour' and expected home later that night. This was something I had not bargained for: had he been there I had somehow foolishly imagined he would know me instantly—despite the fact that he had never seen me before, and was probably totally unaware of my existence. Vaguely I remember looking at the floor for inspiration, and noticing that engraved in it was the game of chopar that my mother had told us about—it was something, she said, that my grandfather had especially made for his wife, my grandmother. Gathering together my courage I said to the three assembled women: 'I'm looking for him because I am his niece, his sister's daughter, come from Delhi.'

Door bolts were drawn and I was invited in. The women were Rana's wife—my aunt—and her daughters—my cousins. To this day

This extract is taken from Urvashi Butalia's *The Other Side of Silence*, published by Penguin Books India.

I am not sure if it was my imagination or if they were actually quite friendly. I remember being surprised because they seemed to know who I was—you must be Subhadra's daughter, they said, you look a bit like her. Look like her? But they had never even *seen* my mother. At the time, though, I was too nervous to ask. I was led into a large, luridly furnished living room: for an hour we made careful conversation and drank Coca Cola. Then my friend Firhana came to collect me: I knew her sister, Ferida, and was staying at their house.

This could well have been the end of the story. In a sense, not finding my uncle at home was almost a relief. I went away thinking well, this is it, I've done it. Now I can go home and forget about all of this. But that was easier said than done. History does not give you leave to forget so easily.

*

Crossing the border into Pakistan had been easier than I thought. Getting a visa was difficult, though, ironically, the visa office at the Pakistan High Commission ran two separate counters, one for people they called 'foreigners' and the other for Indians. At the latter crowds of people jostled and pushed, trying to get together all the necessary paperwork while outside, an old man, balding and half-bent at the waist, offered to take instant photos, using a small bucket of developer to get them ready. Once over the border, however, everything looked familiar at the airport—the same chaos, the same language, the same smells, the same clothes. What I was not prepared for, however, was the strong emotional pull that came with the crossing. I felt—there is no other word for it—a sense of having come home. And I kept asking myself why. I was born five years after Partition. What did I know of the history of pain and anguish that had dogged the lives of my parents and grandparents? Why should this place, which I had never seen before, seem more like home than Delhi, where I had lived practically all my life?

What was this strange trajectory of histories and stories that had made it seem so important for me to come here? Standing there, in the veranda of my uncle's house, I remember thinking, perhaps for the first time, that this was something unexpected. When I had begun my search, I wasn't sure what I would find. But I wasn't prepared for what I did find. This was something no history lesson had prepared me for: these people, strangers that I had met practically that instant, were treating me like family. But actually the frontier that divided us went so deep that everywhere you looked, in religion, in politics, in geography and history, it reared its ugly head and mocked these little attempts at overcoming the divide.

Ranamama, outside whose house I stood that night, is my mother's youngest brother. Like many north Indian families, ours too was divided at Partition. My mother who was still single at the time, found herself on the Indian side of the border. Ranamama, her brother, chose to stay behind. According to my mother and her other siblings, his choice was a motivated one. He wanted access to the property my grandfather—who was no longer alive—owned. With all other family contenders out of the way, he could be sole owner of it. Because of this, and because of the near impossibility of keeping in touch after Partition, the family 'lost' contact with Ranamama. For forty years, no one communicated with him, heard from him or saw anything of him. Until, that is, I went to see him.

*

Ever since I can remember we had heard stories of Partition—from my grandmother (my father's mother) who lived with us, and from my parents who had both lived through it very differently. In the way that I had vaguely registered several of these stories, I had also registered Rana's. Not only had he stayed back but worse, and I suspect this was what made him a persona non grata in our family, he had become a Muslim. My mother made two difficult and dangerous journeys, amidst the worst communal violence, to Lahore to fetch her family to India. The first time she brought her younger brother, Billo, and a sister, Savita. The second time she went to fetch her mother and Rana, the youngest (her father had long since died). But, she said, Rana refused to come, and wasn't willing to let my grandmother go either. He denied that he wanted to hold on to her for the sake of my grandfather's property which was in her name, and promised to bring her to India soon. This never happened. Once the country was divided, it became virtually impossible for people of different communities to move freely in the 'other' country. Except for a few who were privileged and had access to people in power—a circumstance that ensured relatively smooth passage—most people were unable to go back to their homes, which had often been left behind in a hurry. There was deep suspicion on both sides, and any cross-border movement was watched and monitored by the police and intelligence. Rana and his family kept contact for some time, but found themselves constantly under surveillance, with their letters being opened, and questions being asked. After a while, they simply gave up trying to communicate. And for forty years, it remained that way. Although Rana remained in my grandfather's house, no one spoke or wrote to him, no one heard from him in all these years. Sometime during this time, closer to 1947 than not, my family heard unconfirmed reports that my grandmother had died. But no one really knew. The sense of deep loss, of family, mother, home, gave way to bitterness and resentment, and finally to indifference. Perhaps it was this last that communicated itself to us when, as children, we listened to stories of Partition and the family's history.

*

At midnight, the phone rang in my friend Ferida's house. We were deep in conversation and gossip over cups of coffee and the salt/sweet tea the Pakistanis call kehwa. She listened somewhat distractedly to the phone for a minute—who could be calling at this time—and handed it to me, suddenly excited, saying, 'It's your uncle.' As Ferida had answered the phone, a male voice at the other end had said, apparently without preamble, 'I believe my daughter is staying with you. Please call my daughter, I would like to speak to her.'

'Beti,' he said to me as I tentatively greeted him, 'what are you doing there? This is your home. You must come home at once and you must stay here. Give me your address and I'll come and pick you up.' No preamble, no greeting, just a direct, no nonsense picking up of family ties. I was both touched and taken aback.

We talked, and argued. Finally I managed to dissuade him. It was late, he was tired. Why didn't we just meet in the morning? I'd get my friend to bring me over. 'I'll not settle for just meeting,' he told me, 'don't think you can get away from here. This is your home and this is where you must stay—with your family.'

Home? Family? I remember thinking these were strange words between two people who hardly knew each other. Ought I to go and stay with him? I was tempted, but I was also uncertain. How could I pack my bags and go off to stay with someone I didn't know, even if there was a family connection? The next morning I went, minus bags. He remarked on it instantly—where is your luggage? Later that evening he came with me to Ferida's house. I picked up my bags, and we went back together to his home.

I stayed with my uncle for a week. All the time I was aware of an underlying sense of betrayal: my mother had had no wish to re-open contact with her brother whom she suspected of being mercenary and scheming. Why else, she asked, had he stayed back, held on to the property, and to the one person to whom it belonged: my grandmother. Over the years, her bitterness and resentment had only increased. But, given my own political trajectory, this visit meant too much to me to abandon. And once I had seen my uncle, and been addressed by him as 'daughter', it became even more difficult to opt out. So I stayed, in that big, rambling haveli, and for a week we talked. It was an intense and emotionally draining week. For a long time afterwards I found it difficult to talk about that parenthetical time in my life. I remember registering various presences; my aunt, my younger and older cousins, food, sleep—all somewhat vaguely. The only recollection that remains sharp and crystal clear, is of the many conversations my uncle and I had.

Why had he not left with his brother and sisters at Partition, I asked him. 'Why *did* you stay back?' Well, Ranamama said, like a lot of other people he had never expected Partition to happen the way it had. 'Many of us thought, yes, there'll be change, but why should we have to move?' He hadn't thought political decisions could affect his life, and by the time he realized otherwise, it was too late, the point of no return had actually been reached. 'I was barely twenty. I'd had little education. What would I have done in India? I had no qualifications, no job, nothing to recommend me.' But he had family in India, surely one of them would have looked after him? 'No one really made an offer to take me on—except your mother. But she was single, and had already taken on the responsibility of two other siblings.'

And my grandmother? Why did he insist on her staying on, I asked, anxious to believe that there was a genuine, 'excusable' reason. He offered an explanation: I did not believe it. 'I was worried about your mother having to take on the burden of an old mother, just like I was worried when she offered to take me with her. So I thought, I'd do my share and look after her.'

My grandmother, Dayawanti, died in 1956. The first time anyone in our family learnt of this was when I visited Ranamama in 1987 and he told me. For years, we'd heard that she had been left behind in Pakistan, and were dimly aware that rumour put her date of death variously at 1949, '52, '53, sometimes earlier. But she had lived till 1956. Nine years after Partition. At the time, seven of her eight children lived across the border, in India, most of them in Delhi. Delhi is half an hour away from Lahore by air. None of them knew. Some things, I found, are difficult to forgive.

The way Ranamama described it, the choice to stay on was not really a choice at all. In fact, like many people, he thought he wasn't choosing, but was actually waiting to do so when things were decided for him. But what about the choice to convert? Was he now a believer? Had he been one then? What did religion mean to him—after all, the entire rationale for the creation of two countries out of one, was said to have been religion. And, it was widely believed—with some truth— that large numbers of people were forced to convert to the 'other' religion. But Rana?

'No one forced me to do anything. But in a sense there wasn't really a choice. The only way I could have stayed on was by converting. And so, well, I did. I married a Muslim girl, changed my religion, and took a Muslim name.'

But did he really believe? Was the change born out of conviction as much as it was of convenience? It is difficult for me to put down Mamu's response to this question truthfully. When I asked him if I could write what he had said, he said, 'Of course, write what you like. My life cannot get any worse.' But my own feeling is that he wasn't really aware of the kinds of implications this could have. So I did what I thought I had to: silenced those parts that needed to be kept silent. I make no excuses for this except that I could not bring myself to, in the name of a myth called intellectual honesty, expose or make Ranamama so vulnerable.

'One thing I'll tell you,' said Mamu in answer to my question, 'I have not slept one night in these forty years without regretting my decision. Not one night.' I was chilled to the bone. How could he say this, what did he mean, how had he lived through these forty years, indeed how would he live through the next forty, if this was what he felt? 'You see, my child,' he said, repeating something that was to become a sort of refrain in the days we spent together, 'somehow a convert is never forgiven. Your past follows you, it hounds you. For me, it's worse because I've continued to live in the same place. Even today, when I walk out to the market I often hear people whispering, "Hindu, Hindu". No, you don't know what it is like. They never forgive you for being a convert.'

I was curious about why Ranamama had never tried to come to India to seek out his family. If he felt, so profoundly, the loss of a family, why did he not, like many others, try to locate his? Admittedly, in the beginning, it was difficult for people to cross the two borders, but there were times when things had eased, if only marginally. But he had an answer to that too: 'How could I? Where would I have gone? My family, my sisters knew where I was. I had no idea where they were. And then, who in India would have trusted an ex-Hindu turned Muslim who now wanted to seek out his Hindu relatives? And this is the only home I have known.'

And yet, home for him was defined in many different ways. Ever since television made its appearance, Ranamama made sure he listened to the Indian news every day. When cricket was played between the two countries, he watched and secretly rooted for India. Often, when it was India playing another country, he sided with India. More recently, he sometimes watched Indian soaps on the small screen. And, although he had told me that his home in Lahore was the only home he had ever known, it was to India that he turned for a sense of home. There is a word in Punjabi that is enormously evocative and emotive for most Punjabis: *watan*. It's a difficult word to translate: it can mean home, country, land—all and any of them. When a Punjabi speaks of his or her *watan*, you know they are referring to something inexpressible, some longing for a sense of place, of belonging, of rootedness. For most Punjabis who were displaced as a result of Partition, their watan lay in the home they had left behind. For Ranamama, in a curious travesty of this, while he continued to live on in the family home in Pakistan, his watan became India, a country he had visited only briefly, once.

His children and family found this bizarre. They could not understand these secret yearnings, these things that went on inside his head. They thought the stories he told were strange, as were the people he spoke about, his family—Hindus—from across the border. The two younger girls told me once, 'Apa, you are all right, you're just like us, but we thought you know that *they* were really awful.' And who could blame them? The only Hindus they had met were a couple of distant relatives who had once managed to visit, and who had behaved as orthodox Hindus often do, practising the 'untouchability' that Hindus customarily use with Muslims.

*

As the years went by, Ranamama began to live an internal life, mostly in his head, that no one quite knew about, but everyone, particularly his family, was suspicious of. His children—especially his daughters and daughters-in-law—cared for him but they all feared what went on inside his head. For all the love his daughters gave him, it seemed to me there was very little that came from his sons. Their real interest was in the property he owned. Perhaps the one person who, in some sense, understood the dilemmas in his head, was my mami, his wife. She decided quite early on, and sensibly I thought, that she would not allow her children to have the same kind of crisis of identity that Mamu had had. They were brought up as good Muslims, the girls remained in purdah, they studied at home from the mullah, they learnt to read the Koran. For the younger ones especially, who had no memory or reference of Partition, Rana with his many stories of his family, his friends, his home, remained their father, and yet a stranger. In some ways, this distanced him further from the family, and served to isolate him even more. In others, in a curious kind of paradox, his patriarchal authority was undermined, making him a much more humane father than one might normally find in a middle class Punjabi household. But for several of his family members, he was only the inconvenient owner of the property, to be despatched as soon as possible.

I could not understand how he could have lived like this: was there anyone he could have spoken to? He told me no. How could he talk about what was so deep, so tortured? And to whom? There was no one, no one who could even begin to understand. Some things, he told me, are better left unsaid. But why then was he saying them to me? Who was I? One day, as we talked deep into the evening, stopping only for the odd bit of food, or a cup of tea, and he told me about his life since Partition, I began to feel a sense of weight, of oppression. 'Why,' I asked him, 'why are you talking to me like this? You don't even know me. If you'd met me in the marketplace, I would have just been another stranger. Yes, we speak the same language, we wear similar clothes, but apart from that . . .' He looked at me for a long moment and said, 'My child, this is the first time I am speaking to my own blood.'

I was shocked. I protested. 'What about your family? They are your blood, not me.'

'No,' he said, 'for them I remain a stranger. You, you understand what it is I'm talking about. That is why you are here on this search. You know. Even if nothing else ever happens, I know that you have been sent here to lighten my load.'

And, in some ways I suppose this was true. I did understand, and I began to wonder. About how many people had been torn apart like this by this event we call Partition, by what is known as history. How many had had to live with their silences, how many had been able to talk, and why it was that we, who had studied modern Indian history in school, who knew there was something called the Partition of India that came simultaneously with Independence, had never learnt about this side of it? Why had these stories remained hidden? Was there no place for them in history?

*

That first time when I came back to India from Pakistan, I brought

back messages and letters and gifts from the entire family to various
members on this side of the border. Ranamama sent a long letter,
addressed to all his sisters (his one remaining brother was dead by
then). Initially, my mother found it difficult to get over her bitterness
and resentment, and to face the letter I had brought. Her sisters, all
five of them, who had gathered in our house, sat in a row, curious, but
also somewhat resentful. Then someone picked up the letter and began
reading, and soon it was being passed from hand to hand, with
memories being exchanged, tears being shed and peals of laughter
ringing out as stories were recounted and shared.

Tell us, they demanded, tell us what the house looks like, is the
guava tree still there, what's happened to the game of chopar, who
lives at the back now . . . Hundreds of questions. I tried to answer
them all—unsuccessfully. How could I tell them who was in which
room or how the house had changed, when I hadn't seen the original
house myself? Mamu's letter was read and reread, touched, smelt,
laughed and wept over. Suddenly my mother and my aunts had acquired
a family across the border. We kept in touch after that, occasional
letters did manage to arrive. I went several times and met him again.
Once he wrote to my mother: 'I wish I could lock up Urvashi in a
cage and keep her here.' And she told me I had made a real difference
to his life. As he had, I think, to mine, for he set me on a path from
which it has been difficult to withdraw.

But old resentments die hard. And there are many things that lie
beneath the surface that we cannot even apprehend. Once, when I was
going to visit him, my mother said to me: 'Ask him . . . ask him if he
buried or cremated my mother.' I looked at her in shock. Religion has
never meant much to her—she isn't an atheist but she has little patience
with the trappings of religion.

'How does it matter to you?' I said to her.

'Just ask him,' she said, implacable.

I asked him.

'How could she have stayed on here and kept her original name? I
had to make her a convert. She was called Ayesha Bibi,' he said, 'I
buried her.'

*

For some years the border between Pakistan and India seemed to have become more permeable. As a result I was able to make several visits and to cement my relationship with Ranamama. Once, when his second youngest daughter was getting married, I took my mother and her elder sister with me to visit him. There was a great deal of excitement as we planned the visit, for it was really like a visit to the unknown. They didn't know what their brother would look like, how he would react to them, what their home would look like, what their beloved city would have to offer them . . . At Lahore airport Mamu came to fetch his sisters. The last time my mother and aunt had seen their brother was forty one years ago, when he had been a young twenty year old: slim, tall and smart. The man who met them now was in his sixties, balding and greying. He wore an awami suit, the loose salwar and shirt made popular by Bhutto. I tried to imagine what he must have seen: two white-haired women: my aunt, in her seventies, and my mother, in her mid-sixties. The reunion was a tentative, difficult one, with everyone struggling to hold back tears. I stood aside, an outsider now. My friend, Lala, who came to the airport as well, tells me that she has never forgotten the look on their faces—she has no words to describe it. Everyone made small talk in the car until we reached home. Home—this was the house in which my mother and her brothers and sisters had grown up. They knew every stone, every nook and cranny of this place. But now, much of it was occupied by people they did not know. So they were forced to treat it politely, like any other house. My aunt was welcoming, warm, but also suspicious. What, she must have wondered, were these relatives from the other side doing here at the time of a family wedding? How she must have hoped that they would not embarrass her in front of her guests.

For the first two days Mamu and his sisters skirted each other. They talked, but polite, strained, talk. On the third day somehow the floodgates opened, and soon the three of them were locked in a room, crying, laughing, talking, remembering. Mamu took his sisters on a proper tour of the house: they were able to go back into their old rooms, to find their favourite trees, to remember their parents and other siblings. I, who was the catalyst at the airport meeting, was now redundant. Earlier, I had told them that I would stay with Lala, and that's what I had done. But not without a sense of guilt. Now, I was glad I'd done that—they can talk now, I thought, without having me around.

But what I didn't reckon on was that immediately one family bonded, the other grew more distant. For Mamu's own family, the arrival of the two sisters was, quite naturally, something to be concerned about. A girl was being married. What if the potential in-laws objected to Hindus in the family? What if the Hindus were there to reclaim their land? What if the Hindus did something to embarrass the family at the wedding? And, a further complication. My mother and my aunt are the older sisters. Custom demanded that they be given respect. This meant making space for them in the wedding rituals. Yet how could this be done? So, small silences began to build up between 'this' side of the family and 'that', and I was struck by how easy it was to recreate the borders we thought we'd just crossed.

*

Contact with Rana was maintained for some years. I managed, somehow, to go to Pakistan again and see him. But it wasn't easy. He began to worry he was being watched by the police, and he gradually stopped writing. For a while my mother continued to send him letters and gifts, but slowly, even that petered out. Several times, I sent him letters and messages with my friends until one brought back a message—try not to keep in touch, it makes things very difficult. This wasn't just something official, but also within the family, for his sons put pressure on him to break contact with his Indian family. And then, in any case, it became more and more difficult to travel from one country to the other.

It's been many years now since I have seen Rana. I no longer know if he is alive or dead. I *think* he is alive, I *want* him to be alive, no one has told me he isn't, so I shall have to go on believing that he is. And I keep telling myself, if something happened to him, surely someone would tell us. But I'm not even sure I believe myself when I say that. Years ago, when Mamu answered my mother's question about whether he had buried or cremated my grandmother, I asked if he would take me to her grave. I still remember standing with him by his gate in the fading light of the evening, looking out onto the road and saying to him, 'Mamu, I want to see my grandmother's grave. Please take me to see it.' It was the first time he answered me without looking at me: he scuffed the dust under his feet and said: 'No, my child, not yet. I'm not ready yet.'

POSTSCRIPT

Real-life stories don't always have neat endings. I wrote Rana's story nearly a decade ago and, in one way or another, it has stayed with me through all the years that have followed. My visits to Lahore had a difference—for it became a city where I had another family, another home. No sooner would the taxi or auto-rickshaw take the turn from Gulberg to Model Town than I would begin to look out for familiar landmarks. I'd hand out directions, straight, left, right with the confidence of a local, and would wait expectantly for the children to come pouring out of Ranamama's home the moment they got wind that I had arrived. Once, after attending a seminar in another part of Model Town, the private bus carrying all participants passed by Rana's house. It was a winter afternoon. As always, he was out in the garden in his battered, comfortable old chair, reading the papers, a plate of spiced tomatoes and mooli by his side, soaking up the sunshine. On impulse I asked the bus driver to turn into the gate, and a bunch of smiling women climbed out to meet my legendary uncle. Rana was delighted, the entire family was called out, cups of masala chai arrived, and very soon we found ourselves in the middle of an impromptu picnic. My loveliest memory of that time is of my aunt taking me aside and asking me to do something for her (and for him). Would I, she asked, be kind enough to bring some tubes of a whitening skin cream known as Fair and Lovely (my aunt called it 'Flovely'!) for, as she said, there he was sitting in the sun the whole day, and then he would complain that his skin was turning darker! Being an Indian product, the cream was very expensive in Pakistan. So, my next visit to Ranamama included the unusual gift of several tubes of Fair and Lovely cream!

The next visit was memorable for another reason as well. Although I had written Rana's story—he knew this and I knew he knew it—I had not had the courage to show him the book in which it appeared,

and indeed of which it formed the core. Asking someone for permission
to write their story is one thing, showing them what you have done is
quite another. What if you've got things completely wrong? But in
Rana's case, it was not this that worried me. I was concerned that the
book that carried his version of his story, my mother's version of it as
well as my own reading of it could prove hurtful and unfair. But I also
felt I couldn't just get away with not showing it to him. I had to take
responsibility for it somehow. So, in transit one day for several hours
at Lahore airport, I asked a friend of mine to take me to his home.

I arrived, unannounced, book in hand, and immediately lost courage.
I hid the book as best I could under my dupatta and, when I thought
he wasn't looking, slipped it under me and sat firmly on it. Three
hours of conversation and food later, it was time for my flight. As I
prepared to leave, wondering how I could extract the book and hide it
away without him seeing it, he asked me, 'So, when are you going to
give me your book to read?' I hedged, saying I did not have it, that I'd
send it and so on, and he cut me off mid-sentence—'So what is that
you're sitting on?'

And so, years after it was written, Rana read his story. And he read
his sister's version of his story, and her own story. He wasn't happy;
he felt hurt and wounded. He called my friend Lala and talked to her
at length about his feelings. He didn't deny the 'truth' of the telling,
but it hurt nevertheless. The next time I visited him, this was the main
subject of our discussion. If only I had asked him more, he said, he
would have given me other convincing reasons for having taken the
decision he did. How could individuals be held responsible for history,
he asked. How could my mother have thought what she did . . .

Once again, we talked. Of lives and histories and cities and violence
and how all of these were told and retold. I wanted to impress on him
that I had tried hard not to be judgemental, but if his sister felt a
sense of betrayal, it was incumbent upon me to say that. I wasn't sure
he understood or accepted what I said, although he seemed to indicate
that he did. But then, in the way that these things have of never being
simple and straightforward, two days after this conversation, I met a
number of his relatives-by-marriage at his home at dinner. They all
greeted me with affection. 'So, you're the one who's written that

book, *Silence*,' they said. 'Sheikh sahib is so happy with it, he's delighted that someone has written his story at last. We're all waiting to read it!' On the next visit, my gifts included several more copies of the book. Meanwhile, he treasured the copy I had given him—as he put it, for him, it was a gift of love.

Two years ago, Rana died. For me, a whole history died with him. Ironically, I did not know he was gone. Our families retained sporadic contact, the occasional phone call, the once-in-a-while letter. Any time someone went, I would send gifts for my aunt, my cousins, for Rana. I did not think much of the silence from the other side. Visas were difficult again, and too many people had begun to ask me about Rana's story—they wanted to go and film him, to tape his story, to put his picture in the newspapers. I thought it best to stay away for a while. One of his sons lived in Dubai and we were in occasional touch. I asked after Rana each time he called, and he would tell me what I expected to hear, that he was not unwell, but kept indifferent health, and that he often talked about me.

Sometime ago, I heard from Rana's daughter's tutor, who was at the time the only person connected with that household who had e-mail. He wrote, giving me titbits of news, and I passed news back. It was through him that Rana heard of my father's death, and he called and spoke at length to my mother and me. But such contact was sporadic, and so, if there was no news for a long time, it did not seem unusual.

A few months ago, my colleague Jaya went to Lahore for a meeting. There was also a theatre troupe that had been invited there to perform a play on Partition, loosely based on my book. We thought Rana and his family might like to see it, so Jaya undertook to invite him. Repeated phone calls brought no answer, so she and my friend Lala decided to go to the house—perhaps the numbers had changed, they thought.

But it was more than that. They arrived there to find security guards overseeing the destruction of the old haveli. The family had moved out; they were all in small flats, leading their separate lives. The house had been sold. With the patriarch, Rana, gone, the guards told them, there was no one to hold the family together. The property was now slated to have new, modern flats there. Lala and Jaya tried to find out more. With some effort they tracked down the youngest of my cousins and learnt that the transition had not been smooth. My cousins had fought over the property, as families do. The cousin in Dubai, who was in occasional contact with me, was the most difficult one. I thought back to our conversations: all the time he had been talking to me, Ranamama had been dead. Yet, every time I asked after him, he offered me snippets of information that indicated that he was alive. It's difficult to know why. And I'm not even sure I want to. Some histories are best left unsaid.

I have not been back to Lahore since I heard of Rana's death. I'm not sure the city will mean as much to me now. Without the house in Model Town on my map, there will be a strange kind of blank, an absence that I am not sure I know how to deal with. I haven't told my mother about the house being sold and destroyed—I'm not sure she can take it. Sometimes I think, it's only a house, how does it matter? Then I tell myself that it is much more than a house; it's a history. With its most obvious symbol gone, will that history remain only a memory? I'm not sure.

What I do know is that Lahore now holds not one but two graves for me. The next time I go there, I will have to find my way not only to my grandmother's grave that Rana was not ready to show me but also to his own. For me, it's there that this history now resides.

Looking for Home

Meena Arora Nayak

The year Daddy survived the beggar woman's curse, plague struck his village, and his mother perished in it. His father gathered his remaining family and his son's death-defying quilt and went to live with his sister in Lahore. Daddy's aunt turned out to be a mean, childless woman who resented her poor clerk husband and hated her unchanging life. The arrival of penniless relatives was right in keeping with her fare. As soon as she took in Daddy and his sisters, she put the girls to work in the house. All day she made them cook and clean and at meals she cursed them all for leaching upon her. So Daddy's father pawned his deceased wife's gold bangles and bought a barber's kit to set up shop under a peepul tree at the corner of the street.

A beggar used to frequent their street. He was rumoured to be a retired magistrate, and he could well have been one, for he spoke the language of the white sahibs very well. He would sit beside Daddy's father under the peepul tree, lost in meditation, totally without a care. A stray dog bit him once and the wound festered. Daddy and his friends sat and watched the ants climb into the putrefying flesh in his leg. 'They are God's creatures too,' the beggar would say. 'This is God's body. Who am I to interfere?' Sometimes he would pick up mud from the street and rub it into the festering wound. My grandfather would sit with him all day, listening to him, watching him sway with a gentle motion as though a delicate breeze were passing through him. And then miraculously, the beggar's infected wound healed. The boys saw him walking down the street without even a limp. Then one day he was gone, and with him, my grandfather.

This extract is taken from Meena Arora Nayak's *About Daddy*, published by Penguin Books India.

Left alone in his aunt's house. Daddy began to bear the brunt of all her frustrations. She started calling upon Daddy to do all the chores and, eventually, more than the chores. In the morning, while everyone snuggled greedily, grabbing the last cozy moments of sleep, she would wake my father up to fetch ashes to scrub the dirty dishes. Daddy would run to the halwai's shop across the street and scoop out ashes from the furnace left overnight to cool. The rush was to get to the furnace before the halwai's servants cleaned it out. If the ashes were not enough, or were too gritty from unburned coal, she would make him run across town to the other halwai's till she had enough. Soon she started waking him up even earlier so he could clean the dishes before he went to school. Then there was the water to be fetched from the community well. Shivering in just his underwear, he would stand in a queue behind women with large buckets or earthenware jars, waiting for his turn at the well. Hauling buckets of water from the well, he would fill the two he had brought along, and carrying one in each hand, his fingers numb from the cold weight, he would bring them back to the house. On days that his aunt washed her hair, he would have to go back to refill the buckets.

Then one day, Daddy's aunt forbade him to go to school. 'I can't afford the fees,' she said. 'Besides, I need someone in the house to help me with all the chores.' Slowly, the food on his plate began to get more and more scarce till his aunt begrudged him every morsel. One evening, towards the end of his frugal meal, faint memories of his patchwork quilt stirred in his mind. A quilt and a plate full of food begged from the neighbours. He got up and ran to the storeroom where his father's meagre belongings had been put away. He searched the room till he found the quit. It was a little tattered and much too small to be spread across his shoulders, but it was his quilt, nonetheless. He pulled it around his neck, and slipping out of the house, started walking towards the Muslim section of the street. The Hindus, he feared, would know him and would carry tales to his aunt. The first door he knocked on was Amjad's, but he didn't know that, because in all his years of friendship with Amjad, he had never been to his house. He had met Amjad some years ago on the vacant lot in the neighbourhood, where, after school, all the boys used to gather to play. Daddy's favourite game was to watch the kites, his eagle eyes always awaiting that fatal cut which one glass-tinged yarn would inflict on another. Then he would speed towards the path of the kite's rudderless descent and retrieve the prize. There were always others, too, who awaited such booty. And, of course, there was the rightful owner whose sharp flying had initiated the pecha. Swiftness was always the victor, and in that, my father excelled. If was during one such kite race that my father met Amjad.

It was a beautiful kite, not too large to defy the winds, and not too small to fear it. It was a kite that could conquer the skies with its streamlined sides, crafted not with the vanity of a peacock, but for the flight of a sparrow, one half red and one half blue, with a short blue tail like the feather of a blue jay. Amjad's eye was on it as he tightened the spool of his own bigger and heavier yellow kite. He steered towards the soaring blue and red kite. When its owner relaxed the string to allow it more flight, Amjad swooped on it like a vulture. With his nine-thread yarn coated with powdered glass, he severed the other kite clean off its loose spool. For a moment the kite remained at its height then floated towards the ground, disoriented and dislodged. Daddy was already running in the direction he instinctively knew the kite would take. Even before it floated to the ground, Daddy reached for its short, severed lifeline. Bur as he pulled the string towards him, Amjad grabbed the kite.

'It's mine,' Amjad explained to Daddy. 'It's my kata.'

'But I got it first,' my father declared.

'Let go,' Amjad yanked at the thread. It slipped out of Daddy's hand leaving a fine furrow of red across his palm. He looked at his bleeding palm and, enraged, threw himself on Amjad, grabbing the kite. Breaking its fine wooden bones, he tore the blue and red paper into shreds and tossing it on the ground, spat on it.

'Take it now. It's all yours,' he said.

In a trice Amjad was upon him . . . He was a couple of inches taller than my father and half a dozen pounds heavier. In no time at all he had my father doubled on the ground with a punched stomach, a bloody nose and a cut lip. Then he grabbed the front of my father's only shirt and yanked till the buttons flew open, tearing the overwashed, weak material all down the front.

'That's for the kite,' he said and walked away.

Daddy's aunt gave him a beating with a broom for ruining his school shirt. The next morning, she took one of her husband's old khaki shirts, cut off the cuffs to shorten the arm length, and made him wear that to school.

Amjad's mother heard about the fight and sent her son on a mission of truce to the lot. Amjad gave Daddy a sweetmeat and offered to let him fly his kite that day. Amjad and Daddy became the best of friends, but Daddy never forgave his best friend for ruining the only shirt he owned.

And now there he was at his friend's house, begging for food.

Amjad opened the door a slight crack when Daddy knocked. 'What do you want?' he asked.

Daddy hesitated. How could he tell his friend that he was begging? But the tantalizing smell of freshly-cooked curry and whole-wheat chapatis baked on an open fire would not allow him to leave. He stood at the door, fingering the quilt.

'I can't come to play now,' Amjad said. 'We are going to eat.'

'Amjad, who is it?' A woman's voice called from inside.

'It's my friend,' Amjad called back.

'Tell him to come inside. Don't stand at the door.'

'What do you want?' Amjad asked again.

'Can I come inside?' Amjad opened the door wider.

Daddy stepped inside. The fragrance of food grew stronger. A large woman dressed in a loose salwar-kameez walked into the room. She had clear white skin and kohl-blackened eyes that sparkled with love.

'What is your name, beta?' she asked.

'Manohar.'

'Amjad,' she turned to her son, 'go get your friend some mithai.'

Amjad went inside and in a moment reappeared with a plate full of sweetmeats—colourful barfi, layered brilliantly with silver varaq. Daddy pounced on the plate, grabbing two-three pieces in each hand, stuffing his mouth till little morsels spilled out from the corners.

'Manohar, it is very late. Won't your mother worry about you? It is almost time for dinner. Won't she be waiting for you?'

Daddy shook his head. 'My mother is dead,' he said, flicking the clammy paste of the sweetmeat from the roof of his mouth with his tongue.

'Where have you been for so many days?' Amjad asked. 'I won three kites. Wait. I'll show you.'

'Later, Amjad,' his mother said. 'Beta,' she said, bending down to take Daddy's chin in her hand. 'What is the matter? Why are you out so late? Don't you have someone who will worry about you?'

Daddy drew away, jerking his chin out of her hand. 'No,' he said, staring at the floor. 'No one will worry about me.'

'But you must stay with someone. Who looks after you?' she persisted.

For a moment Daddy continued to stare at the wooden floor scrubbed to a dull sheen, then replied inaudibly. 'I stay with my aunt.'

'Won't she miss you?'

'Yes.' He looked up, his eyes angry, his voice bitter. 'My aunt will miss me. There won't be anyone to clean the dirty dishes after dinner.'

Amjad's mother was silent for a minute. Then her eyes clouded over and she took my father's wrist and pulled him closer to her. A warm smell of spices and fragrant hair oil engulfed Daddy.

'Doesn't she give you anything to eat?'

'A little,' Daddy admitted.

'But not enough.'

Daddy shook his head.

'Tell me the truth, beta. What are you doing on the street at this time?'

Daddy pulled the quilt closer, clutching the edges with both hands. 'I came out to beg for food,' he said, raising his chin in defiance.

Amjad's mother gathered him in her arms, tears smudging the kohl in her eyes. In the circle of her soft bangled arms, his face smothered in her ample bosom, Daddy began to tell his story, his voice choking from the reminder of how a mother's love felt.

'You don't ever have to go back to her house,' Amjad's mother promised him. 'Stay here with us. In the morning you can go to school with Amjad and in the evening you can help his father in the shop just like Amjad does.' Amjad's father owned a small jewellery store.

Amjad's house was larger than his aunt's. It had three storeys with the rooms built in concentric circles, leaving the centre open for a three-levelled skylight. Amjad's father made enough money to afford electricity. There were electric bulbs hanging from thin brown wires in the kitchen and living room. Daddy was relieved that he wouldn't have to spend countless daylight hours cleaning the lentils and rice. But the best surprise was a water pump in the yard outside the house. Even if Amjad's mother made him fill water, at least he wouldn't have to carry it two blocks, let alone wait in line for the other women to get their fill.

Amjad's mother took him in like a son. She had always wanted another child, but after Amjad, she had not been able to conceive. Her husband loved her too much to want to marry again for more children, so they had contented themselves with Amjad. She opened up one of the many unused rooms in the house, dusted it clean and set up a bed for Daddy.

His first night there, Daddy lay on his bed, looking out of the open door at the tender brilliance of the stars. He located the family of three stars that shone one beside the other, bonded even in death. His older sister used to sit him on her lap and tell him the story of Shravan Kumar, the loving son, who had sat his blind parents in two baskets and levering the basket's on a wooden plank, had carried them around on a pilgrimage. When he had been killed accidentally by a hunter, his parents had been so heartbroken that they, too, had given up their lives. God had installed this loving family in his skies where they always shone together—Shravan Kumar in the centre, and his parents on either side. Daddy lay staring at the family till his eyes blurred. Then he searched all over the sky, wondering which star was his mother, for hadn't his sister told him that when good people died, God made them stars so they could be beacons for other people and guide them in goodness? He knew his mother had been the best.

The next morning, he woke up early and went down the stairs to the kitchen. He was searching for the box in which to fetch ashes for the dishes when Amjad's mother came in.

'It's early, child. Couldn't you sleep? Don't worry. It was a new place and an unfamiliar bed. You'll soon get used to it. Then you won't wake up till it is almost time to go to school.'

'Where's the box for the ashes? I must fetch them before the halwai's servant cleans out the furnace.'

'What ashes? Why do you need ashes?' she asked.

'For the dirty dishes.'

'I don't need ashes. I clean my dishes with raw mud and I get mine right here in my yard. And you don't need to get that for me; I will get it when I need it.'

'Then what can I do?'

She looked at Daddy, tears making her eyes sparkle brighter than ever. She sat him down on the mat in the kitchen and said, 'Listen, Manohar, you are my son now, just like Amjad is my son. He doesn't have to help me in the housework and neither do you. Now go to the pump and clean up. There are some neem sticks for your teeth lying on that sill. After that, come back here, and I'll give you something to eat. Then you must get ready for school. I have already talked to Amjad's father. He will buy you the books you need and will send your fees with Amjad.'

'I haven't brought my school shirt,' Daddy stated.

'Don't worry about that. I'll give you something of Amjad's to wear. Now run along. I'm going to wake Amjad up. Even the curses of the rising sun don't awaken him.'

Star of Lahore

An Interview with Zia Mohyeddin

EDITOR'S NOTE:

Lahore has been home to a galaxy of poets, but in the dramatic arts one can think of only two megastars: the late Malika-e-Tarannum Nur Jehan, and actor Zia Mohyeddin.

Zia Mohyeddin, currently chairman of the Pakistan Academy of Performing Arts in Pakistan, trained at the Royal Academy of Dramatic Arts in London. Following roles in *Long Day's Journey into Night* and *Julius Caesar,* Zia Mohyeddin shot to fame in 1960 in the lead role of Aziz in the West End hit *A Passage to India.* He returned to Pakistan at the request of the Bhutto regime in the late sixties and set up the PIA Arts and Dance Academy. Finding himself at odds with the political regime, Zia returned to England where he appeared in a number of dramatic productions including the television miniseries *The Jewel in the Crown* (1984).

Zia Mohyeddin brings a rare intelligence and grasp to his roles as actor/interpreter/writer and reader. I have attended Zia's 'readings' in Lahore and Houston. I hesitate to call them 'readings'; they are presentations of artistry that sound the mystical and emotional depths of the Urdu poets and Western writers whose works he reads from. Mohyeddin's diction, in whichever language he uses, has a purity that gratifies the senses. As one British critic noted: 'His voice is worth a profile by itself.' Zia, who prefers to call himself an *interpreter*, subsumes his own persona to the power and imagery of the text he engages. He can transport an audience to a state of exaltation as naturally as he can move it to tears or render it weak with laughter. But enough said —it is difficult to describe the spellbinding effect of Zia's presence on stage. I think it best to let him address some issues to do with his art in his own words. The following excerpt is from an interview by Farid Alvie for *Zameen* magazine.

ON THE MEANING AND SIGNIFICANCE OF LANGUAGE

'What does language mean to me? I think essentially, language means to me . . . culture. Language is nothing but culture. When you use language accurately and when you are able to appreciate a language correctly, you become at ease with that culture. Once you feel that you've acquired not just the rudiments of that language but the expression of that language, then its misuse is a travesty.

'I find perhaps the greatest affinity, and I mean emotional affinity, for example, with Urdu. And it irks me when I am unable to understand a certain passage. Is it because I have not become familiar with the words or because they haven't been a part of my upbringing? Or is it because those words have now gone out of date? What feeling did they represent? What atmosphere did they evoke? Because quite a lot of our Urdu literature is descriptive literature. Urdu is a very recent language. It hasn't got the antiquity that Italian or German or French or English have, so nearly all the experiences of Urdu are either borrowed from the Persian archetypical concepts and allusions or Arabic or in some cases, what we call Brij Bhasha. To some extent, however, we are able to have a kind of an archetypal affinity because it is us: the landscape is ours, the climate is ours, and more or less the continuity of what we wear and used to wear in terms of dress, is familiar to us.

'Language is the only reality I have. Language is the only thing that stimulates me. When I read something which I don't understand— and there are millions of things which I read and don't understand— I don't dismiss it as something which doesn't concern me. It irks me. It bothers me a great deal: is there something wrong with my own comprehension? Is it my lack of knowledge? Is it my lack of a certain kind of experience? I mean I seriously worry and I will then not rest until I have been able to satisfy myself.

'I have always put a great deal of emphasis on the way the language is spoken. Is it because of my initial training as an actor? Is it because elocution is something which comes naturally to me? I don't know. It's been a passion with me. And I think clear and good speech is extremely important because it also means clarity of thought in some way. Language is very important to me. Any language. Especially a language about which I know a little bit. If and when it is distorted or when it is not spoken properly, then, apart from the fact that aesthetically it jars upon my entire being, it also means that I am not getting the real meaning of the sentence and the syntax. I feel that language also enables people to become "humanized". And I am quite sure that one way of softening a society is to make it aware of its own language and the nuances of that language.

'I just finished putting together a compact disc on the life and times of Ghalib and I am very, very serious about making another one on Mir Taqi Mir and one on Iqbal, the three stalwarts of Urdu poetry, as it were: Mir, in the eighteenth century, Ghalib, in the nineteenth century, and Iqbal in the twentieth century. It isn't the way that Mir uses Urdu (which he knew extremely well), or the way that Iqbal has acquired Urdu—it wasn't his mother tongue—and to a great extent Persianized it, but the way thought emerges because of the creative use of language. So it is the thought and the content which I am very keen to bring out while engaging the manner in which I bring it out.

'I would like to be remembered for the kind of things which once belonged to us but which we have chosen for some bizarre reason to discard: the love of language, love of words, and what they mean. And the enormous affection and courtesy which were a part of our language, therefore, our culture, therefore, our heritage.'

ON READING LITERATURE AND THE SANCTITY OF THE TEXT

'I am frequently asked as to why I do not read or why I haven't "done" a certain poet, novelist or critic, and my answer always is that I can only "do" anyone who appeals to me. There are lots of writers who do not appeal to me. Or they do not stimulate me, either in their expression or the way in which they've written their stuff. I am not denigrating them . . . I certainly am not trying to say, therefore, that they are not important.

'First of all, something has to strike me. And strike me in such a way that I feel goose pimples when I read the work of writers. That's my acid test. If a writer or a poet doesn't send those sensations into whatever inner process I have, then I won't "do" that writer.

'But then . . . the curious thing is—I am not a critic. I am not a writer or a dramatist. I am essentially an interpreter. And in my interpretation, I feel very strongly that it is vital that my personal interpretation not matter as much as the truth of the writing itself. And the real strength of that writing must be conveyed. So I must not colour it to the extent where the writer becomes secondary. That is very important. This is why I say that I am reading; I am not acting it.

'In theatre, there are some actors who have become so important that what you go and see is not Shakespeare's *Hamlet*, for example, but Sir John Gielgud's *Hamlet*. But even Sir John would say that what is of primary importance is Shakespeare himself. He cannot just impose or distort Shakespeare at the cost of his supreme voice, because nothing in the text should be sacrificed.

'So I have been a great, great follower of that classical tradition. It would irk me if I were to so personalize a text that the reality and the truth of that text were couched, as it were, in my own histrionics. That is very important. Also I am very firmly of the view that I would be cheapening it if I were to do so. Because my unconscious effort then would be to tell the audience, "Look how wonderful I am." It would be self-indulgence. And I have always loathed, I mean truly loathed, self-indulgence. It is something which we do in our part of the world very frequently, I think. I am very grateful to have worked in a tradition where this thing was looked down upon and where this thing was, by the purists and by those who matter, abhorred.'

ON THE METEORIC SUCCESS OF THE *ZIA MOHYEDDIN SHOW*

'I only did one thing which is still remembered with great affection. And it has never stopped amazing me! Is it that our collective memory of a programme that was shown on the screen for no more than eighteen months twenty-eight years ago is superb, or is it that that memory has been coloured and slightly glamourized as time went on?

'And, of course, it was technically very unsound other than perhaps two or three out of less than, I think, forty-eight programmes that I made in all. Did the three or four programmes "work" because everything gelled? The sound was not good. Every little bit of musical insertion was technically at fault. It's because we just couldn't help it. I suppose in those days, because we had no other standards, it was acceptable as the right thing. But television at that time had a bit of freedom, and it was not so full of the constraints and the strictures that began to be imposed upon it later.

'There were a couple of reasons why I gave up doing that programme. I began to feel very seriously that I would actually begin to believe in the myth which was being created that the programme was pretty good. That would be a highly dangerous thing. Also, it had reached a peak of popularity. It's always good to leave a programme when it's still greatly in demand. And a very real fear that I could sense which was that more and more strictures were going to be imposed. In other words, that I would not have the editorial freedom that I had. If you have to do a programme within the confines of "You can't do this, or you can say this, or you can't have so-and-so saying this, or you must choose your guests with the approval of the authorities etc.", then that would be very counterproductive.'

ON ENGLISH THEATRE, HOLLYWOOD'S STAR SYSTEM, AND THE LURE OF LUCRE

'First of all, I must admit I belonged to, or happened to subscribe emotionally and intellectually to, a generation which grew up thinking that films were a travesty. One doesn't do films. One does serious work. One just does theatre. Films are for the yobs, as it were. Although later on I rationalized that this was a silly notion. And this was absolutely absurd. And all the gods that I had, the gods of my idolatry, the Oliviers and the Schofields and the Gielguds, were themselves deeply involved in films. But somehow it was the theatre. The theatre is what a serious actor pursues. And, of course, a classical actor.

'I was very much moulded as a classical actor. This naturally led to a certain inward resistance to all this. You know, one felt, "Okay, you do a film because you need some money. Films are only for money." And to do anything for money, now that is another thing. I belonged to a family where money was looked down upon as something filthy or something unclean. Maybe my ancestors, all of whom were academics, developed this strange attitude because they never tasted money! Having grown up with this sort of an attitude, it's very difficult to reconcile yourself to accepting money, as one ought to accept money. You do it with a sense of guilt, which I did.

'So all of that being there led to some deep-seated resistance that I had towards becoming involved in . . . what does Hollywood represent? What does it stand for? It's just a big star system, and you do things because you get a lot of lucre. And then I said, "Nothing doing, I must become a little more realistic, money isn't that bad." I rationalized and felt that this attitude of mine was downright silly. And so I have done quite a few films here and there but not in Hollywood, nor in that atmosphere.'

ON THE COMPLEX CRAFT OF ACTING AND THE IMPORTANCE OF TRAINING

'In this part of the world, anyone and everyone who says, *"Jee, mujhe bara shauq hai,"* appalls me. You wouldn't deploy anyone to sit at a desk in an office and be given a computer without having acquired the training for operating it. Acting is the only thing which, it appears, we feel can be done without any attention being given to its training aspects. I wouldn't ask anyone to make me a bookcase unless I knew that he was not just a carpenter but also knew how to handle wood and so on.

'Acting is a craft, and that craft must be learned. I am not suggesting that once you learn the craft you become a good actor. Nothing of the kind—any more than once you learn to become an interior decorator, or have been to a painting school, you become a good painter. You don't. But at least you learn to know how to use a canvas and learn what perspective is and how to use colour or whatever else it entails.

'How does one speak one's lines? That itself is a highly complex process. I don't mean that you need to be able to pronounce the words correctly . . . that's got nothing to do with it, though some people naturally have a very good sense of elocution. It's not just that. The craft is to be able to translate a certain script, as it were, into the reality of a live character. The craft is to be able to speak without hurting your larynx.'

ON COMING HOME TO LAHORE, AND THE STATE OF PAKISTANI SOCIETY

'In the seclusion of my own home, I can perhaps take things. But if I were not to remain as secluded as I am, then I would be extremely uncomfortable. For what I see around is deterioration of everything; not just political life, which is obvious, but the deterioration of taste which I suppose is a natural corollary . . . it's a natural trend given the circumstances, political or otherwise, that we live under and live through. So I tend, perhaps unrealistically, not to leave my own seclusion too often, otherwise it is very painful.

'I do not find encouraging signs . . . and I don't mean in my own profession but about life. I find that people are less kind to each other than they used to be. I find, as I said, deterioration all around. And there is nothing I can do about it. I can't make compromises now. So the best thing is . . . well, to live in seclusion.'

From *An American Brat*

Bapsi Sidhwa

FAREWELL LUNCH AND LAHORI SOUNDS

Feroza sat amidst her well-wishers, too excited to touch the food in the plate, while her voluble aunts looked proud and exhilarated; as if they had a share in the adventure she was embarked upon. Their loud, cheerful voices drowned out the clamour of the scooter-rickshaws and minibuses, and the cries of the hawkers and of men brawling on the street. The Ginwalla bungalow was just off the enormous roundabout of the Main Gulberg Market.

The men strutted on the lawn with their froth-topped beer mugs as if they were toting weapons. They had the jaunty, faintly guilty mien of men who are up to mischief—and that despite the Drinks Permit in their pockets. Pakistan has had prohibition almost from the time of its inception in 1947.

Khutlibai was regaling relatives with the latest family health and news bulletins when an indefinable noise suddenly stopped their breaths. Almost at once they realized that the mosque's stereo system was being tested. The air was blasted by a cough. And when the assistant maulvi cleared his throat in a loud 'ahun-haam!' with impressive squelchy undertones, the feat was broadcast from the eight most powerful stereo amplifiers in Lahore, mounted right on top of the mosque's minaret.

The maulvi made a few announcements that rent the peaceful afternoon: 'A girl, age five, who answers to the name of Shameem, is missing. She is wearing a red cardigan and gold earrings . . . A boy, age three, who answers to the name of Akhtar is missing. He is wearing a white shirt and blue knickers . . .', and then he proceeded to shred the afternoon completely, when, accompanied by a children's choir, he began to sing religious songs.

The guests gathered on the Ginwalla lawn all had their own street-corner mosques with their own resident mullahs and stereo systems, but they had never been subjected to such uninhibited disregard for the aesthetics of a tune. The assault on their ears was intolerable. They could hardly hear themselves speak. Since it was Friday, the head maulvi and his invited cronies, the assistant maulvi and the bearded cheerleaders could be counted on to keep the stereo systems booming all afternoon.

It was pointless to sit outside.

SEEING FEROZA OFF AT THE LAHORE AIRPORT

A little clutch of schoolgirls from the Convent of the Sacred Heart was already waiting at the airport. They held delicate strings of pearly jasmine-buds that curiously matched their own aura of pristine innocence. They clung together, holding on to, or in some way touching each other: fiddling with clothes, adjusting their long chiffon dupatta-scarves, pushing back and smoothing stray wisps of dark hair.

They giggled, nervously remembering to restrain their improper merriment, aware of the eyes attracted like magnets to their sheltered youth, and the wealth that burnished so much unattainable loveliness. Everyone could tell their talk was full of wicked mischief and innuendo.

The party from the house formed another cluster. Suddenly, Cyrus's brother Rohinton, a huge, stern and taciturn man, took a couple of determined strides and planted himself in front of two men who were picking their teeth and ogling the girls with brash, kohl-rimmed eyes.

The men moved away, more stolid than docile. As custodian of the girls, the uncle was within his rights. Next, Rohinton, accompanied by Zareen's brother Behram, who had turned up from Rawalpindi with Jeroo, stalked a wide circle round the girls, demarcating perimeters. Their austere glares peremptorily dispensed with the oglers and loafers.

Arms akimbo, massive chests thrust out, Freny and Jeroo also stood guard. They noticed a bunch of college boys staring at the girls and passing remarks. Mimicking the girls' gestures, two young men draped themselves about their giggling friends, smoothing their cropped hair as if they were long tresses and their imaginary scarves.

The aunts marched up to them. 'Oye, shamelesses! Don't you have mothers and sisters? Go stare at them!'

The students ducked, and pretending to scold and thump their comrades, facetiously saying, 'Sorry an-tee, sorry an-tee,' pushed and shoved each other away, quickly dissolving in the crowd.

They were all grouped in a huge hall, with bunches of people gathered round departing kin like orbiting satellites. Since they were all of them taking the same flight to Karachi—from where some, like Feroza, would fly to other countries—there was a mad and tearful scramble to say goodbye when the flight was announced. Feroza was kissed and hugged and whispered to by every member of the Ginwalla party, and was now absorbed into the Parsee pack. No one was dry eyed. Zareen and Khutlibai daubed their eyes with soggy handkerchiefs; and Cyrus, who had wound his long arms round all three, briefly removed them to blow his imposing nose.

Khutlibai, Zareen and the aunts were whispering breathlessly—as if Feroza's fate hung on the flurry of last-minute instructions they were imparting:

'Don't talk to strangers; and never, ever look into their eyes!'

'A man asked your Behram Uncle, "What is the time?" and when your uncle looked at his watch, he hit him on the head and took away his watch and wallet.'

'Someone asked your Rohinton *kaka* for a cigarette, and when he stopped to say, "Look, my good man (you know how your *kaka* talks) I am a Parsee: Parsees don't smoke," the ruffian pointed a knife at his fly and took away his watch, wallet and Bally shoes!'

'If anyone talks to you, just look straight ahead.'

DINNER PARTY

Zareen and Cyrus were at one of the multitudinous dinners they attended. It was a large party, with about thirty couples. The guests formed groups around four or five sofa sets placed at various angles against the walls, and in the corners of the commodious sitting and living rooms. For the most part the men stood, either with the women, or in groups of three or four, discussing business or politics, and slapping each other's palms as they joked and laughed. Two or three waiters from the Punjab club had been hired for the evening, and they wove between the loquacious guests unobtrusively replenishing drinks.

Zareen, sitting with some women on floor cushions, looked markedly at her watch and raised alarmed eyebrows. A tall woman sitting next to her in a stunning navy-and-silver sari, picked up the cue: 'Good God, it's already eleven,' she said loudly, in a shocked voice, as if it was the first time that dinner had been so late. 'We'd better tell Furrie to feed us, or God knows when we'll eat!'

These were the little ruses the women amused themselves with while trying to wean the men from their evenings Scotch and prime them for dinner.

Their short, roly-poly hostess approached, smiling at Zareen. Zareen pretended astonishment and asked: 'Dinner's on the table? I can't believe it!'

A good-looking man with prematurely white hair, notorious for having to be dragged to the buffet table, cried, 'Have a heart, bibi. Let us finish our drinks at least.'

'Take your time,' Furrie said, 'Nobody's bringing out dinner just yet.'

The women groaned. Furrie laughed, shrugged to express her helplessness, and then leaned towards Zareen to say: 'The guest of honour, an American gentleman, would like to talk to you.'

'Me? Why?' Zareen asked, promptly gathering herself to get off the floor, the lift to her ego at being singled out lending a lilt to her voice.

'Why don't you find out yourself?' her hostess said. 'He's heard you're a Bhutto fan, that you have strong political opinions.'

The wide borders on their silk saris undulating seductively as they moved, Furrie and Zareen walked across the crowded, noisy rooms into the quieter TV lounge. Furrie went up to a large man who sat at one end of a four-piece sofa, an arm stretched out on the backrest. The vast expanse of his chest, his spread thighs, his sloven posture, all bespoke the language of power and possession, and the insensitivity that often goes with them.

Zareen's first instinct was to back off. But her hostess was already saying, 'Here she is. You wanted to speak to her, no?'

The man glanced past her indifferently, and Zareen wondered if he'd asked to see her at all. The guest of honour looked to her like a made-up B-grade movie villain: a pair of thick, brown eyebrows, and then a bald scalp, clean as a plucked chicken's.

A Dutchman Zareen barely knew chivalrously vacated his chair next to the sofa, saying, 'Please, sit down.' He could barely conceal his relief as he withdrew.

Zareen smiled her thanks and, as she adjusted the fall of her sari, wondered what she had let herself in for. Sitting sideways in her chair, she turned to the American expectantly.

From the recesses of the sofa, his impersonal eyes wandering, the man rumbled something indecipherable, and attempted to draw himself forward, as if trying to get to his feet.

'Good God,' Zareen thought. It was as if she had put him to considerable trouble in forcing his reluctant attention.

Zareen lowered her disconcerted gaze.

'You're a social worker?' The man's grating voice appeared to match his other unpleasant attributes. 'They tell me you worked with this Bhutto's wife . . . On some committee or other?'

He made it sound as if social work was despicable and that having once worked with the imprisoned prime minister's wife was something to be ashamed of. Zareen caught herself feeling sheepish and apologetic. Surprised and provoked by her own reaction, she mutinously replied: 'I like to help disadvantaged people. I do voluntary work at the Destitute Women's and Children's Home, and for two orphanages also. I was on many women's committees with Begum Bhutto.'

'And Bhutto—what d'you think of him?'

'He's my hero. The champion of the poor, of women, of the minorities and underprivileged people—of democracy.'

The man went through the motion of clapping softly. Zareen noticed that his cheeks dimpled when he smiled. It was the last gesture Zareen expected of this cynical, bald, villainous-looking character. She found herself relaxing, less defensive. She smiled.

But the instant she met his eyes, her defenses were back in position.

There was no point at which they had made contact, as two equal people, as she had imagined.

'What d'you think will happen if this "hero" is hanged tomorrow? Will there be a lot of trouble? Riots? People making trouble on the streets? Killing?'

The question was weighted with the conceit of a man who already has the answers.

Zareen was acutely aware of the man's insolent demeanour, but courtesy and the tradition of hospitality were too deeply ingrained for Zareen to exhibit her chagrin. She looked away, taken aback in a way she couldn't comprehend.

The man rasped: 'The people here lie a lot. I don't know what to believe.' He raised a shoulder in a disparaging shrug: 'Maybe we Americans gotta stop being so naive.'

Naive? He did not strike her as naive. She felt he had come with preconceived notions about Pakistan and looked only to reinforce them. Nor were some of the other Americans she'd met naive. Or the European, Australian and American hippies who had passed through Pakistan on their drugged pilgrimage to Katmandu before the trouble in Afghanistan had closed the route.

Had anyone told the poor villagers, who fed and sheltered these western wanderers and gave them their pitiable clothes, that the world out there had changed? That these strangers were conditioned to look out only for themselves, and that the villagers' kindness and canons of hospitality were naive?

The man sat up straighter and looked briefly but politely at Zareen. 'Well, what d'you think?'

Zareen found her petrified tongue suddenly loosen, and with her infinite capacity for loquacity and truth-telling, the frightened, desperate words tumbled out: 'There will be a lot of trouble. It will be the worst possible thing, the most tragic thing to happen. He is loved by the masses. The repercussions will be terrible. Horrible.'

'But what about tomorrow? If he's hanged tomorrow, will there be trouble?' he asked in the same emotionless voice.

Zareen felt the tiny hair on her arms stand up. The complete lack of compassion the man projected was chilling. For the first time he appeared to be really interested in what she might have to say.

'No,' she shook her head, thinking hopelessly that all the Peoples' Party leaders, from the mighty to the smallest, were either in prison or under dire threat of some kind or other. Some had been bribed into compliance. 'The immediate trouble will be controllable, I think.' Zareen said simply, wondering how she knew the answer to a question she had not thought to put to herself before.

*

At midnight, as she removed her diamond-and-emerald choker and earrings, unwrapped her sari and unhooked her blouse, Zareen told Cyrus what had happened. 'But why did he want answers from me? Who am I?'

Cyrus looked equally puzzled. 'I guess you've a reputation for shooting your mouth off,' he said. 'And you keep on and on about the masses' feelings, as if you represent them. The fellow must be CIA.'

'You know what I hated most?' Halfway to folding the shimmering, six-yard sari, her arms stretched out, Zareen stood still and thoughtful. 'The man did not think of me as a person, as somebody. I was not Zareen; just some third-rate Third-Worlder, too contemptible to be of the same species.'

Cyrus could see her groping for expression, and he was surprised and touched by the eloquence her distress inspired.

'He was so cynical,' Zareen continued. 'He asked the most simplistic questions, as if the complexity that makes up our world doesn't exist. I've never felt the way he made me feel . . . valueless . . . genderless.'

Zareen jerked her arms to bring the sari edges together. 'The fool! If he had all the answers, why did he ask me questions? Did he have to make me feel so miserable?'

She finished folding her sari with abrupt movements and flung it over the back of the rocking chair. As she turned, Cyrus noticed her blink. Her eyes, large and dark, made more seductive by the unexpected width at the bridge of her nose, were unnaturally brilliant.

Zareen was always meticulous about removing her make-up, but tonight she merely switched out the light and crept wordlessly into Cyrus's arms. Cyrus stroked her hair, nuzzled her neck, and, holding her close, healed the wounds inflicted upon her voluptuous and shaken womanhood, and to her psyche.

Exactly a month to the day after the dinner, they woke up to the news that Zulfikar Ali Bhutto had been hanged at four minutes past two in the morning in the Rawalpindi jail.

PART IV

LAHORE REMEMBERED

Lahore Remembered

Sara Suleri Goodyear

When, in New Haven, I have the occasion to teach the overwhelming
language of *Paradise Lost* to faces very young, a great compassion fills
the classroom. They read and read aloud, forgetting in the process
where the simile began and what could be its possible point of
reference. I try to serve as memory, but when we reach Book VI and
read the lines:

> His Eye might there command wherever stood
> City of old or modern Fame, the Seat
> Of mightiest Empire, from the destin'd Walls
> Of *Cambalu*, seat of *Cathaian Can*,
> And *Samarchand* by *Oxus*, *Temir's* Throne,
> To *Paquin* of *Sinaean* kings, and thence
> To *Agra* and *Lahor* of great *Mogul*
>
> (XI, 385–391)

a certain arrest occurs. I pause to say, 'Lahore—that is my city.' My
students, waiting for explication, look up, both surprised and touched
by this atypical interruption. None is forthcoming, so we proceed
with that uncanny music. Perhaps they know as clearly as do I of my
distraction: some part of me is eighteen again—their age—thus
travelling in my talk, abstracted. Yes, it is my city, and once again,
both willingly, unwillingly, I am in Lahore.

I have often thought that there should be an archaeological map
of the city, one that could do some justice to the centuries of its
transmogrification. Even to begin with Data Ganj Baksh, reputed to
be the first Muslim Sufi saint to have journeyed to Lahore from
eastern Iran, would be an arbitrary starting point. Someone more
learned than I am, however, would have to take charge of this creation,
a person whose hands have long been embedded in history's mind, a

gardener with an equal eye for weeds as well as blossoms. And this archaeology should most categorically not be sanctimonious: the huge and often bloody transitions from pre-Islamic Lahore to Mughal Lahore, from colonized to post-Independence Lahore has to ache, yet somehow be represented with a fleeting sense of humour—sometimes graceful, sometimes crude—that infiltrates the city's gullies and its streets.

Lahore sprawls; its epicentre keeps changing. It is hard to imagine that the town both in itself and as capital of several vagrant empires was once contained within its walls and bustling gates: the Old City, as it is known, has luckily escaped a museum or a mausoleum atmosphere, and remains instead a node of obsessive activity or pleasure. Whether its getting and spending involves wreaths and garlands, jewellery and garments, dancing and singing, piety and prostitution, the Old City of Lahore defies the monotony of centuries. Its economy can be dangerous, but it still approximates what may be best named as a frenetic trading in joy. When the Old City withers, they say, so will Lahore. And thus its gates—such as the Alumgiri Gate, the Bhatti Gate—continue to contain, invisibly, that curious phenomenon, which is the integrity of Lahore.

Epicentres: a few decades ago, the kaleidoscope that represents the city grouped its brilliant shards in a pattern quite unrecognizable from the configurations of today. The artery of the Mall led the traveller from the residential communities of Gulberg beyond, across the canal, and then down the stately road that formed the strange intersection between Mughal Lahore and British Lahore. The cantonment lay across the bridge west of the canal and was then a quiet, tree-lined space: even the military messes seemed orderly in all senses of the word, quite charmingly sedate. Not so now. With a viral energy, the once-new and relatively well-defined Defence Residential Colony has exploded—there are Defences I, II, III and IV, and all divided into B, D, A and BII blocks in a crazy, ungrammatical alphabet. They tell me that nowadays no one bothers to go to the Mall—the traffic is too insane—and why bother, since everything happens in the Defence, anyway? And so the kaleidoscope turns, and turns again. 'You would not *know* Lahore any more!' my friends tell me with a gleam of affectionate malice. 'It is just *not* the same *place* any more!'

Perhaps so. (What was that Persian proverb to the effect of: 'I can deal with my enemies, but God protects me from my friends'?) I would rather believe that Sher Shah Suri has returned to Lahore after five centuries: instead of building his enlightened Grand Trunk Road, he has turned parodic and built the Sherpao Bridge instead. This bridge was designed to connect the outskirts of Gulberg with the now-defunct—except in name—cantonment. It serves its purpose, although with undulations that the River Ravi would envy, and remains the only bridge I have ever seen that really should be graced with not one, but two 'Blind Curve' warnings.

Warnings. In my youth, there was always a madman at one of the innumerable street intersections in Lahore who would stand there directing traffic. The taxis, rickshaws, tongas and cars would simply ignore him and travel on with a laugh—not cruelly, I think, but on in their own ways. They honked, of course, but then they honked at everything—a cat, a mangey cur, beggars galore, or at nothing at all. At the end of the day, no one knew where the madmen went, or the beggars, too, for that matter. Who knows which company they chose to be keeping. Maybe they returned to those colonies of mud huts that crept up distantly from our oases in the most unlikely places. They were made of mud, their sewers were open, but from a distance the colonies could appear quite tidy, until after the white heat of summer the monsoons would arrive to wash away those habitats into the rich alluvial brown of the canal or the shrinking banks of the Ravi. Each year the waters would come to melt that homestead mud; later, in autumn those homes would spring up again in full cognizance of the fact that the next year would see them vanish, in another miraculous and watery disappearance. It was water's way of encouraging the inventiveness of life.

It could make me weep—in private, of course—to hear not only of the even more greatly congested and impossible traffic along the streets of Lahore, but of the dissipation that was its sky. A Lahore sky, no longer blue in a startling winter afternoon that would send each colour dazzling, and then into more dazzlement? No, I am told, with some satisfaction, the pollution is so bad that the sky is only yellow; dust, dust is everywhere. And ashes to ashes. But there were for me other imperatives: memory is useful when it performs such daily excisions, so I am happy to recollect nothing but the geography of the city's grace. There were sounds that suggested the isle is full of noise; the early unmelodious chirrups of birds that somehow made perfect cacophony with the smoke being bestirred in clanking charcoal fires; the yawns of young women rising to the dawn and shaking their thin bodies into a muslin that would die by the end of the day. Yes, there was the noise of colour to the day's awakening. The sun that could be so pitiless by midday was simply a medallion to awaken all thoughts, for the air smelt sweet. And then there was the cry of the milkman.

Despite all information to the contrary, I am convinced that certain sounds in Lahore still exist and perhaps flourish in their own obsolescence. In our home—I may call it such, even if the spaces tended to melt and relocate as though a harlequin energy possessed them—the early-morning cry blended with the sweet woodsmoke at dawn and again at dusk, when the milkman would reappear at each household: did we really need so much milk, it makes me think today. For Lahore could not—cannot—be itself without those noises, the milk people, the doves making dove-sounds, the dhobi/washerman cranking along with his clean bundle of clothes. His bicycle creaked, and I hated having to check off the accounts in the dhobi-book, but how entrancing those clothes could smell! There was little more satisfying to observe than that pile of white cotton sheets, still crisp from the heavy weight of the washerman's charcoal iron. They smelt of charcoal too, after they had been spread out on our beds, latticed rope and wooden frames put beneath the stars of summer sleeping structures. The smell of smoke: no wonder I have retained such a passionate engagement with cigarettes. Lahore is to blame, and Gold Leaf too, of course.

We would buy our Gold Leaf from a kiosk in Gulberg Market, a circular spot of commerce segregated from the then lovely residences that lined the main boulevard in Gulberg. All kiosks of that kind had quite a remarkable character: no sooner had a car paused before one, than it was circled by a bevy of little boys, merchants all, crying out, 'Bibiji, coke-fanta-pepsi?' 'Ten Wills Cigrit-Gold Leaf-Three Castle?' And before we had made our purchases, a gala of beggars would arrive, each one more colourful than the last. They brandished stumps, withered limbs, half-collapsed faces; a particularly athletic one-legged man would hop, skip and jump up to the car with extraordinary speed and dexterity. (It has often occurred to me that if the Special Olympics were opened to the beggars of Lahore, the latter group could gather an impressive array of gold medals that it would smilingly receive, and then melt down and put to far more practical purposes than first-place pride.) And if we had no spare change with which to assuage their desire, we would say, either with apology or with a snarl, 'Ma'af Karo.' *Ma'af Karo*: Forgive me, with dismissal.

Today again, forgive me. I do not wish to mock but merely to record Lahore's ability to bring its populace into a daily jostle with the hideous discrepancies between privilege and its maimed absence. Of course there was destitution outside every doorstep, certainly outside the fancy little café called Go-Go, most popular in the seventies with the leisured youth of Lahore until a rival café opened with the brilliantly original name of Kum-Kum. Yet I must try to articulate and do justice to a peculiarly Lahori aura of democracy without reducing it to some private myth which would have nothing to do with Lahore at all. How shall I do it? A most palatable way would be through food, that famous Lahori cuisine with its splendid demolition of class barriers. Think of the Rao fish at Bhati Gate, or the naan-kebab from Dar-ul-Kabab, situated to the left of Mozang Chungi; remember the vats of nihari breakfasts in the old city, and the glorious copper deghs filled with a most elegant halim. I was never particularly drawn to sweets but most of my compatriots were, so I will leave it to them to describe the mithai shops, with the burfis, the gajrelas, the gulab jamans. A city of beautiful breads that all could enjoy, but what else bespeaks of its democracy? Two possible answers occur to me: the spectacle of cinema, and the spectacle of war.

Where did they find their names, the cinema halls? Odeon, Rialto, Auriga, et al.? Although it was hardly more than a poor relation to Bollywood, the Pakistani film industry certainly clocked up an impressive mileage in celluloid. They churned them out, the Urdu films and the Punjabi films, and since the pantheon of stars was rather slender, no Lahori was unfamiliar with the faces and proportions of the famous five. They couldn't, even if they wanted to, because aside from its most dignified streets, Lahore indulged its film advertisers. The latter erected hoardings of grotesque proportions, so when the average Lahori pulled out his bicycle and set out for a day's work, he was bound to encounter a hundred-foot representation of Shamim Ara or Neelo smiling down at him in bashful but distinctly amorous intent. It must have been good for the economy, however, providing jobs for an army of painters, who had to produce thigh after dancing thigh, breast after bouncing breast. I was always startled by their size, and wondered whether one or two painters worked simultaneously on a ten-by-six-foot breast, to meet in triumph over a foot-long nipple.

Considering that Pakistan is an ostensibly conservative society, it fills me with wonderment to think that it would allow the film industry to litter Lahore's horizons with representations of the female body that, by comparison, make a *Playboy* bunny seem as chaste as Easter's.

Chastity. That really is the impelling goal of the films themselves, although through such convolutions of plot that they could easily accommodate rape, incest and adultery along the way. Of course such high drama is only represented indirectly through song and dance, much to the appreciation of a Lahori audience. When Zeba and Muhammad Ali don matching Fair Isle sweaters and cavort around the Nathia Gail snow singing 'the weather is beautiful, but not as beautiful as you' and the entire cinema hall from the boxes to the pits bursts into an applause of joy—yes, that is democracy. That is the democracy of Lahore. To go to a matinee performance along MacClode Road is to observe a crowd of faces completely given over to the rapture of fantasy that is in its own way quite poignant: an escape from what, one may ask. But at least for an afternoon, virtue has been rewarded, the villain done away with, and even the wicked sidekick who has punctured the film with the refrain, 'Relax, boss. Have a drink. Cheers!' meets his proper, deserved end.

While the end of a film allows one literally to read 'The End' at its conclusion, the end of the spectacle of war brings with it no equal satisfaction. In my girlhood, I lived through two wars in Lahore and neither was any less deranging for their traumatic brevity. The '65 war brought an infusion of patriotic fervour to the city: the same singers who had been crooning filmi love lyrics a week before were now marshalled into singing songs of national identity along with pride, pomp and circumstance of glorious war. The radios and the little transistors that every second man carried blared these tunes incessantly, interspersed with bullet-like bulletins from the war fronts, to which every Lahori listened with erect attention—businessmen and milkmen, democratic again. But there was other music, too: the hideous wail of the air-raid and all-clear sirens, and the constant, sickening thud of artillery fire at the Indian border, seventeen miles from Lahore. At nightfall the adults would crouch in darkened rooms, vainly trying to catch BBC news, finally listening to the crackling declaration, 'Lahore has fallen!' Had we? And if so, into what?

The fall of Dacca in 1971, however, did not leave Lahore the luxury of such questions. A fog of unending separations hung over the city, in which the populace groped towards at least an illusion of conclusiveness. There were some who complained that the '71 war songs had not been half as good as the '65 ones, blaming music itself for its collusion in the bitterness of defeat. The citizenry was indeed lost, although the wisest of its members were heard to repeat: no war is won; all wars are lost. And so Lahore had to redefine its shape again, adding yet another strata to be archaeologized in the times to come. It has been, after all, only seven centuries since the Mongol invasion and pillaging of a city that must now understand how it can, how it will, pillage itself.

It pillaged, I think, its true connection to some poetry that was of Lahore alone. I do not simply refer to the twentieth century, to figures like Iqbal and Faiz, who represent mirror images of nationalistic modernity. No, I think of what could transpire at such shrines as Data Ganj Baksh and Mian Mir in the days when there were still Jamsetjees in the cantonment, Pitmans and Dyal Singh Mansions along the overdeterminedly historical stretch of the Mall. For the *Civil and Military Gazette* was still an actual entity, a newspaper and a building in my youth: now it hardly remains a memory. Do not be concerned; I shall not speak of Kipling, nor of the Lahore Tea House that served cha'i to some of my most admired writers. No, nostalgia is not a healthy route of departure.

But it also remains a moment of glad necessity, for who can conjure up a vision of Lahore without remembering the tiny droplet of beauty that is Iqbal's tomb, resting in the shade of the Badshahi Mosque?

He deserves that spot. Lahore is a city of untold monuments: in other words, a space startling with the stories it can tell. The Badshahi remains for me the most perfect of mosques, so that each time I visit it I am frozen again by the ninety-nine names of God, as though I were reading them for the first time. And Iqbal himself, poet of the great 'Complaint', seems to remind Lahore that its integrity is essentially open-ended: 'Tu Shaheen hai, parvaz hai kam tera,/ Tere samnen asman aur bhi hain.' You are an eagle; your profession is flight,/ In front of you there are skies and more skies.

The sky of Lahore that I wish to remember may be irretrievably lost, but I like to turn back to Iqbal's injunction to envision that there always are, in imperative, more skies. When Faiz made a documentary on Iqbal, he concentrated on the latter's great command towards open-endedness: 'Ankh khol, zamin dekh, falak dekh, faza dekh,/ Mashriq se obharti suraj ko zara dekh.' Get vision, see the earth, see the sky, see the air,/ Notice that the sun still rises from the east. In the context of Lahore, I assume such a scold could imply that the sun is like a window, that there always must be dawnings in the city's history. And thus the literal destruction of the old simply confers a keener responsibility on memory. It also raises the question: can memory be proleptic? Can it anticipate even as it collects? I raised that question with beloved Eqbal Ahmed, who in 1947 walked in a bitter convoy from Delhi to Lahore. 'We were five thousand when we left,' he told me, 'we were a thousand when we reached Lahore.' Memory is worthless, he said, if it does not record a sorrow in order to prepare itself for further sorrows. He loved Lahore, and reminded me that it is very difficult to write about the city without repeating Faiz and his uncanny apostrophe: 'O city of lights.' I have done so, repeatedly.

O city of lights. When I think of what I have left behind—and not only in the Miani Sahib graveyard, home of my mother, my sister, and now my father—I realize that I carry inside me a delicate array of coffins that all pertain to Lahore. They are Muslim coffins, without a nail in them, constructed of finely crafted and unvarnished wood, open to the air. Once, in Lahore, when I was driving with my parents, I saw such a structure being hauled on top of a rickshaw (those gladsome things, so colourful) and exclaimed to them, 'What a funny-looking bed!' It is a coffin, they said. Now I have several of them inside me.

Do Mozzis believe in resurrection, when all the graves pop open and present their contents to their maker? I can't remember, particularly since my coffins simply will not wait for resurrection and press at my ribcage in a demand for immediate recognition. One of those coffins— perhaps the most insistent—is titled 'Women of Lahore'.

Lahori women. I would like to mention Halima, our cleaning woman, Pallas Athene in that straight back and arrogant head. Her husband was an itinerant labourer, which means every time the city chose to tarmac a particular street, Sui Gas was bound to arrive a day later, not merely to lay down a new pipeline, but for the joy of digging the road up again. Halima was proud, and each of her gestures registered to me as an admonishment, whether she was sweeping or emptying wastebins or giving the floors a taki. Taki, that thick grey cloth dipped into some disinfected water and wiped over stone or marble floors each day. Halima will never know the memories of her I carry with me, to this day. But there were other women: I cannot describe how my spine stiffened when I returned to Lahore and observed that its female residents were no longer confining themselves to APWA charitable activities or to constructing dry-arrangements to be auctioned at the next charity fund-raising ball. Worthy activities, no doubt, but in the face of Islamicization of Pakistan and the revisions of the Laws of Evidence, what did Lahori women do?

They took to the streets. Along the Mall, just as the luminous beds of irises were opening, they chose to speak of rights. I found it an extraordinary courageous gesture, to give up cross-stitch and cuisine in order to turn Lahore back on itself and assert the dignity of the female. Admittedly, my words are trite, so that each ghost from that coffin has the right to turn away from me in disgust. But I still salute those women—who will remain unnamed, although eminently recognizable—who opened schools and institutes, who chose to be teachers, writers, lawyers. One wonderful professor decided to adopt all the curs in Lahore, at least any she could find. The vet was first startled, but then became so used to being woken up at all hours of the day and night to tend to another mangey cur that he decided to move his clinic into her rambling house in the cantonment. Still others worked hard to resist the Islamicization of Lahore, asserting their right to sing, to dance, and to create heavenly artifacts, heavenly music. It was not their defiance that so moved me—coffee parties, after all, are hard work, and to move into real work must have been something of a relief. I think what touched me most was their rare blend of intelligence and humour: as beholder, that's what beauty is, I thought. So despite the silliness and jealousies that beset even the most admirable of coalitions, I have only one thing to say when my talking coffin begs a word of me. Lahori women, my salaam to you.

We thought about that uneasy peace, my friend Bapsi and I, when we discussed our frequent revisitings to once and future Lahores. We were meeting in London, or Washington, or Houston, or Miami, or any one of the places where we now collect our thoughts. When she told me that the erstwhile D.P. Edulji alcohol store had been now converted into 'The Crow-Eaters Gallery' for the exhibition of art, I felt heartened. If one form of pleasure has been ostensibly excised from Lahore, how pleasing and appropriate that it should now house a different pleasure, instead of sitting along the Mall in sorry decay. Of course, jokes: once, when a distinguished barrister was absent from his crowded office all morning and his clients queried why, they were told, 'His bootlegger did not deliver.' The clients nodded their understanding to the clerks, for here was a situation far more dire than their petty complaints. But still, I would like to visit The Crow-Eaters Gallery, and see, even in miniature, how new life can begin. 'There *are* young people working in the city,' Bapsi insisted. 'Young, and less jaded than us.' That made me smile, for 'jaded' is the last word to describe Bapsi, who wanders the world as though Warris Road was always around the corner, and has the canal running through her veins and her words. Now is there some peace to that.

Salaam is an appropriate word with which to conclude these scattered comments on Lahore. They are too brief, but the city's stories are too many and too long. There will be a time when surely I will return, in language if not in body. Sometimes, even in Maine, some distant cry will make me think, oh, here comes the raddi-vala, the rag-and-bone-shop man! (Now I must lie down where all the ladders start/ In the foul rag-and-bone-shop of the heart.) Maybe as a raddi-vala I shall return to collect used tales from my friends and acquaintances, and start again, assiduously, to copy the calligraphy of Lahore.

The 'Lihaaf' Trial

Ismat Chughtai

Ismat Chughtai was summoned before the Lahore High Court on a charge of obscenity for her story 'Lihaaf', which hints at a lesbian relationship. Fellow-writer Saadat Hasan Manto was also ordered to appear before the court on a similar charge. These are extracts from Chughtai's memorable account of their court appearances—and much else.

In December of 1944 I received the summons to appear in the High Court. Everyone said that there was no question of being jailed and I would be let off with just a fine. I excitedly started putting together warm clothes for my visit to Lahore.

Seema was very young and frail and cried in a very loud voice. The child specialist assured us that she was perfectly healthy and just had a robust crying voice. But knowing that she wouldn't be able to withstand the sudden change in weather and would not be able to tolerate the cold in Lahore, I left her with Sultana Jafri's mother in Aligarh. Shahid Ahmed Dehlavi came with me from Delhi. His calligrapher accompanied us as well because he too had been declared a criminal. The case had been brought against the collection that Shahid Ahmed Dehlavi had published, not against the journal *Adab-e Latif.*

Sultana was at the station to pick us up. She was working for Lahore Radio Station in those days and lived in Luqman Sahib's bungalow, a grand sprawling place. His wife and children were visiting his wife's parents so we had the complete run of the house.

Manto arrived later, and soon we were attending one reception after another. Most of our hosts were Manto's friends but they invited me because, seeing me as some strange, unusual creature, they were intrigued. Our case was presented on the first day of the court proceedings. Nothing much happened. The judge asked my name and

---

This extract is taken from Ismat Chughtai's *My Friends, My Enemy: Essays, Reminiscences, Portraits*, published by Kali for Women.

inquired whether I had written the story or not. I confessed to my crime. That was it!

I was very disappointed. The rest of the time our lawyer presented a statement, but because we were constantly whispering we didn't catch a word of what he said. And then a second date was set. Feeling liberated we embarked on having a good time. Manto, Shahid[1] and I would get into a tonga and spend all day shopping. We bought Kashmiri shawls and shoes. I was envious when I saw Manto's delicate, fair-skinned feet. The sight of my own uncouth feet made me want to lament like the mythical peacock.

'I'm repelled by my feet,' Manto said.

'Why? They're so attractive,' I argued.

'They're so effeminate.'

'But you have a special interest in females.'

'That's an upside-down argument. I love women as a man. That doesn't mean I should become a woman myself.'

'Well, let's forget this discussion about men versus women. Let's talk about people. Do you know that men with delicate feet are very sensitive and intelligent? My brother, Azim Baig Chughtai, had very beautiful feet but . . .'

I suddenly remembered my brother's repulsively swollen feet just before he died. And the Lahore that was decorated like a new bride with apple and apricot blossoms was transformed into the rocky, sandy cemetery of Jodhpur where my brother sleeps under tons of earth, and on whose grave thorny bushes had been planted to keep away badgers that might burrow through it. Those thorns swam through my veins and I placed the soft lamb's wool shawl I had been fingering back on the counter.

How beautiful Lahore was! Still invigorating, full of laughter, its arms spread out in welcome, embracing all those who arrive here, the city of cheerful people who love unconditionally, without reserve, the 'heart of the Punjab'.

We roamed all over Lahore. Deep in conversation, our pockets filled with pine nuts, we walked and walked. At a street corner we ate fried fish. How much one eats when one is walking! We wandered into a hotel and our mouths began watering when we saw hot dogs and hamburgers on the menu.

'Hamburgers contain ham, which is the meat of the pig, but we can eat hot dogs,' Shahid suggested. So like good Muslims we kept our religious faith intact, and ate hot dogs and drank the juice of Kandahari pomegranates.

Afterwards we discovered that the white race is very crafty. Hamburgers don't have ham and hot dogs contain pork sausage! Even though it had been two days since we had eaten those hot dogs, Shahid suddenly began to feel nauseous. Then a Maulwi Sahib issued a fatwa that if you eat pork by mistake it's not a sin, and only then did Shahid cease to be sick.

But when Shahid and Manto got very drunk in the evening they came to the joint decision that hamburgers are not at all safe and hot dogs are better on all accounts. The argument threatened to take on a rather dangerous turn, and finally it was decided that for the time being we should abstain from eating both because no one can guarantee what the source for either is and which is halal and which haram. So tikkas are the best, we decided. We wandered about in Anarkali, strolled through Shalimar Gardens, saw Nurjahan's mausoleum, and then, by God's grace, attended more receptions and parties.

This was the time when words of praise issued forth spontaneously from my heart for the King of Britain, because he had brought a case against us and thus afforded us the golden opportunity of having a festive time in Lahore. We began to wait impatiently for our second appearance in court. We no longer cared if we were to be hanged. If we were hanged in Lahore we would attain the status of martyrs and the Lahore-wallahs would take out our funeral processions with great pomp and show.

The second appearance was scheduled for the pleasant month of November 1946. This time Shahid was busy with his film. Seema's ayah had become very efficient and Seema was now very healthy and robust, so I left her in Bombay and went by plane to Delhi, from where I travelled to Lahore by train, in the company of Shahid Ahmed Dehlavi and his calligrapher. I felt very embarrassed in the calligrapher's presence. The poor man had been dragged into all this for no reason. He was always very quiet, sat with his eyes lowered, a weary expression on his face. Every time I looked at him I would be assailed afresh by feelings of guilt.

'What do you think?' I asked him. 'Do you think we'll lose the case?'

'I can't say, I haven't read the book.'

'But Katib Sahib, you printed it.'

'I see the words separately and write them, I don't pay attention to their meanings.'

'Amazing! And you don't even read it after it has been printed?'

'Yes, I read to make sure there are no mistakes.'

'Each word separately?'

'Yes.' He lowered his head in contrition. Then he said after a short pause. 'You won't mind if I say something?'

'No.'

'You make a lot of spelling mistakes.'

'Yes, I do. Actually I confuse "*seen*" with "*se*", there's a lot of confusion between "*zuad*", "*ze*" and "*zaal*", and it's the same story with "*he*" and the other two "*hes*".'

'Didn't you write *takhtis*?'

'I did write *takhtis* a lot and often got punished for these very mistakes, but . . .'

'Actually, just as I pay attention only to words and ignore meanings, in the same way you are so involved with what you're saying that you don't pay attention to spelling.'

May God bless calligraphers, they will keep my honour intact, I thought, and dropped the issue.

Shahid Sahib and I were M. Aslam's guests. We hadn't even greeted each other properly when M. Aslam began scolding me, denouncing what he called my obscene style of writing. I was furious. Shahid Sahib tried his best to stop me but I was soon embroiled in a battle.

'And what about the filthy sentences you have written in *Nights of Sin*, actually giving explicit details of the sex act just for titillation?'

'It's different in my case. I'm a man.'

'So is that my fault?'

'What do you mean?' Enraged, he became red in the face.

'I mean that God has made you a man and I have nothing to do with that, and He made me a woman and you have nothing to do with that. You haven't asked me to give you the right to write what you want, nor do I consider it necessary that I should ask you for permission to write freely.'

'You are an educated girl from a respectable Muslim family.'

'And you are educated and from a respectable Muslim family.'

'Do you want equality with men?'

'Not at all. I used to try and get the highest marks in class and often I got more marks than boys.'

I knew that I was resorting to my hereditary penchant for tortuous reasoning. But Aslam Sahib's face had become flushed and I was afraid that he might either slap me or that an artery would burst in his brain. Shahid Sahib was also extremely agitated. He was about to burst into tears it seemed.

Using a mild manner and a tone of entreaty, I said, 'Aslam Sahib, in reality no one told me that writing on the subject dealt with in "Lihaaf" is a sin, nor did I read anywhere that I shouldn't write about this . . . disease . . . or predilection. Perhaps my mind is not the brush of Abdur Rahman Chughtai but a cheap camera instead, which, whenever it sees something, pushes its own button and the pen in my hand becomes helpless. My mind tempts my pen, and I can't interfere in the relationship between the mind and the pen.'

'Didn't you get any religious education?'

'Arre, Aslam Sahib, I read *Bahishti Zewar.* There are such frank matters mentioned in it.' I assumed an expression of innocence. Aslam Sahib seemed disconcerted by this.

I continued. 'When I read those things as a child my heart suffered a jolt. I thought they were filthy. Then I read the book again when I was in B.A. and discovered those things were not filthy at all. They were matters every intelligent person should be aware of. However, if people wish, they can also condemn medical texts and books on psychology as being filthy.'

Once the one-on-one was over we started talking amicably. Aslam Sahib cooled down. Breakfast arrived. The food laid out for the four of us was so elaborate that it could easily feed fifteen people. Three or four types of eggs—plain, *khaugina* and boiled, there were shami kababs and qeema, parathas and puris along with toast, white and yellow butter, yogurt and milk, honey and dry fruits, egg halwa, carrot halwa and sohan halwa.

'O God! Do you intend to kill us?' Because I had tormented him so much I now began to praise some of his work. I had read only *Nargis* and *Nights of Sin* so I spoke about them in glowing terms. Finally he was convinced that in some cases, expressions of explicit sexuality are a lesson in realism and can be instructional. Then he embarked on a glorification of every one of his books, and before long his mood changed and he became very pleasant. Then he said gently, 'Offer your apology to the judge.'

'Why? Our lawyer says we will win the case.'

'No, the wretch is lying. If you and Manto apologize, the case will be over in five minutes.'

'So the respectable class here has pressured the government to build this case against us.'

'That's nonsense!' Aslam Sahib said, but he wouldn't look me in the eye.

'Well, then, did the government or the King of Britain read these stories and decide to indict us?'

'Aslam Sahib,' Shahid Sahib said in a mild-mannered tone, 'it is true that a few writers, critics and some of the respectable citizenry directed the government's attention towards these books, suggesting that they are morally damaging and hence should be seized.'

'Do you think morally damaging books should be exalted instead of being seized?' Aslam Sahib flared up. Shahid Sahib looked stricken.

'Then we definitely deserve our punishment,' I said.

'There you go again with your stubborn arguing.'

'No, Aslam Sahib, it's not right that we commit a crime, lead virtuous people astray and make a clean exit simply by saying we're sorry. If indeed I have committed a crime and it is proven that I have, only punishment will appease my conscience.' I was not saying this sarcastically, I really meant it.

'Don't be obstinate, present your apology.'

'What will happen if we're punished? Fines?'

'And disgrace.'

'There's been enough disgrace already, what else remains now? This court case is nothing. How much will the fine be?'

'About two or three hundred,' Shahid Sahib said.

'That's it?'

'It could even be as high as five hundred,' Aslam Sahib tried to frighten me.

'That's . . . it?'

'So you have a lot of money, it seems.' Aslam Sahib lost his temper again.

'I do, with your blessing, but even if I didn't have so much money, would you not have given me five hundred rupees to save me from going to jail? After all, you are among the wealthy class in Lahore.'

'You talk too much.'

'My mother had the same complaint. She used to say, "All you can do is wag your tongue and fill your stomach."'

Good humour prevailed and the matter was put aside. But it wasn't long before he again brought up the question of an apology.

I felt like bashing his skull and mine, but I controlled myself and said nothing.

We appeared in court on the designated day. The witnesses present today were to prove that Manto's 'Bu' (Smell) and my 'Lihaaf' are both obscene. My lawyer explained carefully that until I was questioned directly I was not to open my mouth. He would say whatever he deemed proper. 'Bu's' turn came first.

'Is this story obscene?' Manto's lawyer asked.

'Yes, sir,' the witness said.

'What is the word that indicates it is obscene?'

Witness: 'Bosom.'

Lawyer: 'My Lord the word "bosom" is not obscene.'

Judge: 'Correct.'

Lawyer: 'The word "bosom" is not obscene, then?'

Witness: 'No, but here it is used for a woman's chest.'

Suddenly Manto jumped to his feet.

'If I don't call a woman's chest "bosom", should I call it "peanuts" then?'

Laughter broke out in the court. Manto was also laughing.

'If the prisoner engages in this type of tawdry humour again he will either be thrown out on contempt of court charges or he will be fined.'

Manto's lawyer whispered in his ear, telling him he should behave, after which he calmed down. The discussion then continued, during which the witnesses kept returning again and again to the word 'bosom'.

'If the word "bosom" is obscene, then why aren't the words "knee" or "elbow" obscene, too?' I asked Manto.

'This is all rubbish!' Manto was angry again. Arguments continued.

We came out and sat down on the wobbly benches in the veranda. Ahmed Nadeem Qasmi, who was with us in court, had brought along a basket of oranges. He showed us how to eat an orange gracefully. Soften the orange gently, make a small hole at one end the way you do in a mango, and then suck on it with ease. We finished off the basket of oranges as we sat there. Once we had eaten all the oranges we felt really hungry, and during lunch break we raided a hotel. After Seema's birth I had lost a lot of weight and now I didn't have to abstain from rich foods. The chicken pieces on our plates were so large they seemed to have come from a vulture or an eagle. Chicken sprinkled with coarse black pepper, eaten with steaming hot qulchas and washed down with the juice of Kandahari pomegranates instead of water—good wishes gushed forth from our hearts for those who had brought us to court.

In the evening, Luqman had invited us to a gathering of some of the poets and writers in Lahore. There I met Mrs Hijab Ali for the first time. A lot of make-up, tons of kajal in her eyes, looking a little melancholy, a little sullen, she responded by staring vacantly into space when you talked to her.

'She's a fraud,' Manto widened his big eyes further and whispered in my ear.

'No, she's lost in the very atmosphere that has emerged from her pen like a dreamy cloud and which has created a rainbow-coloured shell around her.'

Hijab Imtiaz Ali continued staring into space and I sought out her husband, Imtiaz Ali, and struck up a conversation with him. How different the temperaments of husband and wife were. Imtiaz Ali was a very loquacious, jovial and generous man and was responsible for making the evening lively and festive. It seemed as if I had known him for years. His conversation was even more refreshing than his writings. Recently, when I was in Pakistan, I met Mrs Hijab Ali again. She was wearing light make-up up this time, looked younger than before, and was very talkative and relaxed. It seemed as if she had been born anew.

The court that day was packed. Several people had been urging us to offer our apologies to the judge. They were even ready to pay the fines on our behalf. By now the proceedings had lost some of their verve, with the witnesses who were there to prove that 'Lihaaf' was obscene, quite confused and befuddled at this point. No one had succeeded in finding a word that could be easily denounced. After going through the text minutely, a gentleman said, 'The sentence "she was collecting *ashiqs*" (lovers) is obscene.'

'Which word is obscene,' the lawyer asked, '"collecting" or "*ashiq*"?'

'The word "*ashiq*",' the witness said uneasily.

'My Lord, the word "*ashiq*" has been used frequently by the greatest poets, and has also been used in *na'ats*. This is a word that has been afforded a special place by the devout.'

'But it is highly improper for girls to collect "*ashiqs*",' the witness proclaimed.

'Why?'

'Because . . . because . . . this behaviour is improper for respectable girls.'

'It's not improper for girls who are not respectable?'

'Uh . . . uh . . . no.'

'My client has mentioned girls who are perhaps not respectable. So according to you, sir, non-respectable girls do collect *ashiqs*?'

'Yes. It's not obscene for these girls to mention such words, but for an educated woman from a respectable family to write about these girls merits condemnation!' the witness thundered.

'So please condemn as much as you like, but does it merit incrimination?'

The case crumbled.

'If you apologize, we will pay all your fines and . . .' a man came up and whispered in my ear.

'Well, Manto Sahib, shall we offer an apology?' I asked Manto. 'We'll use the money we get to do a lot of shopping.'

'Rubbish!' Manto widened his eyes.

I turned to the man and said, 'I'm sorry, but Manto is crazy, he won't agree.'

'But even if you, if you alone . . .'

'No,' I said in a serious tone, 'you don't know what a troublemaker this man is. He'll make it impossible for me to live in Bombay. The punishment I'm supposed to receive here will be several times better than his fury.'

The case was closed and we didn't receive any punishment. The gentleman's face fell.

Judge Sahib called me to his chambers and greeted me very warmly.

'I've read nearly all your stories and they're not obscene, nor is "Lihaaf" obscene. But there's a lot of filth in Manto's writing.'

'But the world is filled with filth,' I said meekly.

'But is it necessary to fling it about?'

'Flinging it makes it visible and one's attention can be drawn to the process of cleansing.'

Judge Sahib burst out laughing.

We had not been shaken up by the case nor did winning it make us happy. As a matter of fact, we were saddened, because who knew when we would have the opportunity to visit Lahore again.

Lahore. What a savoury word it is. Lahori salt! Like gems. White and pink. I feel like stringing the tiny chunks into a glimmering necklace and draping it around the slender white neck of a Punjabi belle.

'So dim, so dim, the light of the stars.' In Surinder Kaur's throat the gems of Lahori salt have dissolved to become a melody, and with her husband, Sodhi's, voice as it accompanies her like the rustling of satin and silk brocade, it creates a strangely alluring harmony. Surinder and Sodhi's melodies come to life when one sees Lahore, creating a storm of passion so that one is moved to tears. The memory of an unknown beloved rises like bitter-sweet pain in the heart. There is a glow in the atmosphere of Lahore, silent bells tinkle, and the orange blossoms of Mrs Hijab Imtiaz Ali's *afsaanas* fill the air with fragrance. And one remembers that period of life when one used to get lost in her dulcet, sunset-hued *afsaanas*.

—*Translated by Tahira Naqvi*

Note:

1. Chughtai is referring here to her husband, Shahid, who also accompanied her on this first trip, and not to Shahid Ahmed Dehlavi. —TN.

Ava Gardner and I: Post-Partition Lahore

Minoo Bhandara

I was nine years old at Partition—old enough to register events, without necessarily understanding them. I have a vivid memory of the raiders coming to our home in Warris Road. Some half dozen *rehras* trotted down the narrow road, the drivers looking like Roman charioteers from Hollywood movies. As they came face to face with us, one shouted, 'Who art thou?' Defenceless, we stood our ground. 'They are not Hindoos,' replied our saviour, the elderly cook Imam Bakhsh, adding, 'They are Parsees—the ancients of Iran.' Deathly pause. They were sizing us up. We did not look like Hindus or Sikhs. The looters decided to give us the benefit of the doubt. There could be other pickings more profitable than messing around with the 'ancients of Iran' as Imam Bakhsh put it.

By early 1948, the Hindu and Sikh boys had left Lahore and my school, St Anthony's, run by Irish missionary brothers, was left with a majority of Christian pupils. Gone was little Ashok Kumar who also lived on Warris Road; I remember him in his navy-blue shorts going to school perched on the handlebars of his servant's bicycle. One of the new boys, Saad Ashraf, had come from Calcutta. Chubby, gruff Saad was the opposite of the delicate, quietly-spoken Kumar who had vanished in the tumult of the times.

Soon, Saad and I were hop, skip and jumping on the mud rooftops of the servants' quarters. I remember what seemed like a chasm between two rooftops. My friends jumped it. Confronting the void—I froze. Many years later I read the autobiographical novels of Ved Mehta. Before partition, Ved lived in Mehta Gali, next door to Park Lane, where Saad lived. Confronted with the same rooftop dilemma—perhaps the same roof—the friends of the blind Ved holding either hand said, 'Jump, Ved, jump'. He landed safely on the other side.

One of my most vivid teenage memories is of the shake-up that sleepy, slow-moving Lahore received when Ava Gardner and Stewart Granger arrived to shoot *Bhowani Junction*. It was like a monsoon storm invading the stillness of the times.

The done thing was to see them or be seen by them. By luck I found myself seated next to Ava Gardner in a darkened room, known as a 'box' at the Regal Cinema. My father was in the liquor business. In his absence one evening I received a panic phone call from his friend, the owner of the Regal Cinema on the Mall—the best cinema in town. Ava Gardner with other actors were in the cinema watching the movie *The Barefoot Contessa* in which she had starred. The caller hissed, 'Ava Gardner and her friends are drinking gin like water. We're running out of the stuff. Please help. This is a crisis! My prestige is on the line. I can't find English gin anywhere.'

Reacting to his distress call and risking my father's displeasure, I nervously took two bottles of gin to the cinema and handed them over to the owner. He was immensely relieved. To reward me for services rendered, he invited me to sit next to Ms Gardner in the owner's box to view the film. Actually, the owner was at his wits' end trying to handle the motley crowd of actors; he was relieved to vacate his seat for me.

There were about four or five of us in the box watching *The Barefoot Contessa*. Ava Gardner was sitting on a settee, with another actor whose name I forget. I was startled and somewhat discomforted by their compromising position. It was like a 'falabee' of tangled hands and feet; they were least bothered. Suddenly, she turned to me and said something, to which I replied, 'Sorry, Ma'am, I don't understand you.' Question repeated, same answer. Finally she shouted, 'I want to go to the shithouse—do you understand "shit"?'

'Yes Ma'am.'

I had the honour of escorting her to the shithouse with a police battalion and director George Cukor in train. Waiting outside whilst she was in, I attempted some small talk with Cukor. He probably had difficulty understanding my Paki English, and I his American. In exasperation he said, 'If you are looking for a job, young man, I ain't got one.' By now our Barefoot Contessa returned, puckering her nose, declaring that she had yet to encounter a more evil-smelling place.

But the good outcome was that next day I had near-hero status among the friends who had seen me in the Contessa's solemn train walking to the toilets.

By the fifties there was practically no memory of British India for people of my age group. Before Partition, my father's employees had mostly been Hindus. As all had left, my mother was roped in to lend a semi-managerial hand in the liquor business. My father's other business was typewriters. He was agent for the renowned Smith Corona. Both businesses were located on the Mall. In the Second World War, the import of Smith Coronas was not possible but demand had multiplied. So father decided to replicate the Smith Corona in his cavern-like workshops behind the Mall. I remember seeing one of these strange creatures long after its manufacture ceased. Somehow the animal did type, provided one grappled it with all one's strength. Father's lone Muslim mechanic, Ashiq Hussain, who had stepped into the shoes of the Sikh manager, was the sole repository of the technical skills of the project; he was immensely proud of the one machine that survived till the late sixties. I wish our Smith Corona had found a good home in some industrial museum.

Early in the fifties while rickety tongas still trotted languidly on the Mall, foreign ideologies had become a hot topic among the intellectual hopefuls. The avant-garde of those days were the red-hot Stalinists although Marxist opinion varied from delicate pink to brightest crimson. And then there were the Greenies—religious types who were few and far between. Fundamentalist Muslim points of view were rarely aired in our circles. Whilst still at school, I had a pseudo-Marxist argument with Aamer Raza, who later blossomed as a High Court Judge, eminent jurist, author of legal tomes and a dedicated social worker. I don't remember what the pseudo-Marxist arguments with Aamer Raza were about, but the arguments were always convoluted and usually meaningless. Our conversation reflected the culture and mood of the times. 'Where did you get that from?' he might ask me, after I had made some erudite or outrageous comment, and with a smug smirk I'd reply, 'From *Pravda!*' (The absolute gold standard of Stalinism.)

'Not possible,' he would say, 'they don't have an English edition.'

Later I became a habitué of Zelin's Coffee House (our version of a French salon), across the Mall from my father's liquor store. Returning from college I would work in the seedy warehouse of the store for about an hour. My job was to count the liquor boxes. I remember the sherry boxes exuding a very pleasant aroma! What I failed to check was whether the boxes were filled with bottles. By banking successfully on my non-intrusive counts, storekeeper Abrar got away with a huge fraud. He soon set up his own business.

For my part I was itching to get to Zelin's. There, over chicken sandwiches we learnt how to measure life with coffee spoons. At one ferocious discussion I ventured to say that thousands had died in the Great Leap Forward of Chairman Mao. A woman countered: 'Where did you get that bit of propaganda trash?'

'*Time* magazine,' I answered.

'You read *Time?*' A chorus of horrified voices asked and eyebrows were raised in my direction. It was not expected of a leftist cub that he would read 'imperialist' magazines. I was suspect to my peers.

We remained at Zelin's till sundown when it was time to promenade the Mall. We boys, in knots of two and three, would ogle the groups of girls, who in turn would inspect us with oblique glances. We paraded up and down the Mall till our legs were in danger of dropping off. We thought it great fun.

Lahore had a well-known red-light district to the side of the King's Mosque. It was not entirely a sordid place like the brothels of Bombay or Calcutta, but a place of entertainment and culture, vaguely like a Japanese geisha house. An older acquaintance of the family first took me to the district. One dark and dingy lane would open into another. Young men could be seen squatting and peeing in the open drains. Heavily painted ladies offered their wares from dimly lit balconies. I was shocked and scared. We walked up the stairs to one landing. Faint sounds of music could be heard. We entered a largish room with windows tightly shut and were seated barefoot on a dusty carpet with large pillows to support our backs. Since my companion was well known to the Madam of the house, she received us as if at a homecoming. Liquor, tea and snacks were served.

There soon appeared a soft-complexioned young woman, attractively but not immodestly attired. Pleasantries were exchanged. She was cultured. Well spoken. And attractive in every way. As she sang to the accompaniment of two or three musicians playing a harmonium and a tabla, my fears subsided. How could such a nice girl be here? She beamed a smile in my direction more than once. Should she be rescued? I was totally captivated. 'Love passed through the House of Lust', to quote from Wilde's 'Harlot House'; but there was no lust and I never saw her again. Returning home I expressed to my companion an ambition to rescue her. 'Don't be silly,' he said. 'She is just an expensive slut.'

Lahore in the decade prior to Partition had a Bloomsbury reputation. It was multicultural, high-minded, and literary, with romantic affairs abounding. The names associated were Khushwant Singh, the brothers Mahmood and Mazhar Ali Khan, Perin Bharucha, Asghari and Manzur Qadir and many others more or less prominent were mentioned. In the mid-fifties, we were the poor successors of this distinguished crowd.

The poet of this generation was the shy, reclusive, Faiz Ahmad Faiz who was perhaps the epitome of the leftist pre-Partition culture, but a lost soul in the Pakistan that followed. Lahore was his 'City of Many Lights'. He saw these lights from the narrow slits of the Black Maria, which served as his transport for many years.

My first encounter with Faiz Sahib was in the early sixties. I was now only a frequent visitor to Lahore, having moved to Rawalpindi to look after the Murree Brewery which father had acquired soon after Partition. We were watching a play staged by the Government College dramatic society. In the interval, as we were strolling in one of the long corridors, chain-smoking Faiz said that he felt awkward smoking in a room hallowed by the memory of his old teachers.

On another occasion, I drove him and a foreign lady friend in my battered Morris Minor from the Cosmopolitan Club in Bagh-e-Jinnah to his home in Model Town. Faiz was in a nostalgic mood. Shyly, he produced some old photographs of his father at Windsor Castle with members of the British royal family. His father had been Ambassador of Afghanistan to the Court of St James. I was somewhat surprised at first that he showed them to me, because he was such a dedicated communist. But then I realized that it wasn't out of character, because Faiz was so open-minded and non-judgemental. We discussed a multitude of subjects but never argued, because his heart and mind could accept widely different opinions without these upsetting him or influencing his own. Faiz Ahmad Faiz was the gentlest and most soft-spoken man I ever knew, and one of the most compassionate.

The span between the Lahore of Kipling and Faiz and ours today is vast. But while differences appear profound, there are significant continuities. The basic institutions of the British remain more or less intact. A continued thirst for learning the English language ensures that the most thriving businesses in town are private English medium schools. The majestic mock-Mughal High Court buildings on the Mall (Shahrah-e-Quaid-e-Azam) remain the ultimate bastion of our freedoms. Scores of little people still seek justice there daily under the norms of our inherited British law.

And of course there are other unchanging features of life in Lahore. Delightful winters with that magical quality of light and distinctive smell of cow-dung smoke; baking summers with chandeliers of yellow blossoms hanging from laburnum trees; the July breaking asunder of monsoon clouds and the smell of the soil after the first showers.

And if you fancy, you can still picnic by moonlight at Prince Kamran's *baradari* on the banks of the Ravi. It's not all gloom, doom and despondency in the City of Many Lights. Some things do remain the same.

Lahore, Partition and
Independence

Khushwant Singh

Having spent two carefree years in Government College, I was no stranger to Lahore. But coming there to earn my living was a different matter. I had everything laid on for me—a well-furnished flat and office, membership of the two leading clubs, the Cosmopolitan, meant for the Indian elite, and the more exclusive Gymkhana, which was largely an English preserve with no more than a dozen Oxbridge-educated 'natives'. My father's and father-in-law's status opened the doors of judges and ministers to me. With my young and attractive wife, we soon became the most sought-after and photographed couple in Lahore.

The only thing missing was the clientele. I spent a couple of hours in the morning in my office poring over law books, then went to the Bar Room for gossip. I went to the Courtrooms to hear important cases being argued, spent an hour or so in the Coffee House for more gossip, and returned for lunch. For the first few months not a single litigant crossed my threshold. For a while I worked as a junior to Kirpa Narain, who had moved from Delhi to Lahore. One day he collapsed and died while arguing a case. I shifted over as junior to Jai Gopal Sethi, who had the largest criminal practice in the Punjab. He occasionally got his clients to throw a few crumbs as junior's fees at me. I was told that I should acquire a good *munshi*, or clerk. They are quite an institution in the Indian legal profession. Where there are no solicitors, as in the Punjab, they do the soliciting—talking to clients, sorting out their papers, fixing the fee to be extracted,

This extract is taken from Muhammad Ali Siddiqui's *Common Heritage*, published by Oxford University Press.

extracting it along with their *munshiana* of ten per cent. Many did much more. They went to the railway stations and bus stands as hotel agents do, spotted litigants and persuaded them to take on their employer as their advocate. All manner of persuasion was practised: their master's wife was the judge's mistress, or vice versa, or he was the ablest 'England-returned Barrister', who played tennis and bridge with the *Sahibs*, drank and danced with their *mems*.

The first clerk I hired was a sharp little fellow from Himachal. He persuaded me to let him go on tour in Punjab's districts to do propaganda for me. He was away for a month, presented me his travel bills, and assured me that many leading lawyers of the district courts had promised to send their appellate work to me. None came.

The second one was a Shia Muslim. He got me a brief as a junior to a leading lawyer from Lucknow in a case involving two branches of rich Shia *zamindars* of Bahraich over their property in Lahore. I got a small fee but lost the friendship of the Lahore head of the family. We also lost the case. Thereafter having nothing to do, I let my *munshi* hire a *maulvi* who taught me the Koran for an hour every morning. Some time later the *munshi* left me on the pretext that taking a salary from a non-believer who was not only not a Muslim but who did not believe in God was *haraam*, unlawful.

In sheer desperation I hired the most expensive *munshi* in Lahore. He was a strapping, six-foot Sikh Jat who was a renowned tout. I paid him Rs 10,000 as advance—a sum unheard of—to secure his services.

He was familiar with Sikh villages in Lahore district. Whenever there was a murder in any village—and there were at least three or four every month—he went to condole with the bereaved family as well as call on the family whose members had been named as accused. He managed to get a brief from one side or the other. Instead of the tenth due to him as *munshiana*, he took a third of my fee.

However, criminal cases started coming my way. I won some, lost others. I also discovered that hiring renowned lawyers at high fees did not really make much difference in a criminal case. If a magistrate or judge was friendly towards me, I got bail for my clients. And often a lighter sentence. There was an Anglo-Indian lawyer who knew hardly any law but managed to get cases through his touts because he was a *sahib*. Also a Parsee who wore a monocle, hummed and hawed his way through his briefs in a fake upper-class English accent, and managed to make a reasonable living. There was a Muslim lawyer who gained notoriety for never preparing his briefs and throwing his clients on the mercy of the court. 'Who knows the law better than Your Honour? Who am I to tell you the real facts of the case? Your Honour will no doubt grasp them better than I and do justice to my client!' Believe it or not, he did better than most lawyers who burned the midnight oil pouring over their briefs and wrangled with judges.

It was a hard, back-breaking, soulless profession. I took on undefended cases in Sessions Courts for a fee of Rs 16 per day; I appeared free of charge in cases against communists; I took on part-time teaching at the Law College; I was put on the panel of defence lawyers at the High Court and then on the panel of the Advocate General. I hardly ever made more than a thousand rupees a month. My father continued to subsidize me. He bought me a larger apartment with property which brought me some rent; then a large house on Lawrence Road facing Lahore's biggest park, Lawrence Gardens (later renamed Bagh-e-Jinnah). None of this made me change my opinion of the legal profession.

Perhaps it was my failure to make it in a big way that soured me. I kept asking myself, 'Is there anything creative in practising law? Don't I owe more to the one life I have than making money out of other peoples' quarrels? A common prostitute renders more service to society than a lawyer. If anything the comparison with the whore is unfair to her. She at least serves a social need, and gives her clients pleasure for their money; a lawyer doesn't even do that.' I have little doubt that if I had stuck to the law a little longer, I would have made it to the Bench and perhaps even to the Supreme Court. Jokers with less practice than me and lesser legal acumen were elevated to the Bench; a couple ended up as Judges of the Supreme Court. Never did I regret chucking up the law; my only regret was that I wasted five years studying it and another seven trying to make a living out of it.

*

Not having much to do in Lahore and yet possessing a nice home and a lovely-looking (though by now somewhat over-assertive) wife, I had no dearth of visitors. Foremost among these was my friend Mangat Rai, who was posted there. Being in the ICS [Indian Civil Service] he was much sought after by Christian fathers with marriageable daughters. He also wrote pieces which he read out to an ever-admiring circle of friends. One which received encores was about a hen which laid eggs in a drain. It was always heard with open-mouthed admiration. He became a daily visitor to my apartment. Every evening after his office he hauled his bicycle up the stairs and often stayed on for drinks and dinner. Whatever reservations he had about my wife vanished; it was evident that he was getting quite enamoured of her. To leave me in no doubt he wrote me a letter confessing that he was in love with her and seeking my permission to continue visiting us. I passed this letter on to my wife. I could see that she was highly flattered. I treated it as a joke and wrote back assuring him that he would be as welcome as before. I had reason to regret my magnanimity. Mangat Rai had enormously persuasive powers to bring people round to his point of view. Most of it was destructive and designed to reduce others to plasticine that he could mould in whatever shape he wanted. My wife at the time spent some hours every morning at a painting studio run by Bhubesh Sanyal. He began dropping in at the studio and persuaded her that painting was a futile pastime. She gave up painting. She was a very keen tennis player and always spent the evenings playing with me at the club. He persuaded her that cycling was more fun, so she abandoned tennis and went cycling with him. She was very punctilious about religious ritual: opening the *Granth Sahib* every morning, reading a hymn or two, and wrapping it up in the evening. He convinced her of the futility of ritual. She began to miss out on her daily routine of prayers and ritual. He had become a hard drinker. My wife took to drinking hard. He was very open about everything he did. He told my wife that one evening, when seeing off his sister at the railway station, he had run into a young Christian girl known to us. She had no transportation. He offered to ride her back on his cycle. She sat on the front bar. He invited her to his apartment without any conditions attached. She accepted. They spent the night in the same bed. He admitted he felt a little guilty because he loved her and not the girl he had bedded. Instead of feeling let down, my wife admired his candour and was more drawn to him. Inevitably their association came to be much talked about.

Amongst others who became regular visitors to my home were Justice Gopal Das Khosla, also of the ICS, and his wife Shakuntala. He was taken with my wife; I with his. So we were on the level. Then there was the Canadian couple, Wilfred Cantwell-Smith, Scholar of Islamics working on Indian Islam, and his wife Muriel, working for a doctor's degree at the Medical College. There was P.N. Kirpal, then lecturer of history at Dayal Singh College. He was destined to stay in our lives for the rest of our days. There were others like Nawabzada Mahmood Ali Khan and his Sikh wife Satnam; Wilburn and Usha Lal who were distantly related to Mangat Rai; Professor Inder Mohan Varma, lecturer in English at the Government College; Bishen Narain and his wife Shanti, both friends of the Khoslas. Others came and went. Occasionally, when he was in Lahore, there was Arthur's younger brother John Lall, also in the ICS. John was a bit of a playboy with an incredibly British accent. He was given to making wisecracks at my expense. 'Kaval,' he said to my wife one day, 'if you have a sister let her marry your bearded husband and you marry me.' I was the target of witticisms from both the Lall brothers. With John I settled scores when he brought his fiancée Hope, a dark, pudgy girl, to introduce to us. The next day he dropped in and asked me what I thought of her. 'She will be a perpetual exercise in faith and charity,' I told him. He made no wisecracks thereafter. My day of reckoning with Arthur had to wait some years.

Two people who I met in my early years in Lahore deserve mention. One was the painter, Amrita Sher Gill. Her fame had preceded her before she took up residence in a block of flats across the road from ours. She had recently married her Hungarian cousin, Victor Egan, a doctor of medicine who wanted to set up practice in Lahore. Amrita was said to be very beautiful and very promiscuous. Pandit Nehru was known to have succumbed to her charms; stories of her sexual appetite were narrated with a lot of slavering.

I didn't know how much truth there was to gossip of her being a nymphomaniac, but I was eager to get to know her. I did not have to wait for very long. It was summertime. My wife and six-month-old son had gone up to Kasauli to stay with her parents. One afternoon when I came home for lunch I found a tankard of beer and a lady's handbag on a table in my sitting room and a heavy aroma of French perfume. I tiptoed to the kitchen to ask my cook who it was. 'I don't know,' he replied, 'a *memsahib* in a sari. She asked for you. I told her you would soon be back for lunch. She looked round the flat and helped herself to the beer from the fridge. She is in the bathroom.' I knew it could only be Amrita Sher Gill. And so it was. She came into the sitting room and introduced herself. She told me of the flat she had rented across the road and wanted advice about carpenters, plumbers, tailors, and the like. I told her whatever I knew about such people. I tried to size her up. I couldn't look her in the face because she had that bold, brazen kind of look which made a timid man like me turn his gaze downwards. She was short in stature and sallow complexioned (being half Sikh, half Hungarian). Her hair was parted in the middle and severely bound at the back. She had a bulbous nose with blackheads showing. She was full-lipped with faint traces of a moustache on her upper lip. I told her I had heard a lot about her paintings and pointed to some water colours on the wall which my wife had done. 'She is just learning to paint,' I said by way of explanation. 'That's obvious,' she snorted. Politeness was not one of her virtues; she believed in speaking her mind however rude or unkind it might be.

A few weeks later I had another sample of her rudeness. I had picked up my wife and son from Kasauli and taken them up to Mashobra. Amrita was staying with her friends the Chaman Lals, who had rented a house a little above my father's. I invited them for lunch. We were having beer and gin slings on the open platform under the shade of the holly-oak. My son was in a playpen learning to stand on his own feet. Everyone was paying him compliments: he was indeed a very pretty little child with curly hair, large eyes, and dimpled cheeks. 'What an ugly little boy!' remarked Amrita. Others protested their embarrassment. My wife froze. Amrita continued to drink her beer without concern. Later, when she heard what my wife had to say about her manners, and that she had described her as a bloody bitch, Amrita told her informant, 'I'll teach that woman a lesson. I'll seduce her husband.'

I waited eagerly for the day of seduction. It never came. When we returned to Lahore, my wife declared our home out of bounds for

Amrita. Some common friends told us that Amrita was not keeping well. One night a cousin of hers came over to spend the night with us because Amrita was too ill to have guests. He told us that she was in a delirium and kept mumbling calls at bridge—she was an avid bridge player. Next morning we heard she was dead. She was only thirty-one.

I went over to her apartment. Her old, bearded father Umrao Singh was in a daze, her mother in a state of hysterics. They had just arrived from Summer Hill (Simla) and could not believe that their young, talented daughter was gone for ever.

That afternoon a dozen of us followed her cortege to the cremation ground where her husband set alight her funeral pyre. When we returned to the Egans' apartment, the police were waiting for him. England had declared war on Hungary as an ally of Nazi Germany. Egan was an enemy national. He was lucky to have been taken into police custody.

It took some time for Amrita's mother to get the details of her daughter's illness and death. She held her nephew and son-in-law responsible for it. She bombarded ministers, officials, friends (including myself) with letters accusing him of murder. Murder, I am certain it was not. Carelessness, I am equally certain, it was. My version of her death came from Dr Raghubir Singh, then a leading physician of Lahore. He was summoned to her bedside at midnight when she was beyond hope of recovery. He believed that she had become pregnant and had been aborted by her husband. The operation had gone wrong. She had bled profusely and developed peritonitis. Her husband wanted Dr Raghubir Singh to give her a blood transfusion and offered his own blood for it. Dr Raghubir Singh refused to do so without finding out their blood grouping. While the two doctors were arguing with each other, Amrita slipped out of life.

Many people, such as the art critic Karl Khandalawala, Iqbal Singh, and her nephew, the painter Vivan Sundaram, have written about Amrita. Badruddin Tyabji has given a vivid account of how he was seduced by her. Vivan admits she had many lovers. Her real passion in life was another woman—she was also lesbian. And she was a superb painter.

*

Among the guests who stayed in my apartment while my wife and son were away for the summer was the Communist Danial Latifi. He had been in and out of jail and the food they gave him at the Party headquarters did not agree with him. Being at the time close to the Party, I invited him to spend some weeks with me to recoup his health. Danial was then, as he is today, a compulsive talker. His flat, monotone voice retains the same soporific quality. One evening two of my friends dropped in. Both were very drunk. Danial converted their polite queries into a long monologue on dialectical materialism and the class struggle. I went out to take some fresh air. When I returned half an hour later, Danial was still holding forth. Both my friends were fast asleep. Through Danial I received two other visitors in turn. The first was Sripad Dange, then on the run from the police. He had to pretend to be my servant. He spent most of his time reading my books. When anyone came to see me he would disappear into the kitchen. Another was Ajoy Ghosh, also then underground. He was a dour, uncommunicative man. His mistress and later wife, Litto, dropped in every day and spent many hours with him when I was at the High Court. Many years later, in England, I asked my friend Everette of the CID if he had known of these men having stayed with me. He said he had, but it had been decided not to arrest them, only to keep a watch on my apartment and note down the names of people who came to visit them.

*

A person who dominated my life in my Lahore years was Manzur Qadir. He was a couple of years older than me, had done his Bar in England, and had practised in the district courts at Lyallpur. He had picked up a considerable practice and a reputation as an upright man of uncommon ability. His father, Sir Abdul Qadir, had been a judge of the Lahore High Court and a literateur: as editor of *Makhzan* he was the first to publish poems of Allama Iqbal. Manzur had married Asghari, the daughter of Mian Sir Fazal Hussain. She had been married earlier to the profligate Nawab of Hoti Mardan and had a daughter by him. The daughter had died and she had divorced her husband. She was a great beauty—the Russian artist Svetoslav Roerich had used her as a model for his paintings of the Madonna. At the time Asghari considered Manzur below her 'imperial' status and felt she had done him a great favour. He was a short, balding, beady-eyed man wearing thick glasses. He was evidently very much in love with his wife and patiently suffered her tantrums. They moved to Lahore with their daughter Shireen, who was the same age as my son Rahul. In Lahore they had a son, Basharat, who was two years younger than Shireen. It did not take long for Manzur and I to get acquainted and become friends. Fortunately our respective wives, both equally prickly characters, also hit it off well. We began to eat in each other's homes every day. My wife shared Manzur's enthusiasm for the cinema: they saw at least one picture together every week; also his passion for mangoes. Between them they would demolish a dozen at one sitting with great gusto.

Manzur was by any standards a most unusual character. He was without doubt the ablest up-and-coming lawyer in the Punjab. He and his uncle, Mohammad Saleem, the famous tennis player who represented India in the Davis Cup for fifteen years, spent hours arguing points of law after they had done a day's work in the High Court. Both men observed the highest standards of rectitude. They took their fees by cheque, or, when paid in cash, gave receipts for the full amount to their clients. They often paid more income tax than was due from them and had some of it refunded. Manzur was the only person I met in my life who never told a lie and took great pains to avoid hurting people's feelings. In due course, he became a kind of litmus paper by which his friends tested their own integrity. When in doubt over a course of action, we could ask ourselves, 'Will Manzur approve of this?' Like me he was an agnostic.

What Manzur and I also shared in common was a love for literature. In his case it was entirely Urdu poetry, to which he re-opened my eyes. He knew the works of many poets and could recite by the hour. He also tried his hand at writing, but without much success. He was best at composing bawdy verse which he recited with great verve to his circle of male friends, although he was extremely proper when women were around.

We spent many vacations together, sometimes at Patiala, where my father-in-law Sir Teja Singh Malik was a minister; other times in

Delhi or Mashobra with my parents. Our friendship became the talk of the town as instances of such close friendships between Sikhs and Muslims or between Hindus and Muslims were very rare.

What proved to be a turning point in my career was Mangat Rai's desire to score over others of our circle as a man of letters. He suggested that, instead of him alone reading his pieces to an admiring audience, everyone should read something he or she had written. Our first meeting was in his home, a portion he had rented on Warris Road. The theme suggested by him was 'I believe'. We were to write down our beliefs on the values of life. About ten short papers were read out. I put down my reasons for disbelief in God and religion, and talked about friendship, love, marriage, death, and theories of life thereafter. There was nothing very original in what I wrote but just as it came to me. My main achievement was that I emerged as a rival to the hitherto unrivalled Mangat Rai. To be fair to him, he was generous in his praise. The next day I received a note of appreciation from Wilfred and Muriel Smith. It was my first fan mail and did a lot to boost my morale. Perhaps there was a little more to me than I thought.

The literary circle became a weekly feature. We met in different homes by rotation. A lot of liquor (mostly Indian brew) was consumed as poems, short stories, and essays were read and faithfully applauded by everyone. The two who contributed most were Justice G.D. Khosla and myself. Khosla was more anxious to establish himself as a writer than as a jurist. I had much less to do than any of the others. I used my visits to Sikh villages, from where my clients came, as background for my earlier stories.

*

My Lahore days were coming to an end. Almost from the day I had come to live there, war had been raging in Europe and the Far East. I had strong anti-fascist views and was convinced that Hitler, Mussolini, their European allies, and the Japanese had to be defeated before India could become free. Most Indians exulted in the victories of the Axis powers more out of spite for their English rulers than love for Nazis and Fascists. I wasn't quite sure of Japanese intentions after

Subhas Chandra Bose took over command of the Indian National Army. He was too strong a man to be a puppet in anyone's hands. But even about him and his INA I had my doubts. My communist illusions were blown sky-high when Stalin made his pact with Hitler, and only partly restored when they went to war against each other. I did not approve of Gandhi's 'Quit India' Movement. I supported the Muslim demand for a separate state in areas where they were in a majority, believing that India would continue to remain one country with two autonomous Muslim-majority states at either end. I did not share any of the Hindu-Sikh suspicions or animosity against Muslims.

Not many Indians believed that the British would willingly relinquish their Empire in India. They regarded the Cripps and Cabinet Missions as eye-wash. They did not know the English. Young British officers who did their war service in India were a new breed. They refused to join exclusively white clubs, went out of their way to befriend Indians, expressed regret over what some English rulers had done in India, and sympathized with the Congress-led freedom movement. One event which re-assured me that independence was round the corner took place in the summer of 1946. I happened to be with my parents in Mashobra. I had to return to Lahore, so I took the evening railcar to Kalka. There was only one other Indian besides me in the car, the rest were British officers in uniform and English civilians. After a brief halt at Barog for dinner we proceeded on our downhill journey. It was a beautiful full-moon night. At a bend near Dharampur, a wheel of the car came off the rails. The driver told us to wait till he got to the next station to order a relief car to be sent up from Kalka. We sat among the pines on a hillside bathed in moonlight. The English were understandably nervous as some months earlier a railcar had been ambushed by two robbers who had shot six English passengers and then run away without taking anything. It was suspected to be the handiwork of Indian terrorists. Somebody switched on the radio of the derailed car and tuned in to the BBC Overseas Service. Election results were being announced. The Labour Party had won a landslide victory and Clement Attlee was named Prime Minister of England. The English passengers heard the news in grave silence. The other Indian, whom I did not know, and I leapt up and embraced each other. We knew that with the Socialists in power in England, independence for India was indeed round the corner.

I had no illusions about the Muslim-Hindu/Sikh social divide. Even in the High Court Bar Association and Library, Muslim lawyers occupied different corners of the lounge and the library from Hindus and Sikhs. There was a certain amount of superficial mixing at weddings and funerals, but this was only to keep up appearances. After the Muslim League resolution demanding Pakistan, the cleavage became wide and continued to grow wider. The demand for Pakistan assumed the proportions of an avalanche gathering force as it went along. Every other afternoon huge processions of Muslims marched down the Mall chanting in unison:

Pakistan ka naaraah kya?
La illaha illallah

What is the slogan of Pakistan?
There is but one God, He is Allah.

An instance of how deep the poison had spread was a case in which I appeared as Manzur's junior. It concerned a Sikh widow of considerable wealth and beauty named Sardarni Prem Prakash Kaur. She had been married to the only son of a wealthy contractor of Ludhiana. Her husband was a debauchee. He contracted syphilis and died without consummating his marriage. The entire estate came to the young widow. One day, while holidaying in Simla, she happened to be having tea at Davico's. A young Muslim strolling down the Mall saw her sitting alone by the window. Their eyes met and her smile assured him that he would not be unwelcome. He joined her for tea. They became lovers. The young man was handsome, but the good-for-nothing son of a barber. He began to live off Prem Prakash Kaur. They had two sons. Then Prem Prakash Kaur tired of her uncouth lover. Her cousin Gurnam Singh, as handsome as he was cultured, a Barrister-at-law with a large practice in Lyallpur (he was a close friend of Manzur Qadir) decided to rescue Prem Prakash from the clutches of the barber's son. Prem Prakash moved in with Gurnam. Her Muslim lover took her to court over the custody of the two boys. He claimed she had converted to Islam, married him by Islamic rites, and their

boys were circumcised and given Muslim names. Besides marriage
and custody of children, there were criminal cases of trespass and
forcible seizure of property. As these cases moved from the lower
courts to the appellate, the pattern became evident; if the presiding
officer was Muslim, it went in favour of the barber's son; if Hindu or
Sikh, in favour of the Sikh widow. I came in on the scene when the
case of marriage and custody came up for hearing before Donald
Falshaw, then a District and Sessions Judge. I was engaged in order to
give the case a non-communal flavour, as I was known to be friendly
with Donald and his wife Joan.

But for the partition of India in August 1947, the case might still
be going on. Prem Prakash Kaur and all her property were in East
Punjab, which came to India. The barber's son was left in Pakistan.
Gurnam migrated to East Punjab, became its Chief Minister, and
resumed his liaison with Prem Prakash. He was later appointed Indian
High Commissioner to Australia. A few days thereafter, returning
home to collect his belongings, he was killed in an air crash.

*

The atmosphere became so charged with hate that it needed only a
spark to set the Punjab ablaze. The year-long Hindu-Muslim riots in
Calcutta led to massacres of Muslims in Bihar, then to massacres of
Hindus in Noakhali in East Bengal. Then Muslims of the NWFP
[North-West Frontier Province] raided and scattered Sikh and Hindu
villagers and slew as many as they could lay their hands on. Others
fled their homes to safety in Lahore, Amritsar, and East Punjab.

*

Suddenly riots broke out in Lahore. They were sparked off by the
Sikh leader Master Tara Singh making a melodramatic gesture outside
the Punjab Legislative Assembly building. Inside the Chamber, the
Chief Minister, Khizar Hayat Tiwana, had succumbed to pressure
from the Muslim League and resigned. It was now clear that the
Muslims of the Punjab had also opted for Pakistan. As soon as the
session was over, Master Tara Singh drew his *kirpan* out of its sheath

and yelled '*Pakistan murdabad*' (death to Pakistan). It was like hurling a lighted matchstick into a room full of explosive gas. Communal riots broke out all over the province. Muslims had the upper hand in the killings. They were in the majority, better organized and better motivated than Hindus or Sikhs. The Punjab police was largely Muslim and shamelessly prejudiced in favour of their co-religionists. The only organized group to offer resistance to Muslim gangs was the RSS, but all it could do was to explode a few bombs, killing perhaps one or two people. Then it disappeared from the scene. Urban Sikhs were a pathetic lot. They boasted of their martial prowess (they had none) and waved long *kirpans* they had never wielded before.

One day a Bihari working at a petrol station which I used was knifed to death in broad daylight by two Muslim boys aged eleven and twelve. Unsuspecting Sikhs, riding bicycles, were toppled over by ropes stretched across roads being suddenly raised from either side, and stabbed. Our nights were disturbed by sudden outbursts of cries of '*Allah-o-Akbar*' from one side replied to by '*Sat Sri Akal*' and '*Har Har Mahadev*' from the other. Muslims had more confidence. They would come close to Hindu and Sikh localities and shout '*Hoshiyaar! Shikar ka hai intezaar!*' (Beware, we await our quarry.)

Whatever little resistance Hindus and Sikhs put up against Muslim *goondaism* collapsed one hot afternoon in June 1947. We heard no sounds of gunfire or yelling; we saw only black clouds of smoke billowing out of the city. The entirely Hindu *mohalla* of Shahalmi had been set on fire. Hindus and Sikhs began to leave Lahore, taking whatever they could with them. A few days later, they were forced out without being allowed to take anything. Their homes and belongings were taken over by their Muslim neighbours.

I did not know how long I would be able to stay on in Lahore. I had sent my two small children to their maternal grandparents in Kasauli. My next-door neighbours on either side proclaimed their religious identity on their walls; a large cross on the one side to indicate they were Christians; on the other, big letters in Urdu stating *Parsee ka Makaan* (this is a Parsee home). Close by lived Justice Taja Singh. He had often exhorted me and other Sikhs to stick it out. One morning early in August when I drove up to his house, I found it padlocked. The *chowkidar* told me that his master had left for Delhi. It was my college friend from London days, C.H. Everette, then head of the CID, who advised me to leave Lahore for a few days till the situation returned to normal. 'Leave your home and things in the care of some Muslim friend,' he advised. Manzur was at the time doing some case in Simla. I rang him up and we arranged to meet at Dharampur on the Kalka-Simla road, near where the road to Kasauli branches off. The following night my wife and I and our Hindu cook were escorted by a posse of Baloch policemen provided by Everette to the railway station. We left our young Sikh servant, Dalip Singh, in charge of our house till the Qadirs moved in to look after it. We arrived next morning at Kalka without any untoward incident. I had sent my car ahead to meet us there. We drove up to Dharampur. A few minutes later Manzur arrived by taxi from Simla. He told me that some Kashmiri Muslim labourers had been stabbed in Simla and Muslims were pulling out of Himachal hill resorts. I handed him the keys of my house. We embraced each other. I promised to get back as soon as things were more settled.

We spent some days at Kasauli. By then the mass exodus of Hindus and Sikhs from Pakistan and Muslims from East Punjab had begun. There were gory tales of attacks on trains and road convoys in which thousands were massacred in cold blood. Sikhs who had taken a terrible beating in West Punjab were out seeking bloody revenge on innocent Muslims of East Punjab, mopping up one Muslim village after another. I decided to run the gauntlet and get to Delhi. I had to make up my mind about what to do. I left my wife and children at Kasauli. I took a motor mechanic with me in the event of the car giving trouble. Some miles beyond Kalka I discovered that petrol stations along the road were closed. I returned to Kalka to fill up the tank and take a spare can of petrol. On the way I found our servant Dalip Singh walking along the road. He told me that Muslim mobs had come to the house. The Qadirs and their servants had hidden him in an attic for several days. Manzur had removed my name from the gate and put up his own in its place. However, word had leaked out that a Sikh was being given shelter and *goondas* wanted to search the house. Manzur was able to get the police just in time to prevent them breaking in. That night he put Dalip Singh in the boot of his car and drove him to the new Indo-Pak border. He gave him money and instructed him

to board a train going from Amritsar to Kalka. That is how he came
to be there. Not having heard of Kasauli, the fellow had taken the
road to Delhi hoping to catch a bus somewhere on the way.

I put Dalip Singh in the car, took enough petrol to get us to
Delhi, and proceeded on my way. There was not a soul on the road, no
sign of life in any of the towns or villages through which we passed.
It was only after I had passed Karnal, some sixty miles short of Delhi,
that I saw a jeep coming towards me. I pulled up. So did the jeep,
about a hundred yards from me. I took out my pistol and waited.
After an agonizing five minutes of staring at the jeep, I noticed that
its occupants were Sikhs. Two men stepped out on the road with
rifles in their hands. I felt reassured and drove up to the jeep. I asked
them if it was safe to proceed to Delhi. 'Quite safe,' they assured me.
'We have killed the lot in villages along the road.' They used the word
sooar (pig) for Muslims. It churned my stomach. This was no place to
argue with them.

I arrived safely in Delhi, a few days before India was to be declared
independent. I had my father's home to go to. Hundreds of thousands
of others who like me had fled Pakistan had nowhere to go.

Awaaz De Kahan Hai: A Portrait of Nur Jehan

Khalid Hasan

I always found it difficult to imagine a world where there would be no Madam Nur Jehan, but the unthinkable came to pass in the year 2000. Nur Jehan is gone, but her voice lives in the music she left us.

Born in Kasur in 1926 and named Allah Wasai, she was the youngest in a family of thirteen. She had six sisters and of her seven brothers three ended up in mental institutions. Nur Jehan looked after the financial needs of her large family all her life. Once she said, 'People ask me why I don't stop working. Well, how can I? If I don't work, who is going to take care of all these people?'

According to *Film Stars*, a compendium published in Lahore in 1933, Nur Jehan 'is slim, delicate and beautiful. She has soft black hair and bewitching eyes. She joined Kohinoor United Artists and appeared in some of their films. Later, she was employed by Seven United Artists and played the lead in some films opposite Khalil. She recently appeared in *Patit Pawan*.'

Nur Jehan made her first film when she was only four years old.

She always wanted her year of birth to remain a mystery. When I first met her in 1967 in Lahore, she told me, 'People often wonder how old I am. Let me tell you. In terms of experience of life and men, I have always been a hundred years old.'

Her nightingale voice was first heard over sixty years ago in the music halls of Lahore and the smaller towns of Punjab. It was an electrifying voice, never false on pitch, never striking an untrue note. She did not fritter away her gift. She worked indefatigably, always honing and polishing the genius she had been invested with.

Nur Jehan went through good times and bad, marriages, divorces, heartbreaks, casual and serious love affairs, fame, fortune, loneliness and, in the last years of her life, unremitting ill health. She bore it all with quiet grace and never looked for pity.

Shaukat Hussain Rizvi, once her great love, who wrote *Nur Jehan ki Kahani Meri Zubani*, in which he denigrated her origins, she found hard to forgive. I once asked her if newspaper reports claiming she had made up with him were true. 'True?' she exclaimed. 'How can I forgive him after what he did to me? He wails and cries that all he wants is my forgiveness. But how can I ever forget how he treated me, what he did to my children?'

I said, 'I thought you had a soft heart.'

'Not for him,' she replied. 'Not for that woman, Gittho Begum,' she added. Vintage Nur Jehan. Gittho Begum was her name for the actress Yasmin whom Rizvi married after divorcing Nur Jehan. Yasmin was short, hence the name.

After her heart bypass operation she was not sure she would be able to sing again, but six weeks later, assailed by doubt, she sat down one morning and began to sing. 'I sang for forty-five minutes and my voice was good and strong and I was overcome by my gratitude to God. I love my work. When I sing, I feel the presence of God. It is my world, my life, my faith. Only God knows what goes through my heart, how I feel. My only aim now is to bring happiness to others, to serve the people, to build hospitals, to help my children.'

In a conversation with Naveed Riaz in Lahore in the 1980s, she remembered her early years and spoke about them movingly. 'I was only fifteen when I became a mother [she was actually sixteen and a half or seventeen, having married Syed Shaukat Hussain Rizvi in 1943]. I did not know anything about children. I thought of myself as a child. I really was too young to understand anything.' Then she spoke about her mother. 'After my morning *riaz*, a teacher would come to help me learn how to read and write. At times, I found that a bit much, and so, one day, I declared that I was not going to study any more. That was the only time my mother hit me. She struck me just once and said, "*Nahin, Nooriji, tussi parho gai.*" Now that I think about it, had it not been for her, I would not have learnt to read and write. When I record a song, I have the words in front of me on a sheet of paper. And, by God, every time I look at that sheet of paper, I remember and bless my mother. You know, so much time has passed, but I can still feel the thrill of riding on my father's shoulder as he walked through the street. There I am, perched high, looking down on people and shops. O, I remember those days!'

When Nur Jehan first suffered a heart ailment, I remember saying, 'But of course it had to be the heart, considering how many claimants it has had and how often it has fluttered for those on whom she has chosen to smile.' We always believed 'The Madam' to be indestructible. Her death, therefore, was the kind of loss that takes a long time to reconcile with. She suffered much pain in her last years. Now at last she is in peace.

My friend M. Rafiq, who lives in London and who has spent the better part of his working life on researching Indian and Pakistani cinema, is the greatest authority on Nur Jehan's career. He has established that Nur Jehan's family first moved to Lahore from Kasur, where her elder sisters, Eiden and Haider Bandi began a stage career. Nur Jehan accompanied them in a song extolling the Holy Prophet of Islam (may peace be upon him) that became a great hit. Its opening line was: *Hanste hain sitaaare, ya Shah-e-Madina* and it was composed by G.A. Chisti. Around 1930, the family moved again, this time to Calcutta, where, it was hoped, the two older girls would be able to make an entry into films. This did not happen, though they continued to appear on the stage. Nur Jehan won a part in a silent movie called *Hind ke Tare*, made by Indian Pictures, Calcutta. Thereafter, the family moved to Bombay where, in 1931, Nur Jehan made ten silent films: *Brave Warrior, Chandramani, Goodbye Kingship, Heart Thief, Jang-e-Daulat, Magic of Love, Necklace, Prithviraj, Shaliwahan* and *Song of Sorrow*.

The first Punjabi film, *Sheila: Pind di Kudi*, was made in Calcutta in 1936. By this time, Nur Jehan was beginning to be recognized as a singing actress of some merit. The producer, K.D. Mehra, remembering the popularity of the sisters' devotional song earlier, used it in his film. It was sung in Urdu and was a bit of a misfit in a Punjabi film. Nur Jehan was also given a Punjabi song in the film. Her first talkie was *Sassi Punnu*, made in Bombay in 1932 and her last film in India was *Mirza Saahibaan*, released in 1947. Between 1932 and 1947, she sang 127 film songs and appeared in sixty-nine movies that included *Zeenat, Anmol Ghadi, Jugnu* and *Mira Bai*. Fifty-five of her movies were made in Bombay, eight in Calcutta, five in Lahore and one in Rangoon, Burma.

In Pakistan, Nur Jehan starred in thirteen films, starting with *Chanway* (1951) and ending with *Mirza Ghalib* (1961).

In an interview with Naveed Riaz, she said that she did not like to step out of her home and she had never liked parties. She also preferred to avoid hotels and public gatherings. 'I want to lead a simple, uncomplicated life,' she added. Her eldest daughter, Zil-e-Huma, she said, only saw the inside of Shahnur Studio in Lahore after she was married. Her three daughters from her marriage with Ejaz Durrani had never done that even once, she added with a tinge of pride.

For a woman who was a women's libber even before there was women's lib, Nur Jehan was conservative. Her views on women were surprisingly old-fashioned, or perhaps they were cynical. This always surprised me because they came from a woman who had lived life on her own terms and owed little to anyone. Although Shaukat Hussain Rizvi claimed in his book on his former wife that it was he who had made Nur Jehan a star, it was not so. Nur Jehan was a star before she met Rizvi. In any case, who could stop a talent as formidable and unique from universal recognition? She said in an interview in 1981, 'If a woman works, what does she get at the end of the day? The only peace she knows is within the four walls of her home. Who can work harder than I have? And what peace, I ask you, have I known? Once the husband realizes that his wife can earn more than him, he begins to hate her. He wants her to be dependent on him. Totally. She wants to buy a sweater for herself? He would rather that she begged him for it . . . It seems to me that she can only have a good marriage if she has nothing.'

Yet she narrated with pride how one of her daughters was able to learn French, use a typewriter and ride a horse. 'You know what I told her?' she asked. 'I said you should think of making a home. What do you want to be? A polo player? A woman's ultimate fulfilment is her husband, her children and her home. That's what it's all about in this society.'

She talked once about the stirring songs she sang in 1965, at the time of Pakistan's first war with India. 'My musicians used to tell me to get into the trench when our session was on and the siren sounded. I would tell them, "If we have to go, let it be in front of the microphone, singing. Think of the boys who are out there fighting." When I sang *Merya dhol sipahaya*, it was not pre-recorded. I sang it straight into the microphone and it went live because the tape recorder was not working. It was a very poignant moment for me and I cried a lot. Hassan Latif, who was like a brother to me, helped me and gave me a lot of encouragement. He said I was like Umme Kulsum. I have never forgotten his words.'

Rizvi, whom she married after a turbulent love affair in Lahore and Bombay and divorced after they came to Pakistan, recalled the first time he set eyes on her, in his book. She was no more than eight or nine. They were in Calcutta. He was film editor at a movie studio owned by Rai Bahadur Seth Dalsukh Karnani, a colourful and eccentric character who, despite his years, always had an eye out for a pretty girl. Karnani asked the manager of the Corinthian Theatre to go to the Punjab and come back with some girls. The man came back with fifteen to twenty of them, collectively referred to as the 'Punjab Mail'. Among the group were Nur Jehan and her sisters, and one of the girls, Rashida, who was related to Nur Jehan, was installed as the Rai Bahadur's mistress.

When Rizvi was asked to come to Lahore to direct *Khandan* in 1942, Nur Jehan, who with her sisters was in a dance group which performed from town to town, was in Amritsar. He was to choose a heroine for the new movie which was being produced by Dalsukh Pancholi. He recalls that through the help of S.P. Singha, who was vice chancellor of the Punjab University, several girls were sent over for audition but he did not like any of them. He wanted his heroine to look no more than fifteen or sixteen on the screen, which was how old Nur Jehan was at the time. She was sent for but he did not tell her that she was going to play the lead. That was when their affair began. She married Rizvi against the wishes of her brothers who did not wish to lose her. She was the main draw of the roving dance company.

One day, during the shooting, Rizvi said to Nur Jehan by way of a joke, 'What sort of oil do you use on your hair? It smells awful.' He says the moment the words left his mouth she burst out crying and would not stop. 'I should have been warned that she was a very dangerous woman but I was in love. I could not see that.' As a result of this incident, the shooting remained interrupted for five or six days. One day, old Pancholi sent for Rizvi and said, 'Look Shaukat, let this remain a little game between the two of you. Don't let it go too far.' He wrote, 'To this day, his words ring in my ears. But I was blinded by love.'

In Rizvi's words, 'She was having this affair with me on the one hand, while carrying on with some others on the side. One day, I ran into a friend on the Mall [in Lahore] who said there was someone looking for me.' He was led to a house off the Mall where he was surprised to meet Nur Jehan. But she was not alone. In her wake came Hasan Amin. It seems they were having a playful pillow fight. 'I was taken aback,' wrote Rizvi. 'Here was the woman who used to assure me of her love . . . I asked Hasan Amin what it all meant. He replied that it was Nur Jehan's idea. She wanted him to send for me. The idea was to make me jealous.' Her family, he adds, was in on the little game.

I met Hasan Amin at his home in Islamabad in the summer of 1999, when he told me of his lifelong infatuation with Nur Jehan. He told me that Nur Jehan had been his first love. He was a student at Government College, Lahore, when he first saw her, performing with her sisters on the stage. He was smitten. He chased her all the way to Kasur and despite the opposition of her family, Nur Jehan had an affair with him. Earlier that day, there had been a rumour that Nur Jehan had died in Karachi. Hasan Amin said he would phone her which he did. He kept saying to her, 'Nuri, please forgive me.' We were thrilled to find that she was alive, though she was very ill. When I told Hasan Amin, 'We have got to celebrate this', he grandly replied, 'Then we will celebrate it with champagne.'

'Champagne in Islamabad?' I asked.

'Yes, indeed, champagne in Islamabad.' He produced a bottle of fine French champagne with which we toasted Madam's health. I asked Hasan why he was asking her to forgive him. 'She wanted me to marry her, but all I wanted to do in those days was play cricket,' he said wistfully.

But returning to Shaukat Hussain Rizvi. Nur Jehan promised to drop all other lovers and their affair was revived. She told him of her family ill-treating her and of her being beaten up by her brothers. Rizvi told her to make a declaration to that effect (before a judge) but she did not do that. Meanwhile, their affair became torrid. *Khandan* was now near completion. One day, when the studio car went to fetch her from Hira Mandi, Lahore's famous flesh district (where she was staying), there was word waiting that the family had left. Seth Dalsukh Pancholi, being a man of influence, had forty members of her family arrested from Kasur and brought to Lahore. The scene to be shot that day included the actors Ghulam Muhammad, Pran, the hero, and Nur Jehan. Her elder brother made a scene and Nur Jehan began to cry, complaining about the harassment from her family. Rizvi told her to tell the judge the truth and declare that she wanted to marry Shaukat Hussain Rizvi. She promised to do so. Her brother Shafi told the judge that the family was afraid Rizvi would abduct Nur Jehan. But when the judge brought up the matter and placed the case before her, she said that Shaukat Hussain Rizvi was like a 'brother'. This, Rizvi wrote, was typical of her, adding that he could narrate not one but 'two thousand five hundred' such stories.

Khandan was released and it was an immediate hit. Rizvi went home to see his parents in the United Provinces. When he returned to Lahore, Nur Jehan told him that she had been forced to make the 'brother' statement in Lahore because of pressure from her brothers. The two made up and, before long, were married. However, more trouble awaited them. Nur Jehan's parents filed a suit against Rizvi, charging him with abduction. Rizvi sent for her birth certificate from Kasur (reproduced in the book) which listed Nur Jehan's mother's profession as 'tawaif' or prostitute. According to the same document, her date of birth is 21 September 1926.

Rizvi and Nur Jehan's first two children, Akbar and Asghar, were born in Bombay. After *Khandan*, Nur Jehan's career soared and she made several movies. The family left Bombay around the time of Partition and eventually settled in Lahore where Rizvi bought the abandoned Shorey Studio which he turned into Shahnur Studios. Rizvi writes that while he was at work, she would be at play with Ajay Kumar, the male lead in *Dupatta*, her second movie in Pakistan.

Her romance with Pakistan's debonair opening batsman Nazar Muhammad began during the filming of *Chanway*, according to Rizvi. During the 1953 martial law in Lahore after the outbreak of the anti-Ahmediyya riots, Rizvi says that Nur Jehan, who had a curfew pass, would put on a white burqa and go to Hira Mandi to meet Nazar. Rizvi's informers told him of these secret assignations. One day, he followed her and found this was true. Whenever he questioned her about Nazar, she said that he was like a son to her. However, the scandal became so embarrassing that Rizvi decided to take action. One afternoon, when his driver told him that he had dropped off Nur Jehan at a house in Islamia Park where she had a date with Nazar, Rizvi, along with two carloads of friends and helpers, went to the house. It belonged to an old man who sold amulets and traditional medicines. Rizvi knocked at the door—his men had surrounded the place—and when it was answered, demanded to know if Nur Jehan was inside.

The old man pretended that he did not know who Nur Jehan was. The enraged Rizvi began to climb the stairs to the upper floor that had only one room. The old man began to shout and scream to warn the lovers of the raid. Rizvi says he saw the two of them lying in bed. If he'd had a gun, he adds, he would have shot them both. Nazar jumped out of bed and leapt out of the window to fall twenty-five feet below, and broke both his arms. Rizvi's helpers caught him nevertheless. Nur Jehan came down and began to scream, saying it was her husband who was passing her on to other men. She made such a racket that people from the neighbouring houses came out. Soon there was a crowd of about two hundred. Nazar had, in the meantime, lost consciousness. Mian Ehsan of Crescent Films arrived on the scene and took Nur Jehan away. Nazar never played cricket again. It was one of the greatest tragedies of Pakistani cricket.

Rizvi accuses her of having several affairs, one after another. According to him she had an affair with the hero of her first film, Anwar Jahangir Khan as well as cinematographer Raza Mir. Also with M. Naseem, often referred to as Naseem Popularwala, owner of the film distribution company, Popular Pictures, Royal Park, Lahore. This dates back to August 1958 when her marriage to Rizvi was practically over.

Rizvi's account of Nur Jehan is unrelieved by humour or any hint of the love he had once felt for her. It was a little late for him to regret having fallen for the fledgling enchantress from Kasur with a voice like molten silver. In his memoir he repeatedly expresses regret at having married her when he could have married a high-born girl from a nawab or jagirdar family. Perhaps, but Rizvi will ultimately be remembered more for having once been Nur Jehan's husband than for his work.

In Rizvi's small-minded and partisan account of their life together, not once has he acknowledged Nur Jehan's musical genius. Women like Nur Jehan cannot be judged by standards applicable to normal human beings. She was an extraordinary woman whose virtues and failings by the very nature of her greatness remained extraordinary.

I am concerned with the Nur Jehan I admired all my life, with all her faults and failings and all her glorious attributes, not least her music and the professionalism that she brought to her work. She demanded respect and she got it. You could not make one slighting remark about Nur Jehan in the movie industry and get away with it. Madam's network of spies was extensive and their loyalty to her legendary. When I first met the brilliant music director Hassan Latif (*Lat uljhi suljha ja re balam, Meray hathon mein mehndi laggi* and *Ja apni hasraton pay aansoo baha ke so ja*) at Nur Jehan's Gulberg Home in 1969 (now demolished), she introduced him by saying, 'He is my gang.'

Madam's liaisons were part of her legend. Did anyone ever directly ask her about them? One person who did was Raja Tajammul Hussain. 'All half-truths,' Nur Jehan had told him. 'Then let's have some half-truths,' he ventured, 'the serious half-truths, that is.' She was in one of her throwaway moods and said, 'All right then,' and began to pull out names from her photographic memory. After a few minutes, she asked Tajammul, 'And how many affairs have you had?'

'Sixteen, so far,' Tajammul replied with a straight face. Her response in Punjabi remains a Nur Jehan classic: '*Hai Allah! Na na kardian wi solan ho gai nain!*'

Those who knew Nur Jehan will stand witness to the great love she always bore for her children. Her large home in the Liberty Chowk in Lahore's Gulberg, which she had been smart enough to get declared commercial property, was sold for Rs 20 crore. She gave each of her six children—Akbar, Asghar, Zil-e-Huma, Hina, Shazia and Nazia—Rs 2.5 crore. She was truly happy and relieved after she did that.

Madam was a lady who was better not crossed, especially by other ladies. There were stories that she had roughed up the actress Nighat Sultana, who had either said something catty about her behind her back or whom she suspected of flirting with her husband. At that time, she still cared. Another fledgling singer who had bragged about being as good as Nur Jehan was given such a tongue-lashing that she broke down. Around 1994–95, Nur Jehan had a run-in with the singer Tahira Syed who had spoken about her in dismissive terms. She had said she could not listen to more than a couple of her songs at a time as she found her voice tiresome. She had then added that her favourite singers were Nusrat Fateh Ali Khan and Ataullah Khan Isakhelvi and that she could listen to them endlessly. She had also said that Nur Jehan was not a 'professional' singer but only sang off and on to raise money for 'good causes'.

The matter might have proceeded no further, except that when Madam expressed displeasure, Tahira Syed's mother Malika Pukhraj advised her daughter to apologize, adding, 'Everyone knows who we are and everyone knows who *she* is.' The reaction to this remark in the Lahore film circles was immediate. They rose like an indivisible unit in Madam's defence, denounced the two women and declared that there was only one Madam Nur Jehan. And Madam had the last word. Of Ataullah Khan Isakhelvi, the truckers' favourite, she said, 'What he sings does not conform to what I have been taught as music.' And, well, she could say that. Even the great Bade Ghulam Ali Khan recognized her prowess and was proud to accept her as a pupil—it was a gesture of respect Nur Jehan showed to the legendary maestro; the fact was that whatever there was to know about the mysteries and intricacies of music, she already knew. When she died, one of her great aunts said that when Nur Jehan was born, her father's sister, on hearing her wail, said to her brother, 'This one even wails in accordance with the scale.'

Madam also had a famous passage-of-arms with Musarrat Nazir in 1988. Madam was not exactly thrilled that Ms Nazir should have scored one of the biggest popular hits in memory with the song *Mera laung gavacha*. The song is about a girl who drops her tiny jewelled nose-pin as she runs breathlessly through a grove of trees at night. The young man who follows her she consigns to a destiny to forever look for the missing ornament. Madam got so tired of everyone raving about *Laung gavacha* that she recorded her own version of the song which, to her chagrin, sank without a trace.

I recall asking her if she was envious of Ms Nazir's success.

'Envious!' she replied, her voice full of derision, 'I can only feel envious of a singer, but Musarrat . . .?' Later, in Toronto, I asked Musarrat what had happened. She swore to me on oath that messages had been conveyed to her on Madam's behalf that if she did not return to wherever she had come from on the very same pair of feet that had brought her to Lahore, the consequences would not be pleasant. Even black magic (which Shaukat Hussain Rizvi swore Madam was adept at) was mentioned.

I first met Madam Nur Jehan in 1967 when she was going through a messy divorce with Ejaz, an actor who had no talent, only looks, whom she had married some years earlier and whose film career she had helped build. Three daughters and many infidelities later, it was over. During those days I saw a good deal of her. Always smitten with her voice, I came to admire her sharp intellect, her puckish sense of humour and her insight into life and people.

Years later, when Ejaz was picked up at Heathrow airport with a cache of narcotics concealed in film cans and sentenced to four years in prison, it was Nur Jehan who came to his rescue. She paid the lawyers' considerable fees, and this despite her reputation for being tight-fisted. The man who had left her to raise three daughters alone she helped generously in adversity. That was a side of Nur Jehan which was not commonly known. She kept a careful eye on her money but she could also be generous, especially when it came to those she had affection for.

Though it is now thirty-five years since I first set eyes on her, I remember my first meeting with Madam as if it were yesterday. I was doing a story on her divorce for the *Pakistan Times*. Nur Jehan had a listed phone number. Against her name, the telephone department had printed the utterly unnecessary words 'Film Star'.

I found the number either engaged or unattended. But I persisted and was finally rewarded when Madam answered it herself. 'Hello,' she said and I knew it was her. That hello was music to my ears. When I told her who I was and why I had called, she said, 'You people never write the truth.'

'Try me,' I replied quickly. 'What you say will be printed exactly as you say it.' When I told her which paper I worked for, she sounded reassured. The *Pakistan Times* was very prestigious. But I hadn't won yet because the next thing she said was, 'But that is an English newspaper and I can't give you an interview in English.' Then she laughed, a teasing, flirtatious laugh, very Nur Jehan. 'But you know I am not an *anparh*. I can do a bit of *gitter-mitter*.' She also told me I had an honest voice and would I come that afternoon. She asked me if I knew where she lived. 'Yes, Madam, I do indeed. The entire world knows where you live. Bang in front of the United Christian Hospital, the big white house with the black steel gate.' (The Liberty Market came up later on.)

I was shown into the living room which was small but appropriate, with Madam's awards displayed in a glass cabinet. Tea came first on an elegant silver tray. A few minutes later, Madam appeared. She looked stunning in a white sari. She wore diamonds on her fingers and her golden bracelets jangled as she poured a cup of tea for me. I asked her if she always wore white. 'When I entered the film industry, I was very young and uncertain of myself,' she said. 'On my first or second day on the set at the old Pancholi Studio in Lahore, I was struck by a tall, elegant woman, who wore a shimmering white sari. She looked so graceful. She was always in white. She looked so at ease, so much at peace with herself and the world.' What her name was, Madam did not tell me. I guessed she was some producer or director's mistress. 'From that day on, I have worn white. I am a hoarder of clothes and jewellery and I have so much that it is sometimes years before I wear the same sari. I wear colours occasionally, but white is my colour.'

She talked about Ejaz and said she had really loved him when they had got married. He was a nobody, just a boy from Gujarat whom she took under her wing. She asked me if I knew any of his brothers. When I said I did not, she said, 'Well, you shouldn't because no two look alike.' And why was that, I asked. 'Because they are all *haramzadas*,' she replied, sired by different fathers. She laughed, then added, 'I can be very coarse when I want to, coarser than men can ever be. I don't often get angry, but when I do, you would be shocked at the profanities I let fly.' I was to get some evidence of that on a couple of occasions in the next few weeks. She also told me some not-very-nice stories about the women in Ejaz's family. She said I was free to quote her. 'No, thank you, Madam,' I replied, and she laughed again.

She admitted that she had been in a few relationships since Shaukat Rizvi but they had left her unhappy and dissatisfied. Emotionally, she had been adrift. 'I have to be intensely involved with a man, otherwise I cannot sing. My music abandons me.' She said she had helped launch Ejaz's career. Ejaz, his head swollen by success, had begun to drift away from her. He had even hit her on a couple of occasions, but what had broken the marriage was his public affair with the actress Firdaus whom Nur Jehan called 'common'. She predicted that the Ejaz–Firdaus thing would end in disaster. It did.

Ejaz, she said, began to play around with extras and starlets, most of them from 'the area'. As time passed, his escapades became more indiscreet. 'I have been around long enough to know that all men like to play around. A wise woman accepts this and lives with it. But there is one condition which must never be violated. The philandering husband must conduct his liaisons with discretion. He must not flaunt his lechery.' She told me where she had drawn the line. 'Every evening he would drive in front of our house with that woman (Firdaus) sitting next to him. He would stop the car briefly, honk a couple of times and move on. I told him that was where he got off. "Pack your bags and get out," I said, and that was that.' She added, 'I am a fair woman and I was a good wife to him. I never played around while we were married and I tell you all I have to do is to flutter my eyelashes and men come running.'

What sort of men did she like? Would she name someone she found irresistible? 'Yes,' she smiled, 'that American actor in the movie *Ben Hur*.'

'Charlton Heston,' I replied.

'That's the sort of man I like,' she said.

'Tell me more about men,' I asked her.

She smiled coquettishly, threw her head back and laughed. She said in Punjabi, '*Jadon mein koi sohna banda takni aan te mainoon khud bud shooroo ho jandi ai.*' Difficult to translate, but roughly: When I see a handsome man, I experience a restless curiosity in my heart.

Nur Jehan was a woman with an amazing will. On one occasion, she said to me, 'In this society, what is a woman worth? Nothing! She is just a piece of furniture that can be shifted around. She has no power. She lives at the mercy of her parents, brothers, husbands and lovers. I am what I am today because I have struggled. What I have, I have won with my own hard work.' So true.

The late Naseer Anwar once told me a lovely story about Nur Jehan. It was in the 1930s; the city Lahore. The devotees of a local Pir had arranged a special evening of devotional music in his honour. Among those who performed was a little girl who sang some *naats*. 'Sing us something in Punjabi, *beti*,' the Pir said to her. She immediately launched into a Punjabi folk song, a line of which went something like this: 'May the kite of this land of five rivers touch the skies.' As she sang the words in her young, perfectly modulated voice, the Pir went into a trance. Then he rose, put his hand on the girl's head and prophesied, 'Go forth, little girl, your kite will one day touch the skies.' How Pakistan has regressed since then was brought home to me in the late 1970s when a mullah in Lahore issued a fatwa against Nur Jehan, declaring her 'outside the pale of Islam for having said that music was a form of worship'.

At an earlier meeting she tells me about growing up in Kasur. She says she was taught classical music by Ustad Ghulam Muhammad and that her 'film line' ustad was Master Ghulam Haider. She says he also taught her how to stand before a microphone and how to render words such as *hai* and *mohabat*; also how to breathe while singing. She says, 'We were brought up with great love. Our parents doted on us and told us that true joy resides in your own heart and you always carry it with you, no matter where in the world you go. Nobody can bring you joy if you do not have it within your heart.' She says many of the things her parents told her have guided her through life. 'My father used to say, if you cannot help people you should not harm them. I have always remembered that. He also used to recite Kabir: *Aey Kabira teri jhonpari jal-kattion ke paas: Jo karainge so bhariange, too kyoon bhayo udas.* Because of my parents' influence, we grew up honest and hard-working, never greedy or envious of others who had more. We were happy with what we had. We were not ashamed of our slender means. It was not important. When I was a child, there was one prayer I always used to say: O God, do not make me dependent on anyone except on Your own glorious mercy. I have taught the same thing to my daughters.'

Nur Jehan had scored a succession of great Punjabi hits by the time she was cast for *Khandan* in 1942. Her other Urdu hit was *Zeenat*, made in 1945. Everyone remembers to this day the famous qawwali, the first one recorded in female voices, in which Nur Jehan's voice rose above the voices of all others, including Zohra Bai Ambalaywali's and Amir Karnatki's. It was like a flame leaping out. The words were by Nakhshab: *Ahain na bharen, shikway na kiye*. Her other great hits were *Bari Maan, Dost, Lal Haveli* and *Gaoon ki Gori*, the last starring the Lahore-born actor Nazir. One of Nur Jehan's last films in India in 1947 was *Jugnu* that launched the careers of two legendary figures, Dilip Kumar and Muhammad Rafi. The music by Feroz Nizami was a smash, including hits like *Aaj ki raat* and *Yahan badla wafa ka bewafai ke siva kya hai*. Another distinguishing feature of the movie in which Nur Jehan played a college girl who dies of consumption and unrequited love, was a song by one of the great female classical singers of all time, Malika-e-Mauseeqi Roshan Ara Begum. The song she sang was *Des ki pur kaif rangeen si fizaon mein kahin*. The movie was the peak of Shaukat Hussain Rizvi's career. He was never fated to equal that success.

Immediately after the break-up of Pakistan in 1971 (when East Pakistan became Bangladesh), there was a sustained campaign against Nur Jehan for her 'amorous' links with General Yahya Khan. The salacious stories circulated about their relationship had little basis in fact. Yahya enjoyed good company, and there was no better 'company' to be had than Madam's. She used to call him *sarkar*. She told me there was one song he was particularly fond of and she often sang it for him: *Saiyo ni mera mahi merey bhag jagawan aa gya*. Once Yahya Khan said to General Hamid, his friend and evening companion, 'Ham, if I were to make Nuri Chief of Staff, I tell you she would do a damn better job of it than the lot of you put together.' I asked Nur Jehan about Yahya Khan and she said, 'He was a gentleman; kind, humorous and very human. I had tremendous respect for him. I sang at his son Ali's wedding.'

Not long after Zulfikar Ali Bhutto took office, the Pakistan Peoples Party newspaper *Musawat* ran a number of stories about Nur Jehan's close and 'scandalous' association with General Yahya Khan. She was outraged. In a press statement, she said if she really was the sort of woman she was being portrayed as, she would rather leave Pakistan never to return. She also tried to approach Bhutto who did not have time to see her. She called me a couple of times and I said I would do my best. Noor Muhammad Mughal or Noora, Bhutto's personal valet and a man you could ignore only at your peril, was a great admirer of Nur Jehan. One day, he took a copy of *Musawat* that carried a story about Madam complete with pictures, over to Bhutto and said, 'Sahib, why is Hanif Ramay after Nur Jehan? What has she done to him?' Bhutto told Ramay to lay off and leave Nur Jehan alone. Madam always had her way, and she had her admirers.

Which amongst her songs was her favourite? 'They are like my children. How can I differentiate between them?' she had said but when I insisted, she thought long and hard and replied, *Badnam mohabat kaun kare* from the pre-1947 movie *Dost*. She said it was composed by that finicky perfectionist, Sajjad, who, she added, never made a *seedhi* or straight tune. This is quite true, and if you don't believe it, you should try humming any of Sajjad's compositions, say *Darshan pyasi, aayi dasi* or *Aaj merey naseeb ne, mujh ko rulla rulla diya*.

Many people have asked why Nur Jehan was not buried in Lahore, a city she longed for all the time she lay ailing in Karachi. According to well-known Pakistani journalist Husain Haqqani, Nur Jehan's daughter Hina—who he says has inherited her mother's strong will—decided that since Nur Jehan had died on Shab-e-Qadar, a night Muslims believe to be the holiest in Islam's calendar, she was destined to go to heaven and should, therefore, be buried before the night was out. That could only be in Karachi. Lahore would have been too late. When Asghar and Zil-e-Huma proposed to take their mother's body to Lahore for burial, Hina put her foot down. 'Don't you want her to go to heaven?' she asked. And that was that.

Madam Nur Jehan was a great woman and a great artist. She was the toast of India when Pakistan and India were one country. She chose to come to Pakistan because that was where her heart lay. The little town of Kasur where she was born always remained close to her, and Lahore was the city she loved. Malika-e-Tarannum Nur Jehan stands dignified in death as in life, mourned by millions and remembered with love. She was truly blessed, because the devotion that people feel for her is denied by God to all but the elect.

City of Lights

Faiz Ahmad Faiz

Faiz Ahmad Faiz wrote 'City of Lights' while gazing upon the distant glow of Lahore's lights from his prison cell. A dedicated Marxist, he was frequently imprisoned for his political beliefs.

> The greenery is drying in a pallid afternoon;
> Parched walls are wet hued with a lonely poison.
> Far to the heart's horizon shrinks, rises, falls again
> The fog of an undimmed grief, a heavy tide:
> And yet behind this fog rises the City of Lights.
> —O, City of Lights—
> Who can tell how to attain your illuminated paths?
> Here, in broken light, in nights of separation,
> Listless you see sitting the soldiers of desire.

—Translated by Sara Suleri Goodyear

PART V

LAHORE, LAHORE HAI

A Love Affair with Lahore

Bina Shah

'Lahore is a love affair, it has nothing to do with reason' —from Chowk.com

I suspect that the rivalry between Lahore and Karachi began somewhere
in the seventeenth century, when a 'Kurrachee merchantman made his
way to Lahore in a dhow up the River Indus to pay tribute to the
Mughal emperor Shah Jehan at his summer residence. He was thrown
out of the court by a sherwani-wearing eunuch because he smelled
like fish.' The trader must have gone back to Karachi and complained
about the snobbery of the people of Lahore, while the eunuch must
have informed King Shah Jehan that the southern barbarians from
Karachi were uncouth, smelly and lacking in manners.

The seeds of this rivalry, once sown, took root, both in the fertile
soil of the Punjab plains and in the deltas of the Indus, and came to
be passed down through the generations. Today, any red-blooded
Karachi-walla will tell you that Lahoris are 'paindus' (village idiots)
with no sense of culture, class or manners. Similarly, any red-blooded
Lahori will tell you that Karachiites are social upstarts with no sense
of culture, class or manners. Does this mean that Karachi folk and
Lahoris are actually the same people, geographically separated by
chance?

Suggest this to a resident of either city and you'll hear a string of
creative curse words in their respective vernaculars. Karachiites pride
themselves for being sophisticated, modern and forward-looking,
whereas Lahoris, they believe, are content to live on the laurels of the
past and spend their days eating copious amounts of food and ogling
women (in fact they expend so much energy in ogling women that
they have to eat huge quantities of food merely to maintain their
strength). Lahoris, on the other hand, see themselves as the standard-
bearers of gracious tradition and old-world hospitality, and Karachi
people as cold, selfish, stingy and materialistic. They believe Karachiites

don't appreciate either good food or beautiful women because they're too busy dialing their mobile phones and rushing like hyenas from one business meeting to the next.

One individual on the popular website, Chowk.com, put it thus: 'Karachi, in its cosmopolitan disdain, has always looked on Lahore as a provincial cousin, and Lahore has always thought of Karachiites as intolerable relatives.' If you profess to hate your relatives, it probably means that, in reality, you can't do without them. Yet, complaining about them is necessary to one's well-being, like having your colon periodically purged.

Given that neither city has managed to provide the most basic amenities to many of its citizens—like clean water, health care, decent schools, hygienic surroundings and jobs—and both have managed to acquire identical toys, such as spanking new airports and fancy cars, it is difficult to give this rivalry much credence. A restaurant culture has also popped up in both cities to amuse those who can afford to pay five thousand rupees for a single meal. Another similarity: The fashion industry sends its denizens on red-eye flights between the cities ten times a week to cater to the PYTs [pretty young things] and begums in both cities who must have the latest creation from FSH or ARY, that is, home-grown designers trying to imitate YSL (Yves Saint Laurent) or whoever.

Yet, it must be said that no matter which city you belong to, you cannot help but be fascinated by Lahore. A born and bred Karachiite, I decided to don the cloak of neutrality for a while to investigate the causes of the rivalry and to also get a sense of the true character of Lahore in the new millennium. I spoke to people who either know Lahore well or are Lahoris themselves, and in the process discovered what draws them to, or repels them, in this city where the old world and new world meet, collide and create a space unlike any other in Pakistan.

THE CITY OF 'LUV'

One of the few monuments I remember from a trip to Lahore as a child was the famed 'Kim's Gun', immortalized by Rudyard Kipling in his novel *Kim*. In the middle of a very busy Lahori roundabout, the air black with soot, cars and buses competing with donkey carts and tongas, pedestrians and cattle, was a gleaming black cannon, a testament to British rule. A family friend married an American man who was so enraptured by the romance of this landmark and the story behind it that he named his son Kim in its honour.

Perhaps this is the word that best captures the city of Lahore: romance. It is no coincidence that Lahore was founded, according to the Deshwa Bhaga, by a man called 'Luv', the son of Raja Ram Chandar, sometime in the second century AD. Romance floats in the very air of Lahore, between the molecules of pollution and the aroma of food cooking at every street corner. Those who know Lahore intimately can feel its romance as they gaze across the rooftops of the walled city, and glimpse the spires of its colonial-era buildings—the King Edward Medical College, the Aitchison or Chief's College, the Punjab Library—through the haze and fog of a typical chilly Lahore morning, as the sun struggles manfully to shine through. The very climate of Lahore is passionate, whether it's the thunder and rain of a monsoon downpour, the scorching heat of a summer afternoon, or the angry red sky of an approaching dust storm.

Lahoris also experience this romance when they recall the haunts of their childhood. Their memories are laced with sensuality, and not just of the carnal kind. They recall the feel of the grass of the Race Course Park when they ran barefoot across its lawns; the taste of the *jamun* and mangoes they picked from trees planted at their grandparents' houses; or the heavy fragrance of *motia*. Rather less fondly, they recall walking along the street and stepping into a pile of horse dung. Their memories of home are coloured with the remembrance of delicious food, lovingly cooked and forcefully administered to them by nanis and nanas and khalas and phupas and relatives of every gender and age (more about food later). Long naps during stifling summer afternoons, the excitement of the arrival of the monsoon, and the shopping trips to the bazaars of Lahore, are all part of this memory bank. Years later, long after they have left these places far behind, the mere mention of those names—Anarkali, Lakshmi Chowk, Liberty Market—pull at their heartstrings. Lahoris are indeed a very sentimental people.

A KALEIDOSCOPIC CULTURE

The culture of Lahore is not just about its history, although you can find the Mughal influence everywhere you look—in the names of streets, in the monuments and other landmarks—the Shalimar Gardens, the magnificent Badshahi Masjid, the Lahore Fort. Lahori culture is ultimately about being in love with everything around you: 'the gandaa-naala and the long canal, the rishtas and family feuds, the concerts, plays and festivals, the shadis, the dholaks and the mendhis, the chooriyaan, rose petals and khussas, the lunatic buses and frightening policemen'. This quote from Shanzeh Haque, a regular interactor on Chowk, demonstrates the all-inclusive nature of the admiration that Lahoris feel for their city, even for those aspects of it that may seem ugly to a less besotted outsider.

The magic that is Lahore is encapsulated in a story told by another interactor on Chowk, who describes an evening in the lawn in front of the Badshahi Masjid. 'People were busy talking, telling tall tales and reciting poetry. Then suddenly, the azaan was heard, and everyone stopped their "baint-baazi" and turned to the evening prayers.' It seems that life in Lahore is made up of moments like these.

Some fear, however, that in recent years a trend towards commercialization is ruining the character of old Lahore. The arrival of flashy restaurants such as Freddy's Café, Chicago Grill, Pizzeria Uno's, Café Zouk (which has since been turned into the Crow-Eaters Gallery, but remains synonymous with the Lahore social scene), the Avari and Pearl Continental luxury hotels, and multinational fast food joints like Pizza Hut and KFC, threaten the status of the Lahore Fort, the old bazaars, 'the streetside vendors selling kulfis, faloodas, Kashmiri chai and halwa puri', as Shanzeh puts it. Similarly, they worry about a modernization of the city that involves old, historical buildings being torn down to make way for slick glass structures; and movie hoardings depicting 'buxom Pakistani heroines' cavorting with heroes with burgeoning moustaches being replaced by advertising billboards for mobile telephones and electronic appliances.

But others welcome the modernization and believe that it's part of an inevitable transition. There is a new generation growing up in this city that is not content with pleasures such as shopping for ancient books at the Urdu bazaar, or drinking apple sheeshas at St Mary's Park or listening to the hypnotic drumbeats of Pappu Saeen's Sufi musicians. They need places where they can see and be seen in their designer wear, real and faux, where they can flex their muscles and stimulate their hormones by listening to the pulsing beat of the latest club music, played by DJs flown in from Europe for high-energy, high-profile raves. Perhaps muscle-flexing and hormone-stimulating has always been a part of Lahore culture; it's just the venues that are changing.

LIFE IN LAHORE IS ONE BIG DINNER PARTY

Lahore cannot be written about without mentioning the average Lahori's obsession with food. Umer Mughal, a young man born in Lahore, describes this fondness in the reverential tones of a Greek recalling the beauty of Helen of Troy. 'Food is more important than life itself . . . it's the most important thing for a Lahori. You want to go out with some friends, what do you do? Go out for dinner. If you want to escape boredom, what do you do? Go out and eat. If you are happy and want to share it, what do you do? Throw a dinner. Food is the essence of life. Food is the music of a Lahori's soul.'

Sobia Aslam, another young Lahori, shares Umer's opinion. 'Fish need water to breathe, birds need oxygen to survive, Lahoris need food to live. No occasion passes for Lahoris that does not involve food. No conversation ends without mention of food. People go for sehri meals before sunrise in Ramadan; they go to the Walled City at 2:00 a.m. after wedding feasts for food; they plan their lives around dinners, snacks, coffee mornings, breakfasts, brunches, high teas . . . life in Lahore is one big dinner party and everyone's invited!'

It's probably easiest to just list some of the favourite foods of the average Lahori. The list is by no means exhaustive; it's just a starting point. Note how each item of food is linked to the restaurant or area that produces it. Lahoris place great importance on lineage, and the lineage of food is no exception.

- Warris Ki Nihari
- Railway Road Ki Halwa Puri

- Mozang Ki Machli
- Zouk Ke Drinks
- Village Ka Buffet
- Sallo's Ka Steak
- Bundu Khan Kay Bihari Kebab
- Yousuf's Kulfi
- Gawalmandi's Kheer
- Chat-khara's Papri Chaat
- Copper Kettle's Caked Alaska
- Hajji's Nihari

Lahoris pride themselves on their discerning palates and their epicurean talents. This is why, Umer explains, you will find Lahoris on the Champs Elysees making disgusted faces at the bland food they are being served at lavish establishments. (That is if you believe the Lahoris actually leave their 'b'loved L'hore' to travel to Paris.) 'Lahori taste buds are the best you can find in the world; they *know* their food.' It also explains why, when the Gawalmandi area was recently transformed into the dhaba-lined Food Street, the populace, behaving as if it was their last meal before Judgement Day, rioted to gain access to its opening. This fervour has already resulted in another area—from Tollington Market to Anarkali Bazaar—being designated a Food Street; proving the other famous Lahore adage, 'You can never be too fat or too rich.'

BASANT AND THE SINGLE MAN

'AYEE BO!!' This is the shout that accompanies the week of Basant, the holiday that's not marked on any official government calendar, but is branded on the heart and soul of every Lahori. Donning their best yellow outfits (if they are women) and their coolest designer sunglasses (both sexes), people from all over the country travel to Lahore for the week. The days of Basant, a traditional Hindu festival marking the arrival of spring, are characterized by some of the most spirited partying known to man or woman.

A million kites dot the sky, almost eclipsing the sun. The tantalizing smell of fresh barbeque hangs heavy in the air. Thunderous bhangra music blares from every rooftop and the shrieks of *'bo kata!'* when a particularly devastating kite battle is won, are loud enough to drown out the roar of traffic from the streets below. 'You can see children everywhere, their eyes glued to the sky,' says Sobia. To her, Basant means the colour yellow, white kurtas, dhol, dancing, loud music, night lights and rooftops.

Umer Mughal tells me that the number of kites, floodlights, sunglasses and yellow clothes sold for this occasion almost outshine the preparations made for Eid or Pakistan Day. He presents me with a unique idea: 'We should make stadiums to have kite-flying contests on Basant, better yet, install floodlights and have night tournaments. Here's a thought, rename Gadaffi Stadium as Guddi Stadium, and instead of Horse and Cattle Shows have a Basant mela and contests there. The Pakistan Cricket Board will make a fortune in one night!'

Basant has drawn protests from certain religious quarters. They claim that not only does a Hindu festival have no place in an Islamic nation, but the occasion also promotes immorality: it encourages an atmosphere in which men and women intermingle freely, consume alcohol and dance for a longer time than befits the denizens of a Muslim country. Basant even poses physical danger to its participants (this last statement is true; people have died falling off rooftops, and cut themselves severely on the glass-coated strings used to fly the kites). But Umer counters this: 'Basant tells me springtime is here. It brings me to my roots (interior Lahore) and teaches me the importance of sports (kite flying). We learn about life and society, how to enjoy ourselves in large gatherings, the importance of food, and the attractiveness of the opposite sex. It's the best learning experience one could have.'

Islamic or un-Islamic, there is no Lahori who doesn't believe Basant should be declared a national holiday. In fact, if Nawaz Sharif ever makes it back to the prime minister's seat, it probably will.

THE APPRECIATION OF WOMEN—A NATIONAL PASTIME

For all their claims to cultural superiority, there is one trait that tarnishes the Lahori's reputation. This is the habit Lahori men have of staring at women until it seems that their eyes will pop out and roll down along the street, following the women they happen to be ogling.

The men refuse to own up to their odd behaviour: 'So what if they look with hungry eyes, and use purple combs to comb back their gel-slicked hair and wear a red scarf around their neck?' asks Umer Mughal. 'Isn't it what women want? If Lahori women wear tight jeans and skintight sleeveless tops, isn't it because they want to be admired and complimented?' More indignantly he adds: 'If a sleazy Muslim Government College student admires them in his skintight Panorama bazaar jeans and unbuttoned shirts, and fake Ray Bans, they feel sick. But if a school dropout smuggler in his Merc and Gucci and Prada stares at them, they feel flattered and blush and give a hint of laughter.'

Umer quotes Socrates to justify the staring. Apparently the philosopher said that if there is a dog on one side and a beautiful woman on the other, the person who looks at the dog can safely be called demented. (I have no way of verifying this quote, but it proves that the Lahori man will go to any lengths to preserve his right to stare at women.)

Lahori men argue that staring at women is a healthy sport that soothes the mind, body and soul. Given the famed beauty of the women of Lahore, they say that they can hardly help their baser instincts. However, the women of Lahore think that this sport is one that should be shown the red card. Sobia Aslam states boldly, 'Lahori men have a staring problem . . . Staring at women must be a gene that's been passed on from father to son over the generations in Lahore.' And it doesn't matter if a woman is dressed in a burqa, or in jeans!

'I think there's a difference in appreciating a woman by looking at her and liking what you see, and staring at a woman and making her feel uncomfortable,' says Sobia. 'Unfortunately, a lot of men don't know the difference and end up making the woman feel like she's on display.'

In a city where 'to see and be seen' forms a large part of the mentality of its people, this continues to be a sore point between the sexes. I'm sure all can be solved, though, over a romantic dinner on the Gawalmandi Food Street.

KARACHI VS LAHORE—DO WE HAVE A WINNER?

So, back to the question of the rivalry between Lahore and Karachi.
Why does it exist? Whose fault is it, and can we declare a winner?

Opinion is heavily polarized on the issue. Writer and journalist
Amina Jilani asserts that if there is a comparison between Lahore and
Karachi, Karachi comes out on top on every count. When I asked her
to comment on the popular statement that Lahore is the village that
never wanted to be a city, her laconic reply was: 'It has got its wish.'

Umer Mughal believes as firmly in the superiority of Lahore. He
faults the Karachiites for being obsessed with issues of ethnicity and
race. 'It's not an ego issue *ever* for the humble and pious Lahori.' The
Karachiites are the ones who actually fuel the discrimination. 'From
the monitor of your class to the prime minister, should the person be
a Lahori or a Karachiite? I'll let you decide. Myself, I'll kick back,
relax and enjoy the show.' Umer's assertion that the average Lahori
couldn't care less about competition from Karachi stems from the
belief that this is akin to the competition that exists between a Daihatsu
Charade and a Mercedes-Benz.

Sobia, being a gentle soul, attempts to understand the rivalry in a
rational fashion. 'I think the basis for this rivalry could lie in the
language issue: difference in language leads to miscommunication.
Karachiites don't understand why people from Lahore boast about
being "desi", and Lahoris don't understand why Karachiites insist on
sophistication.' This leads to Lahoris insistently speaking their most
parochial Punjabi socially, while Karachiites show off their English
or Hyderabadi-Deccan Urdu in a form of verbal competition that
would put American East and West Coast rappers to shame.

But to speculate on the origins of the rivalry and to try to decide
which city is better than the other is as futile as speculating on whether
match-fixing exists in Pakistani cricket, or who will form the next
government. Ardeshir Cowasjee, the famous columnist, offers what is
probably the most sensible explanation of all: 'Lahoris and Karachiites
have been puzzling since kingdom come as to why they do not like
each other. This frustrates them, and frustration leads to them disliking
each other.'

Perhaps it is sensible not to pick at the rivalry too much for fear of opening wounds that are best left to heal. In the end, even as a hard-core Karachiite, I have to admit that Lahore doesn't sound like such a bad place to fall in love with.

(Many thanks to Sobia Aslam, Umer Mughal, Shanzeh Haque, Amina Jilani, Ardeshir Cowasjee, and the interactors at Chowk.com for their contribution to this essay. —BS)

The Way of All Flesh

Irfan Husain

A first-time visitor to Lahore might be excused for assuming that the international revolution in dietary habits over the last couple of decades has bypassed this city. Judging from the amount of meat that Lahoris consume, and the way they cook it—in copious amounts of oil, and even butter—it seems that the residents of this city are either immune to lethal doses of cholesterol, or live fairly short lives.

However, it's not that Lahoris are completely unaware of medical research on the effects of high amounts of lipids in the bloodstream. The reality is that meat is so essential an ingredient to their cuisine that it cannot be displaced. Any vegetarian unfortunate enough to visit Lahore becomes an object of pity; and if he or she has no choice but to survive on *naan*, *dal* and *raita*, the general perception is that the fault lies with the visitor, for following such unnatural fads.

Where there is meat, there is bound to be ghee. When family elders gather together to moan over the decadence of the younger generation, they ascribe many of today's ills to the fact that young people no longer eat *asli ghee*, or clarified butter—the artery-blocking real McCoy.

When I first moved to Lahore in the late-sixties, the only places that served food after 9 p.m. in the sleepy provincial capital were the joints on Abbot Road or the all-night places in the red-light district of Hira Mandi. The former catered to the late-night movie crowd, while the latter fed people with other appetites. Now, of course, restaurants all over town keep their shutters open until late, and offer a vast choice. But wherever you go, you will still get lots of meat.

For years, my favourite roadside eatery was the old *thaka-teen* (also known as *thaka-thak* or *gurda-kapura*) place on Abbot Road. This style of cooking involves chopping up the ingredients into bite-sized morsels while they sizzle in butter on a large, shallow skillet. The name *thaka-teen* or *thaka-thak* mimics the sound of a pair of choppers being wielded to dice the food. After a few minutes of chopping, the food, still on the fire, is covered with a couple of naans to contain the heat and the flavour. Every few minutes, a cupful of water is trickled on to the skillet to make sure the dish remains moist.

And the ingredients? How to put this delicately? Apart from kidneys, fresh coriander, spices and several pats of butter, the principle ingredient is goat testicles (or *kapuras*). Many people are put off by the thought of eating this delicacy, but take it from me, the flavour is delicate and the texture soft without being slimy. However, for the faint of heart and stomach, the same dish can be prepared with kidneys alone. Both versions contain lashings of cholesterol, and I ascribe my quadruple bypass surgery five years ago to my overindulgence in this and several other meaty dishes in my misspent youth.

The other Lahori favourite, available in the same area, is 'chicken-*chohla*'. This consists of pieces of chicken cooked slowly for hours with chickpeas. I avoided this spicy stew for years because the combination seemed so odd. But I'm glad I did not allow my prejudice against this simple but satisfying dish to last for ever. Eaten with fresh naan, this is a wonderful one-dish meal that makes a change from the normal Lahori all-meat cuisine.

Not far away from these two places is Bhati Gate, one of the entrances to the Old City, where I had my first taste of *karahi gosht*. This dish was the precursor to the *balti* (bucket) style of cooking that became so popular in the UK. Prepared in a large wok or karahi, or a balti, large quantities of diced goat meat are cooked in oil with tomatoes, spices and lots of fresh coriander. When you walk up to the chef, who sits cross-legged before his wok, you find yourself cheek-by-haunch with the several cuts of fresh meat that hang as advertisements for the quality of produce offered by the establishment. After you have selected one, it will be weighed, chopped and cooked before your eyes. As it takes around half-an-hour to cook this dish, your gastric juices will run amok as you wait, with cooking smells wafting up your nostrils. The entire wok is placed before you and your friends, and you attack it with pieces of fresh naan, scooping up the hot meat together with the gravy. The bones invariably end up on the sidewalk. For this dish to be a success, the meat has to be of the highest quality. It takes a connoisseur to choose the best haunch on display.

Bhati Gate is also famous for its *nihari*, a wonderfully satisfying winter dish for which choice cuts of beef are cooked slowly overnight in a deep, thick gravy. Normally a morning treat, it is now served at all mealtimes in other parts of town. But traditionalists queue up at dawn to get the best portions, and the well-known places that offer it run out well before nine. For those who feel they haven't had their full quota of cholesterol, a helping of brain and marrow can be added to the nihari.

Payas, or trotters, have the same status in Lahore's Hira Mandi, which lies in the shadow of the fabled Badshahi Masjid, that onion soup had in Paris's Les Halles district before the old food market was moved outside Paris. And, nobody's payas are better known than Phajja's. Again, these are simmered overnight until the marrow is cooked and the bones have surrendered their gelatine. The chunks of meat attached to the bones melt in the mouth, and the rich soup can be eaten on its own with a spoon. The acid test of a good dish of payas is that the soup must be glutinous enough to make your fingers stick to each other after they have delved into a bowlful. The dish is garnished with a handful of fresh coriander, green chillies, ginger and lemons. Here again, nothing goes as well with a bowl of payas as naan straight from the oven. The addition of brain to this classic dish converts it into *siri-paya*, adding both extra calories and cholesterol.

To redeem Lahore's image in the eyes of the nutritionally conscious, let me add that fish, too, figures among Lahore's best-loved dishes, in the form of deep-fried rohu. However, this river fish is increasingly difficult to find as it is being rapidly replaced by the Chinese carp that was introduced into the Ravi a few years ago. Also, industrial pollution is taking a heavy toll on Pakistan's traditional river fish. Fortunately, fish farming has now become a major source of freshwater fish. The large pieces of rohu are thickly coated in batter and spices, and deep fried in hot oil. When done, the batter is removed to reveal the steaming flesh, which is then dipped in a white, radish sauce. Another Lahori favourite is *bam*, or eel from Karachi. Although it is disdained in Pakistan's port city, Lahoris love its firm flesh and robust flavour.

In Old Anarkali, behind Tollington Market on Lower Mall, a number of wonderful eating places still hold their own against the steady inroads being made by McDonalds and Kentucky Fried Chicken. My favourite in the old days used to be a fish specialist who produced an amazing dish he called *machali ka achar*. This was a river fish cooked in a pickle-flavoured sauce I have never had before or since. Since seating space was limited, we would often pick up a few portions in the old cans he kept for the purpose, and carry them to the nearby residence of Shakir Ali, principle of the National College of Arts, together with a few bottles of Murree Brewery's excellent lager.

Desserts in Lahore are just as sinful as these delectable meat dishes. Most of them are based on thickened buffalo milk cooked gently for a long time until it turns into the thickly concentrated *khoya*. Lahore is also famous for its *jalebis*, best eaten hot from the cauldron. An unsweetened batter is poured into boiling oil to form concentric circles that harden immediately. They are removed from the oil within seconds and dipped quickly into a sugar syrup. These golden delights are crisp and hot with gooey centres. I remember, from my childhood, that cold jalebis would be soaked in milk overnight to form part of the *sahri*, or the meal before the start of the fast in Ramadan.

One Lahori speciality that has added several pounds to my weight and an inch or two to my waistline is *kulfi*. This ice cream, made with thickened milk, and containing pistachios and almonds, was originally made in steel containers (now replaced by plastic cones) and kept frozen in large earthenware *matkas* or pots packed with salt and ice. The kulfi was extracted from its metal sheath and served with cold vermicelli. Currently, some of the best kulfi is sold at 'Benazir Kulfi' in Mozang Chungi, and long lines of cars are parked outside, full of punters who have been gorging themselves on meaty fare and are now on the prowl for dessert.

Lahoris are great snackers, and the innumerable *thelas* or pushcarts are testimony to their day-long appetite for food. Everything from sugar cane to tangerines is piled high and sold in paper bags or newspapers to people just walking from one end of a street to another. Peels are tossed casually over the shoulder as friends chat to each other through mouthfuls of sliced carrots or radishes, dipped in a mixture of salt and white pepper.

Although all kinds of modern restaurants of uneven quality have opened since I first began living in Lahore, their offerings pale into insignificance when compared with the best traditional fare. A first-time visitor would do well to steer clear of the dozens of mediocre Chinese places and burger joints that have mushroomed across the city. A restaurant worth trying, however, is The Village in Gulberg which allows one to taste an entire gamut of local cuisine under one roof. Here, for a flat charge, you can get a battalion of cooks to prepare just about anything you fancy, from fried fish to *seekh* kebabs to kulfi. The quality is uniform, but be prepared for queues and noisy kids.

I cannot end this account of Lahore's gastronomic delights without mentioning Food Street, the unlikely brainchild of a city administrator that has become a huge hit. This is a street in Gawalmandi, in old Lahore, which is blocked to traffic every evening, allowing well-known establishments to set up kitchens that offer a wide array of traditional dishes. You can walk around, deciding what you want to eat, and then sit at a table while your waiter rushes from one cook to the next to bring your order to your table—steaming hot. Almost all the dishes here are authentic, the street is clean and well-lit, and you can eat your fill, and more, without moving an inch from your table. What more could a Lahori want?

(I am indebted to Agha Imran Hamid, a foodie, and my old friend, for reading and correcting this article. —IH)

Lahore, Lahore Hai

Pran Nevile

Wednesday was a great day in Lahore, and one that will be long remembered as a commencement of a new era in the Punjab. On the afternoon of that day, the bulk of the European residents and a large portion of the native inhabitants of the city assembled near the beautiful, but partially ruined, gateway known as the Char-Burje of the Multan Road, where tents had been erected for the accommodation of the ladies and a band of music in attendance for their amusement. After the lapse of about half an hour, a roar of many voices proclaimed the approach of some strange creature that was to astonish the natives, and immediately afterwards, a monster made its appearance in the shape of a steam locomotive. But humiliating to say instead of bounding along with the speed of lightning by its own power, it was being ignominiously dragged at a foot pace by one hundred and two bullocks, and stowed by two elephants. —*Lahore Chronicle*, 1862

Lahore has for long been the nerve centre of political, social, educational and cultural activities. Sir Syed Ahmad Khan called the people the 'Zinda Dillan-i-Punjab' and the Quaid-i-Azam called it the 'Heart of Pakistan'. —*District Census Report, Lahore*, 1972

Mochi Gate was at its prime in the late twenties and early thirties and those who dominated the stage, though they quarreled among themselves had a common foe in the British. Hardly an evening passed without some sort of a political rhetoric which Governor O'Dwyer derisively termed 'frothy'. Iqbal recited his Jawab-i-Shikwa here. It was here that Nehru proclaimed on January 26, 1930 that from that

---

This extract is taken from Pran Nevile's *Lahore: A Sentimental Journey*, published by Allied Publishers Limited.

day onwards India would celebrate 26 January as independence day.

Political meetings, poetic symposiums, religious conferences idlers' rendezvous . . . Mochi Gate offered an inexhaustible source of diversion and education. It supplemented colleges and newspapers. It was not merely a gateway to the city but a passage to political careers as well. —Muhammad Saeed in *Lahore: A Memoir*

That Lahore, the Lavpor and Lohkot of the Hindus, the Lohawar, Lohar, Lahanur or Rahwar of the Mohammedans and possibly the Labokla of Ptolemy was founded by an ancient race of Rajputs towards the end of the first or the beginning of the second century after Christ; that it rose to importance in the eighth and ninth century, becoming the capital of a powerful principality and the parent of other colonies. —Khan Bahadur Sayed Muhammad Latif in *Lahore: History, Architectural Remains and Antiquities*

For the first time in living memory the waters of the river Ravi passed over the railway tracks, cutting off Lahore from the north, when it rose over six feet within 24 hours on Tuesday the 5th September, 1950 AD. The water level of the river was three feet higher than the highest ever recorded at Lahore. The railway tracks beyond Shahdara railway station were submerged. The railway authorities had consequently to suspend the traffic to and from Peshawar and other branch lines. All the trains coming from Peshawar on Tuesday night were sent back to Wazirabad. The trains for Karachi from Lahore were, however, run during the night. The flood water of the Ravi that had submerged by Wednesday afternoon an area of over 50 square miles round about Lahore receded about three to four feet at a place about 15 miles upstream. An appreciable change for the better in the situation in the suburban areas of the city by Thursday afternoon was forecast late on Wednesday night by the Chief Engineer, Irrigation.

It was decided at the conference to issue orders to shoot at persons found indulging in looting. The decision was necessitated following reports of cases of looting in the flood-affected areas. —M. Baqir in *Lahore: Past and Present*

We always looked forward to Basant, the king of all festivals in Lahore.

About two weeks before its arrival, the kite shops were specially decorated and a large variety of shops of different colours, shapes and sizes were displayed along with small and large pinnahs with artistically wound *dore* in numerous attractive colour combinations.

The celebrations on Basant day would commence well before daybreak when specially constructed box kites carrying lighted candles like lantern were set afloat in the sky. These moving lights in the sky made an enchanting sight and signified the inauguration of the great kite-flying festival of Lahore, unmatched anywhere else in the world. A tragic incident that occurred on Basant day has left a lasting impression on my mind. Shiba was a young *khilari* in our mohalla. Tall, handsome and ever-smiling, he was a couple of years older than me. Full of humour, he was very popular and friendly with all boys in the neighbourhood. He was a clever and skillful kite-flyer and had emerged a winner in quite a few kite matches on that day. The winds were quite favourable and the festivities were in full swing. As the sundown approached, Shiba was challenged by another *khilari*, Dwarka, from the next mohalla. In no time Shiba launched his red kite and was ready for the battle. Many of us pulled back our kites and got ready to witness the fight.

After some warming up, we began boosting Shiba's morale by hooting down his rival. Shiba entrapped his opponent's kite and *paicha* was set up. He released the *dore* with measured speed and the fighting kites flew higher and further. The battle dragged on with the approaching evening. We were watching with bated breath and praying for Shiba to come out victorious. The battling kites in the distant horizon now resembled tiny moving specks. Shiba was standing on the rooftop which had a low parapet around it. After some time, finding himself unable to view the progress of his kite, he stepped on to the parapet wall which was less than two feet wide and overlooked the lane below. Soon we saw Dwarka's kite cut loose and drifting away. Shiba was victorious. He shouted *bo-kata*, and in his excitement bent forward, overstepped the wall and tumbled down into the lane more than fifty feet below. There were cries from the housetops in the neighbourhood, 'Shiba has fallen down from the roof.' It was a great tragedy for the entire mohalla. All festivities were suspended and everyone rushed down from the rooftop. Shiba lay dead on the ground a final *bo-kata* of his lifespan.

The Pathos of Exile

Mohsin Hamid

I am dancing with my cousin Omer. My hands and feet are on the ground; my rump is in the air. It is that kind of party—the kind all other parties are measured against. Around us are many of our childhood loves: Ajoo and O.H., Saad and A.T., Shahid and Nippy and Booboo. These are the boys we grew up with. The girls, our sisters and cousins and wives and fiancés, are standing back for a moment, letting us go at it. Our grins are infectious. Some of us are dancing with our eyes shut. Some of us are barely moving, just shaking a shoulder or arching an eyebrow to the beat. I am utterly happy.

Omer's mother was my mother's friend before she married my uncle. When our mothers were pregnant, my mother had a series of dreams. She dreamed she had two mangoes, then two apples, then two oranges. In all of her dreams, my mother gave the larger fruit to Omer's mother. 'I know this,' my mother told Omer's. 'Whatever you have, boy or girl, I will have the same. Only mine will be smaller.'

Omer was born a week before me. As a baby, he drank two bottles of milk and cried for more while I struggled to finish half a bottle. We grew up together, cousin-brothers, in a family with nine aunts and uncles and innumerable cousins. He turned out six inches taller, many, many pounds heavier and several shades darker than I. He held onto his hair better. We shared friends and many nights on rooftops, picking up bad habits from one another, smoking, talking. We left for college in the U.S. around the same time and returned to Pakistan when we were done.

Then I went to the U.S. again, to law school, and Omer stayed behind. I became a management consultant, living first in New York

---

This extract is taken from Mohsin Hamid's 'The Pathos of Exile', published by *Time* magazine.

and then in London. Our lives followed different courses. And now, nine years after we ceased sharing continents, we are back together for his wedding in Lahore, his home and the city he lives in, my home and the city I left behind. We are dancing for the last time as single men. In two days, Omer will marry.

I leave the dance floor and step outside. A tent covers the garden, and a log fire burns in the night. I walk away, around my uncle's house, a house built when we were teenagers, and into the great lawn that curves around what was my grandfather's house. My body steams in the cold air. We played here as children, we cousins. There were more than enough of us at Friday family lunches for any sport that came to mind.

It is February, not long after the kite-fighting festival of Basant. Lahore's winter fogs have given way to the clear nights of spring, but there is still a chill in the air. I sit down on a bench, stroke the wet nose of a dog that comes to me and shut my eyes. This is the passage of time. I am a grown man now, 31, and I am in a place that will always be sacred to me as the place of my childhood. I feel an allegiance to this house, this family, this city, this country. It makes my eyes burn. I do not want to leave. But I know I am a wanderer, and I have no more choice but to drift than does a dandelion seed in the wind. It is my nature. It is in my soul, in my eyes.

Still, Lahore touches me. I am doing well in my career abroad, and I am able to visit often. But there is something about Lahore, something that makes me want to be part of this city's story. Even though I have moved away, this is where I evolved, where my basic notions of love and friendship were formed. A snow leopard can be taken to zoos in other places; it can perhaps even be well fed and content, but it will always wear a coat designed for the Himalayas. I see Lahore when I look in the mirror, and I feel the strength of my attachment at this moment, as my cousin prepares to marry.

My sister and I had arrived on a flight from London that morning. She busied herself with the many errands of the wedding: flower arrangements, tent and lighting designs, food preparations. I, typically and lazily, claimed exhaustion and jet lag as an excuse to go straight to bed. When I woke it was evening. My father was on the telephone from Islamabad, his voice full of excitement at the prospect of seeing me soon. I climbed up onto the roof of my parents' house to watch the sun set and to look out upon my city.

Lahore had changed and was changing. From this rooftop, where I spent many hours struggling to get kites aloft, one used to see only trees and the rooftops of other houses. Now bald patches had emerged where trees had died, and tall office buildings had risen up not far away, almost uniformly hideous in their architecture but robust and healthy signs of life, of growth. I watched them warily and wondered what my house would one day become. A shop perhaps. Or maybe a small museum.

I went down to my room, showered and shaved, slipped on a well-worn pair of brown cords and a brown shirt and a secondhand blazer, and headed out to the party with my sister, who asked me what I had been up to.

'Just thinking,' I said.

'Yeah,' she replied with a grin. 'As usual. While the rest of us were working.'

At 3 in the morning, after half an hour of sitting on the bench by myself, I rise up and return to the party. It is still going strong, but people have begun to leave. I linger until there are just a few of us remaining, the boys, standing around the speakers with our eyes shut, hardly able to move. Then even the boys disperse, and I head back to Omer's room for a chat and a cousin sleepover, an old tradition between us.

The lights are off, and we're under the sheets. Omer's fiancé, Natasha, is a warm, lovely woman, with a doctorate in microbiology and a ready smile. Still, I ask Omer if he's nervous about getting married. I imagine I'd be terrified. But he tells me that it doesn't feel like a big deal, that it just seems natural, what was meant to be. 'I'm calm,' he says, 'calm and happy.' Ah, I think, calmness and happiness. Signs of home. Very welcome to a transcontinental mongrel like myself, soothing me as I drift into sleep.

We're woken by my aunt banging on the door. 'Omer! Mohsin! Do you know what time it is?' We could be 10 years old again. Omer covers his face with his pillow. I yell that we're already up. She opens the door and turns on the lights. 'Up? You're never up. It's 1 o'clock. There are a million things to be done.' And the preparations continue.

My father arrives from Islamabad that afternoon, and I meet him at the airport. He gives me a hug, I pick up his bags and we make our way to the car. He is an economist, and on our drive home our talk turns, as usual, to economics. Things in Pakistan are improving, he tells me. Reserves are up. Property and stocks are soaring. But people are still holding back from investing in new industries. There's a lot of uncertainty and people don't know what's going to happen, so they're waiting and seeing. And while they wait and see, millions of young men and women are trying to enter the workforce every year.

My father takes off his glasses and cleans them with a white handkerchief. His eyes are soft and unfocused, but he seems pleased, perhaps because my sister and I are here. 'You know,' he tells me. 'A year ago, you could see troops passing through the city, heading for the border. Trucks would go by during the day, full of equipment and supplies. And they would come back at night, empty. Our driver used to drive tanks. He was mobilized with the reserves. It was a frightening time.' He puts on his glasses. 'But things are better now. Let's hope they stay that way. Peace is a blessing.'

Later that day, my cousin Omer comes by for tea at our place, grabbing a quick break from the hectic preparations. Omer designs and manufactures furniture. With population growth, he tells me, comes housing growth, and with housing growth comes furniture growth; so he is sitting on many more orders than he can handle. 'You know one thing I really like about what I do?' he says, dipping a *samosa* in ketchup. 'I get to meet all kinds of people. I mean, everything from types like us to families that do full purdah, where you can't even see the women. Sometimes I'll be talking to some guy about furniture he needs and he'll be so nervous, because he's trying to get exactly what his wife wants and she won't come to the showroom and he's terrified of making a mistake.'

'What happens if he buys something and she isn't satisfied?' I ask.

'I let him return it. Customer service, bro. You have to keep the clients happy.'

I think about this, about families with husbands who are terrified of wives who don't go out in public, and I try to imagine the sight of Omer, in his shorts and T shirt, reassuring earnest young men with beards.

*

Lahore has had a difficult decade and a half since I graduated from high school. Many of those who could leave have left, like O.H. and Nippy and I, who have flown in for the wedding from jobs far away. Most of the gang who used to go every summer to the mountains, where we went to flee heat and parental supervision, now live abroad. But we are a tiny minority. And many of those who could not leave have struggled to find work. Some of them now wear the physical uniforms and hard expressions of religious intolerance. I see them on the streets, in the markets, in front of the mosques. They worry me. They are frown lines of disappointment on the face of the city.

I think about why so many of my friends left Lahore and why so few of us returned. None of us seemed to think, at the time, that we were going away for good. The universities were in bad shape, and we went abroad for a better education. But as the economy stagnated and as law and order declined, we delayed our home-comings. We began to work. We began to settle into new lives. And as the years passed, it became harder and harder for us to think of what we would do if we went back to Lahore. The city changed and we changed, and somehow we became voluntary exiles. But at least in my case, the homesickness that resulted from exile, although not fatal, has remained uncured.

As I dash from one friend's house to the next, avoiding wedding chores while catching up with people I haven't seen in a long time, I can't help thinking of Lahore as the girl I first fell in love with. I have fallen in love with other cities since: with New York, the girl I will always lust for but who left me exhausted; and with London, the girl who bored me at first but whose company I have come to savor. But my heart will always have a special place for my first love, for Lahore, the love of my childhood and teens and early 20s.

She has hardened, become more cynical, angrier. She has lost some of her looks. She is less complacent than she was then, less sure of her enduring centrality in her universe. But Lahore is still a charmer, and she is more urbane and cosmopolitan than she was in the days when the opening of a new ice-cream parlor was enough to get her excited for months. Lahore is speckled with Internet cafés, with billboards offering broadband connections, with advertisements for health clubs featuring personal trainers. The students of the National College of Arts have helped restore parts of Anarkali market and a bit of the old city now called 'Food Street'—they look like glamorous backdrops for a period film. The restoration of the palace in the Lahore Fort is also nearing completion, as is the construction of the rather chic new airport, done in a style someone described to me as 'modern Mughal'.

No, Lahore is no longer the same girl she was when we parted ways. And I am no longer the same boy. But even after all these years, even with the scars and frown lines she has acquired, she still makes my heart race, and I can't help wondering what would have happened if we hadn't broken up, what would have happened if I had stayed.

I get a glimpse of it that night. The boys agree to gather after the dancing and ornamental henna-painting activities of the *mahndi* for a late session at my place. I arrive home with my parents, who begin to play cards in the living room while I work with Rahman, a servant I have known for most of my life, to set up the study. We carry cushions up the stairs, move the old boom box in from my bedroom, fetch ashtrays and glasses and ice. I put on a Joe Satriani CD we listened to on our first big trip to the mountains. Then I sit down in the gentle light, surrounded by books and wood paneling, and wait for my friends to arrive.

They come one by one, stopping to chat for a while with my parents and then clumping up the staircase. The study fills. Shahid and Nippy and I discuss women woes, or more specifically my women woes, and the most recent disaster in my romantic life. Booboo and Saad argue about Pakistan's role in the so-called war on terror. Ajoo tells O.H. about his latest hunting outing. A.T. get on his mobile to his wife. The room grows smoky. The music switches to Neil Young. I settle back into my cushion and relax.

This is the magic of Lahore. Maybe because of the heat or the big families or the social restrictions or the relative lack of money, Lahore is a place where bands of friends tend to form and hold together. I would not trade this evening in my long-disused study for a party in the coolest nightclub in SoHo or on the swankiest yacht off Portofino. There is far more pleasure and sustenance to be had here, and I gorge myself on it tonight.

The next day I wander around the city, dropping in on places I once visited often. I buy a pack of cigarettes from the *paan* shop in Main Market, and I'm recognized by Saleem, the kid who used to take my orders and let me run a tab when I was a teenager. He comes over to say hello and ask how London is treating me. 'How did you know I was in London now?' I ask him. He shrugs. From my cousins, he tells me, from my friends, you know, word moves around.

The shopkeeper at the bookstore in the corner of Liberty Market recognizes me, too, and he tells me that my novel is still selling well. 'Yeah, but all your copies are pirated,' I say. He assures me, smiling, that this isn't true, and he also points out that being read is more valuable a reward than being paid.

That evening, I turn on the water in my shower, but the pressure is low because my sister is taking a shower in her bathroom and my mother is taking a shower in hers. I turn off the water and wait. This is what life would have been like if I had stayed, I think: less convenient, perhaps, but more connected to the people I love.

After we have dressed, we meet in the living room, my mother and sister in saris, my father and I in suits. A cousin appears just in time to take our photo, and then we are off to Omer's house, where some of the boys have gathered in a corner of the veranda, smoking. I join their circle. Omer makes his appearance, looking nervous at last and sweating slightly even though the weather is cool.

Then the order is given, everyone disperses to their cars, and we form a massive convoy with the groom's flower-bedecked vehicle in front. We drive slowly, hazard lights flashing, and we block traffic at busy intersections for many minutes at a time. No one honks at us. In Lahore, no one would. Weddings are sacred in this place of bonds, moments for the city to bind itself together even more strongly.

We arrive and pass through a reception line of flowers. Some of the cheekier, and unmarried, girls on their side flick their flowers at some of the cheekier, and unmarried, boys on ours. Then we are inside the tent, which is holding up well against the light rain that is falling. I wander about saying my hellos and thinking how strange it is that just a few nights ago I was working on a PowerPoint presentation in my office in Piccadilly.

The bride and groom sit on a stage, surrounded by family and friends. I stand with my parents and my aunt and uncle. My uncle looks at me, and we share a moment of silent understanding. His son and my cousin, the closest person I will ever have to a twin, is marrying. My uncle's face is full of emotion, and I wink at him to hide the moistness in my eyes.

When I watch Omer walk out of the tent with his wife, I smile, happy for him and for his life, a life much like one I could, perhaps, have led. A wave of nostalgia rises up in me but I wait for it to subside, and I focus on savoring the moment.

I am a wanderer. Soon I will again have left Lahore. There will be time enough then to think about the past. For now, I accept the blessing of the present. This is the gift my city has always given me, a sense of home to sustain me on my travels.

From *Ice-Candy-Man*

LANDSCAPES

My world is compressed. Warris Road, lined with rain gutters, lies between Queens Road and Jail Road: both wide, clean, orderly streets at the affluent fringes of Lahore. Rounding the right-hand corner of Warris Road and continuing on Jail Road is the hushed Salvation Army wall.

Opposite it, down a bumpy, dusty, earth-packed drive, is the one-and-a-half-room abode of my godmother. With her dwell her docile old husband and her slavesister. This is my haven. My refuge from the perplexing unrealities of my home on Warris Road.

A few furlongs away, Jail Road vanishes into the dense bazaars of Mozang Chungi. At the other end, a distant canal cuts the road at the periphery of my world.

*

We cross Jail Road and enter Godmother's compound. Walking backwards, the buffalo-hide water-pouch slung from his back, the waterman is spraying the driveway to settle the dust for evening visitors. Godmother is already fitted into the bulging hammock of her easy-chair and Slavesister squats on a low cane stool facing the road. Their faces brighten as I scramble out of the pram and run towards them. Smiling like roguish children, softly clapping hands they chant, '*Langer deen! Paisay ke teen! Tamba mota, pag mahin!*' Freely translated, 'Lame Lenny! Three for a penny! Fluffy pants and fine fanny!'

Flying forward, I fling myself at Godmother and she lifts me on to her lap and gathers me to her bosom. I kiss her, insatiably, excessively, and she hugs me. She is childless. The bond that ties her strength to my weakness, my fierce demands to her nurturing and my loneliness to her compassion is stronger than the bond of motherhood. More satisfying than the ties between men and women.

I cannot be in her room long without in some way touching her. Some nights, clinging to her broad white back like a bug, I sleep with her. She wears only white khaddar saris and white khaddar blouses, beneath which is her coarse bandage-tight bodice.

In all the years I never saw the natural shape of her breasts.

*

Things love to crawl beneath Ayah's sari. Ladybirds, glow-worms, Ice-candy-man's toes. She dusts them off with impartial nonchalance . . . We no longer use the pram to visit Godmother's house: it is a short ten-minute walk. But when Ayah takes me up Queens Road, past the YWCA, past the Freemasons' Lodge, which she calls 'The Ghost Club', and across the Mall to the Queen's statue in the park opposite the Assembly Chambers, I'm still pushed in a pram . . . The covetous glances Ayah draws educate me. Up and down, they look at her. Stub-handed twisted beggars and dusty old beggars on crutches drop their poses and stare at her with hard, alert eyes. Holy men, masked in piety, shove aside their pretences to ogle her with lust. Hawkers, cart-drivers, cooks, coolies and cyclists turn their heads as she passes, pushing my pram with the unconcern of the Hindu goddess she worships.

Ayah is chocolate-brown and short. Everything about her is eighteen years old and round and plump. Even her face. Full-blown cheeks, pouting mouth and smooth forehead curve to form a circle with her head. Her hair is pulled back in a tight knot.

Queen Victoria, cast in gunmetal, is majestic, massive, overpowering, ugly. Her statue imposes the English Raj in the park. I lie sprawled on the grass, my head in Ayah's lap. The Fallettis Hotel cook, the Government House gardener, and an elegant, compactly muscled head-and-body masseur sit with us. Ice-candy-man is selling his popsicles to the other groups lounging on the grass. My mouth waters. I have confidence in Ayah's chocolate chemistry . . . lank and loping the Ice-candy-man cometh . . .

I take advantage of Ayah's admirers. 'Massage me!' I demand, kicking the handsome masseur. He loosens my laces and unbuckles the straps gripping my boots. Taking a few drops of almond oil from one of the bottles in his cruet set, he massages my wasted leg and then my okay leg. His fingers work deftly, kneading, pummelling, soothing. They are knowing fingers, very clever, and sometimes, late in the evening, when he and Ayah and I are alone, they massage Ayah under her sari. Her lids close. She grows still and languid. A pearly wedge gleams between her lips and she moans a fragile, piteous sound of pleasure. Very carefully, very quietly, I manoeuvre my eyes and nose. It is dark, but now and then a dart of twilight illuminates a subtle artistry. My nose inhales the fragrance of earth and grass— and the other fragrance that distils insights. I intuit the meaning and purpose of things. The secret rhythms of creation and mortality. The essence of truth and beauty. I recall the choking hell of chloroform vapours and discover that heaven has a dark fragrance.

*

It is not yet winter. I have been badgering Imam Din for the past week to take me on his next junket to his village home.

'Lenny baby,' he says, sighing heavily. 'Pir Pindo is way beyond Amritsar . . . Forty miles from Lahore as the crow flies!'

'It may be too far for a little crow; but it's not too far for a strong old ox like you,' says Ayah. She is toasting *phulkas* on the glowing coal fire and deftly flipping them with tongs. 'Poor child,' she says. 'She wants so much to go . . . It won't break your back to take her.'

'Not only my back, my legs too!' says Imam Din. 'I'm not so young any more . . . I'll have a heart attack merely conveying myself there.'

'Go on with you!' says Ayah. 'You should talk of growing old! I'll know that when I know that!'

'I'll never be too old to bother you,' murmurs Imam Din, sighing, pushing his hubble-bubble away and advancing from his corner on Ayah.

Ayah whirls, tong-handed, glowing iron pointed at Imam Din.

'Arrey baba . . .' says Imam Din, hunching his shoulders and holding his hands out defensively in front. 'I still haven't recovered from the last time you scarred me. Aren't you ashamed . . . burning and maiming a harmless old man like me?'

'I know who's harmless and who isn't! Go on, sit down!' she commands.

Imam Din collapses meekly in his corner and drawing deeply on the hookah, causing the water in the smoke-filter to gurgle, offers her a puff.

But Ayah is in a determined mood. 'Will you take her with you or not?' she demands, tongs in hand, and Imam Din capitulates.

'Arrey baba, you're a Hitler! I'll take her. Even though my back snaps in two! Even though my legs fall off! I'll take her.'

I sit on a small seat attached to the bar in front of Imam Din and his legs, like sturdy pistons, propel us at a staid and unaltering pace through the gullies and huddled bazaars behind Queens Road, then along the Mall past the stately pink sprawl of the High Court, and the constricted alleys running on one side of Father's shop. It is an illuminating experience—my first glimpse of the awakening metropolis of two million bestirring itself to face a new day.

At the crack of dawn, Lahore, the city known as the garden of the Moguls, turns into a toilet. Creeping sleepily out of sagging tenements and hovels, the populace squats along alleyways and unpaved street edges facing crumbling brick walls—and thin dark stains trickle between their feet halfway down the alleys.

Cycle bell ringing, Imam Din and I perambulate through the profusion of bared Lahori bottoms. I hang on to the handlebars as we wobble imperturbably over potholes past a view of backsides the dark hue of Punjabi soil—and the smooth, plump spheres of young women who hide their faces in their veils and bare their bottoms. The early risers squat before their mugs, lost in the private contemplative world of their ablutions, and only the children face the street unabashed, turning their heads and bright eyes to look at us.

Past Data Sahib's shrine, past the enormous marble domes of the Badshahi mosque floating in a grey mist, and just before we cross the Ravi bridge, we rattle through the small Pathan section of town. Now I see only fierce tribesmen from the northern frontiers around the Khyber and Babusar Passes who descend to the plains in search of work. They leave their families behind in flinty impoverished valleys concealed in the arid and massive tumult of the Karakorams, the Hindu Kush and the Himalayas. They can afford to visit them only every two or three years. The tribesmen's broad, bared backsides are much paler, and splotched with red, and strong dark hair grows down their backs. In place of mugs there are small mounds of stone and scraps of newspaper and Imam Din sniffs: 'What manner of people are these who don't clean their arses with water?'

A particularly pale bottom arrests Imam Din's attention. The skin is pink, still fresh and tingling from cold mountain winds.

'So. We have a new Pathan in town!' he muses aloud.

At that moment the mountain man turns his head. He does not like the expression on our faces. Full of fury, he snarls and spits at us.

'Welcome to Lahore, brother,' Imam Din calls.

Months later, I recognize the face when I see Sharbat Khan, still touchy and bewildered, bent intently over his whirring machine as he sharpens knives in the Mozang Chawk bazaar.

*

I can't seem to put my finger on it—but there is a subtle change in the Queen's Garden. Sitting on Ayah's crossed legs, leaning against her chocolate softness, again the unease at the back of my mind surfaces.

I fidget restlessly on Ayah's lap and she asks: 'What is it, Lenny? You want to do soo-soo?'

I nod, for want of a better explanation.

'I'll take her,' offers Masseur, getting up.

Masseur leads me to the Queen's platform. Squatting beneath the English Queen's steely profile, my bottom bared to the evening throng, I relieve myself of a trickle.

'Oye! What are you gaping at?' Masseur shouts at a little Sikh boy who has paused to watch. His long hair, secured in a top-knot, is probably already addling his brain.

Masseur raises his arm threateningly and shouts: 'Scram!'

The boy flinches, but returning his eyes to me, stays his ground.

The Sikhs are fearless. They are warriors.

I slide my eyes away and, pretending not to notice him, stand up and raise my knickers. As Masseur straightens the skirt of my short frock, I lean back against his legs and shyly ogle the boy.

Masseur gropes for my hand. But I twist and slip away and run to the boy and he, pretending to be a steam-engine 'chook-chooking' and glancing my way, leads me romping to his group.

The Sikh women pull me to their laps and ask my name and the name of my religion.

'I'm Parsee,' I say.

'O kee? What's that?' they ask, scandalized to discover a religion they've never heard of.

That's when I realize what has changed.

*

There is much disturbing talk. India is going to be broken. Can one break a country? And what happens if they break it where our house is? Or crack it further up on Warris Road? How will I ever get to Godmother's then?

I ask Cousin.

'Rubbish,' he says, 'no one's going to break India. It's not made of glass!'

I ask Ayah.

'They'll dig a canal . . .' she ventures. 'This side for Hindustan and this side for Pakistan. If they want two countries, that's what they'll have to do—crack India with a long, long canal.'

Gandhi, Jinnah, Nehru, Tara Singh, Mountbatten are names I hear.

And I become aware of religious differences.

It is sudden. One day everybody is themselves—and the next day they are Hindu, Muslim, Sikh, Christian. People shrink, dwindling into symbols. Ayah is no longer just my all-encompassing Ayah, she is also a token. A Hindu. Carried away by a renewed devotional fervour she expends a small fortune in joss sticks, flowers and sweets on the gods and goddesses in the temples.

Imam and Yousaf, turning into religious zealots, warn Mother they will take Friday afternoons off for the Jumha prayers . . . At odd hours of the day, they spread their mats on the front lawn and pray when the muezzin calls. Crammed into a narrow religious slot, they too are diminished: as are Jinnah and Ice-candy-man.

Hari and Moti-the-sweeper and his wife Muccho, and their untouchable daughter Papoo, become ever more untouchable as they are entrenched deeper in their Hindu caste. While the Sharmas and the Daulatrams, Brahmins like Nehru, are dehumanized by their lofty caste and caste-marks.

The Rogers of Birdwood Barracks and King George are English Christians: they look down their noses upon the Anglo-Indians, who look down upon all non-Christians.

Godmother and my nuclear family are reduced to irrelevance—we are Parsee.

What is God?

*

Yousaf comes to fetch me. The sun has had time to warm the afternoon. 'Let's go through the Lawrence Gardens,' I urge, and Yousaf, unable to deny anyone, makes the detour through the gardens. We clamber up the slopes of artificial hills and run down bougainvillaea valleys ablaze with winter flowers. Casting long shadows we take a path leading to where Yousaf has parked his cycle.

Our shadow glides over a Brahmin Pandit. Sitting cross-legged on the grass he is eating out of a leaf-bowl. He looks at Yousaf—and at me—and his face expresses the full range of terror, and pain expected of a violated virgin. Our shadow has violated his virtue. The Pandit cringes. His features shrivel into arid little shrimps and his body retracts. The vermillion caste-mark on his forehead glows like an accusing eye. He looks at his food as if it is infected with maggots. Squeamishly picking up the leaf, he tips its contents behind a bush and throws away the leaf.

I am a loathsome maggot. I look at Yousaf. His face is drained of joy, bleak, furious. I know he too feels himself composed of shit, crawling with maggots.

Now I know surely. One man's religion is another man's poison.

I experience this feeling of utter degradation, of being an untouchable excrescence, an outcast again, years later when I hold out my hand to a Parsee priest at a wedding and he, thinking I am menstruating beneath my diamonds and sequined sari, cringes.

*

Late that evening there is a familiar pattern of sound.

Again they're after Hari's dhoti. But instead of the light, quick patter of bare feet there is the harsh scrape and drag of leather on frozen earth.

It doesn't seem quite right to toy with a man's dhoti when it is so cold. It is a summer sport.

Someone shouts, 'Get him before he gets into his quarters!' I hear Imam Din's bullying, bluff *barruk* as he bellows: 'Aha-hurrr! A-vaaaaaaay!' And, closer to his quarry, Yousaf's provocative bubbly 'Vo-vo-vo-vo-vo', as running he taps his mouth in quick succession. Curses! Hair all over my body creeps aslant as I hear Hari's alarmed cry.

Snatching me up and straddling me on her hip, Ayah flings open the bathroom door and runs out. I am struck by the chill, and the approach of night casts uneasy shadows over a scene I have witnessed only in daylight. Something else too is incongruous. The winter shawl wrapped around Hari.

Yousaf is twirling his plume of hair and tugging at it as if he's trying to lift him. I feel a great swell of fear for Hari, and a surge of loathing for his *bodhi*. Why must he persist in growing it? and flaunt his Hinduism? and invite ridicule? and that preposterous and obscene dhoti! worn like a diaper between his stringy legs—just begging to be taken off!

My dread assuming a violent and cruel shape, I tear away from Ayah and fling myself on the human tangle and fight to claw at Hari's dhoti.

Someone pulls off his shawl and it is trampled underfoot. Hands stretch and pull his unravelling mauve lady's cardigan (Mother's hand-me-down) and rip off his shirt. His dhoti is hanging in ragged edges and, suddenly, it's off!

Like a withered tree frozen in a winter landscape Hari stands isolated in the bleak centre of our violence: prickly with goosebumps, sooty genitals on display.

With heavy, old-man's movements, Imam Din wrenches the shawl from under our feet and throws it at the gardener: and the tattered rag that was his dhoti. 'Cover up, you shameless bugger,' he says, attempting his usual bantering manner, but there is a gruff uncontrollable edge to his voice. He is not at ease with cruelty.

I look back. The Shankars stand on their veranda like fat shadows. Ayah has turned her face away. I run to her. I dig my face in her sari and stretch up my hands. Ayah tries to lift me but her fluid strength is gone. Her grip is weak. I hug her fiercely. Her heart beneath her springy breasts is fluttering like Ice-candy-man's nervous sparrows. She raises frightened eyes from my face and, turning to follow her gaze, I see an obscured shape standing by the compound wall. Stirred by a breeze, the shadows cast by a eucalyptus tree shift and splinter, and define the still figure of a man.

The man moves out of the darkness, and as he approaches I am relieved. It is only Ice-candy-man.

PART VI

CHRONICLERS

Kipling's Lahore: The City of Dreadful Night

Ijaz Husain Batalvi

Rudyard Kipling landed in Bombay in October 1882 after an absence of about eleven years from India, a time spent studying in schools in England. In 1882, 'India' consisted not only of present-day India, but also Pakistan, Bangladesh and lower Burma. There was nothing special about the year 1882 except that it was twenty-five years after the so-called Indian mutiny; thirteen years after the opening of Suez Canal and five years after the proclamation of Queen Victoria as Empress of India.

Kipling, while leaving the shores of England, may have skipped the briefing given by the shipping company to newly recruited employees of East India Company and, later, to civil and military servants of the Queen. The briefing was an introduction to India through the experience of those who had survived the India adventure before them. They were shown pictures of the type of houses they would live in; the style of bathrooms, the flora and fauna, the servants: cook, ayah, bearer, syce, dhobi and mali, and what they would look like. They were also introduced to the climate they would face and the diseases they might acquire, like malaria, dysentery and possibly typhoid and cholera.

It was a briefing Kipling did not need because he was not coming to 'India'. He was coming 'home'—a Bombay-born child joining his parents. In accordance with the prevailing English custom in Anglo-India, he was withdrawn from the care of his ayah at the age of six and sent to England, where he spent one of the most miserable periods of his life. Except for a short visit by his mother, he did not see his parents in over a decade. He now returned to Bombay, the city of his birth, as a precocious young man with side whiskers and bad eyesight.

His bad eyesight spared him a career in the Navy or the Army.

This was a return journey to his earliest memories of 'daybreak, light and colour and night winds through palm and banana leaves'. Familiar sounds and smells like a mixture of spice and woodsmoke and jasmine, dust and cow dung, were revived. Forgotten phrases and sentences in the vernacular came back to him without their meanings. He took a train and travelled a thousand miles across the subcontinent to the north-west. After four days, he reached Lahore. In his own words: 'That was a joyous homecoming.' During his absence, his parents had shifted their home from Bombay to Lahore, where his father was a teacher in Mayo School of Arts and Director of the Museum; 'the wonder house' as the Lahoris called it. He wrote: 'I had returned to a father and mother of whom I had seen but little since my sixth year.'

For Kipling, Lahore was going to be a city of destiny, the vibrant life of the walled Mughal city after dark reminding him of an illustration from the *Arabian Nights*; where a mixed population from every part of Asia helped to create an impression of mysterious lives lived in the shadows of domes and minarets. When moonlight fell upon back alleys, squares, old houses with small brick walls or the Shalimar Gardens, he set out on foot to explore the magic and mystery that descended on the city.

Kipling left England after finishing school because his father could not afford to send him to Oxford. His headmaster had recognized that he was 'irretrievably committed to the ink pot' and his parents managed to get him a post on an English daily called *Civil and Military Gazette*, published from Lahore, at a salary of £100 a year.

The daily had been founded ten years earlier by William Ratigan, a leading member of the Lahore Bar. It was a propitious posting; running the paper from Lahore opened up the floodgates of knowledge, information and observation for Kipling, and shaped the writer within him. In November, Kipling commenced work at the *Gazette*. By the end of December, at the age of seventeen, he found himself in charge of the paper because the chief editor, Stephen Wheller, had had a carriage accident.

Lahore was the capital of the Punjab, the last province of South Asia to be annexed by the British in 1849, after the battle of

Chelianwala—one of the bloodiest ever fought by the English in the subcontinent. In the thirty-three years that followed its annexation in 1882, Lahore had started wearing the look of a colonial city with a Mall running through it and with Civil Lines bungalows in which the English lived, outside and away from the walled city. The old city was located at one end of Lahore and the military cantonment at Mian Mir at the other end, five miles away, where the battalion of the British Army was stationed. Kipling left for posterity a magnificent pen-picture of the city divided thus—'the red coats, the pipe clayed belts and the pill box hats, the beer, the fights, the flogging, hangings and crucifixion, the bugle calls, the smell of oats and horse piss, the bellowing sergeants with foot-long moustaches, the bloody skirmishes, invariably mishandled, the cholera-stricken camps, the ultimate death in the work house.'

Kipling travelled comfortably between the two cultural hemispheres and in Kipling the storyteller, East and West were to meet.

If Kipling was going to be chronicler of the Raj, the Raj was lucky to have him. The plains of the Punjab and the city of Lahore provided him with material to write about for the rest of his life. In the words of Phillip Masson:

> He looked always and everywhere for material, and consciously stored it until he could put it to dramatic use. Picking up here one brightly coloured pebble, there another, storing them away and eventually bringing two or three together into one story. Material on that level might be no more than a phrase heard in a bar describing a woman six thousand miles away; it might be the picture of a sentry 'the night dew gemming his moustache, leaning on his rifle at picket'. It might be a few lines of a verse carved on a monument a hundred years ago. The craftsman mind was always at work on these fragments, turning them over, polishing and selecting.

Kipling was not a typical British colonialist and Orwell's depiction of a colonial officer as a 'Pukka Sahib in a pith helmet kicking a coolie' does not fit him. On the contrary, he was a freak and an exception. He had an un-English manner of getting close to the 'natives', of talking to them in their language and getting to know how they lived. For his countrymen, even those who had spent a lifetime in the subcontinent, his description of this strata of Indian society was a revelation.

Who but Kipling would go and sit under the 'pipal' tree with the faqirs, sadhus, sanyasis, mullahs and bairagis. It required a special kind of inclination and courage to get to the 'Chaubara of Dunni Bhagat' which mendicants, charm-sellers and holy vagabonds, from a hundred miles around, used to make their place of call and rest. It is here that he met one-eyed Gobind who told Kipling that 'he was a holy man who lived on an island in the middle of a river and fed the fish with little bread pellets twice a day'. In flood time, when swollen corpses stranded themselves at the foot of the island, Gobind would cause them to be piously buried for the sake of the honour of mankind, and having regard of his own account with God hereafter. But when two-thirds of the island was torn away in a spate, Gobind crossed the river to Dhunni Bhagat's Chaubara. Gobind was nearly blind and his face was seamed and lined and wrinkled beyond belief, for he had lived in his time, which was before the English came within five hundred miles of Dhunni Bhagat's Chaubara. Kipling, the teller of tales, respected his art wherever he found it, and so he reports:

> When we grew to know each other well, Gobind would tell me tales in a voice most like the rumbling of heavy guns over a wooden bridge. 'And what,' said Gobind one Sunday evening, 'is your honoured craft, and by what manner of means earn you your daily bread?'
>
> 'I am,' said I, 'a Kerani—one who writes with a pen upon paper, not being in the service of the Government.'
>
> 'Then what do you write?' said Gobind. 'Come nearer, for I cannot see your countenance, and the light fails.'
>
> 'I write all matters that lie within my understanding, and many that do not. But chiefly I write of Life and Death, and men and women, and Love and Hate according to the measure of one, two or more people.'

'Ay, I was once a famed teller of old stories when I was begging on the road between Koshin and Etra.'

I said: 'But in regard to our people, they desire new tales.'

'But what folly is theirs,' said Gobind, throwing out his knotted hand. 'A tale that is told is a true tale as long as the telling lasts.'

This conversation between two storytellers—one an eighteen year old and the other a holy vagabond of eighty—is recorded by Kipling in a preface to his book *Life's Handicap*, first published in 1891. The last bit of this dialogue has value for storytellers of all lands and all times:

'In what manner is it best to set about the task?' said I. 'Oh, chiefest of those who string pearls with their tongues.'

'How do I know yet?'—he thought for a little, 'how should I not know? God has made many heads, but there is only one heart in all the world among your people or my people. They are children in the matter of tales.'

In Lahore, Kipling encountered two problems for which he was not prepared. One was the heat, and the other the Imperial 'English Caste System'. The English in India were like a small island in the huge sea of an alien population—the natives. This created an oligarchy in which English civil servants were Brahmins. The traders and businessmen, though far richer, were called 'Boxwallahs' and were looked down on by both the civil and military officers. Phillip Masson, who lived for twenty years as part of the system, writes:

British society in India was curiously caste like. There were two great caste groups, 'officers' and 'other ranks', within each of which, marriage was permissible. Marriage between these groups was forbidden. In peacetime, officers and other ranks did not sit down to eat together. All this was like the great Indian castes. And again, like the Indian castes, the two main groups were sub-divided. True, there was no rule that a man in the Indian Civil Service should not marry the daughter of any army officer or a policeman. Nonetheless, these were separate groups arranged in an order of precedence even more rigid than among castes, because it was printed at the end of the Civil List, which everyone had on his desk, it showed everyone's pay and his exact place in the hierarchy. But it did not mention reporters for the *Civil and Military Gazette*.

So one can imagine young Kipling's plight in this class-ridden society and his unpopularity in the Punjab Club, an exclusive haven reserved for the British. Poor Kipling came very near to being thrashed by senior officers for his impudence in speaking out of turn, or not accepting an official point of view.

As for the other problem, over a hundred years ago, with no electricity, the Lahore heat was absolute hell. Senior officials went to Simla or other Himalayan hill stations. For those left behind, the Punjab summer was a test of endurance that made them long for a grey English day. An English woman wrote: 'If fate cast her lot in the North she is called upon to face that pitiless destroyer of youth and beauty—the Punjab hot weather.' Another wrote: 'When the night became intolerable we would wrap ourselves in a wet sheet and lie down in it so as to let evaporation cool us a bit.'

At his parents' bungalow, Kipling had his own quarters, with a personal servant and a horse and a trap in which he drove to office. But while Lahore's winter was glorious with crisp sunshine and flowers in the gardens, summer brought not just heat but also loneliness; he found them both unbearable. His mother had sailed to England and his father went on leave to the hills. Kipling was left alone in the big house with the servants. He worked at the newspaper late into the night, till the last copy was sent to the press and then, as his biographer records: 'He wandered through the lanes of the old city into the small hours.'

Kipling suffered from insomnia. It had set in quite early, possibly as a consequence of his nightmarish stay with his foster-parents in England. Kingsley Amis observes:

By his own account, it was during the couple of months in Brompton Road (1877) that Kipling first suffered from insomnia that stayed with him all his life. 'The night got into my head,' as Kipling put it, and he would wander through the house and round the garden. Such nocturnal rambles became a habit for many years. A poem of 1890 clearly refers to himself; 'We wakeful, oh pity us.' It is not surprising that James Thomson's 'City of Dreadful Night'—with its theme of loneliness and silence, was one of Kipling's favourite poems.

Unable to endure the empty, echoing house and watch the 'punkha' beat the dead air on a stifling August night in Lahore 1885, Kipling went for a walk. He threw his stick in the garden and waited to see how it would fall.

It pointed directly down the moon-lit road that leads to the City of Dreadful Night. The sound of its fall disturbed a hare. She limped from her form and ran across to a disused Mohammedan burial ground where the jawless skulls and rough-butted shank-bones, heartlessly exposed by the July rains, glimmered like mother O'pearl on the rain channelled soil. The heated air and the heavy earth had driven the very dead for coolness sake.

It was a two-hour walk to the Delhi Gate, one of the gates to the old city and on the way he saw, 'string of sleeping camels at rest by the wayside . . . more stretches of moonlight . . . ekka ponies asleep—the harness still on their backs . . . the brass-studded country carts, winking in the moonlight . . . A stifling hot blast from the mouth of the Delhi Gate nearly ends the resolution of entering the city of Dreadful Night at this hour.' But the sleepless night rambler could hardly be deterred by a hot blast and he did enter the city 'where the high house-walls were still radiating heat savagely'. When he reaches the shadows of his favourite Wazir Khan's mosque, his narrative becomes poetically smooth:

'Then silence follows—the silence that is full of the night noises of a great city. A stringed instrument of some kind is just and only just audible. High over head someone throws open a window and the rattle of woodwork echoes down the empty street. It is close upon midnight and the heat seems to be increasing. The moonlight stripes the mosque's high front of coloured enamel work in broad diagonal bands. Is it possible to climb to the top of the great minars and thence to look down on the city?'

He goes up the minar to a cool or, at least, less sultry breeze. 'Seated with both elbows on the parapet of the tower, one can watch and wonder over that heat-tortured hive till the dawn. How do they live down there? What do they think of? When will they awake?'

From that height, Kipling describes the city under the pitiless moonlight. 'Dore might have drawn it! Zola could describe it.' So young Kipling observed looking at the scene but his own descriptive narrative is no less masterly than any of those named by him. And then the muezzin is heard 'a bull-like roar—a magnificent thunder. Even across the courtyard it is almost overpowering. The cloud drifts by and shows him outlined in black against the sky, hands laid upon his ears, and broad chest heaving with the play of his lungs. Allah ho Akbar, then a pause. Again and again, four times in all. The East grows grey and presently saffron. The dawn wind comes up as though the muezzin had summoned it.' His eyelids weighed down with the arrears of long-deferred sleep, Kipling escapes through the courtyard of the mosque into the square—to find that the sleepers have risen and the City of Dreadful Night is awake.

One feels sure that in the morning, after his bath and breakfast, young Kipling, having laid the previous night's ghost to rest through his prose, rode to work in his formal office attire, with the stiff upper lip of an Englishman. He was truly a man who had both the capacity to observe many layers of existence around him and the courage to live them in his own existence.

Mahbub Ali: The Horse-trader

Rudyard Kipling

The hot and crowded bazars blazed with light as they made their way through the press of all the races in Upper India, and the lama mooned through it like a man in a dream. It was his first experience of a large manufacturing city, and the crowded tram-car with its continually squealing brakes frightened him. Half pushed, half towed, he arrived at the high gate of the Kashmir Serai: that huge open square over against the railway station, surrounded with arched cloisters where the camel and horse caravans put up on their return from Central Asia. Here were all manner of Northern folk, tending tethered ponies and kneeling camels; loading and unloading bales and bundles; drawing water for the evening meal at the creaking well-windlasses; piling grass before the shrieking, wild-eyed stallions; cuffing the surly caravan dogs; paying off camel-drivers; taking on new grooms; swearing, shouting, arguing, and chaffering in the packed square. The cloisters, reached by three or four masonry steps, made a haven of refuge around this turbulent sea. Most of them were rented to traders, as we rent the arches of a viaduct; the space between pillar and pillar being bricked or boarded off into rooms, which were guarded by heavy wooden doors and cumbersome native padlocks. Locked doors showed that the owner was away, and a few rude—sometimes very rude— chalk or paint scratches told where he had gone. Thus: 'Lutuf Ullah is gone to Kurdistan.' Below, in coarse verse: 'O Allah, who sufferest lice to live on the coat of a Kabuli, why hast thou allowed this louse Lutuf to live so long?'

Kim, fending the lama between excited men and excited beasts, sidled along the cloisters to the far end, nearest the railway station, where Mahbub Ali, the horse-trader, lived when he came in from that mysterious land beyond the Passes of the North.

This extract is taken from Rudyard Kipling's *Kim*.

Kim had had many dealings with Mahbub in his little life,—especially between his tenth and his thirteenth year,—and the big burly Afghan, his beard dyed scarlet with lime (for he was elderly and did not wish his gray hairs to show), knew the boy's value as a gossip. Sometimes he would tell Kim to watch a man who had nothing whatever to do with horses: to follow him for one whole day and report every soul with whom he talked. Kim would deliver himself of his tale at evening, and Mahbub would listen without a word or gesture. It was intrigue of some kind, Kim knew; but its worth lay in saying nothing whatever to any one except Mahbub, who gave him beautiful meals all hot from the cook-shop at the head of the serai, and once as much as eight annas in money.

'He is here,' said Kim, hitting a bad-tempered camel on the nose. 'Ohé, Mahbub Ali!' He halted at a dark arch and slipped behind the bewildered lama.

The horse-trader, his deep, embroidered Bokhariot belt unloosed, was lying on a pair of silk carpet saddle-bags, pulling lazily at an immense silver hookah. He turned his head very slightly at the cry; and seeing only the tall silent figure, chuckled in his deep chest.

'Allah! A lama! A Red Lama! It is far from Lahore to the Passes. What dost thou do here?'

The lama held out the begging-bowl mechanically.

'God's curse on all unbelievers!' said Mahbub. 'I do not give to a lousy Tibetan; but ask my Baltis over yonder behind the camels. They may value your blessings. Oh, horse-boys, here is a countryman of yours. See if he be hungry.'

A shaven, crouching Balti, who had come down with the horses, and who was nominally some sort of degraded Buddhist, fawned upon the priest, and in thick gutturals besought the Holy One to sit at the horse-boys' fire.

'Go!' said Kim, pushing him lightly, and the lama strode away, leaving Kim at the edge of the cloister.

'Go!' said Mahbub Ali, returning to his hookah. 'Little Hindu, run away. God's curse on all unbelievers! Beg from those of my tail who are of thy faith.'

'Maharaj,' whined Kim, using the Hindu form of address, and thoroughly enjoying the situation, 'my father is dead—my mother is dead—my stomach is empty.'

'Beg from my men among the horses, I say. There must be some Hindus in my tail.'

'Oh, Mahbub Ali, but am *I* a Hindu?' said Kim in English.

The trader gave no sign of astonishment, but looked under shaggy eyebrows.

'Little Friend of all the World,' said he, 'what is this?'

'Nothing. I am now that holy man's disciple; and we go a pilgrimage together—to Benares, he says. He is quite mad, and I am tired of Lahore city. I wish new air and water.'

'But for whom dost thou work? Why come to me?' The voice was harsh with suspicion.

'To whom else should I come? I have no money. It is not good to go about without money. Thou wilt sell many horses to the officers. They are very fine horses, these new ones: I have seen them. Give me a rupee. Mahbub Ali, and when I come to my wealth I will give thee a bond and pay.'

'Um,' said Mahbub Ali, thinking swiftly. 'Thou hast never before lied to me. Call that lama—stand back in the dark.'

'Oh, our tales will agree,' said Kim, laughing.

'We go to Benares,' said the lama as soon as he understood the drift of Mahbub Ali's questions. 'The boy and I. I go to seek for a certain River.'

'Maybe—but the boy?'

'He is my disciple. He was sent, I think, to guide me to that River. Sitting under a gun was I when he came suddenly. Such things have befallen the fortunate to whom guidance was allowed. But I remember now, he said he was of this world—a Hindu.'

'And his name?'

'That I did not ask. Is he not my disciple?'

'His country—his race—his village? Mussalman—Sikh—Hindu—Jain—low caste or high?'

'Why should I ask? There is neither high nor low in the Middle Way. If he is my *chela*—does—will—can any one take him from me? For, look you, without him I shall not find my River.' He wagged his head solemnly.

'None shall take him from thee. Go, sit among my Baltis,' said

Mahbub Ali, and the lama drifted off, soothed by the promise.

'Is he not quite mad?' said Kim, coming forward to the light again. 'Why should I lie to thee, Hajji?'

Mahbub puffed his hookah in silence. Then he began, almost whispering: 'Umballa is on the road to Benares—if indeed ye two go there.'

'Tck Tck! I tell thee he does not know how to lie—as we two know.'

'And if thou wilt carry a message for me as far as Umballa, I will give thee money. It concerns a horse—a white stallion which I have sold to an officer upon the last time I returned from the Passes. But then—stand nearer and hold up hands as begging—the pedigree of the white stallion was not fully established, and that officer, who is now at Umballa, bade me make it clear.' (Mahbub here described the horse and the appearance of the officer.) 'So the message to that officer will be: "The pedigree of the white stallion is fully established." By this will he know that thou comest from me. He will then say: "What proof hast khou?" and thou wilt answer: "Mahbub Ali has given me the proof."'

'And all for the sake of a white stallion,' said Kim, with a giggle, his eyes aflame.

'That pedigree I will give thee now—in my own fashion—and some hard words as well.' A shadow passed behind Kim, and a feeding camel. Mahbub Ali raised his voice.

'Allah! Art thou the only beggar in the city? Thy mother is dead. Thy father is dead. So it is with all of them. Well, well—' he turned as feeling on the floor beside him and tossed a flap of soft, greasy Mussalman bread to the boy. 'Go and lie down among my horse-boys for to-night—thou and the lama. To-morrow I may give thee service.'

Kim slunk away, his teeth in the bread, and, as he expected, he found a small wad of folded tissue-paper wrapped in oil-skin, with three silver rupees—enormous largesse. He smiled and thrust money and paper into his leather amulet-case. The lama, sumptuously fed by Mahbub's Baltis, was already asleep in a corner of one of the stalls. Kim lay down beside him and laughed. He knew he had rendered a service to Mahbub Ali, and not for one little minute did he believe the tale of the stallion's pedigree.

But Kim did not suspect that Mahbub Ali, known as one of the best horse-dealers in the Punjab, a wealthy and enterprising trader, whose caravans penetrated far and far into the Back of Beyond, was registered in one of the locked books of the Indian Survey Department as C.25.1B. Twice or thrice yearly C.25 would send in a little story, badly told but most interesting, and generally—it was checked by the statements of R.17 and M.4—quite true. It concerned all manner of out-of-the-way mountain principalities, explorers of nationalities other than English, and the guntrade—was, in brief, a small portion of that vast mass of 'information received' on which the Indian Government acts. But, recently, five confederated Kings, who had no business to confederate, had been informed by a kindly Northern Power that there was a leakage of news from their territories into British India. So those Kings' prime ministers were seriously annoyed and took steps, after the Oriental fashion. They suspected, among many others, the bullying, red-bearded horse-dealer whose caravans ploughed through their fastnesses belly deep in snow. At least, his caravan that season had been ambushed and shot at twice on the way down, when Mahbub's men accounted for three strange ruffians who might, or might not, have been hired for the job. Therefore Mahbub had avoided halting at the insalubrious city of Peshawur, and had come through without stop to Lahore, where, knowing his country-people, he anticipated curious developments.

And there was that on Mahbub Ali which he did not wish to keep an hour longer than was necessary—a wad of closely folded tissue-paper, wrapped in oil-skin—an impersonal, unaddressed statement, with five microscopic pinholes in one corner, that most scandalously betrayed the five confederated Kings, the sympathetic Northern Power, a Hindu banker in Peshawur, a firm of gun-makers in Belgium, and an important, semi-independent Mohammedan ruler to the south. This last was R.17's work, which Mahbub had picked up beyond the Dora Pass and was carrying in for R.17, who, owing to circumstances over which he had no control, could not leave his post of observation. Dynamite was milky and innocuous beside that report of C.25; and even an Oriental, with an Oriental's views of the value of time, could see that the sooner it was in the proper hands the better. Mahbub had no particular desire to die by violence, because two or three family blood-feuds across the border hung unfinished on his hands, and when these scores were cleared he intended to settle down as a more or less virtuous citizen. He had never passed the serai gate since his arrival two days ago, but had been ostentatious in sending telegrams to Bombay, where he banked some of his money; to Delhi, where a sub-partner of his own clan was selling horses to the agent of a Rajputana state; and to Umballa, where an Englishman was excitedly demanding the pedigree of a white stallion. The public letter-writer, who knew English, composed excellent telegrams, such as: —'*Creighton, Laurel Bank, Umballa. —Horse is Arabian as already advised. Sorrowful delayed-pedigree which am translating.*' And later to the same address: '*Much sorrowful delay. Will forward pedigree.*' To his sub-partner at Delhi he wired: '*Lutuf Ullah. —Have wired two thousand rupees your credit Luchman Narain's bank.*' This was entirely in the way of trade, but every one of those telegrams was discussed and re-discussed, by parties who conceived themselves to be interested, before they went over to the railway station in charge of a foolish Balti, who allowed all sorts of people to read them on the road.

When, in Mahbub's own picturesque language, he had muddied the wells of inquiry with the stick of precaution, Kim had dropped on him, sent from heaven; and, being as prompt as he was unscrupulous, Mahbub Ali, used to taking all sorts of gusty chances, pressed him into service on the spot.

A wandering lama with a low-caste boy-servant might attract a moment's interest as they wandered about India, the land of pilgrims; but no one would suspect them or, what was more to the point, rob.

He called for a new light-ball to his hookah, and considered the case. If the worst came to the worst, and the boy came to harm, the paper would incriminate nobody. And he would go up to Umballa leisurely and—at a certain risk of exciting fresh suspicion—repeat his tale by word of mouth to the people concerned.

But R.17's report was the kernel of the whole affair, and it would be distinctly inconvenient if that failed to come to hand. However, God was great, and Mahbub Ali felt he had done all he could for the time being. Kim, was the one soul in the world who had never told him a lie. That would have been a fatal blot on Kim's character if Mahbub had not known that to others, for his own ends or Mahbub's business, Kim could lie like an Oriental.

Then Mahbub Ali rolled across the serai to the Gate of the Harpies who paint their eyes and trap the stranger, and was at some pains to call on the one girl who, he had reason to believe, was a particular friend of a smooth-faced Kashmiri pundit who had waylaid his simple Balti in the matter of the telegrams. It was an utterly foolish thing to do; because they fell to drinking perfumed brandy against the Law of the Prophet, and Mahbub grew wonderfully drunk, and the gates of his mouth were loosened, and he pursued the Flower of Delight with the feet of intoxication till he fell flat among the cushions, where the Flower of Delight, aided by a smooth-faced Kashmiri pundit, searched him from head to foot most thoroughly.

About the same hour Kim heard soft feet in Mahbub's deserted stall. The horse-trader, curiously enough, had left his door unlocked, and his men were busy celebrating their return to India with a whole sheep of Mahbub's bounty. A sleek young gentleman from Delhi, armed with a bunch of keys which the Flower had unshackled from the senseless one's belt, went through every single box, bundle, mat, and saddle-bag in Mahbub's possession even more systematically than the Flower and the pundit were searching the owner.

'And I think,' said the Flower scornfully an hour later, one rounded elbow on the snoring carcase, 'that he is no more than a pig of an Afghan horse-dealer, with no thought except women and horses. Moreover, he may have sent it away by now—if ever there were such a thing.'

'Nay—in a matter touching Five Kings it would be next his black heart,' said the pundit. 'Was there nothing?'

The Delhi man laughed and resettled his turban as he entered. 'I searched between the soles of his slippers as the Flower searched his clothes. This is not the man but another. I leave little unseen.'

'They did not say he was the very man,' said the pundit thoughtfully. 'They said, "Look if he be the man, since our councils are troubled."'

'That North country is full of horse-dealers as an old coat of lice. There is Sikandar Khan, Nur Ali Beg, and Farrukh Shah—all heads of Kafilas—who deal there,' said the Flower.

'They have not yet come in,' said the pundit. 'Thou must ensnare them later.'

'Phew!' said the Flower with deep disgust, rolling Mahbub's head from her lap. 'I earn my money. Farrukh Shah is a bear, Ali Beg a swashbuckler, and old Sikandar Khan—yaie! Go! I sleep now. This swine will not stir till dawn.'

When Mahbub woke, the Flower talked to him severely on the sin of drunkenness. Asiatics do not wink when they have out-manoeuvred an enemy, but as Mahbub Ali cleared his throat, tightened his belt, and staggered forth under the early morning stars, he came very near to it.

'What a colt's trick,' said he to himself. 'As if every girl in Peshawur did not use it! But 'twas prettily done. Now God He knows how many more there be upon the road who have orders to test me— perhaps with the knife. So it stands that the boy must go to Umballa— and by rail—for the writing is something urgent. I abide here, following the Flower and drinking wine as an Afghan coper should.'

He halted at the stall next but one to his own. His men lay there heavy with sleep. There was no sign of Kim or the lama.

'Up!' He stirred a sleeper. 'Whither went those who lay here last even—the lama and the boy? Is aught missing?'

'Nay,' grunted the man; 'the old madman rose as second cockcrow, saying he would go to Benares, and the young one led him away.'

'The curse of Allah on all unbelievers,' said Mahbub heartily, and climbed into his own stall, growling in his beard.

But it was Kim who had wakened the lama—Kim with one eye laid against a knot-hole in the planking, who had seen the Delhi man's search through the boxes. This was no common thief that turned over letters, bills, and saddles—no mere burglar who ran a little knife sideways into the soles of Mahbub's slippers, or picked the seams of the saddle-bags so deftly. At first Kim had been minded to give the alarm—the long-drawn *cho-or—choor!* (thief! thief!) that sets the serai ablaze of nights; but he looked more carefully, and, hand on amulet, drew his own conclusions.

'It must be the pedigree of that made-up horse-lie,' said he, 'the thing that I carry to Umballa. Better that we go now. Those who search bags with knives may presently search bellies with knives. Surely there is a woman behind this. Hai Hai!' in a whisper to the light-sleeping old man. 'Come. It is time—time to go to Benares.'

The lama rose obediently, and they passed out of the serai like shadows.

Habib Jalib: An Archetypical Lahori

Jugnu Mohsin

Habib Jalib spent almost his entire working life in Lahore, writing his best poetry in this city. He was also part of every protest movement that began in Lahore, from the 1960s to the 1990s. One of Jalib's most famous poems, 'Aisay dastoor ko, subha-e-benoor ko, mein naheen maanta, mein naheen jaanta' (this wayward way, this dark dawn; I do not know and will not own) was first declaimed at a mushaira in Lahore.

He lived in a newly developed colony halfway between Kasur and Lahore. When you got to it, it was a tiny habitation housing no less than ten people. Jalib said the drinking water was brackish and that no natural gas was to be had for miles around. But it was not the state alone which had turned its back on the man who was one of Pakistan's most popular poets. By the time he died in 1993, Jalib had paid a heavy price for constructing the edifice that was his persona.

His greatness appeared to be lost on his family too. His wife was a monumental stoic (he used to say she was a simple woman with simple tastes), his daughters looked at me vacantly when I went over for the interview all those years ago, their features etched with premature cynicism. Jalib languished on a charpai, his frame racked with a persistent cough. 'You can't expect to get my life story over one afternoon. You need six months for that, and you need to be assisted by a lawyer.' That set the tone for the rest of our exchange. All I got was a glimpse of the poet's intellect, his fluency, his sensibility. It was all that I was able to garner on my way across the desert of Habib Jalib's bitterness with life.

Habib Ahmed was born in Hoshiarpur, East Punjab, around 1928. He says his people were of old Punjabi stock and that there was an interesting family fiction which would have them tracing their descent to Mahmud Ghaznavi, one of the earliest Muslim invaders of India.

'I never claimed it as my own. It is nothing to be proud of. The man was a rapacious plunderer.' Habib went to school in Delhi, the Anglo-Arabic in Ajmeri Gate, and was looking for a job when the family moved to Pakistan in 1947. 'I felt like a leaf in the wind. My family roamed Pakistan like beggars. We came first to Karachi, the great white hope, the land of opportunity. We came in quest of the promised resurrection and found death staring us in the face wherever we went. It was the same in the Punjab. In that dreadful winter of '47, while refugees languished in camps, the standard bearers of the Muslim League went on a mad spree. They enriched themselves and their cronies with the abandoned wealth of the Hindus. And we, who were the dispossessed, found ourselves stripped of all hope. It was every man for himself.' Habib Ahmed felt the sharp edge of this betrayal. He decided to speak out against it and in so doing, he became Jalib, the poet, the darling of the masses.

Around then, Pakistan's progressive writers were beginning to band together. Jalib gravitated towards them as a moth to the flame. He found work as a proofreader with the Urdu newspaper *Imroze* and married his cousin. Karachi was a fickle mistress for a temperament such as Jalib's. He felt himself drawn to Lahore where there was a larger population of disenchanted non-affiliates. His talent was in greater demand, too, and he was able to get supplementary work as a film songwriter.

It is not wholly correct to bracket Jalib with the real non-affiliates. Jalib had long been a committed revolutionary and it was in the early '50s that he first voiced such concerns. While still at Karachi, he had worked actively as a leftist participant in peasant leader Haider Baksh Jatoi's struggle against the Sindhi feudal lord-cum-chief minister, Ayub Khoro. A vicious witch-hunt followed and it may have contributed in part to his departure for Lahore. Jalib's poems of that period, published collectively in *Barg-e-avara*, are a testimony to the infant Pakistani state's reprisals against dissenters.

In true poetic tradition, Jalib talked of his persuasion as one would of the beloved. 'Mujhe jamhooriat ka rog lag gaya,' he said. ('I was afflicted by a longing for democracy.') He also joined the Azad Pakistan Party. Its founder, Mian Iftikharuddin, had clearly made an impression on him. 'Iftikharuddin was the first oppositionist to the state. He started this honourable tradition and no one can take that away from him. He was a rich man, yes, but he chose to employ his wealth for a cause. He also published newspapers when he could have done things far more lucrative.'

Jalib was in great demand wherever he went. He said unabashedly, 'Mujhe harr mushaira mein bulaya jaata tha. Baqi doston kay saath, hum nay is shehr mein baghavat ki lehr dora di.' ('I was invited to every mushaira in Lahore. My friends and I sent a wave of defiance surging through the city.') His circumstances were, as usual, destitute. He lived on the edge in the working-class Sandah district of Lahore, 'in a room and a half', and had a child every year.

Those were trying times, Jalib said, there was plenty to rebel against. Instead of addressing the infant state's socio-economic problems, Pakistan's rulers were busy shoring up their short-term interests by offering to become America's lackeys. 'Those were the days of SEATO and CENTO. Our rulers had become mercenaries and we, the people, unwitting pawns in their game. I was disgusted.'

The Azad Pakistan Party had by then merged with the National Awami Party (NAP). Jalib was much taken with Maulana Bhashani and Abdul Ghaffar Khan, the NAP's leaders in East Pakistan and the North-West Frontier respectively. And while he may have been following a party directive when he opposed Ayub Khan, Pakistan's then military dictator, it was also as a matter of conscience that Jalib supported Fatima Jinnah, around whom the entire opposition to Khan had coalesced. It was for this act of independence that Jalib first saw the inside of a jail. They took him to the old Borstal in Lahore and flung him into a cramped and fetid cell with common criminals. Jalib's only consolation was that he was in the very place where the British Raj had hanged the freedom fighter Bhagat Singh. And it is his memory the Pakistani state desecrated when it eventually demolished the jail to make way for the upmarket Shadman Colony. The irony of it was not lost on Jalib.

I asked him when it was that he next went to prison. He didn't like that at all. He sat bolt upright, his brow knitted and his eyes flashed. It was as if I had insulted him. 'When have I not been to prison? All Pakistani rulers have jailed me, from Ayub Khan to Zia-ul-Haq. Benazir did not arrest me, I suppose she was too busy with her battles on other fronts.' Having had his impassioned say, Jalib sank back against the bolsters and declaimed from the depths of his bed, 'I'll tell you a story. There was this bard at the court of a king. The king fancied himself a poet. He recited a pathetic little verse and asked the bard to comment upon it. The bard said it was awful. The king condemned him to the dungeons for a year. Next year, he had the bard hauled up again. The king recited the same poem. The bard told him again that it was awful and was sent off for another year. The following year, the bard was brought to the king and before he could go through the whole exercise again, the bard asked to be sent back to the dungeons. In a nutshell, that's the story of my life. I have never been able to give a bad thing a good name.'

In the mid-sixties, Jalib came out with his next book of poems, *Sar-e-maqtal*, which went into its fourth edition within a month of publication. He spoke out against the army action in East Pakistan and was arrested. Zulfikar Ali Bhutto, who rode to power on the backs of the people, delivered Jalib his most crushing blow. 'It was a betrayal, nothing short. I wrote *Zikr Behtay Khoon Ka* and Bhutto it was who proscribed it. When he dismissed the NAP ministries how could I, in all conscience, sit it out? I condemned Mr Bhutto's high-handedness both as a member of the party and as a citizen of Pakistan.'

It was on the day Jalib's twelve-year-old son died for lack of medical attention that he was arrested and transported to Hyderabad to be tried for treason by a special tribunal. 'I remember that day. My small house was full of mourners. The police came to get me. Every face in the police had become well known to me. I asked if they'd come to condole. They looked a little shamefaced and said they'd come to arrest me. I asked to be allowed a few hours with my family. The police refused to give me more than half an hour. I asked them to pick me up and throw me into the police van, which they did. They took me to the Federal Investigation Authority's office behind a cinema and asked me to sign on the dotted line. I refused and they packed me off to Hyderabad.'

In 1977, with General Zia's coup, the Hyderabad detainees were let off. Jalib came back to his beloved Lahore but he could not remain a silent spectator for long. It flowed out of him, that poem, full of irreverence and sarcasm:

Zulmat ko Zia,
Sarsar ko saba,
Banday ko khuda kya kehna?

(Can cruelty be kindness, a dust storm the morning breeze, can man be God?)

And as if that wasn't enough, Jalib marched in Lahore in support of the Women's Action Forum and their demand for the repeal of Zia's retrogressive laws. It was a sight to behold. A fragile old man stood in the middle of a group of 200 women, surrounded by a police cordon. Jalib raised his arm, invoking all concerned to listen. He then let rip a devastating attack on those who would deny the rights of women. A hushed silence fell upon his audience. The women raised their voice as one. A current of energy seemed to pass through the crowd. One woman threw her weight against the police cordon. Others followed. The cordon was broken. And as the women ran free with their placards on the road, Jalib was struck repeatedly on the head with batons. Blood poured down his face and on to his modest white clothes. A photographer's lens froze the moment forever.

This, the least of the man's offerings at the altar of democracy, was nonetheless typical. Habib Jalib was never the silent spectator, he fought for every cause worth the name, his poems were heard everywhere, in the unlikeliest of places. He paid for his conscience. And if he tended to knock it back, it must have been because he never took the opium of the masses.

Dastoor

Habib Jalib

Deep jis ka mehlaat hee mein jalay
Chund logoon kee khushioon ko lay kar chalay
Voh jo sayay mein har muslehat kay chalay
Aisay dastoor ko subha-e-benoor ko
Mein naheen maanta, mein naheen jaanta

Mein bhi khaif naheen takhtaa dar say
Mein bhee mansoor houn keh do aghyar say
Kyon Dartey ho zandaan kee divaar say
Zulm kee baat ko, jail kee raat ko
Mein naheen maanta, mein naheen jaanta

Phool shakhoon peh khilnay lagay, tum kaho
Jam rindoon koe milnay lagay tum kaho
Chak seenoon kay silnay lagay tum kaho
Iss khulay jhoot, zehain kee loot ko
Mein naheen maanta, mein naheen jaanta

Tum nein loota hai sadiyoon hamara sakoon'
Ab naa hum par chalay gaa tumhara fasoon'
Chaaragar mein tumhein kiss tarah say kahoon'?
Tum naheen charagar ko manay, magar
Mein naheen maanta, mein naheen jaanta

He whose light shines only in palaces
Who seeks only to please the few
Who moves in the shadows of compromise
Such a debased tradition, such a dark dawn
I do not know, I will not own.

Like audacious Mansoor I declare
I have no dread of the hangman's plank.
Why do you fear the prison walls?
These acts of cruelty, these nights in jail
I will not accept, I will not condone.

You say: flowers are blooming on branches.
You say: the deprived are receiving wine.
You say: their bruised breasts are healing.
This blatant lie, this corruption of the intellect
I will not accept, I do not accept.

For centuries you robbed our peace
Your spells can no longer bedevil us.
Know you as the saviour some proclaim?
I do not own, I will not allow.

—*Translated by Bapsi Sidhwa and Parizad N. Sidhwa*

Pavement-pounding Men of Letters: Intezar Hussain's Lahore

Khaled Ahmed

When Baghdad was bursting with a renaissance of Islamic knowledge in the ninth century, Lahore did not have a single Muslim inhabitant. Some kind of an earthenwork fort was in existence under the satrapy of the ruler of Multan, a place better known than Lahore in the old records. At first, the city was called Loh. It acquired its present name when the epithet 'fort' (awar) was attached to it. Biruni noted this name in the eleventh century. Mahmud Ghaznavi took Lahore in 1021 and his general, Malik Ayaz, built the citadel, complete with brick boundary walls. Lahore was actually this fort, and the mound on which the fort is perched is the archaeological city we want to celebrate. The great gardens of Shalimar fell outside this early Lahore, as did the mausoleum of the other great saint of Lahore, Mianmir. The premier saint of Lahore, Data Sahib Ali Hujviri, was once considered to be buried outside Lahore, but today his tomb is just on the edge of the mound that was ancient Lahore.

The Fort as we see it today was the work of Akbar the Great, supplemented by his descendants, Jehangir and Shah Jehan. Aurangzeb built the Badshahi Mosque and the Hazoori Bagh garden, which lies between the Mosque and the Fort. After the end of the Mughal era, the Fort and its prized residential features began to decline. In the chaotic Sikh period, the Lahore Fort began to be stripped of bricks and much of its precious stonework. Maharaja Ranjit Singh gifted some of its embellishments to the Golden Temple in Amritsar.

The British, the next inheritors of the Fort, caused more damage to it than anyone in the past. They stationed troops inside the residential area and built barracks in front of its most important feature, the *Diwan-e-Am* or Audience Hall. Lord Curzon finally rescued the gem-like Moti Masjid within the Fort from the abuse of the troops and, in 1903, transferred the Fort to the Archaeological Department. The Lahore Fort also has a part to play in the story of the *Koh-i-Noor*, the most precious diamond of India, which was kept in its treasury from 1813 to 1849. Sir Henry Lawrence got hold of the gem and passed it on to the then Governor General of British India, Lord Dalhousie. Soon thereafter, it landed in England to become a part of the Queen's regalia.

The treatment the Fort received after 1947, at the hands of the Punjab government, took the British legacy quietly forward. The police shifted its notorious Special Branch to the Fort and built torture cells within its precincts for political dissidents. The government finally rid the Fort of this curse in 1997.

LAHORE AND NOSTALGIA

Pre-Partition Lahore arouses a great deal of nostalgia. Literary memoirs of the city remember the Lahore of the early twentieth century as the 'bride of the cities', where poets and grammarians consorted in an environment of enlightenment. 'Foreigners' like Agha Hashr, scriptwriter from Bombay's famous Parsi Theatre, playwright Imtiaz Ali Taj (his ancestors had shifted here after the 1857 rebellion of Delhi), and Urdu's greatest humorist, Patras Bokhari, made Lahore their permanent home; the writings of Rajinder Singh and Krishan Chandar were 'introduced' by Maulana Salahuddin, the editor of *Adabi Duniya*. Pakistan's poet-philosopher Allama Iqbal and leader of the grassroots Khaksar Party, Allama Mashriqi, rose to fame in Lahore, as did the orator-journalist Zafar Ali Khan. Faiz Ahmad Faiz came to Lahore from Sialkot and 'grew up' in Government College in the company of grammarian-poet Soofi Ghulam Mustafa Tabassum and the founder of the Progressive Writers' Movement, Dr M.D. Taseer. Lahore was also Saadat Hasan Manto's city.

These days nostalgia seems to belong exclusively to the living Hindus and Sikhs who had to leave in 1947 and never really took to Delhi. Som Anand, in his *Lahore: Portrait of a City*, is just such a 'mourner' for Lahore, the city where he grew up. Som was the son of Faqir Chand Anand, a banker whose liberal outlook compelled him to marry a Muslim lady. Lalaji stayed in Lahore beyond 1947. Som lived in aristocratic Model Town and grew up totally without religious prejudice. He believed that the Hindus were locked up within the confines of their own ancient religion and saw Muslims as the deprived majority over whom Islam held sway, making them an emotional, easily provoked community. He lived through days when the clash of religions and 'separation of communities' was accepted as a way of life. It took little to make the two communities square off and confront each other as enemies.

This confirms the memories of Khushwant Singh who lived in Lahore as a lawyer in the years leading to Partition. Hindus, Muslims and Sikhs lived in 'separation' with a small community of 'floaters'—individuals who fraternized across the communal divide. Som Anand despised the Rashtriya Swayamsevak Sangh (RSS), the Arya Samajis and Mahasabha-ites of Lahore, convinced that they perpetuated inter-communal hatred. Strangely, he didn't feel threatened by the Khilafatist religious organizations; what perturbed him was the Muslim League, whose separatism had sowed the seeds of the communal riots that came in early 1947. Although the mullahs were friendly, the Muslims had by this time converted to the two-nation theory, the cornerstone of Muslim League's campaign that India contained not one but two nations. In this environment, the one set of people truly innocent of all communal prejudice were the communists—Hindus, Sikhs and Muslims bound together in humanity and by Marxist ideology.

Som tells many stories. The story of Ustad Daman, the Punjabi poet of the inner city, who would quieten unruly crowds with his Punjabi poems before leaders like Nehru could hope to address them. Sikhs, Hindus and Muslims admired him to the point of worship. He lived like a rustic in a city of scholars, but the enlightened Lahoris recognized him for the man of learning he really was, beneath his rough exterior. He spoke in Bengali at a meeting addressed by Bengali leader, Maulana Bhashani; he knew Russian and could speak it, without having ever been to the USSR.

There is also a story about Maulana Salahuddin, who put up a Hindu nameplate outside his house to escape the attention of RSS hooligans—only to have the house burned down by Muslim hooligans in 1947. Another personality of the time was Imtiaz Ali Taj, who wrote the best plays in Urdu, and was the best narrator, besides. Without him as a narrator, no radio-play was worth listening to. Today, a grandson of Maulana Salahuddin is a judge at the Sindh High Court; and a granddaughter, Asma Jehangir, is an internationally renowned human rights activist. The daughter of Imtiaz Ali Taj, Yasmeen, is as renowned for her radio voice as her father was.

PAVEMENT-POUNDING MEN OF LETTERS

Earlier, a different strand of nostalgic writing about the city, and perhaps the most significant, was produced by the pavement-pounding men of letters who frequented the tea and coffee houses of Lahore, remembering their salad days. How rich it was, this tea-house-hopping way of life of the fifties and sixties that is no more today. The literary life of Lahore was at this time ideologically divided among two *adeeb* (men of letters) groups, Anjuman-e-Tarraqi-Pasand-Mussanafeen and Halqa-e-Arbab-e-Zauq, the first a Progressive left-wing writers' group, the second right-wing, and very nationalistic. Various literary personalities belonging to these adeeb groups could be found huddled in different tea houses with their admirers.

When one establishment, simply called Coffee House, had to shut shop, thanks to the parsimony of the adeeb types, another called Pak Tea House took them in. Men like Ijaz Husain Batalvi, Qayyum Nazar, Zia Jalundhari, Yusuf Zafar and Mukhtar Siddiqi attended Halqa meetings in the YMCA, then betook themselves to the uncomfortable seediness of Pak Tea House.

Intezar Hussain stands out in this constellation of literary stars. Intezar's life—or the little that he allowed to escape from his inner fastness of memory and words—was spent walking the streets of Lahore with variable and varied companions. That's what he has written about. The relationships he formed in the tea houses of Lahore are all he can write about. Those who think he has left out his private life need to know that he either had no other life, or that he never discovered a method for writing about it. He mentions his sister's sons just twice, in passing, in his writings. His nephew, Hassan Zaheer—a brilliant civil service officer who was later to be held as a prisoner of war in India—wrote two books that changed Pakistan's

history, the first on the separation of East Pakistan and the second on
the famous Rawalpindi Conspiracy Case, in which Faiz Ahmad Faiz
and his leftist companions were convicted for trying to overthrow
the government of prime minister Liaquat Ali Khan. He arouses no
response in Intezar, perhaps because he never visited the tea houses
where Intezar lived.

Pakistan's literary personality number one has always aroused
resentment at home and admiration abroad. Pakistani men of letters
are dismayed by his imperviousness to nationalism and revolution.
The Left found him cold when the Progressives tried to impose
revolutionary tenets on society. The Right found him flaccid in the
face of their ideological demands. When India-inspired nationalism
peaked, friends found Intezar walking around in his personal bubble
of nostalgia about his old home in 'enemy' India.

Intezar Hussain deceives through his mute presence. He listens
and rarely challenges, as if he doesn't care. He remains sealed to the
outside world, as if guarding something within that would wilt if
allowed airing. He writes prose that has nothing to do with the
idiom favoured by Lahori writers. In fact, the new writers thought
his Urdu was strange. In his memoirs *Chiraghon ka Dhuan*, Intezar
recalls his meeting with one Maulana Mahir-ul-Qadiri in Lahore
who said, 'Aren't you from Buland Shehar?' The maulana was himself
from a village near Dubaee, a town close to Buland Shehar, where
Intezar was born. He had identified his dialect. A believer in the
new Urdu style decried Intezar's throwback to his Buland Shehari
idiom by telling him that his accent reminded him of the speech of
the butchers' wives of Rampur. It is obvious that Intezar didn't care
what people said. Many people from Buland Shehar had abandoned
its colloquialisms and had begun writing the new Urdu, in which
clichés masqueraded as idiom.

But Intezar's memoirs are stubbornly couched in the speech of
Dubaee. Every page has a word that you can't find in the bowdlerized
post-1947 dictionaries of Pakistan. But that's where Intezar's spice
is. He is generous about his 'committed' contemporaries, in a slightly
chiding tone, flecked with the acid of his Dubaee slang. There is
hardly anyone among his friends who was not, at one time or another,
riled by his lack of commitment. He observed, went along, but reserved

his judgement. The men of letters who believed in causes betrayed them, because of own their lack of character and vision. Intezar was lucky; he never really believed.

INTEZAR AND ASKARI

Living in Krishan Nagar in Lahore, Intezar found a day-long companion in Muhammad Hassan Askari, Pakistan's most sensitive literary critic, who tragically turned to fundamentalism in his senility. Idiosyncratic and full of Muslim League passion against the Progressives, Askari got Intezar addicted to long walks at a time when Lahore was beautifully walkable. It was also Askari who put him in the habit of tireless tea-house hopping. The two would travel from Mian M. Aslam's haveli at Baroodkhana—where they patiently heard him read out his latest romantic-historical novel—to Landa Bazar, to Radio Station, where Askari read his speeches; and to Café Orient, where men of letters sat self-consciously facing the Anglo-Indian lady at the counter.

This portrait of Askari foreshadows the chaotic Askari who savaged friend and foe alike later in Karachi, under the influence of the very seminaries that were to figure prominently in the terrorist jihad of fifty years later.

While Intezar, who edited the leftist *Nizam*, sinned by publishing non-revolutionary articles, Askari was up to his mean tricks against the Progressives. He wrote about the bellwether of the Progressives, Ali Sardar Jaafri, whom he ridiculed for flaunting his good looks before the lady who sat behind the counter at the Café Orient. A fervid Abdullah Malik, the Communist foot-soldier of the Left, lost his cool over the article and threatened to collar Askari. After that, Askari got together with another idiosyncratic genius, Manto, who, too, had become a thorn in the side of Progressive hegemony in Lahore. From Karachi, critic Mumtaz Shirin joined the ideologically indeterminate duo.

At times, conservative reaction to the Progressives bordered on lunacy: Dr Syed Abdullah, who taught Urdu at the Oriental College, first made himself famous by writing a pioneering revivalist book on the classical poet Mir Taqi Mir, then opined that his complete works should not be published because he was too 'pagan' for Pakistan's new ideological environment.

These were times when the Right and the Left clashed not just intellectually but physically as well. From *Nizam*, Intezar moved to another left-wing journal, *Imroze*. When a reactionary rightist poet Saifuddin Saif came to its premises with his hoods to thrash the 'Commies', he found Intezar cowering in the newsroom. Under General Ayub Khan, senior civil servant Qudratullah Shehab was Malraux to the De Gaulle of the military dictator, a position later appropriated by an intellectual factotum, Altaf Gauhar, while Gauhar's brother, Tajammal, set the cultural tone in Lahore.

Journalist and Marxist critic Safdar Mir found Intezar ready to join him in his organizational adventures because Intezar was such a deadlines man, something that the other literary critic, the colossally learned Muzaffar Ali Syed, could never be. The days of Safdar Mir gave way to the supremacy of despotic ideologue Aziz-ul-Haq at the Pak Tea House, whose 'revolution' was preceded by his violent death.

Apart from the coffee houses, writers in Lahore also gathered at the poet and feminist Kishwar Naheed's unpretentious house in Lahore, which served as an informal literary salon. Intezar is ambivalent about Kishwar Naheed's salon—like most adeeb types who frequented her house, ate her food, but came out abusing her. Famous painter Shakir Ali was one such, but he had nowhere else to go after Pakistan's only history-of-ideas man, Sibte Hassan, died. Zahid Dar was to be the only adeeb to rise above the inner male chauvinist tumult, but then he was helplessly in love with Kishwar Naheed. Literature takes its revenge: every time an adeeb wrote verses to rubbish her after getting his ego bruised at her house, she came off looking a worthier human being. Intezar escaped getting tarnished because of his light touch.

Intezar's association with Askari prepared him for his friendship with his last soulmate, Nasir Kazmi, the poet who keeps on being partially discovered by critics who have tired of the heavily Persianized ghazal and want poetry they can sing. He was as eccentric as Manto but less prickly—spoke like an angel when he wanted to—and engaged editor Shaikh Salahuddin and painter-editor Haneef Ramay in philosophical discussions when he was not dozing off or pounding the pavement with Intezar in search of cups of tea and paan. When he finally went back to his room in the Old Anarkali area late at night, Intezar would go through the ritual of seeing him off in front of Tollington Market.

Intezar finally landed up in Sheikh Enayatullah's *Mashriq*, writing columns that pleased with style. He kept his real idiom in check to find favour with the world of journalism but his columns were still the best written in town. He tried to scrounge for subjects in the cultural happenings of Lahore, but Sheikh Sahib wanted the column read by the layabouts of Badshahi Mosque. So Intezar obliged by producing one on actress Nilo, which won him a new lease of employment. Yet, when modernist free verse advocate Iftikhar Jalib attacked Hayat Ahmad Khan's classical music from the point of view of 'people's culture' and Hayat wrote a very effective rejoinder, Intezar felt compelled to reproduce the exchange in the journal.

There is sadness in Intezar—a sadness that comes from his prescience about the futility of the revolutionary fervour of the adeeb who abandons his world of imagination for that of politics. Intezar calls it *chautha khoont*, the delimitation of the province of creativity beyond which the adeeb demeans himself and his trade. People like Fazlur Rehman Khan of Lahore lived in their world of the mind and produced worthy fiction, but when made to react to the literary politics of Pak Tea House, nothing they said made sense. On the pavement outside the YMCA lay the reputation and failed genius of many adeeb types, who ventured out of their inner world and tried to impose their defective understanding of the outer world on others.

All literature, after all, is words. Intezar wrote them carefully, and guarded them against Lahore's contamination. His Buland Shehari speech, sealed against miles and miles of dull prose surrounding his journalistic career, is powerfully evocative. There is no one who writes like him, unless it is someone like the humorist Mushtaq Yusufi who uses tweezers to pick his words and produces his verbal mosaic once in a decade. All revolutions have come to grief at the end of the century. Intezar survives them, but not without a touch of sadness about what, to him, was always predictable.

The Cool Street

Intezar Hussain

The Mall in those days, say during the fifties and early sixties, was a peaceful road suitable for strolling. It was better known as 'Thandi Sarak' or 'Cool Street'. The noisy scooter and the equally noisy rickshaw had not yet made their appearance. There were very few motor cars to be seen and, because of the slow traffic of cycles and tongas, they were not able to speed or otherwise disturb the peace on the Mall. As for tongas, their leisurely pace punctuated by the *takh-takh* of the horses' hoofs, they were in tune with the tranquility pervading the area. Cycles, because of their sheer abundance, appeared to rule the road. A ladies' cycle had a charm of its own—and in the early hours the Mall appeared to be flooded with girls cycling to Government College and the Punjab University.

Unfortunately the ladies' cycles did not last long. The girl students, bowing to increasingly conservative pressure from the religiosity, were soon seen bidding farewell to their cycles—although their favourite teacher in Government College, Dr Nazeer, stayed with his low-slung racing cycle even after he got posted as principal of the college.

The last cycle from among the literary circles to be seen on the Mall was the one owned by Mubarik Ahmad. Although he kept pace with the changing trends in Urdu poetry, he stuck fast to his old rusted cycle.

The pervasive quiet and sparse traffic on the Mall encouraged the gentlefolk living nearby to take advantage of the 'Thandi Sarak' and come out of their houses for an evening walk. Every evening, Professor Siraj, accompanied by his wife, would emerge enthusiastically from the gates of the Principal's House and walk swiftly along the footpath that accompanied the road, all the way to the Bagh-e-Jinnah Gardens. He would be followed equally energetically by Mrs Siraj, who somehow managed to keep up with his pace.

In fact, a number of gentlemen were seen to appear on the Mall at an appointed hour with the punctuality of clocks. Maulana Salahuddin Ahmad, editor *Adabi Duniya*, left his office (situated near Regal Cinema) exactly at noon. Twirling a stick, elegantly attired in tie, suit and hat—even in the scorching heat of May and June—he could be seen walking towards Old Anarkali, where his friends Maulana Hamid Ali Khan and Dr Ashiq Hussain Batalvi sat waiting for him in the Nagina Bakery.

With the approach of evening, a tonga carrying Maulana Chiragh Hasan Hasrat, the veteran journalist, made its appearance on the Mall. Its destination was Zelin's Coffee House. Maulana had to be there at an appointed hour to savour his cup of coffee in the company of Shorish Kashmiri, Abdullah Butt and Abdullah Malik. At a fair distance from this group of journalists sat a group of young artists animatedly discussing abstract art over their frugally nursed cups of coffee. The celebrated artist Shakir Ali went straight to the Coffee House on the very day he arrived in Lahore. He sat down with this group of fledgling artists and stirred them to the core with his revolutionary ideas and visionary dreams. Within a month or so, the discussions and discourse turned into a fully-fledged movement of modern art.

In a corner was a table reserved for the redoubtable scholar Riaz Qadar. He arrived at Zelin's at 9 a.m. without fail and left at 9 p.m., the time the Coffee House closed. An intellectual who occasionally also dabbled in writing, he spoke incessantly, from morning till night, enthusiastically discussing every subject under the sun.

Almost next door to the Coffee House we had India Tea House, which, after Partition, turned into Pak Tea House, a favourite haunt of every variety of writer in the city. A large group of writers sat around a table headed by Qayyum Nazar, who in those years was the Secretary of Halqa-e-Arbab-e-Zauq. He too was firmly committed to his cycle, perhaps more than to the Halqa. But some young writers staged a revolt against him in Halqa. In disgust, he withdrew from Halqa as well as from the Tea House.

Adiba: A Storyteller's Tale

Aamer Hussain

Aamer Hussein visited Lahore as a guest of the Pakistan Academy of Letters in 1996, and fell in love with the city. He wrote the first draft of 'Adiba' a year and a half later. The story was inspired by the work—and loosely based on the life—of the popular Urdu novelist A.R. Khatun (1900–1965), who migrated to Lahore from Delhi after Partition and continued to write there with even greater success than she'd had in India. Khatun is increasingly recognized for her witty, perceptive pictures of pre-Partition India and post-Partition Pakistan and for the beauty and imaginative range of the magical tales she wrote for children.

1945

Adiba, alone. She's lived in a grey world since her husband went to the front: suspended for four years (she writes later) between despair and hope. War over, they send her a wire:

YOUR HUSBAND WAS KILLED ON THE WAR-FRONT FIGHTING THE JAPANESE IN MALAYA ON 25 FEBRUARY 1942.

She observes the mourning rituals—prayers said on the third day and the fortieth, food distributed to the poor. She doesn't even know where her husband's grave is, but her grief, restrained so long, is threatening to spill over.

His Majesty's Government had called Adiba's husband up to fight in 1941. Though he was way past the age for war, he'd put himself on the reserve list and asked to be remembered. He'd asked to go to the

This extract is taken from Aamer Hussein's *Turquoise*, published by Saqi Press.

Middle East, but they'd sent him to Southeast Asia. He wrote to her for some months and then she had no more letters. Only a message that he was reported missing in Malaya.

She hates the Raj, but that's nothing new; in the thirties, in those years before the war, they'd said the Imperial sun was setting, and the women avoided talking to English memsahibs. Adiba has always advocated freedom from the British yoke, taking the part of the rebels and the nationalists even from a distance. But patience is her second name, perseverance her creed. In her husband's absence, she'd started to write again, at first because she had to, and then she couldn't stop. They pay her for every instalment she writes. She needs the money. Her four children are far away, in schools and colleges. A kind publisher from Lahore, who'd admired her first book, came and bought all the copies she had left in store. That helped her, for a while. Then she wrote a new version of a romance she remembered from her childhood, about a brave princess who went out disguised as a soldier lad to rescue her lover from captivity.

Her story came out as a book this year.

The British authorities won't be giving her a pension.

1947

Adiba, alone, makes her choice: She'll migrate, follow the crescent moon, to the new country. It's 1947. The hated Britons are on the move. Terrible things are happening here—homes and villages set on fire, people herded and chased across the border by armed men who don't ask them whether or not they want to leave. Though she's quite protected, and she isn't afraid, she believes that Delhi's no longer her home: it's time to leave, start a new life. Later, she writes: *The earth of our homeland didn't want us and the sky was saying farewell.*

Her second son is working in a hospital in Lahore. She travels to join him, in a toy plane, carrying what she can in two suitcases and a cloth bundle. She comes to this city by a river, with its bright bazaars, great marble-domed mosque, and many leafy lanes. On its outskirts, there are tombs and a pleasure garden built by a king for his consort.

It's a hard life in this city she's chosen to settle in. She moves from home to temporary home. The first is a cattle shed, a mere store for cakes of buffalo dung. She has two rooms in the next. She hopes or waits for the property the authorities had led her to believe they'd offer her, to compensate for all she's lost. She moves three times in five years. *People who once paid obeisance to your rank now refuse to recognize you. Those who owned a guava tree have claimed an orchard here, and those who owned a brick wall have asked for marble mansions.* She isn't young: but she'll spend the next fifteen years writing novels, and fighting for the property she feels the new country owes her to replace what she left behind in the old land.

Many, she sees, are luckier than she has been. She tries to consider the even less fortunate.

1956

Adiba dismisses young writers as anarchists and rebels. Many writers dismiss Adiba as feudal, old-fashioned. *She's a traditionalist,* they say. *She writes in the mode of the past. Her characters are dolls dressed up in finery. Home and hearth suffice for her heroines. She can't speak English. She's never read Russian, French or English novels.* It isn't modish to write without a purpose or a desire to change the world; to speak of war and strife and oppression and abuse with laughter and irony, as she sometimes does, is considered frivolous. Now righteously indignant young women thirty years younger than she is, equipped with university degrees, carry off the critical acclaim and the literary prizes. But her publishers press for new work. They tell her she has ten thousand readers a year. Adolescents and housewives can't wait for her novels. A celebrated woman writer comments: *We win the literary awards, she wins the hearts of the young. We're writing of the same matters; but so, so differently.* She tells stories of youths summoned to war by the cruel, pale rulers. Of girls who join caravans to cross the new border, escaping mad uncles and careless aunts, to live separated from all they know until rescued from refugee camps. She writes about the brooding young men who pine for these maidens, driven to madness or drink by disappointment and separation. She writes about women whose men fight to free the land from the British, and of the scripture-abusers with long beards, who clip youth's wings, try to stop it from soaring. She tells stories of women who bring up their children alone, earning their wages cooking and sewing, or teaching the alphabet and the Holy Book. She writes about the wives of heroes; she writes of heroic wives.

Soldier boys write to her from the front. They ask what happens later, when the honeymoon's over, to her heroes: Does Shaad's brother marry Azra's cousin? They ask for continuations, sequels, autographs, letters. They tell her, *When we read your stories we find our way home.*

Her daughters, like some of her heroines, graduate. One son becomes a doctor. That way, he says, he can take care of her. She has high blood pressure and a tricky heart.

Critics still make light of her writing. She's a peddler of romances, a teller of tales. But sometimes, when she looks at new stories, she sees young writers are learning from her, writing about the world she once delighted in painting, but their colours are sombre, and hers layer pastel on bright, like muslin scarves hung out to dry on a line in the sun. Some of the stories could be her own: of betrayal and loss, of the ignominy of men and women. Others sometimes repeat her phrases, the phrases she borrowed so blithely from life, but to different ends. They write about poverty and pain. She says she only wants to give pleasure. She's written about the wars in the world and the struggle for freedom and Pakistan, about borders and partition and the bruises and scars of arrival in a promised land, but that's only the bloody backdrop to stories of hope: she prefers happy endings.

She writes about love.

1960

Alone, as you can be when your children are children no longer with children of their own, when they still surround you but remain far away, Adiba grows tired of looking at poverty and pain. She begins to write romances, tales to read out loud to her grandchildren. She still says her prayers five times a day. Though her God hasn't always been good to her, she invokes his blessings on others. She admires the young general who came to power and will rule the land for the rest of her days. She remembers him in her prayers.

Her children are always in need, her publishers want her to write a book a year. But she can't. She treasures her craft, treasures her time. She continues to love cooking and sewing; her mind's always on chores and tasks. She makes delicacies from leftover bread; cuts up a worn-out jacket into patches for a quilt, stitching purple to orange and scarlet and green, peacock colours for a cradle or an orphan.

Some critics will say her wonder tales are her life's best work. They never give her a prize but across the whole land they call her their teller of tales. She tells the nation its stories: the stories they've forgotten, the stories they're waiting to hear.

Each book makes her feel as she felt when the last of her children was cut out of her womb.

1962 (and 1939)

Adiba, now sixty-two, has been ill for years. Struggling with the novel she feels may be her last, she's rebuilding, again, the homes that have slipped away from her hands, or chasing glimpses of blue mirages before the sun goes down. She writes letters to those journals she once often wrote for telling readers the stories of her life. She writes about migration and her own woes in the new land: how she was cheated of a property allotted to her by the authorities; robbed of her furniture and chased away by relatives from a house she'd divided and shared.

Sometimes, though, she recalls youth and joys, writes of her days in the old land. Her husband had been an official in the Indian Civil Service. She'd travelled with him from city to city. Each one of her children was born in a different town. She missed the city where she'd come of age and married, but life and her children kept her occupied. She read many books.

One day her husband gave her a story by a friend of his to read, a romance called *Shamim*. She recognized some people in it, and some places. I can do better than this, she thought. She wrote for a month, in secret. Sometimes she snapped at her children, if they pulled at her skirts while she wrote. Her daughter remembers the pencil she used, new when she began, worn out when she came to her story's end. When she'd filled three notebooks, she showed her story to her husband. She'd titled it *Andaleeb*, for the nightingale and her heroine. I'll publish this for you, he said. He chose her pseudonym—Adiba. She was Badar Zamani till then. They were in Delhi. He had a thousand and one copies of her book privately printed, and sent it out to his friends; one was a well-known writer who edited a journal. Her story ran as a serial in eleven instalments. Later, when readers pleaded for more, he would publish a second edition of her book. *Andaleeb: A Tale of Love and Woe* first appeared in 1939. In distant places, the world was preparing its wars. Indian cantonments emptied themselves, one by one, of white men. The war came much closer. And her husband was taken for a soldier.

1965

To the end, young women come to see her, to learn the art of writing romances, but all she can tell them is: *I write what I see and I write from my life*. She doesn't like similes or elaborate figures of speech; her stories have no message, no goal. In writing, as in life, she prefers the middle path. But some of the girls who approach her think her life is her finest piece of work: they come to learn how to live.

People remember a quiet small woman in white, with fragile hands and flesh scarce on her fine bones. Fans often saw her emerge from her kitchen, wiping her hands on her clothes, or they'd find her, shears in hand, deadheading roses. There are no known photographs.

On the airwaves, from the old country, a woman writer she once met in Delhi, their home town, calls her the last chronicler of a lost world. That's three days before her death. She's still writing.

There'll be a war this September, and the nation will call her favourite general its hero, but she's been gone eight months by then. She won't live to see the worst wars between the old land and the new, or the bloody struggle for the distant east. She's had no regrets about moving. She has missed the old city, but ceased to set her stories there a decade after she landed in the new, because sometimes the light in Lahore reminds her of home, when it falls on a marble floor and picks out the gold of a dome or silvers a pigeon's wing, and here, too, you can smell jasmine and roses and the rain on the breeze, or watch kites—purple and orange and scarlet and green—fly peacock-bright against the horizon. She has found the warm, loud people around her enchanting, though she hasn't been able, so late in her life, to twist her tongue around their words.

But her ancestors knew Lahore. They built a fort here, in which there's a mirrored chamber. The Empress Nur Jehan is buried on the outskirts of the city with a poem engraved on her tomb. A dancer, walled alive for belonging to a father and loving his son, gave her name to a district: Anarkali, Pomegranate bud. (Queen and dancer loved the same man, one to exile, the other to death. Both lie in this city, and so does he, the World's Conquerer, Emperor Jehangir.)

They bury Adiba in this place of intimate strangers. Another woman writer, who'd known her and loved her, washes and shrouds her body for the journey to the grave.

There are many obituaries, on both sides of the border. Many cite *Andaleeb* as her best work; others praise her stories for children. Veterans (some came from the old land) remember:

> Adiba was a descendant of poets and remotely related to the last emperor, the one deposed in 1858 after the First War of Independence, who'd died in Rangoon, the one who'd written these words: *Father, my home is slipping from my hand, four palanquin bearers are bearing my palanquin away, I'm losing my kin and my strangers.*
>
> In 1959, after twelve years in Lahore, Adiba was allotted five rooms in a house. Though she tried to buy the rest of the house from them, her neighbours were litigious and the property remained contested.

1985

Adolescents laid fresh-cut flowers on her grave. Her daughter completed Adiba's last story and went on to write many more books than her mother's six or seven. She never took Adiba's place. People mourned their teller of tales.

Twenty years after her death, a poet exiled to Delhi with only a knapsack says she's carried two of Adiba's books back to her native city. The poet, when she grows tired of the poverty and pain surrounds her, reads Adiba for succour.

She understood pain, the teller of tales. *Hardship,* she wrote, *will be your best teacher, but never let hardship bring you to your knees.* And she stitched strands of sentences, patterns of phrases, now pastel, now bright, so carefully into the crisp muslin of her pages.

Her best-loved book is about a soldier taken prisoner by the Japanese in the Second World War. His wife is told he's dead but she doesn't believe the news. But the soldier finds his way home. He's been blinded by the enemy. His wife, in his absence, has given birth to twins. One for each lost eye.

2000

Dear Adiba:

This is a tribute on the hundredth anniversary of your birth from a writer who has spent thirty-one of his forty-six years in a foreign city. He first read your books seven years ago and is writing to tell you of the inspiration he draws from your tales, of the great pleasure they continue to give him. When he reads you, he finds his way home. He asks forgiveness for playing games with the stories you told, for occasionally reordering the events of your life.

Here is a story he invented in your name. He tells it in your voice.

A young man who wore a circlet of gold with a ruby that shone on his brow saved a kingdom from an evil ogre. As a reward, he claimed the hand of Nilofar, the king's beautiful youngest daughter. 'Who are you?' the king asked. 'I am Prince Ahmar,' the young man replied. 'My father is the king of a faraway country, but I have sworn to stay away from my land for seven years because my brother accused me of a crime I did not commit, and I am not at liberty to say where I come from.'

The nuptials took place with pomp and splendour.

Now, Nilofar's stepmother and stepsister, who envied her fortune and her handsome bridegroom, sowed the seeds of doubt in her heart: Where did the young man come from? To what clan did he belong? But most of all, they wanted the ruby that shone on his brow.

They sent an old courtier disguised as a holy man to tell Nilofar that she must travel on a pilgrimage to a shrine a night's journey away to pray for her bridegroom Prince Ahmar's health and his future. While she was gone, they put poppy juice in the golden chalice of milk Ahmar drank from before he slept. Then Nilofar's stepsister crept into the bridal chamber and stole the ruby from the sleeping prince's brow. Ahmar uttered a great cry, and with blood pouring from his nose and his mouth, he fell to the earth and died. But as he fell, Nilofar's sister saw the chaplet of gold disintegrate into dust in her hand, and in place of the ruby a tiny drop of blood shone on her palm. Then she heard a great fluttering of wings and she looked up to see, in the darkness, two white birds flying up into the air and out into the night through the wide-open window.

Nilofar's stepmother and sister, afraid of the dire consequences of their deed, had Ahmar's body secretly removed and buried in a wild remote place a day and a night's journey away.

When Nilofar returned, her stepmother and stepsister told her that her bridegroom was an impostor, an evil trickster. He had stolen her jewels and fled to his land.

But Nilofar didn't believe their lies. She dressed in a suit of clothes he'd left behind, concealed a sharp gold dagger in her bosom, and went out in search of Ahmar.

Nilofar wandered a day and a night. She encountered many obstacles placed in her way by her sisters. As night fell, she came upon a garden enclosed in marble walls. It was a place of lush green grass and many flowers. A tall cypress tree grew there between two pools of clear blue water. She drank from one pool, washed her hands in another, and then she sat down beneath the cypress tree, her head against its trunk, to rest a while before she resumed her journey. A round gold harvest moon travelled low in the sky.

She was drifting into sleep when she realized she could understand the language of the pair of white birds that softly sang above her head in the tall tree's branches.

'Tell me a tale,' said one of the birds.

'Of what shall I sing, my love?' her mate replied. 'Of my own travels, or of the world's woes?'

'Sing to me of what you have seen in the world today.'

'I will tell you of the prince of a faraway land and his young bride who has been betrayed,' said her mate. So Nilofar heard them tell the whole story of her sister's perfidy, and learned that her husband's life lay in the enchanted ruby she stole from his brow.

Then one bird, weeping, said to the other, 'Can the young man never be brought back to life?'

And her mate replied, 'The prince lies within these marble walls. His garments are the green, green grass and his eyes pools of blue water. His mouth is a deep-red hibiscus. His body is this cypress tree, his hair its green leaves.'

'But if his bride were to catch us, and hold us close, heart to heart, and with one stroke of his sword separate our heads from our necks, so that one of us should not die before the other, and hold our heads above the ground where the prince lies, our blood will spill on the earth and its drops will become rubies more bright than the ruby the wicked woman stole from the prince. Then the prince's heart will beat again in his breast, and he'll return to the land of the living. But if one of us dies before the other, the prince will always lie sleeping.'

Nilofar called up to the pair of white birds. They flew down from the high branch and

bent their heads before her. 'Soon,' she said to herself, 'I'll see my beloved lying asleep
beside me beneath this tree, with a ruby shining on his forehead, and I'll wake him with
a kiss on his cheek.'

She took out the sharp golden knife she had hidden in her bosom. Soon the green grass
grew red with the blood of white birds.

CENTENARY

Adiba, teller of tales, was born with the twentieth century. She died
when she was sixty-five. Came to her new homeland when she was
forty-seven. Last saw her husband when she was forty. Published her
first novel when she was thirty-nine. Gave birth to her first daughter
before she was twenty. Married her mother's brother's son when she
was nineteen and he twenty-nine. It was a happy marriage.

The Sun, My Companion

Kishwar Naheed

My city is hot;
That's perhaps why my hands burn.
My city is hot;
That's perhaps why my feet scorch.
My city is hot;
That's perhaps why my roof melts.
My city is hot;
That's perhaps why my walls are ignited.
My country is hot;
That's perhaps why children are parched.
My country is hot;
That's perhaps why I am forced to go naked.
My country is hot;
That's perhaps why
I cannot know of rains, or floods.
And self-styled masters
Come to ruin my crops.

Tell me not to hate my country.
Let me dry my wet clothes in these courtyards.
Let me grow old in these fields.
Let me quench my thirst in its rivers.
Let me breathe in the shade of its trees.
Let me wear Lahore's dust and its weariness.
I do not want the shelter of lengthening shadows,
For the sun spends itself in my country.

This poem is taken from *The Price of Looking Back: Poems of Kishwar Naheed*, published by Mustafa Waheed Book Traders.

The sun and I
And you
Cannot walk together,
For the sun is my companion.

—Translated by Baider Bakht and Derek M. Cohen

PART VII

RELATIONSHIPS

Poems

Madho Lal Hussain

ON SEPARATION

The nights loom and slip into each other
as I stay waiting for him.

Ever since Ranjha turned yogi,
I have scarcely been myself

and people call me mad.
My youthful flesh has wasted into creases,

leaving my bones a clicking skeleton.
I was too young to know the ways of love;

and now as the nights loom and slip into each other,
I play host to that heartless guest—Separation.

*

TELL ME, MY HEART

Tell me, my heart, who am I?
This heart is not that heart; this flesh

is not that flesh. The heart
just beats, and beats the air.

Man was made to worship,
and he has gone to sin.

Hussain only knows what there is to know.
All else a dimming caravan.

*

FULL OF FAILING AM I

O God, do not mind my faults;
full of failing, I am without virtue.

O God, from within, show compassion,
and enlighten me.

To the men of the world, the pride of the world,
to the recluse, renunciation—

all masks, masks, masks!—
Neither a man of the world, nor a

recluse am I, and they laugh at me, at me,
who has befriended the Terrible one.

—*Translated by Bapsi Sidhwa with Rich Levy*

From *The Pakistani Bride*

Bapsi Sidhwa

NIKKA PEHELWAN'S FALL FROM GRACE

In his new self-importance, Nikka turned insufferably arrogant. To quote a Punjabi proverb, he would not let a fly alight on his nose.

He became a bully. He described graphically to those he wanted to intimidate what he would do to their balls and the chastity of their women. He bought a shop next to his for much less than the going price and expanded his business to include a provision store. He sat solidly on his charpoy outside and lorded it over the alley.

'O, ay, you one-eyed jinx, if I see you bring your solitary eye into our mohalla again, I'll thrash you,' Nikka threatened once, and sure enough, when he noticed the half-blind man a month later, he chased and thrashed him.

He forced the milkman to take a circuitous route because the jangle of cans suddenly jarred his delicate senses.

He was feared and even the police could not control him. Their reports, though, reached the man in the scented, luxurious room. At first he regarded his protégé's antics with indulgence. 'Leave him alone—the man means no harm.' But the complaints grew urgent, and Nikka's high-handed conduct ceased to please. The weary black brows atop the blood-shot eyes of the politician puckered. 'If that's the case, let's put him right. To be sure, he has his uses, but rough him up a little. Show him his place . . .'

*

His masseur gossiping next to him, Nikka sat upon his sagging charpoy, blocking the pavement. He was in a foul mood. Somehow he sensed trouble. The evening traffic rushed by in a tangle of cycles, tongas, bullock-carts and trucks, squashing the dung on the wide road. Nikka glared at the traffic, his shifting eyes intent on mischief.

In one leap, suddenly he stood plumb in the path of a galloping horse and cart. Trucks came to a screeching stop, tongas reined in, cyclists wobbled to one side, and men on the pavement shifted to the edge. The cart-driver yelled, rising and trying to draw his stampeding animal to a halt.

Mouth foaming, head high, the horse towered above Nikka who firmly seized the bridle. The animal's momentum staggered him, but not letting go, he slipped to one side. With a palm over the scraping wooden wheel and wrenching at the bit, he stopped the beast.

The cart-driver glared at Nikka in disbelief:

'What's wrong with you, you crazy fool! You want to die?

Nikka held the reins just above the horse's heaving neck.

'Come on. Get down,' he commanded.

'Why?'

'Because I'll castrate you for driving recklessly in our mohalla.' Nikka was fiendishly calm.

The driver glanced around into a swarm of inquisitive faces. He raised his whip and struck the horse and Nikka in a panic to charge through. The crowd pushed apart slightly. Cursing furiously, Nikka pulled the man from the cart and struck him.

There was a surprised rustle. Shouts of 'Police! Police!' rose hysterically.

Qasim, on his way to work, looked over the heads in amazement. Policemen came running with sticks. Something was amiss. They never interfered in Nikka's brawls. He shouted, 'Watch out, Nikkayooooo! The police are here!'

Nikka, busy with his work, heard Qasim dimly. 'So what?' he thought. The battered man was crying piteously. And then, Nikka was wrenched away.

Whirling in a hot rage, he looked in disbelief at the handcuffs clamped on his wrists. The swelling crowd pressed forward.

'Why, what's this? A joke?' asked Nikka.

'You're under arrest for assault,' said a policeman he had never seen before. The man pulled him along by a chain while another pushed him into a few bewildered steps forward.

Stung into a sudden realization of his position by this indignity,

Nikka roared, 'You pimps. You bloody swine. Don't you know who I am? I am Nikka Pehelwan! Nikka Pehelwan of Qila Gujjar Singh! How dare you . . .'

Ignoring the outburst, the policemen dragged him off the road.

'Where is the SSP Sahib, you bastards, where is my friend?' he screeched, trying to intimidate the policemen by his acquaintance with the Senior Superintendent of Police.

An inspector, distinguished by a trim, belted coat, stepped forward.

'Come on, Nikka, don't throw a tantrum. No one's going to help you. At least keep your dignity.'

Nikka glared at him. 'Why, you unfaithful dog! Don't you know whose protection I command? Ask the SSP Sahib . . . he'll tell you.'

'We're arresting you on the Superintendent's orders. Now shut up!'

'The pig's penis! I'll have him hanged—all of you,' Nikka roared, slashing about blindly with his manacles.

Screaming threats, delighting the children and the crowd with his colourful invective, he was thrust into a van with wire mesh at the windows and was driven away.

The Gate-keeper's Wife

Rukhsana Ahmad

Annette's short sun-bleached hair spiked wispily away from her face as her weary fingers pushed through it. She felt wizened and faded as she rubbed the sides of her cotton skirt down with the palms of her hands in a vain attempt to push out the creases. Time to go. It was nearly five o'clock. But the sun, not seeming to notice this, still blazed down vengefully on the breathless, parched scene below.

She dropped back the corner of the heavy curtains flinching from the glare, cherishing the last few moments of the cool darkness left to her before she had to face its white hostility. Two people had died of heat stroke the day before. It was a record summer for sweltering temperatures. She felt irritated by the mindless cruelty of the sun, remembering how hushed and still all the birds in the aviary had been the day before, how listless all the magnificent cats had seemed. Surely it had to stop. 120 degrees fahrenheit was a ridiculous peak to maintain . . . enough to turn the most dedicated of sun worshippers into apostates. At the best of times Lahore Zoo was not a perfect place for animals; these temperatures were putting their lives at serious risk. Surely it must stop soon.

'*Sahib aa gaya?*' she asked in her heavily accented Urdu as the lime juice with soda appeared from behind the curtain magically. Kammu's timing was always perfect.

'No, Memsahib,' his tone was mildly apologetic as he answered, eyes averted respectfully, holding the tray out before her.

'Thank you, tell driver, five minutes,' she sought the aid of her hands to gesticulate her meaning this time.

Not back yet. Won't see him now till dinner time. He was supposed to go for golf at five-thirty. Maybe he's changing at the club again.

This extract is taken from Rukhsana Ahmad's *The Inner Courtyard*, published by Virago Press.

He could have telephoned. Nine years of this and it still hurts. She tried to block the hurt from her mind as she got her things together. A little navy parasol, beige straw bag, sunglasses and the vet's handbook permanently borrowed from the British Council Library. The heat outside lashed her face as she hastened into the cool protection of the blue Toyota.

The zoo was not far from their house on the G.O.R. estate. Thirty-seven years after the British had left it was still the most privileged address in Lahore with its awesome Government Officers' Residences, faded but desperately holding on to the aloofness of their old masters, as they stood in their vast lawns behind exclusive boundary walls.

It was past locking-up time at the zoo, five o'clock; but in the absence of the threatening finality of a bell it took the efforts of the entire staff to persuade people to believe that the gates would shut at five and that they must head for the way out or be locked in. Reluctant children sucking ice lollies which dribbled down their fingers in the intense heat faster than they could gulp them down dragged their feet accompanied by relieved adults, ready for the shade, hurrying for whatever transport (or the lack of it) awaited them outside the gate.

The gate-keeper interrupted his role of town crier to open the gates for Annette's car. They drove past the last few stragglers towards the depot and the superintendent's residence located at the far end. Hussain was all prepared for her arrival, books and registers, buckets and pans laid out in the verandah where he sat on what looked like a dried-out chair, his feet, dry and dusty, sticking out of his thonged chappals. He got up quickly to receive her. Brief formalities exchanged, his daily offer of a cold drink declined as usual, they got down to business.

Annette now sat on the dried-out chair and looked through the entries in all the ledgers whilst Hussain rummaged about in the store weighing up and measuring out the grain for the birds and the fruit for the monkeys. Madam preferred to check the weight of the fish and the meat herself, so he would only weigh that when she'd finished reading all the entries of food delivered into the stores that day. It took about forty minutes to get all the food ready and then the two boys who also assisted the head gardener to keep the drying lawns tidy would come to help him feed the animals under the watchful eye of the Memsahib.

He wondered about her sometimes. Who she was, where she came from and what kind of love of animals this was that brought her out in the afternoon sun when most other women of her class still drowsed in darkened rooms. He knew that he had this job because of her in a way. It was common knowledge that the previous superintendent had been sacked because of her intervention. The gate-keeper had told him the story many times . . . how she came to visit the zoo about two years ago, saw that the animals looked thin and under-fed and decided to complain. She wrote letters, made approaches and got them to change the super. She was there with a letter from the governor himself the day Hussain took charge saying she had permission from him to 'inspect' the food before it was given to the animals and that she would personally make sure that the animals had a proper diet. To this day she had not been late. Hussain got into a routine of being ready for her, terrified of what might happen if she became angry again. The gate-keeper, Maaja, thought her an interfering busybody. 'Poor Nawaz Sahib who got turned out with his family of eight in such disgrace had still not found a job, and was such a good man really!' he always ended with a sigh. At this point in the conversation Hussain would lose interest in the story and walk off remembering something important that needed doing.

Annette, exhausted with the heat that day, summer dress clinging to her body stickily, sat down to rest herself on a bench shielded by a grove of jasmine and hibiscus bushes, as she trailed Hussain on his round to feed the animals. The heavy perfume battled with the odour of the animal cages; water was a problem in the summer months and the cages smelt foul two-thirds of the time. She was worried about Heera. He seemed even more listless than he'd been the day before, quite disinterested in the meat that had been pushed unceremoniously by Hussain into the cage. She opened her manual wondering if they should be getting in touch with the vet, or whether she should just observe him more closely. She was fond of him. He was popular with many of the staff too. It was they who had nicknamed him Heera because of the diamond glint to his eyes at night. He was as lively and mischievous a cheetah as any you could find in the Sundarbans, but this summer had really knocked it out of him. She picked up her bag and started walking slowly, unthinkingly, back towards his cage, her footsteps muffled by the soft mud.

Instinctively she drew back out of sight when she saw the woman. She had not seen or heard Annette. She was intense, absorbed, circling the cage slowly, carefully moving round inside the forbidden inner perimeter of the white railings. Only the staff were allowed into that area. Even Annette respected that boundary. She watched awestruck.

The woman had an eye on Heera but she didn't seem unduly worried. Annette almost gasped as she saw her lower her body, lean forward and put her arm through the bars to lift a couple of hunks of meat and slip them speedily into a limp polythene bag. She was a tall woman, thin, lithe; her mission accomplished she rose and dashed swiftly away with a speed that would have done Heera some credit. In the dusky gloom Annette felt aware of a frantic need to sit down as her body swayed, liquid and weak. She waited to collect herself for a few moments wondering what had held her back from challenging the woman. Surely she should have yelled at her. That was what she was supposed to be doing, preventing the pilfering and thieving that had been going on in the place. Heera got up slowly and ambled towards his dinner, sniffing the meat delicately before applying himself to the effort of eating. It was later than usual when she finally summoned her energies to leave. The men were hanging about the gate waiting to wish her and see her off. It wasn't altogether unusual for her to leave a little late. She found the quiet and peace of the after hours at the zoo sustaining and sometimes sat watching the animals settle down as long as the light permitted.

Darkness always fell suddenly as the sun dropped behind the high mud walls of the aviary at the western boundary of the zoo, forcing her to drag herself slowly away. Today she felt drained as the car drove past the gate and she lifted a limp hand to acknowledge their salutes.

She found herself desperate to talk it over with Saleem that night. He seemed absorbed and distant over dinner, but she raised it all the same. His laugh sounded curt and cold, 'Didn't you ring the police?'

'No.' Annette felt uncomfortable as she faced his sardonic amusement.

'What's so funny?'

'Your policing: the kind of moral crisis you've come to.' His laughter had an unpleasant chilly edge to it, widening the distance between them.

'Moral crisis?'

'I think that's what they call it.' He seemed intent on the food, picking the bones out of his fish with his fingers. She looked away. He added after a pause, 'Did I ever tell you the story about Mrs Howe?'

'I don't think you did. Who is she?' Annette was beginning to feel irritated by his tone of superior detachment.

'Was. Yes. Mrs Howe, was the wife of the Consul-General in Mashad, when Papa was posted there, back in the forties. She loved horses; loved them very much indeed. Her routine was to go out every afternoon, round the city, such as it then was, in search of any sick and maltreated horses and take them in. She'd go round in her jodhpurs, whip in hand, personally whiplash the guilty owner, and then take the horse away. She became a dreaded sight. The owners usually got treated worse than the horses, ended up in jail, and lost a working animal without recompense.'

'So?'

'So, nothing.' The tension mounted. Then. 'Mind you those were days when a British man-of-war would steam up to the shores menacingly, if, say, five men gathered in protest over the price of sugar.'

'I don't know what you're suggesting Saleem. What I'm trying to do here is different.'

'Yeah. I hope so. You weren't in your jodhpurs and you didn't get the police down. I was only eleven then, much purer in my sense of iniquity than I am now; always for the underdog. I can tell you though that I, for one, was never sure if the horses were the real underdogs.'

Annette felt a hopeless, voiceless rage against his cruel remoteness from her own feelings. Hostility, polarisations, oversimplifications. What had happened to them? She hated scenes. But her chair scraped angrily as she dropped her napkin and rose to leave the dining table. She stepped out onto the verandah gazing abstractedly at the fireflies in the still, suffocating darkness outside, remembering the past. The radicalism of their Cambridge days had faded for both of them. In her case it had dissolved into a vague defensiveness about her own realities. It had become his style, she thought angrily, to rub in the entire guilt of the white nations into her soul with a personal venom. Controversies and anger rankled, hung solid in the air between them.

He knew well enough, she thought sadly, how she felt about the animals at the zoo. They were special to her, like family, her babies almost. It was as if someone had deprived one of her own children. A wrong had been committed, and here he was confusing issues, blurring the boundaries between wrong and right, trying to set up a parallel which wasn't really a parallel at all. Just to humiliate her, show her up. Not a glimmer of the old passion remained between them to buffer differences of opinion.

There were other women in Lahore she knew, white women she could have talked to, but there, too, were gaps in convictions and assumptions that always yawned in the space between them intensifying her aloneness in this teeming, torrid city. He was reducing her, cutting the ground from under her feet, putting her on the defensive again. She knew now that she'd been foolish and weak. She really should have called, well, the men, the staff, if not the police; that was the logical course of action. That night she decided she'd take it up with Hussain first thing tomorrow.

Her resolution wavered the next afternoon though, as she looked for a suitable moment to raise the question. She forced herself to utter, almost under her breath, 'There's something I need to ask you, Hussain.'

'Yes, Madam,' he was alert and politely attentive.

'How many families live inside the compound of the zoo?' she asked.

'Three, Madam. Mine, the gate-keeper's and the gardener's.'

He'd anticipated her next question correctly. Somehow she could not connect that woman with Hussain. She began reluctantly, 'I saw a woman stealing meat from Heera's cage yesterday.'

He seemed genuinely shocked. 'A woman? Was she tall or short, madam?' he lowered his voice carefully.

Annette was aware of the curious eyes of the two boys who were hovering in the verandah. 'Tall,' she said briefly. 'That's Tara, madam, Maaja the gate-keeper's wife. Shall I call her?'

'Yes, please. Afterwards. But you'll have to stay and talk to her for me.'

She was already dreading the interview.

It was certainly not easy. Tara came, a poorly dressed but strikingly good-looking woman. A mangy, snot-stained baby perched on her hip and a dust-encrusted toddler trailed by her side holding on to her faded yellow shalwar. She stopped to deposit them both on the patch of grass outside before she came in and stood before them, looking rebellious and defiant rather than evasive or contrite. For a few moments it seemed as though she would say nothing by way of explanation or apology. She had turned her face away. Annette could feel a righteous throb of anger building up inside her head. But then, quite suddenly, the woman launched into a voluble emotional speech. Annette could not make much of the words. She looked at Hussain for explanation. He coughed in some embarrassment and tried to respond to Tara, but Annette held him back. 'Tell me first,' she spoke imperiously.

'She says something about Heera, madam; she says he wants her to take some of his food,' Hussain muttered, his disbelief of that theory filtering clearly through his intonation.

'What makes her say this?' The angry throb pounded even more impatiently in Annette's head. She looked intently at the woman's face as she chattered on whilst Hussain looked more and more irritated and anxious to dissociate himself from this episode.

'She says, Heera won't go near his food, till she's taken some it and, she says, madam, you can stay tomorrow night and see for yourself.'

'That's maybe because of the heat and partly because he's not been well.' Annette gestured to Hussain to interpret; but her mind latched on to those words. She was less sceptical than he was. Before her eyes was a picture of Heera, sitting in the shadows, seemingly disinterested in the food, allowing the woman to pinch it without pouncing or even batting an eyelid.

'Madam, she says Heera is an animal with the spirit of a saint. He knows that her children often have to go hungry, so he can't eat. He waits for her to take something and if, if, she doesn't take it the meat will lie around and rot.' Hussain's lip was distinctly curling up with cynical disbelief even as he narrated this fantastic story.

A part of Annette wanted to believe it but, officially, she felt obliged to contradict the proposition. 'Tell her she's mistaken, would you Hussain. And tell her she mustn't do it again,' she repeated in an attempt to bring the incident to a dignified close.

Hussain felt disappointed at a certain lack of firmness in Madam as he conveyed this to the woman. She was not impressed. She was arguing, torrents of words pouring out of her, as if she were egged on by the success of her initial defence. Annette looked at her face once again, more closely. It was an open, honest face, her dark skin glowed with an earnest intensity which completely banished the righteous throb from her head. Her story about Heera was like the confirmation of genius in a child prodigy to an admiring doting mother. Annette concluded the interview with a mild warning and turned to leave, intrigued but more satisfied with the outcome than she had expected to be.

That day was Thursday, barbecue night at the Lahore Gymkhana Club. She usually joined Saleem there for dinner at about eight and they returned late in the evening, together. She sat nursing her soft drink, waiting for him to come out of the showers. He'd been playing golf. The usual crowd was there, usual gossip, usual meaningless pleasantries. Annette waited with some impatience, her spirits sodden with the emotional exchange of the evening and her mind tortured by the larger question mark which hung over her marriage, a question she had blinked away for so long. Plain as daylight that it was all over. Children and mortgages, the aspic which magically holds marriages together, had both been denied them. The house they lived in had belonged to Saleem's father and came to them unencumbered; and children they could not have . . . It had not really been a deep regret, not to her, not so far, but she felt aware of a secret fear that in this society it could easily become one. She'd thrown herself with energy into other things, the zoo had been one of them. But Tara had shaken all her certainties. And Heera, of course. She thought of her coming up the burning concrete pathway with her two children, of her conviction that Heera wanted them to share his food. She saw herself in the verandah of the depot, with Hussain, checking, weighing, inspecting all the food and cringed a little.

Saleem, forgetting her dilemma of the night before, asked her absently about her day as the waiter piled the barbecued dishes in ritualistic sequence before them; chicken breasts followed by kebabs and spicy lamb tikkas, maybe worth a day's wages for Hussain, two days' wages for the gate-keeper.

She watched the food mesmerised as the appetising glaze vanished along with the charcoal flavour and it turned into bloody hunks of tough fibrous beef. She could smell the raw wetness dripping down its sides. The morsel nearly stuck in her throat choking her with the obscenity of it all. She rounded on Saleem with a bitter vehemence.

'It's over, isn't it?' was all she could manage to say.

Snapshots of Love in Shalimar

Bano Qudsia

The entire party entered the gates for a picnic. In the front were Professor Aijaz, Professor Zia and Professor Baig, and on either side of them, Dimple and Tayyiba. Of the four other girls who followed them, two—T and Z—were dressed in identical clothes. Behind the girls were Ghazi and Zafar, who were carrying most of the party's bags. The rest of the party trailed behind.

The group made its way to Miana Mahal, the middle terraces. Professor Aijaz stood before the marble *jaali*. Here was the water cascade that had inspired such deep reflection in Zaib-un-nissa, the daughter of Alamgir. It was well known that she came to Miana Mahal to look at the waterfall. She would watch the disintegrating pearls of water and compose tragic verses; imagine the daughter of such a mighty emperor thinking such heartrending thoughts. It is said that the original struggle is for food and sustenance, and once you have these, your troubles are over. Zaib-un-nissa had everything, and yet . . . ?

Professor Aijaz had his back to the cascade as he spoke, 'In your dreams your wishes are always fulfilled; our id controls the ego and superego by day, but at night it breaks loose and fulfils its wishes. You understand what I'm saying?'

The girls closest to him nodded.

'Though the superego does not relinquish its hold completely even during sleep, the id, without hurting the superego, disguises its wishes to the point of hurting them and gets whatever it desires. Am I right, Professor Zia?'

Professor Zia said *yes*, slowly. He was preoccupied with worrisome thoughts about his baggage labels, foreign exchange, and the BOAC ticket which had not yet arrived.

'Though all the Mughal princes had grandiose dreams, Shah Jehan's dreams were made out of marble. Do you know that Shah Jehan had this building constructed?'

The girls smiled. Who didn't know that?

'Maybe you don't know that this garden is a dream come true, Shah Jehan's dream . . . I will tell you about the dream, if you like.'

Yes, yes, everyone cried.

'It is said that Shah Jehan once spent a night encamped at his father's tomb. He was comfortably ensconced in Bagh-e-Dilkusha, the Garden of Open Hearts. As morning approached, he saw a garden in which the water flowed from the upper level down and then flowed under. Somebody in the dream told him this was the garden of Eden. So when he woke up, he decided to make an Eden on earth—and succeeded.'

Professor Baig, who taught English literature instead of id, ego and superego, and was infatuated with Hamlet and Browning, quickly interjected in English, 'If Ali Mardan had not been alive, Shah Jehan's dreams would never have been realized. Such a man of genius is born once in centuries. The continuum of his craft transformed the dusty land of Hind into lush greenery.'

Zafar and Zia's group, having passed through the side passages of Miana Mahal, had reached the Bagh-e-Hayat Baksh, the Life-giving Garden, where there was Maqam Sawan Bhadon, the place of rain and shine, and two beautiful *baradaris*, or summer pavilions. They used to be covered in marble, but Maharaja Ranjit Singh liked them so much that he stripped the marble off them and installed it in the Ram Bagh in Amritsar. Now both the baradaris were covered in dust.

Zafar went to the stone throne with its perforated marble grill. 'This throne should be considered a special memorial for Shah Jehan, for he often used it during his lifetime.' Sitting on the throne, Zafar fixed the aperture of his camera, turned the lens towards the middle terraces, and called Professor Aijaz, 'Professor Sahib, turn this way. You too, Professor Zia.'

The girls feigned to move away, some turning their faces, but they were not fast enough, and, from the royal throne, Zafar shot not one but five photographs. The tussar chaddar-clad Rasheeda was in each one of them.

The party camped out in the Bagh-e-Hayat Baksh to eat. There was a clump of trees to their left, and spreading their rugs in its shade, they opened the tiffin baskets. A week ago, each of them had

contributed five rupees towards the food and had given the money to
Zafar. The boys fell to eating immediately, and even challenged one
another to eat more. The girls, apparently reluctant, coaxed each
other to eat and quietly ended up eating twice as much as the boys.
Professor Aijaz, who had diabetes, pulled out Sweetex from his pocket
and said, 'Dimple, put these pills in my tea . . . two . . . thank you.'

Dimple took the Sweetex bottle and put it in her purse. It wasn't
teatime yet.

'Zia, when do you reach America?' Professor Aijaz questioned.

'The ticket is not even here yet, sir, but I will probably stay in
Beirut for two days. I have an uncle there. From there I go to London
for ten days, and from there to Minnesota.'

'You will meet Dr M. Rose there. I'll give you an introductory
letter and she will help you in every way.'

Professor Aijaz, Ghazi, Rasheed, Iftikhar and Zafar were sitting at
a little distance from the others. Their plates had chicken bones,
peppercorns, tomato skins and some potatoes left on the edges. They
had eaten so much that it wasn't possible for them to even eye the
girls or take a walk. The rest of the boys divided themselves into
small groups; some went to the water tank and some down to the side
terraces.

Having eaten their fill, the girls left for the Mughalia Hammam.
Dimple looked down and said, 'God, how impossible it is to bathe
here—no tub or sink! These Mughals, they did so many wonderful
things, but if you look at their bathhouses, you realize how uncivilized
they really were.'

T said quickly, 'Why would they need tubs or sinks, when they
have water fountains to bathe in? What is so civilized about stagnant
tubs of water?'

The conversation turned from Mughal Hammams to Turkish
Hammams to Japanese bathhouses, and from Japanese bathhouses to
Hindu water jugs, and from water jugs to sand scattered around
oceans, and arrived at the bodies of sunbathers stretched out on the
sand. Only Rasheeda was quiet. Her head covered by her tussar chaddar,
she was staring down intently. The bathhouses had transfixed her.

The bathhouse was proof of Emperor Shah Jehan's exquisite taste.
This three-part marble structure, in which dripping water sounded

like rain, had arched niches in its walls. These were so numerous and
so well placed that when the Mughal princesses bathed, the shimmering
candles kept in the niches must have appeared like lightning. And in
the centre, five fountains sent up sprays of cool water, the droplets
looking like moonbeams. The servants' station facing the Hammam
was where the slave girls stood holding silken garments and trays
filled with flowers—which they tossed into the Hammam. Above the
Hammam, which one can now look down into so easily, stood woman
sentries with swords on their ebony shoulders. No one would dare
look past them at the bathers. Heap upon heap of dresses would
arrive, which the slave girls would receive on all four sides of the
water tank. By the time the dresses reached the princesses bathing in
the scented water, hundreds of hands had touched them, and thousands
of lewd eyes had gazed upon them. The same gaze that had been kept
away from the bodies of the princesses reached them in this way,
wrapped up in these clothes.

When the evening shadows reach Shalimar, there is an eerie chill
in the perfumed air. The shadows lengthen, and the garden, which in
daylight resembles a blooming Gul Dawoody, appears pale, like
Rukmarkhi. The wall of Bagh-e-Hayat Baksh, which has two side
doors that go up to the middle terraces, resembles, in the dark of the
evening, the red stone walls of the dungeon where Shah Jehan spent
his days after losing his throne to Aurangzeb.

At the canteen, located on the side where the riverbed of the Khoie
used to be, Zafar and Ghazi ordered tea. Visitors were sitting around
on woven chairs, enjoying bottles of Coca-Cola. Stale cakes and
braided pastries arrived with the tea. In the Nigah Khana, the seeing
room, there were bottles of pasteurized milk, crates of Coca-Cola,
empty boxes of tea leaves and the bicycles of workers. It is said that
an English tourist stayed here. He would sleep on the roof of the
Nigah Khana in a netted bed for fear of mosquitoes, and with a pistol
under his pillow so that he could tackle any possible rioters. He
dreamed of ballroom dancing in the middle terraces, where, wearing
Mughal dress, he would walk on the garden paths.

Dropping two tablets of Sweetex into his cup, Dimple offered tea
to Professor Aijaz. The only noise to be heard was the clattering of

utensils. Zafar, moving the pastry tray towards Rasheeda, said softly, 'Have one, you haven't touched anything.'

Rasheeda raised her lashes, her gaze soft as cream, sweet as honey. She slowly selected a pastry, and for a moment their eyes met, then turned towards the east and west gates.

To Zafar, the eyes that looked up for a moment before being veiled by their lashes, were much prettier than the three-terraced Shalimar Bagh, the three-sided Hammam, Sawan Bhadon, or the Chaddar of Miana Mahal.

All the girls, even those used to two teaspoons of sugar, refused to put any in their tea, so Rasheeda didn't put any in hers either. She gagged, however, with the first sip. She had never had such a tasteless warm drink. Moving the cup away and starting to look around, she suddenly gazed in front of her. Zafar, with his legs dangling off the platform of the water tank, had his camera pointed towards her. Rasheeda tried to get up, wanted to run, but in the interval between wanting and running, the picture was taken. Zafar thanked her silently with his eyes, put the camera over his shoulder, and went towards the Baradari.

When Zafar returned home after the picnic, he felt like he had the whole world's wealth dangling over his shoulder. For the first time, he didn't want to take the spool out of his camera and hand it over to some studio to develop into negatives. But then, he also had a desperate desire for the pictures to be developed so that he could see the tussar-wrapped girl . . . How different she was from all the other girls. Bahawalpuri kooza amidst stainless steel utensils, delicate like glass, seductive like Chinese art, and mysterious like the Harrapan civilization.

—*Translated by Shaista Parveen*

Air-conditioning

Mohsin Hamid

Your robes are itching and you crook a finger at one of your clerks.

'Have we considered air-conditioning?' you ask him.

'One moment, Milord,' he says, scurrying off.

He returns in a few minutes, hands you a sheaf of papers, and bows repeatedly. You are about to commence fanning yourself when the title page catches your eye: 'Air-Conditioning,' it says. Intrigued, you begin to read and encounter the following:

Anticipating your Lordship's request, an investigation was conducted into the role air-conditioning may or may not have played in the lives of the various witnesses expected to testify before your Lordship during the course of this trial. Clearly, the importance of air-conditioning to the events which constitute the substance of this case cannot be overestimated.

The pioneer of academic commentary in this field is Professor Julius Superb. Although his ideas received a cool reception when first aired, they are now widely influential and are discussed not only in doctoral dissertations but also in board rooms and living rooms throughout the land. Indeed, Lahore will not soon forget the Superb paper presented at the Provincial Seminar on Social Class in Pakistan.

Professor Superb walked to the auditorium with a determined smile on his face and a growing ink stain on his shirt pocket, the work of the unsheathed fountain pen he had used to add the final touches to his speech. Those of his students who saw him at the time recalled that he seemed distracted. This did not arouse their curiosity, as the professor was known for his absentmindedness.

Reaching the doors of the auditorium, he attempted to hurl them open, failed, and then struggled unsuccessfully until he realized that

This extract is taken from Mohsin Hamid's *Moth Smoke*, published by Farrar, Straus and Giroux.

he was pushing, not pulling. His awesome mind broke the problem into discreet parts, solved each with the inhuman speed and precision of a supercomputer, and he was inside before fifteen seconds had passed.

Professor Superb then waited in the hushed gloom until it was his turn to speak. When the time came, he strode to the front of the auditorium, mounted the stage, cleared his throat, and delivered a few introductory remarks. Finally, he was ready.

'There are two social classes in Pakistan,' Professor Superb said to his unsuspecting audience, gripping the podium with both hands as he spoke. 'The first group, large and sweaty, contains those referred to as the masses. The second group is much smaller, but its members exercise vastly greater control over their immediate environment and are collectively termed the elite. The distinction between members of these two groups is made on the basis of control of an important resource: air-conditioning. You see, the elite have managed to re-create for themselves the living standards of say, Sweden, without leaving the dusty plains of the subcontinent. They're a mixed lot—Punjabis and Pathans, Sindhis and Baluchis, smugglers, mullahs, soldiers, industrialists—united by their residence in an artificially cooled world. They wake up in air-conditioned houses, drive air-conditioned cars to air-conditioned offices, grab lunch in air-conditioned restaurants (rights of admission reserved), and at the end of the day go home to their air-conditioned lounges to relax in front of their wide-screen TVs. And if they should think about the rest of the people, the great uncooled, and become uneasy as they lie under their blankets in the middle of the summer, there is always prayer, five times a day, which they hope will gain them admittance to an air-conditioned heaven, or, at the very least, a long, cool drink during a fiery day in hell.'

Smiling, the professor walked out of the hushed auditorium, his footsteps echoing in the silence.

Most of the students present were either asleep or too bored to pay attention. Others had not heard a word, because Professor Superb eschewed the use of a microphone, thinking himself a great orator when in actuality he had a faint and unsteady voice. However, some of those who were awake and listening in the first three rows later said they were transfixed by the speech. Among them was the professor's former pupil, Murad Badshah, who regularly attended the Provincial Seminar Series.

Murad Badshah was never very fond of ACs. He was a man who liked to sweat, and he sweated well and profusely. In his own opinion, he had supremely athletic pores and a finely honed sweat distribution system which sent trickles of coolness wherever they were most needed.

He also enjoyed the natural aroma that clung to him like pollen to an errant bee.

But Murad Badshah was in the rickshaw business, and he had to accommodate passengers whose opinions (at least on this subject) often differed from his. Accordingly, he bathed three times a day in the summer: morning, midday, and evening. He found bathing almost as effective as sweating in its ability to cool his body, and thought of his combined bath-sweat cooling regimen as a way of augmenting rather than diminishing his body's natural cooling capacity.

ACs, on the other hand, he considered unnatural and dangerous. Your pores will get out of shape if you rely on ACs for your cooling, he would say. It's fine as long as you stay in your little air-conditioned space, but one day you might need to rely on your body again and your body won't be there for you. After all, fortunes change, power blackouts happen, compressors die, coolant leaks.

He loved load-shedding for this reason. It amused him to see the rich people on the grounds of their mansions as he drove past their open gates, fanning themselves in the darkness, muttering as they called the power company on their cellular phones. Indeed, nothing made Murad Badshah more happy than the distress of the rich.

Lazy pores, he would say to himself, and laugh joyously. And the rich people would stare at the retreating lights of his rickshaw on their darkened streets and wonder what anyone could possibly be so happy about when it was so damn hot.

Murad Badshah was a firm believer in the need for a large-scale redistribution of wealth. After Professor Superb's speech, he vowed to break the barriers that separated the cooled from the uncooled, like himself. Indeed, he used this principle to justify his piracy campaign against yellow cabs, since they were not only taking market share from rickshaws but were air-conditioned as well. He was fond of asking his victims, 'Why should you be cooled?' A populist, he rebelled against the system of hereditary entitlements responsible for cooling only the laziest minority of Pakistan's population, and he embraced Darashikoh as a partner when the latter fell from cooling.

But in the Shah household, in the compound financed by the corrupt millions of Aurangzeb's father, the hum of the air conditioner was sucking the life out of a marriage. For air-conditioning can be divisive not only in the realm of the political but in the realm of the personal as well.

Aurangzeb loved ACs with a passion unrivalled by his love for any other species of inanimate object. He insisted that his father install central air-conditioning in their new house, that the system be supported by a dedicated back-up generator, and that he have a master remote control for the entire upstairs portion. He was never happier than when his bedroom was so cold that he needed a heavy blanket to avoid shivering in the middle of summer. Conversely, he liked it to be so warm in winter that he could comfortably sleep naked without so much as a sheet. Aurangzeb, more than most men, sought to master his environment.

Mumtaz hated ACs with the sort of hatred one normally reserves for members of other religions and ethnic groups. An AC had almost killed her when she was young. She came home from a school football match (she was a star midfielder with a vicious left foot), took off her clothes in front of the AC, caught pneumonia, and spent two weeks in a hospital with a tube draining her lungs, battling for her life. Although Mumtaz was only fourteen at the time, and although people told her she had brought her illness on herself, she swore never to forgive and never to forget. Having once been betrayed by an AC, she branded them all traitors, and avoided their use except under circumstances of egregious warmth.

And so it was that the marriage between Aurangzeb and Mumtaz was doomed from the start.

In New York, a city of hot, muggy summers, Aurangzeb insisted that only an insane person would sleep with the air-conditioning off. Mumtaz disagreed, but baby Muazzam settled the question: he would cry all night unless serenaded by the cool hum of the air conditioner.

A triumphant Aurangzeb agreed to Mumtaz's terms of surrender: the AC would he left on in night, but at a thermostat setting of no more than three (with nine, of course, being the coolest).

When the couple returned to Lahore, where young Muazzam had his own room and a nanny, Mumtaz renewed her campaign. 'We have to conserve electricity,' she would say. 'The entire country suffers because of the wastefulness of a privileged few.'

'I couldn't care less about the country,' Aurangzeb would reply. 'Besides, you have a delusional and obsessive fear of pneumonia.'

'I think you underestimate the risk pneumonia poses to all of us. Besides, I really do feel that we have a duty to use electricity responsibly.'

'Then sleep outside. The AC is staying on.'

The results of Mumtaz's renewed attempts to reduce the air conditioning in the life she shared with Aurangzeb were minimal in terms of any change in the temperature. But her relations with her husband had grown chilly since their return from America, and his persistence on the AC issue did nothing to restore the warmth that had disappeared. In fact, now that they were back in Pakistan, Aurangzeb was far less conciliatory toward her than he had been before. For his part, he felt that she should be grateful for the style with which he (actually his father) supported them. He felt that the cars and clothes and dinner parties made him a good husband, and he resented her inability to demonstrate gratitude through obedience as his wife.

Mumtaz would later wonder whether Darashikoh's lack of air-conditioning played a role in attracting her to him. No one will ever know the answer to that question, but it must be said that if air-conditioning doomed her relationship with her husband, it doomed her relationship with his best friend as well. You see, Mumtaz was over-air-conditioned and longed to be uncooled, while Darashikoh was under-air-conditioned and longed to be cooled. Although they walked the same path for a while, Mumtaz and Darashikoh were headed in opposite directions.

Yes, and no matter how important air-conditioning was to Mumtaz, to Aurangzeb and Murad Badshah and Professor Superb, it was more important to Darashikoh Shezad, for it took his mother from him and propelled him inexorably toward a life of crime.

On a midsummer night that followed a day when the temperatures spiked into the hundred and teens, much of Lahore was plunged into darkness. The pull of innumerable air conditioners stressed connections and wires and the systems that regulated the eddying currents of electricity past their capacities, and one after another, they failed. The wind chose that night to rest, and neighborhoods baked in the still heat.

Perhaps it was not surprising that Darashikoh's mother decided to sleep on the roof on that tragic night. After all, she had often done so as a child growing up in Khanewal with no air-conditioning. She told her son and servants to carry two charpoys up to the roof, and such was her command over her household that they managed to do so.

Darashikoh would remember having a cup of hot tea with her before lying down on his charpoy, his arms crossed under his head, staring up at the stars. He fell into a deep sleep, so deep that he never heard the firing of the bullet that would claim his mother's life.

His mother may have been asleep as well, for when her son found her dead the next morning, she was lying on her charpoy with her eyes shut. Or she may have been awake. She may have heard the repeated coughing of a Kalashnikov being fired into the sky. But even if she did, she probably thought nothing of it: there were two weddings in the neighborhood that night, so the celebratory sound of automatic gunfire was only to be expected. Of course, the bullets might not have come from those weddings. Someone might have fired a Kalashnikov in the air to announce a victory in a kite fight, a job promotion, or the birth of a child. A young man may have fired just to fire, or to let the neighborhood know that his was not a house to be robbed. Perhaps the weapon was fired at the moon, a metallic human howl.

Indeed, it is possible that only the one bullet was fired that night, for only one was found in the morning. It pierced Darashikoh's mother's throat from above, passed through the charpoy, and rolled, spent, to the edge of the roof. Her death was probably not instantaneous, since her spinal cord was not severed by the injury. The coroner was of the opinion that she bled to death in silence over the course of some minutes, unable to get up or to make a sound. The pool of her blood was already dry when the lightening sky roused Darashikoh from his sleep.

After that night, Darashikoh would have a recurrent vision which came to him not only when he was asleep but when he was awake as well. Once he was sitting with Mumtaz when the vision came, and he described it to her in this way: 'I imagine Lahore as a city with bullets streaking into the air, tracers like fireworks, bright lines soaring into the night, slowing, falling back on themselves, a pavilion collapsing, the last dance of a fire before its fuel is consumed. And I lie on a field in the center of town, on grass fenced in by buildings, looking up at the stars with a sweet stem in my mouth, watching the brilliant arcs descending toward me.'

Mumtaz could not understand why people fired into the air as though the bullets would never come down again. She said, 'People don't believe in consequences anymore.'

But Darashikoh believed in consequences. He knew that his mother would not have died if the AC had been cooling her room that night, and when he lost his job and had his power disconnected, he felt more than just the discomfort of the heat in his house. He felt an insecurity, a dis-ease that gnawed at him day and night. Perhaps he merely feared the loss of social status that the end of his air-conditioning represented. Or perhaps he feared something more profound and less easily explained. He needed money to have his power and air-conditioning and security restored, and he swore that nothing would stand in his way. He, a man who hated guns, came to accept that he would have to use one.

It is possible that Darashikoh could have learned something from his young servant, the mystically minded Manucci.

If one had asked Manucci during his days as a street urchin, as he sat, in defiance of municipal orders, astride the gun Zam-Zammah, Manucci would probably have said that ACs were hot. The first time he saw one jutting out into the street from the wall of a shop in the old city, he walked up to the noisy box and was amazed at the blast of hot air it sent straight into his face. Why do people turn on hot air in the middle of summer? he often wondered.

When he asked, people thought he was crazy. 'What do you mean ACs make hot air?' they would say. 'They make cold air. Everyone knows that. That's the way it is: ACs make cold air. That's what they're for.'

'Do you have an AC?' he would ask. 'No,' they all had to admit. No one had an AC. The other beggars, the vendors, the runners at paan shops, the ne'er-do-wells: none of them had an AC. But they all knew ACs made cold air, everyone knew that. That's what ACs were for.

One day Manucci met an AC repairman. 'You don't seem to be doing a very good job,' Manucci told him. 'All the ACs around here are making hot air.'

'You're crazy, boy,' the AC repairman said.

Manucci realized what all this had to mean. It meant people thought what he called hot air was cold air. So whenever he walked down the street past the back of a protruding AC, he would smile and say, 'What cold air it makes. Wonderful.'

And people would shake their heads.

But Manucci knew they would call him crazy if he said this air was hot, so he always said it was cold. And when they shook their heads at him he shook his head right back.

It was not until the day that Darashikoh's mother grabbed Manucci by the ear as he was trying to slip her wallet out of her purse and, deciding what Manucci needed was a home and some discipline, brought him back to her house, it was not until that day that Manucci finally went inside a building that had an AC. When it was turned on, he felt cold air blowing right into his face. And that is why he said, without blinking an eye, 'This air is hot.'

He was very pleased with this statement.

But Darashikoh, just in the door from his first college boxing practice, was surprised, and strangely unsettled.

The Old Mansion

Ikramullah Chaudhry

The three lived in a single room. There was a room above it and another below. Every time the tenant in the upper room chucked out some water, the three occupants of the room below were shouted at and cursed. Only after they explained that they were not to blame would the man go for the real culprit. Likewise, when the man below turned on the faucet, which cut off the supply to the man on top, it was the three in the middle who were called to account. They would then point at the door of the offender, and the man on top would fall on him like a maniac. The three were quite fed up with the location of their room. A couple of times they even brought up, among themselves, the idea of moving out, but stopped short, for they were not likely to find another room with such low rent and, more importantly, one that was right in the heart of the city. And since the man above and the one below weren't exactly living in paradise either, it didn't make sense to look for a room on the top or the ground floor. No place came without its peculiar problems. Why court new troubles? Why not quietly endure those they already had? They had gotten used to them after all, hadn't they? Let it be. No harm done.

The three had identical names. Then again, they didn't. Only the first names were the same, the rest different. People called them *Chota* (the youngest), *Manjhla* (the middle one) and *Bara* (the oldest) for convenience. I guess that'll do for us too. No compelling reason to use the names their respective parents had given them in the hope they would turn out to have the qualities the names implied. Wishes are like flowers. By the end of the day only the stem remains, the petals fall off or are plucked out and scattered. The men looked no different from a naked stem—dried up, shrivelled, scrawny. So people dropped the formality of calling them by their names.

Bara had been around for the last sixty, maybe seventy years. 'Around' in a manner of speaking—he seemed to merely roll in whatever direction he was pushed in this noisy and crowded world. When the massacres started in Bihar and his people fled, he fled with them. Some were killed on the way, others made it to the safety of East Pakistan in dire straits, and he with them. When death sentences were doled out to people for the sole crime of being Pakistani, they fled East Pakistan, and he with them. He boarded a ship and, buffeted by the waves of the inner and outer sea alike, made it to Karachi. When Biharis became the target of frequent arrests and other punishments in Karachi, he moved to Lahore. The frequent divisions and partitions had taught him that the most effective strategy for survival in such situations was to make a run for one's life. Groups would round up members of the opposite group and make short work of them, fully convinced that this was the easiest, most expeditious way of ridding society of impurities. Also, it was entirely possible that one of his own group might confuse him with the opponent and kill him. He had seen that happen, though, for his part, Bara was not a staunch Muslim, Pakistani or even Bihari Muhajir. All he had ever wanted from the world was to be able to make ends meet, or if that was too much, then perhaps to have a meal a day.

One could see just by looking at his face that he was still ashamed of the event of his birth sixty or seventy years ago. The shame simply wouldn't wash away, even though he had not been a participant in this crime, but only its result. It was as though he were trying to hang his own dead body for murder. If anything, his embarrassment grew worse with time. It seemed he'd never die. In the end, he would simply liquefy from shame and flow like water into the sewer, careful not to bubble out of the gutter and get in anybody's way. He exuded his sense of shame before one and all—except for his two companions— as if guilty of some misdeed. Had it occurred to him that his life was the constant source of his shame, he would certainly have ended it. His mother had died when he was still a child living in his village. People would commiserate, 'How sad, your mother died,' and he would feel it was his fault that she died. He fled Bihar as a young man, made his escape from East Pakistan in his middle age, and took flight from Karachi as an old man, and throughout these vicissitudes remained steadfastly shame-ridden; there was no need for his mother to die each time.

Manjhla had found him sitting at Data Sahib's *darbar* (shrine) one day, immersed as usual in shame. It seemed he had no one to look after him. Afraid that without proper care or protection the old man might die at the shrine, Manjhla had brought him along to the room with smoke-blackened walls and chipping plaster where he and Chota had been tenants for the past several years.

Bara told Manjhla his name and stuck 'Azimabadi' at the end of it. Azimabad was a good 200 miles from his village and he had never been there in his life. Why did he always indulge in these unnecessary forms of misrepresentation? Oddly enough, they never caused him any shame. After all, one needed a bit of pride to live, never mind how you got it, otherwise there would be no difference between a human being and dirt.

Manjhla was a frightened man. Frightened of what? He couldn't tell. But he was up to his ears in fear. Anything that entered his mind was instantaneously transformed into fear. He was even afraid of himself. Anybody might do anything, at any time, like a loaded shotgun. And so could he.

He came from a small village in Gilgit in the foothills of a large mountain that was a two-day journey from Skardu. A trip either way required a night's stop en route. He didn't like living in Lahore. But he did like helping his old father stay alive, along with his two young orphaned nephews and himself. Since his native Gilgit had no jobs to offer, he had to accept both together—his 'dislike' and his 'like'. At the end of each trip to the village, he would return more convinced than ever that the mountain would have vanished by the time of his next visit, as well as the orchards, the river, even the village itself. If he couldn't go home one summer, fear ran in his veins instead of blood for the rest of that year. Two fears especially plagued his life, and thanks to them he would never step out of the house without wrapping a piece of cloth around his head and face. He feared that his eyes might accidentally fall on a woman he did not know, and in punishment, he might have to burn in Hell in the afterlife. That he was already in Hell in this life, without having eyed a strange woman, meant nothing to him. His other fear was related to the feeling that his face and bearing somehow looked different from the general population of Lahore. God knew what this might prompt the locals to do to him. In reality, nothing untoward had ever happened to him. Fears, however, follow their own paths, and past experiences rarely manage to hold them back.

One reason why he took a liking to Bara was that his short, sparse beard (never mind that it had turned grey) and the features of his face resembled his own, except that his complexion was darker. It was entirely possible that at some point in the distant past people from Gilgit had ventured forth to Bihar and settled there, or maybe it was the other way round. The human breed is like the wind: it can strike out in any direction and end up anywhere at all. Whether this had actually happened or not, the fact is that both had started out from faraway regions and ended up together in Lahore looking for work. Manjhla was mortally afraid of dying in Lahore and being buried there. Bara, on the other hand, couldn't care less. He no longer had a native place to feel passionate about. Sure he remembered now and then the streets and lanes in which he and his little friends had played together naked. What of it? One remembers a lot of things, does one die over each and every memory?

Chota, too, was blissfully free of such hang-ups. He was a native of Punjab, and enjoyed the rare distinction of being homeless in his own home. He wore a perpetual smile on his face, which bore a scar from a cut about a half-inch wide extending from the left corner of his lips across the jaw, past the ear, and all the way to the base of his neck. Since the facial muscles had been pulled taut to the left, it gave him a permanently smiling expression. When wracked by worry over some matter, he appeared rather to be smiling; when he cried, he seemed to be laughing, and when laughing, crying. He had obliterated the difference between the two acts in one fell swoop. Whether he laughed or cried, the sounds that came out of his mouth resembled those of a toothless hyena staring with hunger and longing at the half-eaten carcass of an animal and laughing—or crying (your guess). His grandfather had owned four acres of land and made do with the yield all his life. He had adopted two sons and a daughter and married them off. When he died, Chota's father and uncle were worried that two acres apiece wouldn't be enough to feed their families. The uncle sold his share to Chota's father in instalments and struck out for Karachi in search of work, taking his family along. He never returned, and nor did he have any further contact with the village. When Chota's *phupha* died without leaving an heir, his wife inherited four acres of land from him. And when she too died, Chota's father went to claim it for himself and his younger brother, maintaining they were their sister's heirs. But the deceased sister's *devar* confronted him with, 'When your father died, did you remember to give your sister, and my sister-in-law, her share of the land? Instead, you dragged her to the *tehsildar* and had her relinquish her claim in your favour. Some cheek you've got now to come and claim her share of the inheritance according to the *shari'at*.'

Chota's father wouldn't budge and insisted on taking possession of the land then and there. In the ensuing scuffle, he was murdered on the spot, and the murderer went after Chota to finish him off too, as he was the last surviving heir. His mother was hacked to death with swords as she tried to shield him, her only child, from the attackers. He received several wounds and the attackers left him for dead. His maternal grandfather took him to his own village. He was fifteen when this grandfather died and his maternal uncle made him leave the house. He drifted off to Lahore, looking for work, and started living with Manjhla in a room in this crumbling mansion, which some Hindu had built in the beginning of the twentieth century. Chota owned six acres of land—on paper, that is. In reality, he could neither take possession of it nor raise any crops on it. Indeed he couldn't even set foot in his native village without risking death at the hands of his enemies, one of whom had now become a Member of the Provincial Assembly to boot.

This mansion, constructed with outsize bricks laid with red lime mortar, had a *devrhi* tall enough to allow an elephant, *hauda* and all, to pass through easily. At the time it was built, the days of travelling on elephants had long been over, but humans usually take their time perceiving change, adjusting to it and freeing themselves of old habits of thought. The devrhi led to a spacious courtyard bordered by verandas on three sides with rooms directly behind them. The same floor plan was repeated exactly on the second storey, but only partially on the top floor, which had galleries roofed with corrugated metal in place of verandas. Drainage ditches ran along the edge of the courtyard and the walls of the devrhi and emptied into the main gutter outside, into which the garbage from the upper floors was also channelled through steel drainpipes. Where the pipes had ruptured, the broken or missing portions had been repaired by nailing metal foil to the walls. Thanks to this novel solution, all day long filthy, stinking water dribbled down the walls where the pipes ran and emptied into the ditches. If a careless tenant upstairs dumped a large amount of water all at once, the half-clogged pipes overflowed into the courtyard. Stepping inside the devrhi, one felt one had walked into the middle of an open sewer. The red lime mixture continually filtered down from between the bricks of the ceiling and walls in a fine, powdery shower. During the British period the devrhi had had a massive main gate that was regularly closed every night. Now, however, it gaped open night and day, like a sleepless eye. Most likely, rioters had smashed the gate in 1947, or the immigrants had used it for fuel. Something had happened to the gate, but no one knew exactly what.

There were about as many families living in the mansion as it had rooms. Some were the children of former allottees—those allotted these rooms as compensation for property left behind in India— some were tenants of the heirs of allottees who had made their way out of the cycle of poverty and moved to better places. The women carried out their household chores or work—mostly handicrafts, which they made on commission for local merchants—perched on charpais laid out across their rooms, in the verandas or the courtyard. Their filthy-looking children frisked about in the courtyard without a scrap to cover their bodies. A woman dared not intrude upon even an inch of space in another's room, for this, like countless other trifles, could lead to fights that lasted the entire day. Sometimes the men would be dragged in as well. Perhaps these rows acted as a safety valve, releasing the pressures accumulated in the mind due to such hardships as cramped space, an over-abundance of children, the crush of tenants, poverty and disease. The number of hearths in the verandas and courtyard matched the number of rooms. A few old women worked as domestics in the homes of families in the neighbourhood, for wages and for meals. The men sold all kinds of wares on pushcarts, pulled rickshaws, did odd jobs, ran shops, or worked for hire.

The despondency, dissatisfaction and uncertainty about the future that had haunted the refugees who were resettled in the mansion in

1947 still dogged its current occupants, the only difference being that now even people native to the city had begun to feel the sting of these worries. Like the immigrants who missed their former homes, the ill-fated crumbling mansion looked homeless, and seemed to miss its former occupants. Nobody took care of it, because they were all supposed to—collectively.

A large, octagonal bay window jutted out of the three men's room a couple of feet into the street like a miniature balcony. Seen from the street, it seemed to have four sides growing out of a large lotus flower made of stucco, a pattern repeated both above and below the window. The window had panels of stained glass and was permanently sealed from the inside with wooden boards nailed in the shape of a cross, because it might, like any of the other bay windows in the building, come crashing down any time. If it could have been opened, it would have opened on to the street like a royal enclosure of exquisite latticework from which a king might give audience. And if it had been the old times, one could even imagine the three men giving audience to their subjects: Bara shyly, Manjhla terrified, and Chota smiling. After all, Bara and Manjhla had something of the Mughals in their haggard faces.

A narrow walkway, no more than a couple of feet wide, its corroded metal roof supported by a wooden frame and thin, carved pillars, began at the side of the bay window and ran along the row of rooms. Its flooring was missing in many places and one could see the street below through the gaping holes. The metal roof had come undone in spots and slapped in the wind like a spring; the stronger the wind blew, the more it rattled. The wooden frame and the delicately carved supports had turned white like desiccated bones strewn across a stretch of desert. The boards of the frame, too, had come loose and hung down or curved upward here and there. Above the devrhi's arch, a pair of lions, carved in red stucco and only dimly visible through years of smoke and dirt, stood catlike on their hind legs; like two friends being photographed together, they looked helplessly into the camera lens with the portions of their eyes still intact. Their tails had chipped away almost entirely, and their manes partially. The artisan who fashioned them had given them bodies like that of a she-goat, so that they appeared, strangely and simultaneously, a little ridiculous, a little pitiable and a little mean. Nowadays one can see any number of such one-eyed, truncated lions roaming the streets of Lahore, some of them even called 'Lions of Punjab'.

The evening had deepened, and the encroaching darkness had hushed the bustle and noise of the day. The three sat in their room talking. Without the straw of their friendship, they would have drowned long ago in this sea of people called Lahore. Evening was the only time when each could forget about his defining traits and feel the taste of life on their tongues, bittersweet. And they liked it.

The heavy, late-evening air pressed down the stench rising from the courtyard, packed with charpais on which young and old, women, men, children, slept away as though drugged, as the empty pushcarts, large upturned wicker baskets, ropes lying coiled like snakes, and cold hearths waited in immobility for their owners to rise. And under some cots, cats and dogs were seen lying side by side in peace, rooting for bread crumbs or bones from which the last fibre of meat had been sucked off.

'Bare Miyan,' Chota began, 'you didn't marry?'

'I wanted to, *yaar*, but it just didn't happen,' Bara cooed like one of the pigeons that roosted in the balcony for the night.

'"Didn't happen"—how so?' Manjhla asked.

'Well, you see, when I'd just arrived in Dhaka, I found myself a place in the area where a lot of Bihari immigrants had set up homes. There was this girl there. She too came from Bihar. I liked her a lot. Whenever we ran into each other in the lane, we would stare at each other. This went on for quite some time. One evening, when the lane was deserted, I saw her coming along and accosted her. "Listen," I said.

'"Go on," she said.

'"I will die without you."

'She drew back from modesty, gave a little smile, scratched the ground with her big toe, and said, "Well, then, talk to my Baba."

'In that single instant the scent of her body permeated my whole being.'

'So did you go see her father?' Chota asked impatiently.

'Yes, sir, I did. He asked me what I did. I told him that I pulled rickshaws.

'"Do you own the rickshaw?" he asked.

'"No. I rent it."

'"All together, how much money do you have?"

'"Forty, maybe fifty rupees."

'He said, "Come back when you have your own rickshaw and a thousand rupees in your pocket."

'Well, I left. Soon, she got married and I gradually forgot about the matter. Not her scent though. That stayed with me.'

Chota was smiling as he sighed. A sudden commotion in the veranda outside interrupted them just as they were about to break into hearty laughs. It sounded like a woman being murdered and screaming for help. They hurriedly pasted their dominant traits back on their faces. Chota opened the door, smiling as usual, and peeked out. 'Nothing!' he said. 'Some cats are having a fight.' Then, sitting down, he said, 'Is that all, Bare Miyan? Just once in seventy years? You didn't try again to get married?'

'As a matter of fact, I did. One more time. But never mind. It's getting late and tomorrow is a working day. Go to sleep!'

'No, Bare Miyan, finish your story.'

'Well, then, in Karachi I met up with a woman, an immigrant from Bihar like myself. Her husband had been murdered in East Pakistan. She had three children, the oldest about ten years old. I started to frequent her hut. She was extremely poor. Well, who wasn't? But she showed me great hospitality. I was sort of leaning towards it, and a couple of friends encouraged me besides, but this one had no scent. I refused.'

Once again there was noise outside, but this time it sounded muffled, like the moan of a child, followed by the sobs and cries of a woman. The three perked up their ears again, but Chota tried to put their minds at ease. 'No call for fear or shame,' he said. 'That's just the way cats wail at night. They'll move on. Sleep now.'

The three fell asleep. In the morning they found out that an eight-month-old infant had died in the room next door for lack of medical attention, in the arms of his teenage mother, recently arrived from Swaat. The mother kept crying, while the father, who must have been in his mid-twenties, lay in a drugged sleep on the adjoining cot after a shot of heroin. So it had not been cats after all.

The three men had no worries. But that didn't mean that they were a happy lot, either. Happiness doesn't really exist in the world. Let's just say they did not or could not indulge their misery. Their ability to feel anything at all had been snuffed out. Driven from pillar to post the whole day long like pack donkeys, they had come to look upon life as an arduous journey through very rough terrain. Hardship was a necessary component of the journey. A crumbling, filth-ridden mansion, hunger, disease, drugs, children dying like flies, the life-squeezing suffocation of cramped space, fights over trifles, and worse yet, daily visits by the police, the obscenities they shouted at the tenants and the way they humiliated every man, woman and child—through it all, the three would just sit, with their differentiating traits plastered across their faces, and look on in total indifference. So did the others, as though it were all happening to someone else, in some other city, while they were merely reading an account of it in the newspaper.

Fifty years had gone by; the country had passed through several governments, but the mansion and its residents remained without a home, without a country. It seemed that the rulers, all of them, were identical siblings in every respect, and these residents of the mansion were their stepbrothers. But why the jealous mistreatment? The mansion dwellers weren't exactly Yusuf in beauty. Here, even a twenty-year-old woman looked like an old hag and a prepubescent boy of ten, a mature young adult. The stepbrothers had robbed them of their innocence, beauty, youth—everything!

The night felt close and stuffy. The light from the street lamps filtered in through the remaining windowpanes and reached their eyes in shades of red, blue and green, which irritated them. They cursed the man who had thought of putting in stained glass, to make it all look fetching, no doubt. Bara said edgily, 'I feel like smashing the panes that are left. That would let in some breeze at least.'

'If you feel so hot, we can go and stand on the veranda,' Chota offered.

But the usual glut of charpais greeted their eyes down below in the courtyard. A child would ask for water, the mother would get up cursing, walk over to the pitcher, drink a glass herself first, then give some to the child and fan him to cool him off. Slowly she'd succumb to sleep and her hand would stop moving. The child would start crying again, and she would hurriedly resume fanning. Meanwhile the Swaati youth returned from somewhere, removed the padlock from the door and went in. Chota remarked, 'When he left here in the evening he had his wife with him. How come he's returning alone?'

'Maybe she wanted to go back home and he went to put her on the bus or something,' Manjhla ventured in explanation.

Chota began, 'This Moti Begum . . .'

'Moti Begum, who?'

'Oh, the fat one. You know her. The one who sometimes comes here in the afternoon all powdered and rouged to visit the women in the courtyard when they do their embroidery and needlework. I know she's lured two or three women into going out with her for six, seven hours at a time.'

'So?'

'Don't you understand? She takes them out to turn tricks. All the other women know that too. But they keep quiet. They're afraid that if they spill the beans, all hell will break loose. Or maybe as a precaution: what if they themselves needed her help at some point?' Chota laughed in his peculiar way.

'Their men don't know about it?' Manjhla asked.

'God knows. But if they see a hint of prosperity suddenly appear in their homes and want to keep quiet, well, that's their business.'

'Chota, you're in on all the gossip!' Manjhla said.

'Of course. You know why? Because I socialize with everyone. All you ever do is tremble from fear, and you, Bare Miyan, can never have enough of feeling ashamed.'

'And what do you do—smile?'

Chota laughed his hyena laugh, then he said, 'You can buy anything in the mansion—liquor, heroin, hemp, women, labour, you name it.'

'You're too suspicious, Chota,' Manjhla said. 'You *will* go to Hell. That's enough. Go to sleep.'

'Don't get angry,' Bara said. 'Maybe Chota is telling the truth. I've seen this happen before. First in Dhaka, then in Karachi, maybe here too. Misery and helplessness always drive people to sell themselves.'

A few days later, when the three returned from work in the evening they found the residents standing in small groups and talking on the street outside the mansion, inside in the courtyard, and in the verandas. Manjhla, quaking with fear, said, 'It looks like something terrible's happened.'

Chota, smiling, joined one of the groups and promptly returned to fill in his companions: 'Rumour has it that the City has declared the mansion dangerous and ordered its demolition.'

'These rumours always turn out to be true in the end,' Bara remarked, in deep shame.

Chota continued, 'Someone was saying it will be torn down tomorrow, but another man said nothing of the sort was about to happen, that it was all a lie. Somebody else said that Sardar Rustam Khan's *qabza* men had met some of the allottees and offered to buy their rooms at a thousand rupees apiece, plus permission to live rent-free for six months. They refused, saying the offer wasn't good enough. The men taunted, "Okay, wait until tomorrow. When the City pulls it down, you won't get even a penny, and you and your families will have to sleep on the pavement, in the bargain. Only Sardar Sahib can stop the demolition. He's already bought up the shares of other allottees." Only God knows whether this was some kind of ploy or was true. Anyway, they left asking them to think it over, and promised to return at midnight to get their answer.'

Just then the Swaati girl, lovely as a doll, came daintily down the stairs, alone, clip-clopping in her fancy sandals. Draped from head to toe in her chaddar and looking straight ahead with her clever black-bee eyes, she sped past them to the devrhi and then out onto the street, where she waved down a rickshaw. She had a brief exchange with the rickshaw-puller. Both smiled, and she hopped in and left.

The three looked at each other. Was this the same mother who had sat the whole night long holding her dying child, too frightened even to cry in a loud voice? Or walk out onto the veranda and shout for help in her native Pushtu, because she was a stranger here? Or muster the courage to kick her drugged husband awake? Bara said, 'If only hands meant to fan babies weren't lifted to hail rickshaws for such purposes!' And the three went back to their room.

A commotion continued inside the mansion throughout the night. People kept coming and going, talking among themselves. Schemes were hatched. The three couldn't sleep well. When they set out for work in the morning they saw armed police and City forces standing outside the mansion, ready to move in with their pickaxes, bulldozers, trucks and bobcats. An officer from the City was in charge of the operation. Some of the residents of the mansion were talking to him, thrashing their arms about and beating their chests.

'Why weren't we given advance notice?'

'We posted notice three times on the mansion.'

'It's plastered with notices. How did you expect us to see it there?'

'Well, that's not our fault, is it?'

'If Sardar Rustam Khan had bought out the mansion, you'd go back quietly. But you won't listen to us.'

'That's not true. Anyway, you have three hours to clear out. After that, I'm not responsible for any damage.'

The three immediately returned to their room and started packing. Just then the man who lived in the room above them came stomping down the stairs and straight into their room, and asked, 'No water and electricity again today?'

'That's right,' Chota answered, smiling.

'That fellow below you is a real bastard. He isn't going to give up until we give it to him.'

'He didn't cut them off. Not today. It's the City. They're tearing down the mansion.'

'Why?'

'It's dangerous.'

'So what? If it fell, it would have crushed us. Maybe a few cats and dogs as well. The pigeons roosting on the balcony wouldn't have gotten hurt; they'd have flown away. If the mansion collapsed, it wouldn't have done those stinking City bastards any harm, just like the pigeons.'

The three went on packing their belongings.

'This mansion is rock solid. It'll last another hundred years. You hear me? All it needs is a little bit of repair. Where will we go? The City doesn't understand.'

The man stomped down the stairs. The three picked up their belongings and strode out of the mansion—Bara shyly, Manjhla fearfully, Chota smiling. Once again they stood on the street, wondering where to go next.

—*Translated by Muhammad Umar Memon*

Mohsin Mohalla

Ashfaq Ahmed

No one could remember when Master Ilyaas had begun to rent the small room in their neighbourhood. However, everyone seemed to know that Master Ilyaas was an immigrant and that he came from some part of Ambala; the dialect he used was spoken around Ambala and Patiala. Master Ilyaas lived in the rented room, and the boys from the neighbourhood came to him for help with their maths and multiplication tables and to practise their writing on wooden slates.

Master Ilyaas owned two fighter quails and one pure-bred rooster. The quails remained locked up in their cages, but the rooster stayed just outside the door of his room. Master Ilyaas had put a copper ring on one of his legs and tied a strong string to it; the other end of the string was tied to a nail he had hammered into his doorframe. Master Ilyaas was respected by everyone in Mohsin Mohalla and they never failed to greet him when they passed by his door. They were sure Masterji worked, but no one knew exactly what he did. Perhaps he was a bookkeeper for tradesmen in the vegetable market in another neighbourhood, or he laboured for daily wages in some factory or the other; whatever it was he did, they knew he barely managed to get by on what he earned.

As it happened, Master Sahib was a simpleton who didn't know how to look out for himself in a metropolis like Lahore. His plain looks inspired little love or compassion, and his manner of speaking little confidence. Since he did not lie or cheat or exaggerate, or boast or try to bully others, no one believed what he said, and his speech was so full of grammatical and linguistic errors that his listeners would abandon his company in frustration. So guileless, so undemanding was he that he did not appear to belong to the human species. And because no one likes to associate with such people, he did not have any friends. His presence had become a burden to the neighbourhood and to its societal structure. And, ironically, that is precisely why the people of the mohalla respected him; bowed and said their 'salaam', before moving on when they passed by his door. One winter evening, Master Ilyaas's landlord castigated him loudly. Using harsh language, he threatened to throw out all his belongings if he didn't pay the rent he owed him for the past six months within three days. Masterji froze with fear; he didn't have the required one hundred and eighty rupees. He had only forty rupees. He attached to it a ten-rupee note from his wallet to add it up to fifty. Up until now, the landlord had accepted the twenty, thirty, forty or fifty rupees that Masterji handed over each month and had extended the rent deadline. This time, however, he appeared to be adamant about getting his money. Flinging the fifty-rupee bundle, tied with thread, in front of the rooster, he shouted: 'Bugger off! I will not accept this. Give me the full amount; the one hundred and eighty rupees you owe.' Master Ilyaas picked up the bundle of notes from the floor and put it in his pocket. Since he was unaccustomed to showing his emotions, he was not able to weep. He went to his charpai and sat down on it despondently.

At the end of three days, the landlord removed Masterji's belongings from his room; he placed Master Sahib's charpai behind the two transformer poles near the sidewalk and the rest of his possessions around it. He clamped a new Chinese lock on the door and, climbing onto his scooter, rode away. The landlord's house was at some distance from this mohalla, but he visited it each month in order to collect the rent due to him from the rooms he had let out.

Master Sahib managed somehow to pass the night under the transformer. The next day he went to the haveli of Sheikh Karim Nawaz to request a loan of two hundred rupees. Knowing him for the simple and docile fellow he was, Karim Nawaz brushed him off; lending money to the likes of him was not a good idea. Then Master Sahib went to Ismaeel the merchant and, reducing his request to one hundred and fifty rupees, asked him for a loan. The merchant, too, turned him down. Master Sahib approached everyone: the barber, butcher, doctor, lawyer, baker, but was disappointed by each in turn. They all told him the same story; faced with inflation, they did not have anything leftover to lend him.

Master Ilyaas spent eight nights in the open, beneath the flimsy shelter of the transformer, before going to the homeopathic doctor to have his pulse taken. The doctor examined him with his stethoscope and announced: 'Master Sahib, you have pneumonia. I will give you some medicine, but you should consult another doctor as well.'

Saying 'Very well', Master Sahib left him and went to Jabbar's bakery to buy hot milk. He drank the milk and, showing his racing pulse to Jabbar, begged the baker to loan him two hundred rupees. Jabbar began to laugh: nobody in his right mind would lend such a fool a rupee and here he was asking for two hundred! The thought was so preposterous that even Jabbar, who rarely laughed, could not contain himself.

With a quilt wrapped around his head like an igloo, Master Ilyaas sat on his charpai for three consecutive days. Those who passed by greeted him and remarked: 'Getting some sun, Masterji?' and from inside his quilt, in a muffled voice, Masterji would reply, 'Yes, I am feeling a bit cold.'

On the fourth day, at dawn, around the time of Fajr prayers, Masterji died. Every inhabitant of Mohsin Mohalla was deeply grieved by his death. After breakfast, they gathered outside and, wrapped in silence and sadness, stood in the sun. Masterji's quail were given a bowl of birdseed and his rooster was fed flour and sugar balls. Sheikh Karim Nawaz Sahib came out of his haveli to sit under the transformer. A big rug was spread on the ground and somebody placed two or three newspapers on it. People gathered around the rug.

Sheikh Karim Nawaz took out two hundred-rupee notes and, giving them to Saeed and Bilal, sent them off on their scooters to arrange for the grave. He gave three hundred rupees to Babu Jalal to go with Rehmat to arrange for the white burial shroud, incense, rose water and flowers. Jabbar the baker prepared a big pot of tea and served it to the gathering of mourners. People started collecting money for the Qul ceremony and before long the residents of Mohsin Mohalla had collected eight hundred and eleven rupees to hand over to Sheikh Karim Nawaz Sahib.

—*Translated by Shaista Parveen*

A Long Wait

Zulfikar Ghose

He ought not to have slept, for he was awake now and it was only eight o'clock in the evening. He had to wait another eleven hours for the train, and knew that he would not be able to sleep now for much of the night. He went to the refreshment room and had a meal. It seemed the same plate of rice and curry which he had eaten some four hours earlier. After eating, he wandered back to the platform. An express had arrived, from Karachi or from Peshawar, from one end or the other of the country, he did not know. The whole station, and not just the platform on which it stood, was crowded. The train stopped at Lahore for a whole hour. People who were catching it at Lahore had already settled in. The first-class passengers had rolled out their bedding on their berths and, wearing pyjamas, were standing outside their compartments, smoking and chatting with friends who had come to see them off. For the third-class passengers, there was no hope of a seat for anyone who had not been at the platform the moment the train arrived at the station. Those who had managed to enter the large compartments had locked the doors from the inside and hung out of windows in order to block any entrance to the dozens of passengers who were fighting to get in. Those who could not enter the train were shouting at those who had done so, abuse was being exchanged along the entire length of the platform, except at those places where the pyjama-clad passengers were smoking and chatting. Threats mingled with the abuse, threats to call the police, to report to the station-master. Several policemen, however, were walking about the platform and listening to the people who were threatening to call the police. At one point, two passengers had come to blows, for a man

This extract is taken from Zulfikar Ghose's *The Murder of Aziz Khan*, published by Oxford University Press.

who was denied entrance to a compartment had dragged down a man who was hanging from a window. Porters, who, with special commissions in mind, had managed to find seats for the inter-class passengers were finding it difficult to get the luggage of the passengers in and were abusing the passengers for expecting too much of them. In the six-berth second-class compartments, the passengers who had reserved their berths had rolled out their bedding, but more passengers had turned up with second-class tickets but without a reservation for a berth. Those who had reserved the berth, claimed full right to it while those who had not made a reservation demanded their right to sit at the end of the seat. No one was prepared to make compromises, however, and obscene language was exchanged when appeals to the spirit of Islam and democracy had failed. Finally, the train slowly moved out of the platform with many people hanging onto the doors, and the station seemed suddenly silent. It reminded Aziz Khan of the silence on his own land; but the arrivals and departures of people, whose destinations were unfamiliar to him, continued to distract him.

It was a long night. He should have gone to Shahid's, or even to a hotel, and rested properly. But he had not been able to leave the station although the thought of finding a bed for the night had occurred to him. He was afraid of over-sleeping and missing his train, afraid that Shahid might talk him into staying on in Lahore. He wanted to return to his land. It was a long night on the platform, now sitting upright and now lying down on the bench. Occasionally he had walked up and down the platform. On one or two benches, men lay asleep, curled against the hard wood. Sometimes a group of railway workers would walk silently, sleepily past, one carrying a lantern, walk to the end of the platform where the platform sloped down to the level of the tracks and gradually disappear into the night; until he could see only the lantern, its little spot of light becoming tiny as a speck of dust. He sat again on his bench, dozed off and shook himself awake to lie down before dozing off again. He was woken by the sound of a locomotive, steaming, puffing in spasmodic bursts and then easing off. He saw it through half-open eyes. There was no train attached to it. As it went past him, he saw two faces in the driver's cabin, black and glistening in the glow of burning coal. Images and fantasies, reality and unreality kept him awake and asleep, there and not there. Afterwards, he could not tell what he had seen and not seen. Red lights turned to green and green to red and when he looked in the distance, the platform seemed to have become longer in the darkness, he could not tell whether the light he looked at was red or green. Once, he must have slept for a long time, though he could not tell for how long; it could be that he had just fallen off asleep and woken a minute or two later and the duration of being asleep had seemed a long time; or it could be that he had slept for much longer, an hour, two hours, or even longer; how could he tell? He had not observed the time when he had fallen asleep and now there was no way of ascertaining the time unless he walked down the platform to the point from where he could see the station clock. But if he did go to see the clock to see the time, it would mean nothing, for he had not seen the time when he had fallen asleep. He heard crows cawing somewhere far in the distance, distinctly cawing somewhere in the open air. And then they stopped. He wondered whether it had been crows cawing. Nobody else cawed, it must have been crows. Perhaps the men he had seen disappear down the line were making some noise which for a moment had reached him and had seemed to be like crows cawing. No, he was certain it was crows. If it was important and if it mattered to his destiny, he would affirm that he had heard crows cawing soon after he had woken up after a long or a short sleep, the duration of which was not as important as its soundness, its dreamlessness. Where was he? Yes, Lahore, there was the sign in front of him saying Lahore in Urdu and in English. He looked at the English letters and tried to work out how they could mean Lahore. The English word was longer than the Urdu word, though the word was the same. He looked hard at the English letters, tried to give a sound to each letter which would add up to the word Lahore. But no, the word was not the same, for in Punjabi you pronounced it as Lowr and in Urdu as La-whore. How did the English pronounce it? They must pronounce it either as Lowr or as La-whore, very probably as La-whore, for Urdu had always been the fashionable language, its accents had always been imitated. But whichever way the English pronounce Lahore, their word for it was longer physically. He realised he had been making a mistake, for, following the Urdu habit of reading from right to left, he had been looking at the English word from the right to left. The sign was some distance away from him, far enough for him to see the whole signboard as a complete unit, but he had been looking only at the English word and although he had been seeing it as a whole, he had been looking at it from a certain point of view, that of seeing the constituents of the word, and consequently he had been seeing the English word in reverse, that is to say, although his eyes saw LAHORE, they did not see LAHORE because they had been looking at EROHAL. Now he would have to start again if he wanted to work out how the English letters could add to the word Lahore. He must shut his eyes, forget that he had ever observed the English word for Lahore in reverse, open them and examine the letters with a new interest. He shut his eyes. He had not heard what he ought to have been hearing, what he would have heard if he had not been so preoccupied with one word, which had been a useless preoccupation because he already knew the meaning of the word, that it was the name of the city he had come to and which he was leaving, and what else mattered about a word apart from the thing which it named, he had not heard that the sparrows were chirping, twittering, squeaking, tweeting, as though the station were an old spring mattress on which he lay and he was turning restlessly and the rusted old springs were chirping, twittering, squeaking, tweeting like sparrows waking up. He had not been deceived about the crows. He was positive that he had heard crows cawing earlier, for now the sparrows were raising a din, he could see them fluttering about the station, making long journeys within the station, travelling the great distance of the platform, flying down and landing on the platform, turning their heads to the right and to the left in order to look straight, picking up bits of paper, bits of straw, flying up, stopping in mid-flight and alighting upon posts, signboards, any object which had a protuberance wide enough for their claws to grip, and cleaning their beaks like a barber sharpening a razor on the palm of his hand, now one side and now the other, their little heads saying no to the thing on which they were wiping or polishing or sharpening their beaks. There were other noises now, people, porters, coolies, coming and going on the platforms, carrying buckets, brooms, brushes; soon taps were turned on, there was water flowing on the platforms, the brooms were sweeping, the brushes were scrubbing. It was dawn. It was still dark enough for the lights to be on and yet there was

enough daylight for the lights to be purposeless, like the eyes and the
limbs of a body which was certain to die in a moment or two, another
breath and perhaps another, and then the breath would be exhausted,
the body would be useless and if the eyes remained open, someone
would remember to draw down the eyelids. Sooner or later, someone
would remember to switch off the lights. Had the night passed, was
the waiting over? He rose from the bench and walked to the public
lavatory. Sweepers were busy there, the smell was like a fist which hit
you in the face as soon as you entered. He withdrew as hurriedly as he
could and found a tap on the platform which had been turned on to
wash the platform. He cupped his hands under it and washed his face.
He went to the refreshment room and saw that there was a crowd of
people there. It was six o'clock. And now that he entered the lit room,
he saw that outside the daylight had increased. The sun must have
risen somewhere. He sat drinking tea. He drank two cups. He did not
eat anything. He returned to the platform and again sat down on the
bench. The station began to be crowded. Boys were selling newspapers;
other boys were going from person to person, offering to shine their
shoes, their cry of *boot-polish* condensed into a drawn-out *pleeesh*.

Again he could not find a seat and had to sit on the floor and,
when the train moved, again he had no way of telling which way he
was going. He dozed off, his body shaking to the movement of the
train. He woke up and could not tell for a moment whether he was
going to Lahore or coming from it, whether his journey of two days
ago was over or whether it was still the same journey and he had not
as yet reached Lahore. The people around him could be different or
they could be the same; if different, he could not tell how different
for he had not closely observed the former people from whom these
people must be different. He concentrated. He thought of the three
police officers, of the judge, of the woman in the witness box with
her jewellery and heavy make-up, her air of being perfumed for the
visual seduction of passers-by. He thought of the men he had passed
in the streets, the suited ones. The chained dog of a sentry outside
the high court. What could he tell Rafiq and Javed when he reached
home? He had forgotten to take a gift for Zakia. They do not want
you, my sons, they do not want you. Harvest time was approaching,
there would be work to do. His head nodded, the train spoke, they do

not want you, his head nodded, the train spoke, they do not want you, then faster, they do not, they do not, they do not, his head nodded, his head nodded, his head nodded, the whistle, his head jerked, his ears listened, the whistle again, the darkness, the train was shouting, the whistle again and then the bursting into light, and then the same rhythm, the same, steady reproachful voice, they do not want you, they do not want you, they do not want you, his head nodded, his head nodded.

'Bulla Ki Jaana Main Kaun'

Bulleh Shah

Says Bulla, who knows who I am?
I'm not a momin in the mosque,
Or a believer in false rites.
Not impure among the pure.
Nor Moses or Pharaoh.
Says Bulla, who knows who I am?

I am not in the vedas or holy books,
Not in drug or wine.
Not in the drunk's wasted intoxication,
Not in wakefulness or sleep.
Says Bulla, who knows who I am?

I am not in sorrow nor in joy,
Neither in piety nor in inequity.
I am not water, I am not earth,
I am not fire, I am not air.
Says Bulla, who knows who I am?

I am not from Arabia or Lahore,
Nor from India or Nagaur.
Neither a Hindu or a Muslim from Peshawar,
Nor do I live in Nadaun.
Says Bulla, who knows who I am?

I do not know the subtleties of religion.
I was not born of Adam and Eve.
I am not the name I assume.
I am not in stillness, not in movement.
Finally, I know only myself.

I cannot recognize any other.
Who could be wiser than I?
Bulla, who then, stands here?
Says Bulla, who knows who I am!

—*Translated by Bapsi Sidhwa*

Notes on Contributors

Rukhsana Ahmad's first novel, *The Hope Chest,* was published by Virago in England. Her short stories appear in several collections and have been commissioned by BBC Radio 4. Her plays, for stage and radio, have been shortlisted for The Writers' Guild of Great Britain awards. She has edited and translated into English a collection of feminist Urdu poetry: *We Sinful Women,* and a novel: *The One Who Did Not Ask* by Altaf Fatima.

In 1990 Rukhsana co-founded Kali Theatre Company with Rita Wolf and was its Artistic Director for several years. She is a founding member of the Asian Women Writers' Collective as well as a founding trustee and the current Chair of SALIDAA. She is a Fellow of the Royal Literary Fund based at Queen Mary and Westfield College, University of London.

Zulfiqar Ahmad is currently serving as accounts officer at IPRI. Previously he served with the Foundation for Research on International Environment, National Development and Security (FRIENDS), Rawalpindi, Pakistan, as Manager (Admin. and Finance) for nine years. He holds MA (Political Science) from the University of Punjab, Lahore and MBA (Finance) from AIOU, Islamabad.

Ashfaq Ahmed (1925–2004) edited *Laillo Nehar, Dastango* and was the director of the Urdu Science Board for twenty-five years. He wrote and broadcast 'Talqeenshah', a hugely popular weekly Punjabi radio programme for thirty-three years. His television plays, *Aik Muhabat Sau Afsane, Tota Kahani* and *Kila Kahani* have been played and replayed on TV channels in Pakistan. His TV programme *Zaveye,* about life, religion and society, produced since 1998 has had a positive impact on making people realize the value of a moral and ethical society.

He received the Pride of Performance award in 1979, was associated with Pakistan Academy of Letters, Institute of Modern Languages, Islamabad University, and National Council of Arts.

Khaled Ahmed was born in 1943 in Jallandhar (India), and after 1947 moved to Pakistan, where he grew up, went to school, and ultimately to college and completed his education. He is currently the consulting editor, the *Friday Times,* a popular weekly newspaper based in Lahore, Pakistan. Previously, he has worked as editor for the *Frontier Post* and as joint editor for the *Nation,* both Pakistani English dailies. He received a postgraduate diploma in International Affairs from Punjab University in

Lahore and a diploma in Interpretership in Russian from Moscow State University. While at the Stimson Center, Khaled investigated South Asian interpretations of Western deterrence theory with particular attention to religion.

F.S. Aijazuddin, OBE, FCA, was educated in the UK. Although a chartered accountant by profession, he is widely regarded as an authority on the art history of the subcontinent, especially on Pakistan. He has written eleven books on such diverse subjects as Pahari miniature paintings, Sikh portraiture, rare maps, and topography as reflected in the works of British and European artists and lithographers. He has also published several essays on politics, economics and social issues and is the author of two volumes which dealt with the secret diplomatic negotiations during the 1970s between the United States and China through Pakistan.

Aijazuddin is the Honorary British Consul in Lahore and Chairman of the Executive Committee, Lahore Museum. He is also an International Councillor of the Asia Society, New York.

Saad Ashraf was born in 1937 in Peshawar and did his schooling from St Anthony's High School in Lahore. He graduated from Government College, Lahore, and took a degree from the Engineering College, also in Lahore. He retired from government service a few years ago, and now lives in Islamabad. He is the author of a collection of poems, *Fifty Autumn Leaves*, and *The Postmaster*, a novel published to acclaim by Penguin in 2004.

Baider Bakht is Adjunct Professor of Civil Engineering at the Universities of Toronto and Manitoba, Canada. He translates modern Urdu poetry into English in collaboration with Canadian poets and scholars of English. He lives in Toronto, Canada.

Ijaz Husain Batalvi (1923–2004) was one of Pakistan's most eminent lawyers and a well-known literary figure. He was born in Batala, India. He received his BA from Government College, Lahore, and in 1944 joined All India Radio, Delhi. He migrated to Pakistan in 1947 and in 1949 enrolled at Lincoln's Inn for his Barrister-at-Law degree. In 1954, Batalvi returned to Pakistan to practise law; and taught law at the University of Punjab from 1957 to 2001. He was an active member of Halqa-e-Arbab-e-Zauq in Lahore where he read out his Urdu short stories and poetry. He was also a literary critic. A collection of his writings is to be published.

Minoo Bhandara, businessman, politician and writer, graduated from Punjab University in 1956. After studying philosophy, politics and economics at Brasenose College, Oxford, he joined the family business in Rawalpindi. In 1978–79 he attended the Advanced Management Programme at the Harvard Business School.

Bhandara served as Adviser to the President of Pakistan on Minorities Affairs 1981–1985. He was elected to the National Assembly of Pakistan in 1985 and also in 2002 and currently serves as a parliamentarian. He has visited China, Japan and Russia as a delegate. Since 1985, Minoo Bhandara has written extensively on regional and political issues for *Dawn* newspaper, and has also frequently contributed op-ed pieces to it.

Urvashi Butalia was born in Ambala, India, in 1952. She has worked as an editor at the Oxford University Press and ZedBooks. Urvashi is the director and co-founder of Kali for Women, India's first feminist publishing house. Her writing has appeared in several newspapers including the *Guardian*, the *Statesman*, the *Times of India* and several magazines including *Outlook*, the *New Internationalist* and *India Today*. Urvashi is very active in India's women's movement; she is a consultant for Oxfam India and holds the position of Reader at the College of Vocational Studies at the University of Delhi. Her main areas of research are Partition and oral histories. She has also written on gender, communalism, fundamentalism and media.

Ikramullah Chaudhry was born in 1930 in Jandiala, a village in the Nawan Shehr District of Jallandhar (India). He finished his high school studies in Amritsar. After Partition his family moved to Multan where he received a bachelor's degree in 1953. Two years later he took a law degree from University Law College at Lahore. After practising law in Multan for a few years, he went into the insurance business and retired in 1990. He has been writing fiction since 1962 and has published several collections of short stories and, more recently, a novel *Sa'e ki Avaz*. He lives in Lahore, Pakistan.

Ismat Chughtai (1915–1991) was born in Badayun, UP. She grew up largely in Jodhpur where her father was a civil servant. She began writing in secret because women writers in India were not taken seriously at the time. In 1941 she wrote 'Lihaaf' (The Quilt), a story which hints at a lesbian relationship between a Muslim woman and her maid. It brought her both notoriety and fame. She was charged by the British government with obscenity, but won the case because her lawyer argued that the story could be understood only by those who already had knowledge of lesbianism, and thus could not be a corrupting influence. In 1943 she turned completely to a writing career.

Derek Cohen is the author of *The Politics of Shakespeare* (1993), *Shakespearean Motives* (1988) and *Shakespeare's Culture of Violence* (1992). He has co-edited (with Deborah Heller) *Jewish Presences in English Literature* (1991). His other interests include South African literature, on which he has published widely.

Emma Duncan previously worked at ITN before joining the *Economist* as Media Editor. She went on to become Asia Editor and South Asia Correspondent before being appointed Britain Editor. She is the author of *Breaking the Curfew*, which examines Pakistan politics and society.

Faiz Ahmad Faiz (1911–1984) was born in Sialkot of pre-Partition Punjab. He grew up surrounded by literature with a father who was a friend to many writers, including Muhammad Allama Iqbal. He began his career as the editor of the leftist English-language daily, *Pakistan Times*, as well as the managing editor for the Urdu daily, *Imroze*. Although his first volume of poetry, *Naqsh-e-Faryadi*, was published in Lucknow in 1941, he became widely known after the 1952 publication of *Dast-e-Saba*, poems written during his imprisonment by the Pakistani government. Faiz was also a journalist, songwriter and activist.

Zulfikar Ghose is a Pakistani-American English-language writer. He was born in the 1920s in Sialkot and moved to Bombay in 1942. After Partition, he migrated to England and then to the US in 1969. He lives in Texas and teaches in a university.

He has written poetry and prose (fiction and non-fiction) equally. *The Loss of India*, *Jets from Orange*, *The Violent West*, *A Memory of Asia* and *Selected Poems* are some of his poetry books. His work in prose includes *The Triple Mirror of the Self*, four books of criticism, and an autobiography, *Confessions of a Native-Alien*.

Sara Suleri Goodyear was born in that part of British India that is now Pakistan. She received her BA at Kinnaird College, Lahore, in 1974. Two years later, she was awarded an MA from the Punjab University, and went on to graduate with a PhD from the University of Indiana in 1983. Sara is currently professor of English at Yale University and a founding editor of the *Yale Journal of Criticism*. She is also the author of *The Rhetoric of English India* (1992) and *Meatless Days* (1989).

Mohsin Hamid grew up in Lahore and later studied at the Princeton University and Harvard Law School. His first novel, *Moth Smoke*, was a *New York Times* Notable Book of the Year, a winner of a Betty Trask Award, and a runner-up for the PEN-Hemingway Award. It has been published in eleven countries and nine languages, and is a cult best-seller in Pakistan, where it has also been made into a TV miniseries. His articles and essays have appeared in publications such as *Time*, the *New York Times*, *Smithsonian Magazine*, the *Guardian*, the *Friday Times*, *Dawn* and *Outlook India*. He divides his time between Lahore, London and New York.

Khalid Hasan is a senior Pakistani journalist. He lives in Washington and works as a correspondent of the Lahore-based *Daily Times* and weekly *Friday Times*.

He has written over thirty books, which includes *Scorecard*, *Give Us Back Our Onions*, *The Umpire Strikes Back*, *Private Views* and *Question Time*. One of Pakistan's best-known columnists, Khalid Hasan worked for a specialized international news agency in Vienna from 1981 to 1991 and was Zulfikar Ali Bhutto's first press secretary.

Irfan Husain, whose popular columns appear regularly in *Dawn, Daily Times, Khaleej Times* and other foreign publications, was born in Amritsar in 1944. His family migrated to Pakistan in 1947 and he went to school in Karachi and Paris. He got a master's degree in economics from the Karachi University before joining government service in 1967 and moving to Lahore. He now divides his time between London and Pakistan, and keeps in touch with the culinary scene there. He enjoys cooking and often writes about food.

Aamer Hussain was born in 1955 in Karachi, Pakistan, where he lived till 1968. He moved to England via India two years later. He graduated in Urdu, Persian and History from SOAS. His first published story was 'The Colour of a Loved Person's Eyes' in 1987. His fiction has since been anthologized in Pakistan, England, the USA, Italy, Canada, India and Bangladesh, and translated into Spanish and Arabic. He has published four volumes of stories: *Mirror to the Sun* (Mantra London 1993), *The Blue Direction* (Penguin India 1999), *Cactus Town* (OUP Pakistan 2002) and most recently the highly acclaimed *Turquoise* (Saqi 2002). He is a Fellow of the Royal Society of Literature and is at present a lecturer on the National and International Literatures MA at the Institute of English Studies (London University).

Intezar Hussain, born in Dilai, received his early education in Hapur, UP. He migrated to Pakistan in late 1947 and took up residence in Lahore. He worked briefly for *Imroze* and *Afaq*, before joining *Mashriq* as a columnist. He also wrote for the *Civil and Military Gazette*, Lahore, in the early sixties; *Frontier Post*, Lahore, in 1989–90; and is currently writing for *Dawn*.

His vast literary works include *Galli Koochay* (Lanes and Streets), *Khali Pinjra* (Empty Cage), *Chand Grahan* (Lunar Eclipse), *Aagay Samandar Hai* (The Sea is Ahead), *Zamin Aur Falak Aur* (The Earth is Different from the Sky) and *Chiraghon ka Dhooan* (Smoke from Lamps).

Shah 'Madho Lal' Hussain (1538–1599), Lahore's romantic Sufi saint, added *'masti'* (rapture) to his Punjabi lyrics or kafis. His love for his Hindu disciple Madho Lal was so intense that he added Madho Lal's name to his own and became known as Madho Lal Hussain. They are buried together in Bhagbanpura, in Lahore. Madho Lal Hussain is credited with introducing the love legends of Heer and Ranjha, Sohni and Mahiwal to Punjabi verse and using them as metaphors and motifs for the Sufi's longing for union with the One.

Muhammad Allama Iqbal (1873–1938) was born in Punjab. He received his early education in Sialkot, and proceeded to Europe for higher studies, where he stayed for three years. Iqbal returned to India in 1908, and practised as a lawyer till 1934, when ill health compelled him to give up his practice.

The epoch-making poems, 'Shikwa' and 'Jawab-e-Shikwa', which he read out in the annual convention of Anjuman Himayat-I-Islam, Lahore, sparkled with the glow of his genius and made him immensely popular. His other poems 'Tarana-e-Hind' (The Indian Anthem) and 'Tarana-e-Milli' (The Muslim Anthem) also became very popular among the masses and used to be sung as symbols of National or Muslim identity at public meetings.

Habib Jalib was a populist poet. He was a clear departure from the mainstream Urdu poetic tradition where the poet preferred to live in his ivory tower away from the rough and tumble active life. He was in fact much closer to the Punjabi tradition where the poet was also an activist fighting on all fronts, usually either landing in jail or forced into exile.

A totally dispossessed man, he was fearless in his confrontation with the government and was therefore much feared by the powers that be. He was topical and engaged the anti-people policies in his verses which became instant slogans and were more deadly than the deadliest of bullets. His verses galvanized scattered opposition and inspired hope among the common urban dwellers. These easy-to-understand verses were thus more effective as their outreach was more than that of the more respected poets.

Daud Kamal (1935–1987) won accolades for his many collections of verse translations and original poems in the English-speaking world. His anthology of Pakistani English poetry, *The Blue Wind*, was recently published in England, and his work was selected for broadcast by the BBC. Kamal graduated from Peshawar and Cambridge Universities, and was Professor and Chairman of the Department of English at the University of Peshawar. He died in New York during a USIS-sponsored tour.

Sorayya Y. Khan is the author of *Noor* (Penguin India, 2004). She was a Fulbright Creative Writing Scholar in Pakistan and Bangladesh in 1999–2000 and won The Malahat Review Novella Prize in 1995. Her work has appeared in the *Kenyon Review*, the *North American Review*, the *Asian Pacific American Journal*, and several anthologies of Pakistani writing. She currently lives in Ithaca, New York, with her husband and two children.

Krishen Khanna, b. 1925, is one of India's most reputed artists. He worked as a banker from 1948 to 1961 before deciding it was far better to follow his destiny as an artist than to stay in a secure job. A member of the Progressive Artists Group, Bombay, he has held more than forty one-man exhibitions in India and abroad, and participated in all the important Triennales and Biennales in the world—at Sao Paulo, Venice, New Delhi, Tokyo and elsewhere. His work is represented in several major museums including the Museum of Modern Art, New York, and the National Gallery of Modern Art, New Delhi. A recipient of the Padma Shri, he divides his time between Delhi and Simla.

Rudyard Kipling (1865–1936) was born in Bombay, but educated in England at the United Services College, Westward Ho, Bideford. In 1882 he returned to India, where he worked for Anglo-Indian newspapers. His literary career began with *Departmental Ditties* (1886), but subsequently he became chiefly known as a writer of short stories. A prolific writer, he achieved fame quickly. Kipling was the poet of the British Empire and its yeoman, the common soldier, whom he glorified in many of his works, in particular *Plain Tales from the Hills* (1888) and *Soldiers Three* (1888), collections of short stories with roughly and affectionately drawn soldier portraits. In 1894 appeared his *Jungle Book*, which became a children's classic all over the world. *Kim* (1901), the story of Kimball O'Hara and his adventures in the Himalayas, is perhaps his most felicitous work.

Kipling was the recipient of many honorary degrees and other awards. In 1926 he received the Gold Medal of the Royal Society of Literature, which only Scott, Meredith, and Hardy had been awarded before him.

Shahnaz Kureshy was born in Hyderabad, India, in 1939 where she attended St George's Grammar School. She moved to Pakistan in 1950. After graduating from Kinnaird College, Lahore, she went to Tunis, to teach English at the Berlitz and the Bourguiba Schools of Languages and also studied French. She received a scholarship at Ball State University in Muncie, Indiana, where she completed her master's in Education in 1963. She taught English at the Indiana Institute of Technology, Fort Wayne, and has since taught in several countries including Iran, Denmark, Pakistan, and the United States. She has three children and lives with her husband in Houston, Texas.

Rich Levy has been the executive director of Inprint, a non-profit literary arts organization that champions creative writing and reading in Houston, since 1995. His poems have appeared in *Boulevard*, *Gulf Coast*, *High Plains Literary Review*, *Intro*, *The Texas Observer*, *The Texas Review*, and other magazines. He received his MFA from the Iowa Writers Workshop.

E.D. Maclagan (1864–1952) served as lieutenant governor of Punjab from 1919 to 1921 and as governor from 1921 to 1924. According to Zulfiqar Ahmad, editor of Notes on Punjab and Mughal India, a collection of scholarly historical articles selected from the Journal of the Punjab Historical Society, E.D. Maclagan was secretary to the state of India and later became governor of the Punjab. The essay which appears in this anthology is an excerpt from Maclagan's article, an English translation (from the original Spanish) of one chapter (chapter LXVI) from the 'Itinerario' of Manrique (an Augustinian Friar's account of his travels in the East).

Saadat Hasan Manto (1912–1955) was the leading Urdu short-story writer of the twentieth century. He was born in Samrala in the Ludhiana district of Punjab. He worked for All India Radio during the Second World War and was a successful screenwriter in Bombay before moving to Pakistan after Partition. During his controversial two-decade career, Manto published twenty-two collections of stories, seven collections of radio plays, three collections of essays, and a novel.

Ved Mehta was born in Lahore, Punjab, in British India, and was educated in the United States and Britain. Encouraged by the success of his early autobiography, *Face to Face* (1957), Mehta published more than a score of books, including experimental books in which he created his own brand of intellectual journalism. He has written about events and personalities in India, Great Britain and the United States, and also on philosophy, religion and linguistics. He is renowned for his series of eleven books with the omnibus title *Continents of Exile*. The series was launched with *Daddyji* (1972) and concluded in 2004 with *The Red Letters*, a portrait of his father. Ved Mehta has been the staff writer and reporter on the *New Yorker* magazine, and in recent years, has taught writing and history at the Yale University and Williams College. He lives in New York City.

Muhammad Umar Memon was born in Aligarh (India) and left for Pakistan in 1954, where he completed his education and for a few years taught at Sindh University. He moved to the US in 1964. He has written fiction in Urdu and has translated Urdu fiction into English. He has compiled several anthologies of fiction by contemporary Urdu writers. At present he is Professor of Islamic Studies, Persian and Urdu literature at the University of Wisconsin, Madison, and is editor of *The Annual of Urdu Studies*.

Jugnu Mohsin is the publisher of the *Friday Times*, who fought to assert freedom of the press in the face of Nawaz Sharif government's increasingly brutal efforts to control the media.

Kishwar Naheed was born in Bulandshahr, India, in 1940. She is one of the best-known feminist poets of Pakistan. In a field dominated by traditional male voices, Naheed, writing in Urdu, was a pioneer of a new, distinctively feminine voice and has produced over the span of thirty years a body of work that is innovative, defiant, political, and self-aware. Her first collection of poetry, *Lab-i goya*, published in 1968, won the prestigious Adamjee Prize of Literature. This collection of traditional ghazals was followed by a collection of nazms, translations of foreign poetry, and by many works in free verse.

Kishwar has held the position of Director General of Pakistan National Council of the Arts before her retirement, has edited a prestigious literary magazine *Mah-i naw*, and has founded an organization named Hawwa (Eve), whose goal is to help homebound women become financially independent through cottage industries and the marketing of handicrafts.

Tahira Naqvi is a New York-based Pakistani author who writes in English and translates from Urdu. She has published short stories and a novel. She also teaches Urdu at the New York University.

Meena Arora Nayak is the author of two novels, *In the Aftermath* and *About Daddy*. She is an assistant professor of English at a community college and lives in Virginia, USA. Meena is working on her third novel.

Pran Nevile is a former diplomat and UN adviser, who writes frequently on subjects relating to the British Raj. He is widely travelled and has produced several works, including his much-acclaimed study, *Lahore: A Sentimental Journey*.

Munir Niazi, equally proficient in Urdu and Punjabi, has been writing poetry for a long time. In the sixties he contributed songs to Pakistani films. '*Us baiwafa ka shehr hay*', sung by the late Nasim Begum, for the film *Shaheed*, still stirs up memories of a period gone by.

Shaista Parveen was born and raised in Karachi. Although she is a physician by profession and works as a paediatrician in the Houston area, writing poetry is her first passion. She writes both in Urdu and English and has read her poems at various art venues, and as part of multimedia performances.

Bano Qudsia, born in Ferozpur in 1928, has published several short stories, novels and plays for television. She is known for her forthright style that analyses human emotions and psychology and examines the influence of religion on middle-class values. *Tawajju Ki Talib* (collection of short stories), *Raja Giddh* (novel), *Adhi Baat*, *Tamasil*, *Chaatan Par Ghonsala* (TV plays) are some of her famous works. She received Tamghe-e-Imtiaz, best playwright Taj award and Graduate award for best playwright 1986, 1988–1990.

Samina Quraeshi, the Henry R. Luce Professor in Family and Community at the University of Miami, is an educator, author, designer and artist who has devoted her career to exploring and demonstrating the importance of art and culture in educational, corporate and governmental environments. She is also a member of the steering committee of The Education for Family-Centered Community Development Initiative, which has been working with former Vice-President Al Gore. Her experience in education has exposed her to students at the University of Miami, Harvard University, Boston University, and The Rhode Island School of Design.

Author of two award-winning books, *Legacy of the Indus* and *Lahore—The City Within*, Samina Quraeshi's photographs and paintings have been exhibited at the Zamana gallery in London; at the S. Dillon Ripley Center, The Smithsonian in Washington DC; at the MIT Museum in Cambridge; and at the Carpenter Center for the Visual Arts at Harvard University.

Bina Shah was born in Karachi and was raised both in America and Pakistan. She received a bachelor's degree in psychology from Wellesley College and a master's in Education from the Harvard University, and worked with several IT publications before moving into freelance writing. She writes for the websites Chowk and Naseeb, and is the author of *Animal Medicine*, a book of short stories, and two novels: *Where They Dream in Blue* and *The 786 Cybercafe*. She lives and works in Karachi.

Bulleh Shah was a Punjabi Sufi poet, believed to have lived from 1680 to 1758. As is a common practice in Indian poetry, his poems include a signature line which contains his name. His spiritual master was Shah Inayat Qadiri of Lahore. Bulleh wrote primarily in Punjabi, but also in the local spoken language, Siraiki, which is a dialect of Sindhi. His style of poetry is called Kafi, which was already an established style with Sufis who preceded him. Several of his songs are regarded as an integral part of the traditional repertoire of Qawwali, the musical genre which represents the devotional music of the Sufis. The tomb of Bulleh Shah is in Kasur, where he lived, and he is held in reverence by all Sufis of India and Pakistan.

Parizad N. Sidhwa was born and brought up in Lahore, Pakistan. She graduated in the US in 1990, and lives and works in Houston TX. An avid fan of Urdu poetry, she writes poems both in Urdu and English.

Khushwant Singh is India's best-known writer and columnist. He has been the founder editor of *Yojna*, and editor of the *Illustrated Weekly of India*, the *National Herald* and the *Hindustan Times*. He is also the author of several books, which include the novels *Train to Pakistan, Delhi* and *The Company of Women*; the classic two-volume *A History of the Sikhs*; and a number of translations and non-fiction books on Sikh religion and culture, Delhi, nature and current affairs. His autobiography, *Truth, Love and a Little Malice*, was published in 2002.

Adam Zamizad was born in Pakistan and spent his early childhood in Nairobi. He went to the university in Lahore, Pakistan, becoming a lecturer there, and later came to live and work in the UK. Adam Zamizad is one of the most exciting and fascinating authors at work today and has been described as a 'jewel in the crown of English literature'. He has had five novels published to great acclaim, and has been translated into many languages.

Copyright Acknowledgements

Grateful acknowledgement is made to the following for permission to reprint copyright material:

Nasira Iqbal for Muhammad Allama Iqbal's poem 'On the Banks of River Ravi', first published in Urdu in *Bang-e-dara*, by Sheikh Ghulam Ali and Sons Ltd, Lahore, 1989

Sang-e-Meel Publications for the extract from E.D. Maclagan's 'The Travels of Fray Sebastian Manrique', from *Notes on Punjab and Mughal India: Selections from Journal of the Punjab Historical Society*, edited by Zulfiqar Ahmad, Sang-e-Meel Publications, Lahore, 1988

Fakir Syed Aijazuddin for the extract 'Akbar's Capital: Jewel in the Sikh Crown', from his book *Lahore: Illustrated Views of 19th Century*, Mapin Publishing, Ahmedabad, 1991

Sorayya Y. Khan for 'The Beginning of Five Queen's Road'

Khushwant Singh for the extract 'Lahore, Partition and Independence', from *Common Heritage*, by Muhammad Ali Siddiqui, Oxford University Press, Karachi, 1997; and his translation of 'Toba Tek Singh' by Saadat Hasan Manto, from *Orphans of the Storm: Stories on the Partition of India*, edited by Saros Cowasjee and K.S. Duggal, UBS Publishers' Distributors Ltd, New Delhi, 1995

Penguin Books Limited, London, for the extract 'The 1988 Show', from *Breaking the Curfew: A Political Journey through Pakistan* by Emma Duncan, 1989

Saad Ashraf for 'The Postal Clerk'

Samina Quraeshi for the extract 'The City Within', from *Lahore: The City Within*, first published by Concept Media Pte Ltd, Singapore, 1988

Pran Nevile for the extracts 'The Splendours of Hira Mandi or Tibbi' and 'Lahore, Lahore Hai' from *Lahore: A Sentimental Journey*, Allied Publishers Limited, New Delhi, 1993

Adam Zamizad for 'Kanjari'

Shahnaz Kureshy for 'The Legend of Anarkali'

Munir Niazi for the poem 'Thought-Nymph', from *The Poetical Works of Munir Niazi*, edited by Suhail Safdar, Pakistan Writings, Lahore, 1996

Krishen Khanna for 'I Went Back'

Ved Mehta for 'A House Divided', from *Time* magazine issue, 18–25 August 2003

Urvashi Butalia for the extract 'Ranamama', from *The Other Side of Silence*, Penguin Books India, 1998

Meena Arora Nayak for the extract 'Looking for Home', from *About Daddy*, Penguin Books India, 2000

Sara Suleri Goodyear for 'Lahore Remembered'; and her translation of Faiz Ahmad Faiz's poem 'City of Lights'

Tahira Naqvi for her translation of 'The "Lihaaf" Trial', from *My Friends, My Enemy: Essays, Reminiscences, Portraits*, by Ismat Chughtai, Kali for Women, 2001

Minoo Bhandara for 'Ava Gardner and I: Post-Partition Lahore'

Khalid Hasan for 'Awaaz De Kahan Hai: A Portrait of Nur Jehan'

Bina Shah for the extract 'A Love Affair with Lahore', from Chowk.com

Irfan Husain for 'The Way of All Flesh'

Mohsin Hamid for the extract from *Moth Smoke*, Farrar, Straus and Giroux, New York, 2000; and 'The Pathos of Exile' from *Time* magazine issue, 18–25 August 2003

Ijaz Husain Batalvi for 'Kipling's Lahore: The City of Dreadful Night'

Jugnu Mohsin for 'Habib Jalib: An Archetypical Lahori'

Khaled Ahmed for 'Pavement-pounding Men of Letters: Intezar Hussain's Lahore'

Intezar Hussain for 'The Cool Street'

Aamer Hussain for 'Adiba: A Storyteller's Tale', from *Turquoise*, Saqi Press, London 2002

Kishwar Naheed for the poem 'The Sun, My Companion', from *The Price of Looking Back*, Mustafa Waheed Book Traders, Lahore, 1987

Rukhsana Ahmad for 'The Gate-keeper's Wife', from *The Inner Courtyard*, Virago Press, London, 1990

Bano Qudsia for 'Snapshots of Love in Shalimar'

Ikramullah Chaudhry for 'The Old Mansion', part of *The Annual of Urdu Studies* No. 14, 1999

Ashfaq Ahmed for 'Mohsin Mohalla'

Zulfikar Ghose for the extract 'A Long Wait' from *The Murder of Aziz Khan*, Oxford University Press, 1998